Clearing the Path for First-Generation College Students

Clearing the Path for First-Generation College Students

Qualitative and Intersectional Studies of Educational Mobility

Edited by Ashley C. Rondini, Bedelia Nicola Richards, and Nicolas P. Simon

Afterword by Jenny Stuber

LEXINGTON BOOKS
Lanham • Boulder • New York • London

Published by Lexington Books
An imprint of The Rowman & Littlefield Publishing Group, Inc.
4501 Forbes Boulevard, Suite 200, Lanham, Maryland 20706
www.rowman.com

6 Tinworth Street, London SE11 5AL, United Kingdom

British Library Cataloguing in Publication Information Available

Library of Congress Cataloging-in-Publication Data
Names: Rondini, Ashley C., editor. | Richards, Bedelia Nicola, editor. |
    Simon, Nicolas P., editor.
Title: Clearing the path for first generation college students : qualitative
    and intersectional studies of educational mobility / edited by Ashley C.
    Rondini, Bedelia Nicola Richards, and Nicolas P. Simon.
Description: Lanham : Lexington Books , [2018] | Includes bibliographical
    references and index.
Identifiers: LCCN 2018011191 (print) | LCCN 2018016778 (ebook) | ISBN
    9781498537025 (Electronic) | ISBN 9781498537018 (cloth : alk. paper) | ISBN
    9781498537032 (pbk. : alk. paper)
Subjects: LCSH: First-generation college students–United States. | People
    with social disabilities—Education (Higher)—United States.
Classification: LCC LC4069.6 (ebook) | LCC LC4069.6 .C65 2018 (print) | DDC
    378.1/98—dc23
LC record available at https://lccn.loc.gov/2018011191

Contents

Acknowledgments

FROM THE EDITORS

In curating this collection, we shared a commitment to including both established, canonical works in the study of first-generation college students, and the critical, cutting-edge work of emerging scholars in the field. Each of the chapters featured in this book underwent a rigorous double blind external peer review process, in addition to an editorial review. To that end, we would like to acknowledge and sincerely thank the scholars who took time to carefully review contributions to the book and provide insightful feedback to authors: Roberto Gonzalez, Terrell Strayhorn, Alma Garza, Amy Stich, Laura Nichols, Stephanie J. Waterman, Ken Sun, Desiree Zerquera, and Jessi Streib. We have also collectively benefitted from the editorial support and guidance of Sarah Craig, Julia Torres, and Brighid Stone at Lexington Books.

FROM BEDELIA NICOLA RICHARDS

This project would not have been possible without the support of many people. Many thanks to Dr. Marilee Mifsud, who suggested Lexington Press for this project, for recommending our excellent editor, and for providing much insider knowledge on how to curate an edited volume. I am also thankful to my former Dean, Kathleen Skerrett, for providing generous financial support to hire our editor Laura Holliday and her colleague Berkeley Goodloe, who have provided professional and timely assistance with this project.

FROM ASHLEY C. RONDINI

My commitment to multidimensional scholarship that "does justice" to the experiences of first-generation college students draws inspiration from the experience of bearing witness to the incredible educational journeys of Justin Zullo and the students comprising Brandeis University's Posse 7, Posse 10, and the Myra T. Kraft Transitional Year Program. I have been privileged to receive ongoing support, personally and professionally, from far more people than I have space to name here. From this project's inception, guidance and critical feedback was generously provided by a cadre of advisors and mentors: David Cunningham, Carol Auster, Celina Jeffery, David Embrick, Jenny Stuber, and Donnell Butler. For their endless support of my professional endeavors, I am indebted to Anita Hill and Peter Conrad. I have been deeply grateful for the generous expressions of collegial encouragement that I received from Maria del Carmen Flores-Mills, Leanne Roncolato, Miranda Waggoner, and Meg Day throughout this process. We are indebted to Madeleine Peck Wagner for her beautiful original cover art, "Farther, Further." Finally, my own work on this book was directly facilitated by the invisible labor provided through the familial support structures that made it possible for me to complete it. As with so many other aspects of being both a parent and an academic, this labor of love has truly been a team effort. For this reason, I offer my humblest and deepest gratitude to my family: my partner, Richard Marsden, my son, Kailen Rondini-Marsden, my father, Donald Rondini, and, most of all, my mother, Marie Rondini—a resilient first-generation college graduate whose legacy cleared the path and paved the way for her own children and grandchildren to follow proudly in her footsteps.

FROM NICOLAS SIMON

I would like to thank all my colleagues of Eastern Connecticut State University for all their support to my dissertation, this edited volume, and our students who are mostly first-generation college students. I especially would like to thank Jasmine K. Carvalho, Liselotte J. Hammer, Mallory S. Papp, and Brianna M. Zecchini for helping us to edit the contributions' references. Their work was greatly appreciated. I also would like to thank Miriam and Arthur for their unconditional support and encouragement.

ORIGINAL COVER ART "FARTHER, FURTHER," BY MADELEINE PECK WAGNER

A Note from the Artist:

In thinking about the work "Farther, Further" I thought about what it meant for me to get to college, how initially school seemed like a hopeful—yet still large and looming—entity. While I was a small cog trying to figure a way through the social and academic structure. It was a joyous and sometimes painful time—and I grew immeasurably. With this work I hoped to capture that tension between hope and fear, work and freedom . . . and navigating in new waters with unfamiliar routes and rules.

Introduction

Clearing the Path: Situating First-Generation Students' Experiences in Qualitative, Intersectional Scholarship

Ashley C. Rondini, Bedelia Nicola Richards, and Nicolas P. Simon

An April 2015 *New York Times* article headlined "First Generation Students Unite" described the emergence of a "first generation student movement" at and across college and university campuses throughout the United States. This piece is one of many stories from news sources all across the country—including *The Washington Post, The Chronicle of Higher Education, The Huffington Post,* and *The Chicago Daily Herald*—that have reported on the challenges, experiences, and successes of first-generation college students in the past several years. The term "first-generation college student" has been most typically used to describe young people of traditional college age from families wherein neither parent has completed a baccalaureate degree (Carnevale and Fry 2000; Pascarella and Terenzini 1998; Terenzini et al. 1996), although—as is demonstrated by the chapters that follow—there is variation regarding how scholars and institutions may operationalize the concept. Increasing media attention to this population reflects its rapid growth in the past several decades. Honing in on the specific profiles of several first-generation college students at elite universities, the *Times* article (and accompanying video, in the online version) detailed a coalition of first-generation college students working with "1vyG," a thriving multicampus organization that hosted its fourth annual conference focused on "empowering and supporting" first-generation Ivy League students, in 2018. Its goals, and other similarly themed initiatives by and for first-generation students at a wide variety of academic institutions, include an emphasis on building community and elevating the collective visibility of shared "first-gen" identities.

Perhaps not surprisingly, first-generation college students themselves have been at the forefront of efforts to organize and mobilize around their shared status and experiences within institutions of higher education. These

1

students conceptualize their activism as part of what IvyG's organizers refer to as a growing "movement, not a moment"—which is a perspective that the institutions that serve them are now compelled to share. Integral to the resulting student-led organizations and initiatives is an asset-based framing of first-generation students' journeys that acknowledges obstacles while celebrating individual and collective perseverance. In different phases of their development and in different institutional contexts, first-generation student communities and organizations may be variably focused on support and resources for first-generation students and/or education and advocacy about and for first-generation student issues for the wider campus community. As the Facebook page for Cornell University's student-run First Generation Student Union (FGSU) reminds its members, they are "First, but not alone." The Working Class Student Union (WCSU) at the University of Wisconsin, Madison describes its purpose as "to advocate and provide resources for Working Class and First-Generation college students at UW–Madison while educating the entire university population on the benefits of recognizing and celebrating class diversity," based on the belief that working-class students "share a unique identity that has traditionally been silenced," and the desire to "break that silence and the stigma that it has created so that we can advocate for ourselves and the issues that are deeply impacting us" (WCSU, 2017). The emergence of these efforts is not limited to the campuses of Ivy League or large research universities. At Franklin and Marshall College, the fledgling First Generation Diplomats group focuses on support and advocacy, while pledging to approach first-gen student status through an intersectional lens that will encompass, as the FGD's website puts it, first-gen "students from diverse backgrounds, recognizing a need to respect individual differences of students from all races, socioeconomic statuses, ethnicities, genders, sexual orientations, nationalities, and abilities."[1] The group's founding coincided with the efforts of faculty and staff members at the college to establish a "First Gen Student Allies" organization, support for which is visually symbolized through "First Gen Student Ally" stickers displayed on faculty and staff members' office doors across the campus. The institutionalization of efforts to support first-gen students—whether led by students; by faculty, staff, and administration; or by both—manifests in a variety of other ways as well.

Community colleges serve the vast majority of matriculated first-generation college students. Yet, due to the imbalance of funding and infrastructural support opportunities for faculty research across different institutional contexts, the majority of recent scholarship focused on first-generation student experiences—including that which comprises this volume—has been conducted by scholars at four-year, disproportionately private colleges and universities, and thus is more likely to focus on the experiences of first-generation students at these types of institutions. Although first-generation students comprise a dramatically smaller proportion of the student body at four-year institutions than they do at community colleges, both public and private four-year colleges and universities of all sizes have developed, or are in the process of developing, a range of mechanisms to address the specific needs and experiences of this growing population in their midst.

At all schools awarded competitive, federally funded TRiO Student Support Services Program grants, resources are explicitly devoted to academic and social supports for first-generation college students, low-income college students, and/or college students with disabilities. A steadily increasing number of schools are also adding complementary programs, events, and organizations centered on first-generation students' experiences and identities. On the small private campus of Clark University in Worcester, Massachusetts, the student-led First Generation Student Union organization is supported by the overtly titled "Office of Multicultural and First Generation Student Services." Every spring at Brandeis University in Waltham, Massachusetts, as end-of-semester due dates approach and final exams loom, the Student Support Services Program (SSSP) organizes a celebration of first-generation students, faculty, and staff entitled "I am the First," which is funded by the Office of Academic Services and a grant from the Brandeis Pluralism Alliance out of the Dean of Arts and Sciences Office. Attended by one hundred or more members of the campus community, the dinner event includes an introduction by the university's president noting the accomplishments of first-generation students, as well as student testimonials that describe their social and academic obstacles and triumphs with poignant candor and pride. At Loyola Marymount University in Los Angeles, the First To Go Scholars program includes a four-day summer retreat, a single-unit seminar course on the first-generation college student experience, and a year-long structured program focused on connecting first-generation students with resources, tools, and strategies for success in college. Institutions such as Endicott College Boston (a satellite campus of the original Endicott College in Beverly, Massachusetts) and Empire State College (a division of the SUNY system, with thirty-four campuses throughout the state and extensive online course options) are specifically focused on serving student populations that are first-generation and/or of nontraditional age as they work to attain their academic and professional goals. Off campus, the last two decades have seen a proliferation of local and national nonprofit organizations focused on increasing college access and college success for first-generation students, in addition to the older "tried and true" programs such as Upward Bound. Since its founding in 2004, Class Action, a national nonprofit organization, has offered support and resources to first-generation college students to "ease their transition to college" while also collaborating with college and university administrations to identify gaps in services for first-gen students. The organization has hosted the First Generation Student Summit since 2012, wherein "First gen students and their allies come together to identify problems, discuss grassroots solutions and share what's working on other campuses."[2]

While most Americans perceive education as the "great equalizer" in attaining upward mobility, research points to enduring economic, social, and cultural barriers encountered by first-generation college students (see, e.g., Wilbur and Roscigno 2016; Armstrong and Hamilton 2013; Aries 2008; Mullen 2010; Stich 2012; Stuber 2011). The paths forged by first-generation students in pursuing their aspirations are often obstructed in both obvious and subtle ways. Our goal in this book is to provide tools with which to more clearly understand the various forms that the obstacles on those paths may take, while at the same time illuminating the myriad strategies that trailblazing first-generation students employ as they encounter them, as well as the practices undertaken to support these students by the institutions that serve them.

Although academic engagement with and reflection on issues of educational mobility and identity have a much longer history, our contribution to the pursuit of these understandings comes at a sociohistorical moment when scholarship on first-generation status within the sociology of higher education has more recently come to the fore. Contemporary scholarship on first-generation college students has its intellectual roots in the "working class academic" literature that emerged during the 1980s—a genre primarily comprising compelling, retrospective, first-person accounts of individuals who had been the first in their families to get a college degree and had chosen to enter academia as a profession (see, e.g., Adair and Dahlberg 2003; Dews and Law 1995; Grimes and Morris 1997; Muzzati and Samarco 2006; Oldfield and Johnson 2008; Rodriguez 1982; Ryan and Sackrey 1984; Shepard, McMillan, and Tate 1998; Tokarczyk and Fay 1993; Welsch 2005; Zandy 1990). This literature contributed valuable insights into first-generation college students' experiences and the social processes that accompanied upward mobility for individual scholars.

An abundance of quantitative academic and policy-focused work has significantly contributed to our understandings of the issues facing first-generation college students, illustrating economic (Lundberg et al. 2007; Lyons 2004; Pascarella et al. 2004), academic (McCarron and Inkelas 2006), and experiential (Allan, Garriott, and Keene 2016) inequalities between these students and their counterparts with college-educated parents. The National Center for Education Statistics (Chen and Carroll 2005) analyzed data from the National Education Longitudinal Study to reveal that in comparison to their peers, first-generation students (a) declared majors later; (b) did not accumulate as many academic credits in the first year; (c) were more likely to require remedial courses; (d) were less likely to take courses in mathematics, science, computer science, social science, humanities, history, and foreign languages; (e) had lower GPAs; and (f) were more likely to withdraw from or repeat courses. Not surprisingly, as each of these individual indicators is associated with higher risks of attrition, the report demonstrates that first-generation college students persistently experience higher rates of attrition than their peers, and are subsequently less likely to complete their degrees. The Pell Institute for the Study of Opportunity in Higher Education has pointed to similar indices of differentiation between low-income first-generation students and their more privileged peers, citing disparate persistence and degree attainment rates after students have matriculated (Engle and Tinto 2008) while also spotlighting the importance of comprehensive precollege services and programs in facilitating college access for first-generation students (Engle, Bermeo, and O'Brien 2006).

More recent research has demonstrated the persistence of these trends, while also highlighting the extent to which first-generation status itself conveys various forms of disadvantage, even when other factors are accounted for. First-generation status has long been understood to be negatively associated with a variety of academic performance measures, such as GPA (Strayhorn 2006), even as it intersects with other kinds of social identity statuses and risk factors for academic difficulty. For example, while all students with disabilities are at higher risk than students without disabilities for poor academic performance, first-generation college students with disabilities demonstrate lower levels of academic performance than do their continuing-generation peers with disabilities (see Lombardi, Murray, and Gerdes 2012). While students of color, immigrant students, and students from low socioeconomic status (SES) families are overrepresented among first-generation college students, first-generation status itself acts as a predictor of higher attrition risk when other demographic factors are controlled for (see, e.g., Ishitani 2003, 2006; Wilbur and Roscigno 2016). Wilbur and Roscigno (2016) found that first-generation students, on average, enroll in four-year colleges at rates of 70 percent less than their continuing-generation college student peers. Further, first-generation students who enroll in four-year colleges are 60 percent less likely to complete their college degrees than are their peers with college-educated parents (Wilbur and Roscigno 2016, 9).

Importantly, when first-generation status is disentangled from low socioeconomic status (with which it is significantly correlated), "college-specific disadvantages" and family stressors, "while certainly related to more general SES disadvantage, also have a unique and independent first-generation character" (Wilbur and Roscigno 2016, 8). Although students who are both of low socioeconomic status *and* first-generation status are "surely at the greatest system of disadvantage," Wilbur and Roscigno found that the "first-generation disadvantage" was not alleviated when they controlled for SES in their study (see Wilbur and Roscigno 2016, 9). When compared to their continuing-generation college student peers across racial and socioeconomic lines, first-generation college students were "less likely to be involved in [the] extracurricular and high impact activities" that would normally be positively associated with retention, and more likely to experience circumstances that are negatively associated with college completion such as working longer hours, residing at home during college, and personal and family-related events that are stressful (Wilbur and Roscigno 2016, 9).

This volume focuses on qualitative works, even as we recognize the critically important work that quantitative researchers have contributed to charting the "lay of the land." Our aim here is to build upon the valuable contributions that can help to tell us *which* variables matter and *to what extent*—to explore *why* and *how* the variables identified in quantitative works matter in the meaning-making processes that inform first-generation students' experiences, taking into account the unique social locations of individuals and groups. The crucial work of quantifying these differential risks and outcomes lays the groundwork for qualitative investigation of the mechanisms and social processes that undergird and perpetuate educational inequities and for documentation of the strategies and tools with which first-generation students confront the challenges that they encounter. The meaning-making processes through which selected variables are experienced may otherwise be difficult to extrapolate from numbers alone. Collectively, the chapters herein enhance the depth and nuance of understandings drawn from quantitative data. Centering first-generation students' voices, these studies provide "insider" perspectives presented within the contexts through which students encounter their experiences of educational mobility.

We contend that qualitative analyses can illuminate the strategies and tools developed by first-generation students, their parents, or the institutional actors who occupy decision-making positions related to programs and services serving first-gen students. For example, longitudinal research on children of parents with low educational attainment levels has demonstrated that the educational expectations of parents act as a significant predictor of college attendance for first-generation students (see Bui and Rush 2016). When they do matriculate, survey data demonstrate that first-generation students are less likely to confide in parents, family members, and professionals about the stresses of college life than are their continuing-generation peers (see Barry et al. 2009), even when their difficulties intensify as time goes on. However, these findings cannot tell us *how* parents convey educational expectations and/or *how* their children received and interpreted the messages about educational expectations with which they were presented, nor can they illuminate the ways in which students navigate their communication with parents (or others) regarding their college experiences, in light of the limits of what they disclose. To return to the understanding that the communication of academic expectations is an important aspect of parental support in predicting future enrollment in higher education for first-generation students, the qualitative literature illustrates the interactive processes through which these expectations are communicated.

At the same time, qualitative scholars have also documented the conflicts that students experience in attempting to navigate the institutional environments of their college or university campuses when the cultural capital of their families and communities of origin differs from that which is valued or required in their new institutional environments (Lee and Kramer 2013; Lehmann 2013). A number of relatively recent works have contributed to deeper understanding of the ways in which students navigate the experiential core of college life at the intersections of their social identities. Jenny Stuber's *Inside the College Gates: How Class and Culture Matter in Higher Education* (2011), Amy Stich's *Access to Inequality: Reconsidering Class, Knowledge, and Capital in Higher Education* (2012) and Elizabeth Lee's *Class and Campus Life* (2016) have illuminated the ways that inequities in socioeconomic class and cultural capital differentiate first-generation students' outlooks toward, and experiences of, the academic, social, and extracurricular aspects of their campus experiences from those of their peers. In another example, Armstrong and Hamilton (2013) collected data for their influential book, *Paying for the Party*, in a residential women's dormitory, placing the classed experiences of female students at the center of their analyses. Nonetheless, much of the literature on first-generation students systematically neglects to engage the relevance of gender, gender identity, or sexuality as meaningfully relevant to lived experiences of first-generation student status.

Our collection of studies engages the experiences of first-generation college students at the intersections of race, gender, citizenship/immigration dynamics, and socioeconomic status, drawing from and building upon the nuanced dynamics underscored through the qualitative empirical work of the past decades' scholarship. The first-generation student population is in no way a monolith, despite the shared experience of navigating academic environments without the benefits yielded by parental educational experience from which to draw. Race, class, gender, sexuality, disability, nationality, and citizenship status unavoidably constitute meaningful dimensions of social difference that inform educational outcomes as well as overall opportunities for social mobility. As in the study of any dimension of social inequality, it is crucial to engage intersectional approaches to the study of first-generation students' experience because individuals occupy multiple identities and social locations simultaneously (Crenshaw, 1989). Elizabeth Aries's (2008, 2012) work provides an example of intersecting race and class dynamics as they pertain to lower- and middle-class Black *and* lower- and middle-class White undergraduates at an elite liberal arts college, including those that are first-generation students. First-generation students face distinctive challenges, even as their shared first-gen status intersects with other aspects of their social identities and educational backgrounds in particular ways. The benefit of engaging nuanced, intersectional analyses of student experiences is demonstrated by Anthony Jack's (2014) work on the "privileged poor" and the "doubly disadvantaged," wherein differences in secondary institutional experiences mediated significant disparities in relevant cultural capital for college success among low-income Black students, despite their shared racial, socioeconomic, and first-generation student identities. Collectively, research on low-income White students (Lehmann 2013; Stuber 2011), Black students (Jack 2016; Owens et al. 2010) and Latinx students (Saunders and Serna 2004) allows for comparisons across groups of differing racial, ethnic, and immigration statuses. Nonetheless, there is comparatively less scholarship in the first-gen literature that meaningfully engages racial and ethnic identity dynamics for students of Asian and Native American descent or the significance of immigration and citizenship status in simultaneous relation to first-gen student status.

For example, although Native American student enrollment in higher education has increased by more than 200 percent since the 1970s—the majority of which comprises first-generation students (Brayboy et al. 2012)—existing scholarship on race, culture, and first-generation students pays scarce attention to the experiential factors bearing on the higher education experiences and retention of this population. Further, examinations of the impact of the legacy of settler colonialism on Native youths' racial identity formation experiences within predominantly White institutional environments in the United States—and higher educational institutions particularly—remains largely disconnected from the literature on educational mobility (see, e.g., Horse 2012). In addition, much of the sociological literature on Asian Americans is located within the immigration literature in part because Asians are one of the fastest growing immigrant groups in the United States (Lee and Zhou 2015), and the majority of Asian American children have immigrant parents (Passel 2011). Accordingly, this literature tends to focus on issues of assimilation and cultural adaptation. Immigration scholars are more likely to engage with debates about the role of Asian Americans in reshaping the color line, noting evidence of Asian Americans' growing acceptance into predominantly White spaces (Alba and Nee 2003; Lee and Bean 2010). It is rare for immigration scholars who focus on Asian American students to highlight how their status as immigrants intersects with their status as first-generation college students. Although there is an abundance of studies in the sociology of education literature that seeks to critically engage the construction of Asian Americans as "model minorities" (Lee 2015; Lee and Zhou 2015), this trope continues to shape popular discourse about this population (Breitenstein 2013; Kristof 2015). The model minority narratives of Asian American success and acceptance are not compatible with the narratives of struggle, marginality, and resilience that characterize both the literature on first-generation students as well as the literature about racial and ethnic minority college student experiences more generally. Yet, dominant constructions of Asian America that are consistent with the model minority stereotype obscure the experiences of students from less advantaged Asian American ethnic groups (Lee 2015). For example, while almost 50 percent of Asian Americans have a bachelor's degree or higher (higher than the US average), as of 2011 this was true for only 16 percent of Cambodians, 14.8 percent of Hmong, and 13.2 percent of Laotians (SERAC 2011). For Asian, Latinx, and other immigrant groups, immigration status may complicate how we as scholars in the United States tend to define first-generation status as a function of educational attainment. First-generation college student status among Asian American students is rarely addressed in immigration or education scholarship, and immigration and citizenship status are rarely central issues in studies of first-generation college students.

This edited collection builds on the momentum of earlier qualitative literature by placing first-generation status at the center of inquiry, while at the same time engaging intersectional analyses of the heterogeneity within that population. *Clearing the Path* comprises a range of peer-reviewed studies that explore social processes and meanings germane to the experiences of first-generation college students with timely, empirical examinations of the ways that first-generation college students negotiate dynamics and dilemmas of structural inequities, identity transformation, social and cultural capital, ongoing relationships with families or communities of origin, and the pursuit of community and belonging that characterize their educational mobility trajectories. Our hope is that these studies will serve to engage existing questions in the field of first-generation student scholarship in meaningful ways, while at the same time raising new critical questions for further examination in the future.

The navigation of identity dynamics for first-generation students is a complex process, to which several of these chapters speak directly. Allison Hurst's *The Burden of Academic Success: Managing Working Class Identities in College* (2010), from which her chapter in this book is excerpted, provides a framework through which to conceptualize the various identity management strategies—that of class "loyalists," "renegades," or "double agents"—that working-class first-generation students adopt in confronting these inequities. Another chapter, Lee and Kramer's "Out With the Old, In With the New? Habitus and Social Mobility at Selective Colleges" (2013), has quickly become a landmark text in the scholarship on first-generation students, examining the ways in which first-generation students are incentivized to develop a "cleft habitus" as they navigate the social distance between their home and school environment. Rondini's chapter in this volume, "Cautionary Tales: Low-Income First-Generation College Students, Educational Mobility, and Familial Meaning-Making Processes," further explores these issues within the family context, drawing on qualitative interviews with first-generation students and their parents to examine one mechanism through which parental encouragement and educational expectations are conveyed, understood, and applied to the formation of social meanings attached to intergenerational educational mobility.

How might differing institutional contexts and processes inform differentiated first-generation student experiences at the college level? In a key study of one particularly successful program's efficacy in supporting the success of underrepresented first-generation students of color in the sciences, Godsoe's chapter, "Science Posse: The Importance of the Cohort in Normalizing Academic Challenge," examines the significance of the cohort structure for students in the STEM Posse program, with particular attention to the role that this program plays in normalizing experiences of academic challenges or difficulties that might otherwise make individual students feel isolated. In another examination of institutional dynamics and practices, "First-Generation Students and Their Families: Examining Institutional Responsibility During College Access and Transition," Kiyama, Harper, and Ramos turn an analytic lens to the ways that colleges and universities inclusively engage (or dismissively fail to engage) the parents of first-generation students before and during the critical college transition process.

Of course, institutional dynamics matter in ways that shape educational outcomes long before students even arrive to campus. In his early work, Jack (2014) found that even among Black students who originate from the same neighborhoods and inhabit the same social class positions, those who attended elite boarding schools gained cultural capital that contributed to a more positive and successful college experience. In Jack and Irwin's chapter in this volume, "Seeking Out Support: Looking Beyond Socioeconomic Status to Explain Academic Engagement Strategies at an Elite College," the researchers examine the ways in which these dynamics differentially inform students' strategies for seeking out institutional support during their college careers. If secondary school context alone can contribute to such meaningful differences within a population that appears so homogeneous on the surface, what does that mean for differences across racial and ethnic groups whose histories of marginalization and relationship to the dominant group differ in meaningful ways? In Beard's chapter, "Toward a Local Student Success Model: Latino First-Generation College Student Persistence," the author critically engages this question as it pertains to Latinx first-generation students at predominantly White institutions. Beard's work pays particular attention to the ways in which these students "capitalize on community cultural wealth," among other resources and strategies, in ways that bolster their educational persistence. For other first-generation student-of-color populations, how do the particular socioenvironmental dynamics of predominantly White college campuses shape experiences of belonging—and pose challenges to thriving? For example, there are few scholarly studies that engage the intergenerational effects of settler colonialism that may uniquely inform Native students' negotiation of familial, cultural, and institutional identities as they undertake their college experiences (Reyes 2014). In their contribution to this volume, "Demystifying Influences on Persistence for Native American First-Generation College Students," Youngbull and Minthorn engage, in nuanced and groundbreaking ways, the multidimensional dynamics that particularly shape Native first-generation students' experiences and obstacles to educational attainment. In addition, the authors provide an inventory of programs and models that they identify as best practices for the support of Native first-generation students.

Given that immigration as a sociohistorical process has been critical to how racial and ethnic groups have been incorporated into the United States, how does immigration as a process at the macro level intersect with citizenship status at the individual level to influence what it means to be a first-generation college student? Because international degrees are devalued in the US economic market (Buenavista 2010) and cultural capital is context specific, some children of immigrants with college-educated parents may nonetheless experience challenges similar to those of their peers whose parents do not have advanced degrees (Chou and Feagin 2015), despite the ways in which their parents' contextual educational attainment experiences may benefit them in other ways (Feliciano and Lenuza 2017). This transnational intergenerational dynamic is one of several explored in Piñeros Shields's chapter in this volume, "Rethinking First-Generation College Status among Undocumented Immigrant Students," wherein he examines how premigration parental educational attainment level informs the college-access and college-going experiences of undocumented Latinx immigrant students at the intersections of class, race, and citizenship. Relatedly, as Yeung points out, English language proficiency may limit even college-educated immigrants' ability to cultivate and transfer valuable forms of cultural capital useful in the US context. In her chapter on interdependent relationships and family responsibilities for low-income Asian American students who are also second-generation immigrants, she examines the multidimensional ways in which family immigration history shapes students' experiences of higher education in the United States.

Given the extant literature on the ways that gender influences the educational experiences of students (Dumais 2002; Lopez 2003; Morris 2011; Ostrove 2003), to what extent does gender—either as an ideological construct or a feature of one's identity—intersect with first-generation status and socioeconomic class to shape students' experiences? Ann Mullen's *Degrees of Inequality: Culture, Class, and Gender in American Higher Education* (2010), from which her chapter in this volume, "Choosing Majors, Choosing Careers: How Gender and Class Shape Students' Selection of Fields," is drawn, brings intersecting gender and socioeconomic class dynamics into critical focus in ways that bear significant implications for our understanding of first-generation students' experiences and trajectories.

The body of work presented here is designed to function as a tool for dialogue between first-gen student communities, scholars, practitioners, and administrators who have the power to enact meaningful change in institutions that serve first-generation college students. This volume balances a focus on the challenges that first-generation students encounter in making successful transitions with an attention to the assets that contribute to their resilience, as well as potential policy and programmatic approaches to bolster first-generation students' likelihood of success. These chapters bridge a conversational gap between the production of scholarly research germane to experiences of first-generation college students and the implementation of evidence-based practices aimed at effectively supporting the success of this population.

Even so, we offer this collection of works as only a starting point that bears its own limitations. As noted earlier, the scholarship herein disproportionately examines the experiences of first-generation students at predominantly private, four-year institutions, reflecting the comparatively scant body of first-generation student research conducted within the community college systems that serve this population in far greater numbers. While it is our hope that this volume will provide fertile ground for the continuing cultivation of sociologically informed understandings of first-generation students' experiences, we also recognize that there are far more dimensions of identity beyond those explored herein—disability, religion, sexuality, and gender identity/expression, to name a few—that intersect with first-generation status in addition to those informed by race, gender, class, citizenship, and immigration dynamics. There are, as always, more unanswered questions to explore. There is, as always, more critical work to be done.

REFERENCES

Adair, Vivyan C., and Sandra L. Dahlberg, eds. 2003. *Reclaiming Class: Women, Poverty, and the Promise of Higher Education in America.* Philadelphia: Temple University Press.

Alba, Richard, and Victor Nee. 2003. *Remaking the American Mainstream: Assimilation and Contemporary Immigration.* Cambridge: Harvard University Press.

Allan, Blake A., Patton Garriott, and Chesleigh Keene. 2016. "Outcomes of Social Class and Classism in First- and Continuing-Generation College Students." *Journal of Counseling Psychology* 63, no. 4: 487–96.

Aries, Elizabeth. 2008. *Race and Class Matters at an Elite College.* Philadelphia: Temple University Press.

Aries, Elizabeth. 2012. *Speaking of Race and Class: The Student Experience at An Elite College.* Philadelphia: Temple University Press.

Armstrong, Elizabeth A., and Laura T. Hamilton. 2013. *Paying for the Party: How College Maintains Inequality.* Cambridge: Harvard University Press.

Barry, Leasha M., Cynthia Hudley, Melissa Kelly, and Su-Je Cho. 2009. "Differences in Self-Reported Disclosure of College Experiences by First Generation College Student Status." *Adolescence* 44, no. 173: 55–68.

Brayboy, Bryan M. J., Amy Fann, Angelina Castagno, and Jessica Solyom. 2012. *Postsecondary Education for American Indians and Alaska Natives: Higher Education for Nation-Building and Self-Determination.* San Francisco: The ASHE Higher Education Series.

Breitenstein, Dave. 2013. "Asian Students Carry High Expectations for Success." *USA Today*, August 4. http://www.usatoday.com/story/news/nation/2013/08/04/asian-students-carry-high-expectations-for-success/2615483/.

Buenavista, Tracy Lachica. 2010. "Issues Affecting US Filipino Student Access to Postsecondary Education: A Critical Race Theory Perspective." *Journal of Education for Students Placed at Risk* 15, no. 1–2: 114–26.

Bui, Khanh, and Ryan Rush. 2016. "Parental Involvement in Middle School Predicting College Attendance for First-Generation Students" *Education* 136, no. 4: 473–89.

Carnevale, Anthony P., and Richard A. Fry. 2000. *Crossing the Great Divide: Can We Achieve Equity when Generation Y Goes to College?* Princeton, NJ: Educational Testing Service.

Chen, Xianglei, and C. Dennis Carroll. 2005. *First-Generation Students in Post-Secondary Education: A Look at Their College Transcripts.* (NCES 2005–171). US Department of Education, National Center for Education Statistics. Washington, DC: US Government Printing Office.

Chou, Rosalind S., and Joe R. Feagin. 2015. *The Myth of the Model Minority: Asian Americans Facing Racism.* Boulder: Paradigm Publishers.

Crenshaw, Kimberle. 1989. "Demarginalizing the Intersection of Race and Sex: A Black Feminist Critique of Antidiscrimination Doctrine, Feminist Theory and Antiracist Politics." *University of Chicago Legal Forum* 1: 139–67.

Dews, C. L. Barney, and Carolyn Leste Law, eds. 1995. *This Fine Place So Far From Home: Voices of Academics From the Working Class.* Philadelphia: Temple University Press.

Dumais, Susan A. 2002. "Cultural Capital, Gender, and School Success: The Role of Habitus." *Sociology of Education* 75, no. 1: 44–68.

Engle, Jennifer, Adolfo Bermeo, and Colleen O'Brien. 2006. *Straight from the Source: What Works for First-Generation College Students.* Washington, DC: The Pell Institute for the Study of Opportunity in Higher Education.

Engle, Jennifer, and Vincent Tinto. 2008. *Moving Beyond Access: College Success for Low-Income, First Generation Students.* Washington, DC: The Pell Institute for the Study of Opportunity in Higher Education.

Feliciano, Cynthia, and Yader R. Lenuza. 2017. "An Immigrant Paradox? Contextual Educational Attainment and Intergenerational Educational Mobility." *American Sociological Review* 82, no. 1: 211–41.

Grimes, Michael D., and Joan M. Morris. 1997. *Caught in the Middle: Contradictions in the Lives of Sociologists from Working Class Backgrounds.* Westport: Praeger.

Horse, Perry G. 2012. "Twenty-First Century Native American Consciousness: A Thematic Model of Indian Identity." In *New Perspectives on Racial Identity Development: Integrating Emerging Frameworks (Second Edition),* edited by Charmaine L. Wijeyesinghe and Bailey W. Jackson III, 108–20. New York: New York University Press.

Housel Heinz, Theresa, and Vickie L. Harvey, eds. 2010. *The Invisibility Factor: Administrators and Faculty Reach Out to First-Generation College Students.* Boca Raton: Brown Walker Press.

Hurst, Allison L. 2010. *The Burden of Academic Success: Loyalists, Renegades, and Double Agents.* Lanham, MD: Rowman and Littlefield Press.

Ishitani, T. T. 2003. "A Longitudinal Approach to Assessing Attrition Behavior Among First-Generation Students: Time-Varying Effects of Pre-College Characteristics." *Research in Higher Education* 44: 433–49.

Ishitani, T. T. 2006. "Studying Attrition and Degree Completion Behavior Among First-Generation College Students in the United States." *The Journal of Higher Education* 77, no. 5: 860–86.

Jack, Anthony A. 2014. "Culture Shock Revisited: The Social and Cultural: Contingencies to Class Marginality." *Sociological Forum* 29, no. 2: 453–75.

Jack, Anthony A. 2016. "(No) Harm in Asking: Class, Acquired Cultural Capital, and Academic Engagement at an Elite University." *Sociology of Education* 89, no. 1: 1–19.

Kiyama, Judy M. 2010. "College Aspirations and Limitations: The Role of Educational Ideologies and Funds of Knowledge in Mexican American Families." *American Educational Research Journal* 47, no. 2: 330–56.

Kristof, Nicholas. 2015. "The Asian Advantage." *New York Times*, October 10. https://www.nytimes.com/2015/10/11/opinion/sunday/the-asian-advantage.html?_ r=0.

Lee, Elizabeth M. 2016. *Class and Campus Life: Managing and Experiencing Inequality at an Elite College*. Ithaca: Cornell University Press.

Lee, Elizabeth M., and Rory Kramer. 2013. "Out With the Old, In With the New? Habitus and Social Mobility at Selective Colleges." *Sociology of Education* 86, no. 1: 18–35.

Lee, Jennifer, and Frank D. Bean. 2010. *The Diversity Paradox: Immigration and the Color Line in Twenty-First Century America*. New York: Russell Sage Foundation.

Lee, Jennifer, and Min Zhou. 2015. *The Asian American Achievement Paradox*. New York: Russell Sage Foundation.

Lee, Rachel C., and Sau-Ling Wong, eds. 2013. *Asian America. Net: Ethnicity, Nationalism, and Cyberspace*. New York: Routledge.

Lee, Stacey J. 2015. *Unraveling the "Model Minority" Stereotype: Listening to Asian American Youth*. New York: Teachers College Press.

Lehmann, Wolfgang. 2013. "In a Class of Their Own: How Working-Class Students Experience University." In *Contemporary Debates in the Sociology of Education*, edited by Rachel Brooks, Mark McCormack, and Kalwant Bhopal, 93–111. Houndmills: Palgrave.

Lombardi, Allison R., Christopher Murray, and Hilary Gerdes. 2012. "Academic Performance of First-Generation Students with Disabilities." *Journal of College Student Development* 53, no. 6: 811–26.

Lopez, Nancy. 2003. *Hopeful Girls, Troubled Boys: Race and Gender Disparity in Urban Education*. New York: Routledge.

Lundberg, Carol, Laurie A. Schreiner, Kristin Hovaguimian, and Sharyn Slavin Miller. 2007. "First-Generation Status and Student Race/Ethnicity as Distinct Predictors of Student Involvement and Learning." *National Association of Student Personnel Administrators* 44, no. 1: 57–83.

Lyons, Angela. C. 2004. "A Profile of Financially At-Risk College Students." *The Journal of Consumer Affairs* 38, no. 1: 56–80.

McCarron, Graziella P., and Karen K. Inkelas. 2006. "The Gap Between Educational Aspirations and Attainment for First-Generation College Students and the Role of Parental Involvement." *Journal of College Student Development* 47, no. 5: 534–49.

Morris, Edward W. 2011. "Bridging the Gap: 'Doing Gender,' 'Hegemonic Masculinity,' and the Educational Troubles of Boys." *Sociology Compass* 5, no. 1: 92–103.

Mullen, Ann L. 2010. *Degrees of Inequality: Culture, Class, and Gender in American Higher Education*. Baltimore: Johns Hopkins University Press.

Muzzati, Stephen L., and Vincent C. Samarco, eds. 2006. *Reflections from the Wrong Side of the Tracks: Class, Identity, and the Working Class Experience in Academe*. Lanham: Rowman and Littlefield.

Oldfield, Kenneth, and Richard G. Johnson, eds. 2008. *Resilience: Queer Professors from the Working Class*. Albany: State University of New York Press.

Ostrove, Joan. 2003. "Belonging and Wanting: Meanings of Social Class Background for Women's Constructions of Their College Experiences." *Journal of Social Issues* 59, no. 4: 771–84.

Owens, Delila, Krim Lacey, Glinda Rawls, and JoAnne Holbert-Quince. 2010. "First-Generation African American Male College Students: Implications for Career Counselors." *The Career Development Quarterly* 58, no. 4: 291–300.

Pascarella, Ernest, Christopher Pierson, Gregory Wolniak, and Patrick Terenzini. 2004. "First-Generation College Students." *The Journal of Higher Education* 75, no. 3: 249–84.

Pascarella, Ernest, and Patrick Terenzini. 1998. "Studying College Students in the 21st Century: Meeting New Challenges." *Review of Higher Education* 21, no. 2: 151–65.

Passel, Jeffrey S. 2011. "Demography of Immigrant Youth: Past, Present, and Future." *The Future of Children* 21, no. 1: 19–41.

Reyes, Nicole Alia Salis. 2014. "The Multiplicity and Intersectionality of Indigenous Identities." In *Intersectionality and Higher Education: Theory, Research, and Practice*, edited by D. Mitchell, Jr., 45–54. New York: Peter Lang Books.

Rodriguez, Richard. 1982. *Hunger of Memory: The Education of Richard Rodriguez*. New York: Random House.

Rondini, Ashley C. 2016. "Healing the Hidden Injuries of Class?: Redemption Narratives, Aspirational Proxies, and Parents of Low-Income First Generation College Students." *Sociological Forum* 31, no. 1: 96–116.

Ryan, Jake, and Charles Sackrey, eds. 1984. *Strangers in Paradise: Academics from the Working Class*. Boston: South End Press.

Saunders, Marisa, and Irene Serna. 2004. "Making College Happen: The College Experiences of First-Generation Latino Students." *Journal of Hispanic Higher Education* 3, no. 2: 146–63.

SERAC (Southern Asian Resource Action Center). 2011. *Southeast Asian Americans at a Glance*. Washington, DC: SEARAC.

Shepard, Alan, John McMillan, and Gary Tate, eds. 1998. *Coming to Class: Pedagogy and the Social Class of Teachers*. Portsmouth: Boynton/Cook.

Stich, Amy E. 2012. *Access to Inequality: Reconsidering Class, Knowledge, and Capital in Higher Education*. Lanham: Lexington Books.

Strayhorn, Terrell L. 2006. "Factors Influencing the Academic Achievement of First Generation College Students." *NASPA Journal* 43, no. 4: 82–111.

Stuber, Jenny M. 2011. *Inside the College Gates: How Class and Culture Matter in Higher Education*. Lanham: Lexington Books.

Terenzini, Patrick T., Leonard Springer, Patricia Yaeger, Ernest Pascarella, and Amaury Nora. 1996. "First Generation College Students: Characteristics, Experiences, and Cognitive Development." *Research in Higher Education* 37, no. 1: 1–22.

Tokarczyk, Michelle M., and Elizabeth A. Fay, eds. 1993. *Working Class Women in the Academy: Laborers in the Knowledge Factory*. Boston: University of Massachusetts Press.

Wang, Tiffany. R. 2014. "'I'm the Only Person from Where I'm From to Go to College': Understanding the Memorable Messages First-Generation College Students Receive from Parents." *Journal of Family Communication* 14, no. 3: 270–90.

Welsch, Kathleen A. 2005. *Those Winter Sundays: Female Academics and Their Working Class Parents*. New York: University Press of America.

Wilbur, Tabitha G., and Roscigno, Vincent J. 2016. "First-Generation Disadvantage and College Enrollment Completion." *Socius: Sociological Research for a Dynamic World* 2: 1–11.

Working Class Student Union, 2017. Facebook, September 21, 2017. https://www.facebook.com/pg/wcsuuw/about/?ref=page_internal

Zandy, Janet, ed. 1990. *Calling Home: Working Class Women's Writings*. New Brunswick: Rutgers University Press.

NOTES

1. https://www.fandm.edu/campus-life/clubs/first-generation-diplomats
2. http://www.classism.org/programs/resources-generation-college-students/

1

"Cautionary Tales"

Low-Income First-Generation College Students, Educational Mobility, and Familial Meaning-Making Processes

Ashley C. Rondini

What they said was, "You need to get an education, to get a career because that is the only way you can be someone in the future." They always put themselves as an example. Like my mom said, "This is what I do for a living. You don't want to do this; this is because I didn't go to college. This is because I don't have an education." All my aunts told me the same thing. I always understood, because their lives were not easy.

—Lydia (21-year-old Latina of Dominican descent)

Familial habitus is shaped by the structural and material conditions within which family life is contextualized, at the intersections of stratification systems based on socioeconomic status, race, gender, and immigration history. Familial cultural norms—and specifically parental messages—surrounding education have a significant impact on the development of children's motivations for and orientation toward educational persistence and, ultimately, social mobility (Goldsmith 2003; Kao and Tienda 1998; Lareau 2003; MacLeod 2009). This chapter examines specific intersubjective processes through which successful low-income first-generation (LIFG) college students and their parents participated in the construction of meanings associated with academic persistence and, ultimately, intergenerational educational mobility. My research engages and expands upon the work of scholars who have contributed to existing research on education, habitus, parental support of LIFG students, and intergenerational mobility. The data illuminate a particular strategy employed by low-income parents in cultivating worldviews conducive to high educational aspirations and strong motivation for academic persistence for their children, despite the structural obstacles faced by these families in providing material resources with which their children can actualize their goals. These findings lend insight into the ways that macrolevel social and economic forces and microlevel systems of meaning converge to inform the cultivation of shared familial orientations toward higher education.

LOW-INCOME FIRST-GENERATION COLLEGE STUDENTS

From an early age, class-based habitus is understood to impact the relative advantages and disadvantages that children across racial groups bring with them to the process of navigating educational institutions (see, e.g., Lareau 2003; Neckerman, Carter, and Lee 1999). Beyond the experience of obvious material disparities, research has indicated that a more subtle but also significant point of class-based differentiation is manifest between the working-class "natural growth" vs. middle-class "concerted cultivation" cultural orientations toward parenting (see Lareau 2003). Within this framework, explicit intentionality is solely attributed to middle-class parents' efforts to instrumentally equip their children for academic success, as juxtaposed with the seemingly less strategic or intentional characterization of efforts by parents who are navigating socioeconomic constraints as they focus on providing their children with basic necessities. While this critical comparison regarding the cultural dynamics of class differentiation does serve to highlight the practical life skills and independence developed by working-class children in various ways, it also lends itself to an interpretation that parental efficacy in support of children's academic pursuits is limited to that of the socioeconomically advantaged parents to whom "concerted" intentionality to "cultivate" children's talents and academic skills is exclusively credited. Importantly, these concepts are framed in terms of the role that they play in the reproduction of educational and social inequalities. While a few studies have touched upon the ways in which parents' low educational attainment and/or lack of knowledge regarding higher education may negatively impact children's levels of academic engagement in college (Kenny and Stryker 1996; London 1989; McSwain and Davis 2007), little has been understood about the relevance of *successful* LIFG students' parents' participation in the construction of social meanings associated with their children's educational trajectories vis-à-vis their concerted, intentional efforts to encourage academic persistence. In the absence of such an analysis, it is possible to draw the problematic conclusion that the parents of LIFG students are involved in their children's educational trajectories only to the extent that their own "deficits" (see, e.g., Cabrera and Padilla 2004) constitute obstacles to success for the next generation.

The literature focused on structural mechanisms of social reproduction in educational settings seems to bear out presumptions of low-income parents' incompetence with regard to effectively contributing to their children's successes; in terms of social network connections, access to community resources, or access to educational and occupational resource distribution and opportunity structures, families with wealth, high income, and high parental education levels are better positioned to bolster their children's academic success than are families with fewer assets, low income, and low parental education levels (Belley and Lochner 2007; Filmer and Pritchett 1999; Fine 2003; Karagiannaki 2012; Pfeffer and Hällsten 2012). Yet, the attributes of *resilience* and the capacity to "cope with adversity"—both conceivably attributable to examples set by parents who have endured structural constraints—have also been found to positively correlate with the success of underrepresented student populations (Reay, Crozier, and Clayton 2009, 1107).

More generally, research has demonstrated that supportive familial relationships have a positive influence on college students' academic achievement, self-efficacy, and intrinsic motivation for scholastic success (Strage and Brandt 1999; Turner, Chandler, and Heffer 2009). Research also suggests that supportive familial relationships may have a more significant influence on the educational persistence of college students from underrepresented racial and socioeconomic backgrounds than they have for White and/or middle- or upper-class students (Guiffrida 2006; Lee and Kramer 2013; Melendez and Melendez 2010; Nora and Cabrera 1996). LIFG students—across racial lines—are disproportionately more likely to struggle with strains in their familial relationships when they undertake their college careers at elite institutions, wherein the dominant habitus significantly differs from that of their home environment (Lee and Kramer 2013).

Particularly in light of these understandings, data concerning the perspectives of the parents of LIFG students is notably absent from much of the scholarship that addresses intrafamilial dynamics. The foundational literature on working-class experiences in academia—largely comprising first-person narratives rather than systematic or empirical study—primarily addressed familial dynamics insofar as scholars provided their own retrospective accounts of interactions and relationships with their own families (see, e.g., Adair and Dahlberg 2003; Dews and Law 1995; Grimes and Morris 1997; Mahony and Zmroczek 1997; Ryan and Sackrey 1984; Muzzatti and Samarco 2005; Tokarczyk and Fay 1993: Welsch 2005). Similarly, with few exceptions (see Gofen 2009; Rondini 2016), the burgeoning contemporary literature engaging intergenerational educational mobility is limited to analysis of students' interpretations regarding their parents' perspectives (see, e.g., Hurst 2010; Lee and Kramer 2013; Lehmann 2014; Reay, Crozier, and Clayton 2009; Stuber 2006), in the absence of data based on parents' own accounts. In recent research engaging the processes through which first-generation students construct college-going as a way to avoid the difficulties faced by previous generations, and thus view themselves as "family pioneers," parents' perspectives are only represented through the ways that students characterize them (see Langenkamp and Shifrer 2017). This is not to dismiss the contributions made by these studies; arguably, the impact of students' ideas about their parents' thoughts, feelings, and opinions is significant enough to their navigation of academic experiences to merit inquiry. However, the overall erasure of parents' voices in the study of intergenerational mobility limits understandings of the agency and subjectivity with which parents may actively participate in relevant familial meaning-making processes regarding their children's education, even in the absence of material resources. The separate student and parent interviews in this study allowed me to link intersubjectivities (see Weiss 1995) within family systems, facilitating the identification of overlap and tensions in interpretations and understandings of the same topics.

Several empirical studies address patterned ways in which aspects of familial experiences based on race, class, and immigration shape educational expectations, sources of motivation, and aspirations (see, e.g., Connell 2004, Neckerman, Carter, and Lee 1999; Hochschild 1995; Kao and Tienda 1998), without directly engaging the complex intrafamilial processes through which these perspectives are cultivated. Socioeconomically and/or racially disadvantaged parents are not less likely than White and/or middle- and upper-class parents to place a high value on education, or to espouse the "American dream ideology" (see Hochschild 1995). Given the contemporary pervasiveness of "college-for-all" as a hegemonic cultural frame, social class is less likely than ever before to differentially predict educational aspirations (see Langenkamp and Shifrer 2017; Goyette 2008). Despite being often mismatched to resources and opportunities through which to realize them, particularly high educational aspirations for children are held by immigrant parents at all socioeconomic levels (Cheng and Starks 2002; Feliciano 2006; Kao 2004; Kao and Tienda 1998; Kim 2008; Louie 2006; Ogbu 1978; Portes, McLeod, and Parker 1978), and racial minority students are likely to have higher educational aspirations than those held by their White counterparts when socioeconomic status is taken into account (Cheng and Starks 2002; Feliciano 2006; Goyette and Xie 1999; Kao 2004; Kao and Tienda 1998; Kim 2008; Portes and Zhou 1993; Qian and Blair 1999). While some studies have addressed the specific occupational outcomes to which parents encourage their children to aspire (Cheng and Starks 2002; Hochschild 1995; Louie 2006), none have sought empirically to gain more nuanced, qualitative understandings of the specific *mechanisms* through which socioeconomically disadvantaged parents actively co-construct social meanings related to their children's educational mobility. In addition, the literature exploring how gendered experiences inform the parenting approaches and strategies of low-income women (see, e.g., Edin and Kefalas 2005; Silva 2013) is largely disconnected from the limited scholarship that explicitly engages gender in relation to LIFG student experiences (see, e.g., Mullen 2010; Tokarczyk and Fay 1993).

Bourdieu's concept of *habitus* comprises the implicitly understood cultural norms of a collectivity in relation to which identity is conceptualized. Bourdieu's (1996) discussion of the significance of habitus arises in his examination of the structured and structuring aspects of the family, wherein he examines how particular dispositions may evolve within family systems. Despite his characterization of dispositions as "durable and transposable" (Bourdieu 1979, vii), Bourdieu's conceptualization of habitus and dispositions is *not* that of monolithic forces foreclosing the exercise of individual agency or subjectivity. In fact, Bourdieu (1990) discussed habitus as a conceptual response to what he viewed as a problematic erasure of subjectivity within quantitative, structuralist studies of social reproduction and mobility (see, e.g., Blau and Duncan 1967; Duncan and Hodge 1963; Hauser 1978). For members of low-income families, these structural forces are likely to inform the formulation of a worldview shaped by shared experiences of constraint and deprivation. However, there is a range of different ways that such experiential influences may manifest, not limited to those which lack subjectivity, agency, intentionality, and strategic orientation toward disrupting intergenerational processes of social reproduction. That said, differently formulated worldviews within similarly socioeconomically situated populations are not *in and of themselves* sufficiently powerful to yield divergent educational or occupational pathways to mobility in the absence of structural conditions or "mobility ladders" (Portes and Zhou 1993) through which material access to opportunity can be attained (see, e.g., MacLeod 2009).

Nonetheless, the study of habitus as it relates to processes of social reproduction has not been matched by similar degrees of scholarly engagement with the mechanisms through which habitus might contribute to, or at the very least be consonant with, social mobility. Embedded implications of absolute mutual exclusivity in the utility of habitus across class-differentiated environments have thus traditionally precluded the exploration of possibilities regarding how habitus might reflect "the generative capacities of dispositions," which Bourdieu describes as "functioning on the practical level as categories of perception and assessment or as classificatory principles as well as being the organizing principles of action" through which individuals constitute "acting agent[s]" (Bourdieu 1990, 13). For example, in relation to the experiences of LIFG college students, previous scholarship has described how familial habitus can be antithetical to the types of habitus that are most highly valued by institutions of higher education. As such, research has il-luminated processes through which LIFG students experience cleavages in the habitus with which they identify (Lee and Kramer 2013), and/or are required to "discard" or "transform" the habitus of their families in order to succeed (Lehmann 2014). Research has also demonstrated that working-class college students, who are disproportionately likely to share first-generation student identities, may employ a variety of strategies to navigate their edu-cational experiences in relation to their class-based familial identities. Hurst characterizes these strategies as those of nonassimilationist class "loyalists," assimilationist class "renegades," and chameleon-like "double agents" who adapt their behaviors and choices in accordance with the different contexts within which they are operating at any given time (Hurst 2010). The latter, nonetheless, is characterized as an "alternating" of presumably mutually ex-clusive forms of embodied habitus between contexts.

While this chapter does not contest the important understandings that past scholarship has yielded regarding experiences of conflict and disconnection based on mismatched aspects of habitus for LIFG students at elite institu-tions, my research provides insight into an additional dimension of these processes: the ways in which *some* specific aspects of familial habitus for LIFG students may act to support their academic persistence, even as other aspects of familial habitus may well be as incompatible with their academic engagement as previous work has demonstrated. While the latter is useful to an understanding of the cultural dimensions of social reproduction, the former lends insight into some of the cultural dimensions of social mobil-ity. I posit that these dynamics may coexist, if in tension with each other, in complicated and important ways. We cannot assume that cultural dynamics cease to relate to outcomes of mobility while at the same time examining in so many ways their role in social reproduction. As Streib (2017) points out, the extensive scholarship on the cultural mechanisms through which culture and habitus informs social reproduction has not been matched by an analogous scholarly investigation of the cultural mechanisms (in this case, the habitus cultivated within families of successful LIFG students) that could potentially be relevant to processes of social mobility. The habitus within a low-income family, by the very virtue of its development in the context of structural con-straints, may provide fertile ground for the cultivation of aspirations toward increased opportunities. To understand intergenerational educational mobil-ity (and, consequently, socioeconomic mobility), I argue, it is necessary to contextualize the concept of habitus within families not only insofar as it has the capacity to *inform* social reproduction, but also in the simultaneous ex-tent to which it can be creatively reappropriated in attempts to *disrupt* social reproduction, through what Bourdieu would call "the agent's practice, his or her capacity for invention and improvisation" (Bourdieu 1990, 13). To this end, attention to the function of "cautionary tales" within familial meaning-making processes regarding intergenerational educational mobility highlights one manifestation of the arguably underresearched agency employed by low-income parents in actively working to inform such processes in intentional and strategic ways.

The idea of higher education as a "way out" of difficult circumstances has been identified in previous studies (Langenkamp and Shifrer 2017; Lee 2016; Rondini 2016), as has the significance of familial storytelling about past generations' fortunes as a source of inspiration for academic success (see, e.g., Gándara 1995). Previous work has also described the processes through which parents of low-income first-generation students attribute social meanings associated with personal "redemption" to their children's educational mobility and/or view their children's educational achievements as a proxy for their success as parents (Rondini 2016). In this chapter, I turn to the specific intersubjective processes through which LIFG college students *and* their parents actively co-cultivate motives for academic persistence despite challenges and constraints by drawing on their families' intergenerational biographical narratives of struggle and sacrifice. Despite the lack of material resources upon which to scaffold their children's aspirations, many of the parents in this study described conscious efforts that constituted the cultivation of a culture of motivation for, and expectations of, academic persistence. The meanings and motivations associated with the educational persistence of students in the study were developed in relation to the ways in which they, and their parents, understood the limitations constituted by their familial socioeconomic status, and subsequently sought to transcend them, despite the persistent lack of material resources that contextualized their efforts to do so.

STUDY DESIGN, SAMPLE, AND RESEARCH METHODS

Data for this study were gathered through in-depth interviews (n = 30) with low-income first-generation college students (n = 16) and their parents (n = 14). I was unable to interview a parent for three of the students because they declined or were unavailable to participate. In the case of one student, both parents participated in the interview. The students were undergraduates at a small, private, elite research university. All student respondents (1) were over the age of 18, (2) had graduated from public high schools, (3) were members of the first generation of their families to pursue a baccalaureate degree, and (4) were eligible for federal Pell Grant financial aid. It should be noted that Pell Grant eligibility is only extended to those students whose family income is less than 150 percent of the poverty line. In 2009, the federal poverty line was calculated at $22,050 for a family of four; during the 2009–2010 academic year, the combined expenses of tuition, room, and board totaled more than double that amount, at $48,332 per year. My sample criteria were designed to cultivate what Frankenberg (1997, 26) calls "a purposive rather than random strategy for gathering interviews" wherein particular experiences are intentionally overrepresented for the purpose of gaining specific insight into the range of perceptions constructed by individuals who share those experiences. The qualitative, conceptual exploration of nuanced "meaning-making" processes (see Denzin and Lincoln 1994) within a specific subpopulation facilitated by the study design is neither intended nor well-suited to broad generalizability or statistical measurements. All student interviews were conducted on campus. The student participants were the point of contact from which I then set up interviews with their parents, when it was possible to do so. In all cases, I interviewed students first, and then traveled to their communities of origin to interview parents, at a location of their parents' choosing. In most cases, parent interviews took place in their homes. The study received IRB approval from the appropriate institution, and all participants are represented herein by pseudonyms.

Beyond the broader parameters for selectivity, I utilized the programs offered by the university's Office of Academic Services as a venue for recruiting my sample, through snowball sampling methods and recruitment fliers posted in the student lounge of the Student Support Services center. As a result, the students are disproportionately representative of the population of LIFG students on campus that is actively connected to these services. As a part-time employee of the Office of Academic Services and an adjunct instructor at the university, I had various connections with students who participated in Academic Services Office programs. While I did not include in the study any students with whom I had a direct teaching, mentoring, or advising relationship, students' general familiarity with me as a visible participant in the office's programs likely enhanced my opportunities to connect with potential participants for the study.

Given that LIFG college students are not as statistically likely to matriculate or persist in their studies at elite four-year institutions as they are at public two-year institutions (Chen and Carroll 2005; Strayhorn 2006), the criteria for participation in this study delineated a very particular subset of the broader population of LIFG students. Specifically, while the focus of this paper is understanding a particular mechanism of familial meaning-making processes experienced by the successful LIFG students regarding their academic mobility, there are multiple structurally based factors relevant to the outcome that all of the participants in the study have gone on to complete their degrees since this research was conducted. While this outcome could not have been not known at the time that interviews took place, it should be noted that ultimately, albeit not intentionally, the data in this paper therefore overrepresents experiences of LIFG who were successful in their academic pursuits. Because recruitment for the study was largely conducted through the office of Academic Services, the students who elected to participate overrepresent those who were already connected to a strong network of academic and peer advisory structures, tutoring, and mentoring, including those encapsulated with the school's TRIO student support services program. It is particularly important to note that there is significant overlap between the population of the university's targeted college access and diverse leadership recruitment programs and initiatives, and the population of students who participate in the programs of the Academic Services office. That this network of services, institutional structures, and programs reflects evidence-based understandings of best practices for supporting the academic persistence low-income and/or first-generation students (Engle, Bermeo, and O'Brien 2006; Engle and Tinto 2008; Muraskin 1997) constitutes important context for the interpretation of findings in this study. To be clear, the findings presented here are not intended to advance an argument that any essentialist understanding of "culture" (whether understood as delineated by class, race, ethnicity, immigration, or any other such forces) *in itself* constitutes sufficient explanation of what was required to overcome the structural barriers faced by these LIFG students; familial meaning-making processes do not occur in a vacuum of structural mechanisms and systems relevant to college access and institutional support for academic persistence.

While a fully comprehensive, comparative investigation of how race, gender, class, and immigration dynamics shaped participants' experiences is beyond the scope of this sample, the discussion presented herein engages the ways in which participants themselves articulated the salience of these dynamics in the course of their narratives. I interviewed a racially diverse sample,[1] while remaining attentive to how racialization and racism informed students' and families' constructions and articulations of social meanings by situating the microlevel experiences of racialization processes within the broader intersections of race, class, gender, and immigration as they emerged through participants' narrative accounts of educational experiences, perceptions of mobility structures, and identity formation processes. Students of color and immigrant students are both overrepresented in this study and overrepresented among the overall population of LIFG college students in the United States.[2] Respondents self-identified their racial and/or ethnic backgrounds with varying terminology, and the labels used herein represent an effort to present this information as clearly and consistently as possible without erasing their preferred identifiers or ignoring the salience of immigration dynamics in the ways that racial and ethnic identities were articulated. As such, participants who specified an ethnic group identity as salient to them or their families are labeled as "of [a particular ethnic label] descent" if they were born in the United States, or "[national/ethnic group] immigrant" if they were born outside of the United States. Respondents who did not identify themselves in relation to a particular ethnic group are labeled only in relation to the racial groups with which they self-identified. One family—Ron and his parents, Peter and Sara—identified as "Guyanese" both racially and ethnically, and their identities are accordingly listed as "of Guyanese descent," with intergenerational distinctions in immigrant status also noted.

Student interviews were conducted in English. For interviews with five of the parents in the study, I employed the services of Spanish-speaking translators, who later assisted with transcription of the audio recordings. I analyzed the data from these semistructured interviews using a grounded theory approach whereby I continually compared transcripts between interviews as my data collection process continued. In so doing, I identified and coded emergent themes in the data utilizing ATLAS.ti qualitative data management software, and built upon developing understandings throughout the project.

FINDINGS: EXPANDING OUR UNDERSTANDING OF PARENTING STRATEGIES

The parents in the study, most of whom lived paycheck-to-paycheck, were aware that they did not have financial assets to pass on to their children. They were aware that their children's future financial stability and prospects for social mobility would rest upon their educational attainment. The urgency with which many attempted to instill high educational aspirations in their children was often framed in terms of being the "only" thing that parents could "give" their children that would insure them a "better life" than what they themselves had had.

A consistent thread throughout the students' accounts was a layer of meaning attached to their educational experiences which operated not despite the structural disadvantages that they faced, but rather *because* of them. Specifically, in various ways, the students described conceptualizations of their educational achievements as being connected to a deeper sense of personal responsibility to not only succeed for their own sakes, but for the sake of the parents, families, and communities with whom they identified. Scholarship on the "immigrant bargain" (see Louie 2006) has explored some of the ways in which such dynamics are typically manifest between immigrant parents and their children, and this theme resonates here even as this chapter builds on understandings of the specific mechanism involved in such processes. That said, the strategies outlined in this chapter manifested similarly in both immigrant families and families of US-born parents in ways that merit further examination. Education was repeatedly characterized not just as *an* option that they chose to pursue, but rather as *the only* option that they had to pursue the hope that they, and their families, would make gains in status and economic stability. The desire to graduate from college was marked by a strong sense of urgency, which directly reflected the structural positions, and subsequent needs, of the families in which the students had been raised.

The interviews with students' parents demonstrated that the development of this sense of urgency directly reflected the social meanings of education constructed by students' parents and families. Specifically, familial narratives framed the social meanings of children's postsecondary education as protection against social reproduction processes that otherwise threatened to create vulnerability to similar hardships and struggles as those endured by their parents.

Cautionary Tales: Education as a Safeguard Against Social Reproduction

Higher education was conceptualized by students and their parents as a means through which to which safeguard against the likelihood that future generations might otherwise confront struggles similar to those that past generations had to endure. Previous research has demonstrated that parents of LIFG students often disparaged their own educational and occupational trajectories but maintained their commitment to the American dream ideology by viewing their children's academic success as tantamount to "redemption" for their own perceived failures or shortcomings (Rondini 2016). At the same time, students' interpretations of these "redemption narratives" were often fraught; they often identified their parents more positively as important sources of support and motivation for their educational aspirations, even as they recognized the ways in which structural constraints may have limited their parents' capacities to provide financial and cultural capital commensurate with that to which their more privileged peers had access.

Parents described worrying about what the alternatives for their children's futures would be in the absence of a college degree, in light of how difficult their own life experiences had been. In explaining their motivations for achievement, several students described formative childhood experiences of poverty and household instability, with great emphasis on their desire to insulate themselves from struggles during adulthood that might otherwise be similar to those that shaped their parents' low educational and occupational outcomes. The collective identity of each student's family was contextualized by that family's intergenerational biographical narrative. In several families, students developed insights into the significance of education by framing their family struggles in the context of previous generations' limited educational attainment and, subsequently, limited employment prospects. Students' educational aspirations and achievements were often tied to a sense of responsibility to "vindicate" their parents' struggles and sacrifices on their behalf. These themes were particularly pronounced within—albeit not exclusive to—immigrant families, in ways that echo evidence of the "immigrant bargain" dynamic (see Louie 2012). As such, several of the students were acutely aware of how the resources and opportunities to which they had access were far more plentiful than those that their parents had experienced. Generally, parents' discussions of education were centrally framed in terms of wanting "more" for their children than they themselves had had, in terms of material resources, educational opportunities, and occupational choices, and parents' educational and occupational trajectories were significantly co-constructed (by parents and children) as "cautionary tales" from which the next generation could learn valuable lessons about what pathways should be avoided.

Students' awareness of the hardships that their parents had undergone in order to provide for them to this point in their lives was translated into a compelling motivation to differentiate their own life "paths" from those that had been modeled for them, to the greatest extent that they could do so. For example, Roberto (18-year-old Latino of Dominican descent) recalled periods of his childhood when his parents would unfold cardboard boxes on the floor of the factory that they worked in, for him and his siblings to sleep on, while they worked overnight shifts during which they did not have other options for childcare. Reflecting on what this may have been like for his parents, he stated assuredly that *his* life would be "very different, because my parents worked in a factory. My parents sacrificed a lot, and they lived a really difficult life. I don't think I'll have to make some of the sacrifices that they did."

This theme of parental sacrifice and struggle in the hope of a better life for the next generation emerged in multiple ways. Consistent with previous research (see Louie 2012), students who had either immigrated to the United States or were children of immigrants generally described clear awareness that their parents had largely based their decision to come to the United States on the prospect of their children becoming well educated. Roberto's mother, Elizabeth (42 years old, Latina immigrant of Dominican descent), began explaining her purposeful decision-making with regard to her children's educational opportunities before the formal interview even began, as soon as she met me at the door to her home. She cited her own biographical narrative in explaining her strong desires for her children to achieve higher levels of educational attainment than she and her husband had. Recalling her decision to come to the United States from the Dominican Republic, she explained:

> As a parent I have to motivate my children in order for them to achieve a level that we haven't achieved before in order to go to university to study and graduate and have a better future so they can give their children a better future so they will not have to suffer what we have already suffered and gone through. . . . I know that having an education will allow them to get better jobs. I do not want my children to be a repeat of my life. I want them to have the things that I could never get. . . . I want his life to be different. I want his life to be easier. I don't want him to work as hard as I did and as hard as his father did in order to bring his children into a better life or future. I don't want him to work so hard. I don't want him to have to be like us who immigrated into another country for a better future.

A similar narrative emerged in conversations with Gabriel (19 years old, Black of Ghanaian descent) and his father, John (47 years old, Black immigrant of Ghanaian descent). John recalled that a similar thought process informed his decision to bring his family to the United States from Ghana; he explained, "My motive was not first to come and make money, but rather to come and afford them opportunities." Awareness of his parents' purposeful decision-making was not lost on Gabriel. In response to a question regarding how his life might be different from his parents' lives, Gabriel expressed cognizance of how the difficulties his parents faced in their immigration experiences were endured for the sake of his own acquisition of opportunities. He reflected:

> Being in this country I would be a lot more prepared and a lot more suited to be able to pull myself up and progress in this nation than they did. . . . Just being conscious of certain things in this society, being that I came here at a young age . . . the way the system works . . . I would be more knowledgeable than they were.

In addition to the "knowledge" of cultural expectations and institutional systems to which Gabriel refers here, students who had immigrated with their families or were children of immigrant parents frequently referenced another dimension of advantage that they had over their parents' generation, in relation to educational and economic opportunities available to them in the United States as compared to the opportunities that had been available within their respective countries of origin. Ken (21 years old, Asian immigrant of Chinese descent) also juxtaposed his parents' circumstances with his own, expressing that he felt he has "been given" many more resources and opportunities than his parents had, despite the disadvantages he faced in comparison to many of his more privileged peers:

> Well in the time they grew up they didn't have very much. China [was] a third world country; they didn't have a lot of things to grow up on. But the next generation should be better than the first one. That is the kind of thought I grew up on. I expect to do better than my parents because I have more opportunities than them. So that is how I feel. . . . I don't really know what kind of things they didn't have—I know that money was really a big problem; they didn't have money to go to school. They had to begin working full time when they were 15 years old on the farms and stuff. I don't have to deal with that. That is one big factor. Going to school is really expensive; they didn't have the opportunities that I have.

Ken, an honors student who works thirty-five to forty hours per week in a combination of his three jobs, went on to downplay his own considerable efforts and accomplishments by highlighting the extent to which his own upbringing provided him with tools that he feels would have enabled "anyone" to succeed. Ken's family's immigration history significantly shaped his perception of academic success as a "responsibility." As characterized in Louie's (2012) discussion of the "immigrant bargain," academic success was often positioned as a "trade" that students owed to their families, in exchange for the parental sacrifices that had yielded the provision of their educational opportunities. Ken has internalized the implications of these dynamics, as reflected in the following matter-of-fact commentary;

> I think it is almost expected. When you are given so many things and so many opportunities you don't have to do a lot to be successful. When you are not given very much then you have to be exceptionally smart to accomplish something. But when you are given so many opportunities it almost takes effort to fail.

The family of Ron (19 years old, of Guyanese descent) employed a philosophy similar to the one that Ken espoused; that is, when one generation has suffered to provide more opportunities for their children than they themselves had, that sacrifice should straightforwardly yield the children's successful academic outcomes. Upon arrival to the United States, the "better" and more "stable" employment opportunities that Ron's grandparents had come in search of took the form of low-wage factory work. Ron's mother and stepfather envisioned that their own parents' hopes would come to fruition through the educational and occupational attainments of Ron and his siblings. Subsequently, they made conscious efforts throughout his schooling to bring about this result. As Ron explained,

My parents always held high expectations for me. There was never any excuse about us failing; they felt they gave us everything we needed so why should we mess up? If we got a job, they always told us, "you have a lot of time; you have no bills or other responsibility, so just get your school work done." They were always influential about getting good grades. "Work hard and don't mess around." They would always speak to us about little conversations and lectures: "it is worth it because later on you will not have to struggle, like us, but you *have to* get good grades." They really wanted us to do better than they did. . . . They don't want to see me struggling.

Ron's mother and stepfather look to him to "make good" on the potential and promise that they feel they might have shown themselves, if they had been guided to do so in their youth. His mother Sara (38 years old, immigrant of Guyanese descent) recounts:

I said you have to go to school—we will take care of you—you don't have to work full time and then go to school. We will give you the opportunity to do this. You have to put school as your first focus—that is something no one else can take away from you. And I don't want to hear anything else about it.

When asked the age at which they began to have conversations with Ron regarding education, his stepfather Peter (40 years old, immigrant of Guyanese descent) emphatically interjected, "We *always* talked to him about school. *Always.*" Their explicit hope is not that Ron will *not* "follow in their footsteps," but rather that he will surpass them in his own educational and, ultimately, occupational attainment. Ron's mother stated,

I want to see him make more money than we do when he graduates. He will have a profession—a real profession like a doctor or a lawyer—something that you would call a *profession*. If he becomes the first one to do it—that is all I could ask; that is all I want. If he could become a profession like a doctor or a lawyer, if he can do it, it is like peace of mind.

In response, Ron's stepfather Peter immediately added, "One of my philosophies is we have to be better than our parents and they have to be better than us. . . . It is important to me because of all the stuff I haven't achieved—they can achieve it and I will be happy about it." The sternness with which both of Ron's parents described their messages to him conveyed the urgency with which they imbued the academic orientation that they were actively trying to cultivate.

In turn, students like Ron framed their own goals in terms of surpassing their parents' levels of educational and occupational attainment, albeit with some occasional discomfort. The discomfort that manifested seemed to hinge

on students' desires to convey the respect and gratitude that they held for
their parents' sacrifices and struggles, rather than risk articulating their goals
to surpass their parents in a manner which might lend itself to an interpretation that they were "putting down" their parents or taking for granted the opportunities to which their parents had never enjoyed access. These processes
sometimes created conflicting feelings for the students as a result of their
desire to convey loyalty to their families and deference to their parents while
at the same time consciously attempt to fulfill the expectation that they would
differentiate their own life paths from those of previous generations. For
example, Alejandro (18-year-old Latino of Mexican descent) described with
nostalgic reverence how he viewed his father's management of a garment
factory when he was growing up, recalling that

> I always wanted to do what my dad did. My dad was the boss. . . . I thought it
> was really cool and he would go out and make the contracts, make the clothes
> and I felt there was so much respect in it. . . . It was stressful; looking back at it
> now it wasn't as glamorous as I made it out to be, but I always wanted to have
> that respect.

Alejandro's recognition of his father's leadership in a grueling work environment was informed by his recognition of how difficult and "stressful"
factory work was, even as he clearly admired his father's demonstration of resilience and dignity in this challenging context. However, when asked about
the point at which he became aware of wanting his own life to be different
from his parents' lives, he replied without hesitation, "College, as soon as I
got here." Importantly, his father had also encouraged him to differentiate his
own educational and occupational trajectory from (and, in fact, surpass) that
of his parents; Alejandro explained,

> My dad even tells me, "I want you to be better than me; I want you to do what
> you love so that you won't kill yourself doing something that you don't love."
> He encouraged me to do whatever I wanted.

Alejandro's mother Roberta (37 years old, Latina immigrant of Mexican
descent) described the difficult financial decision that she made to quit one of
the two jobs that she held when her children were young, in the aftermath of a
parent-teacher conference in which she was advised that it would benefit her
children for her to be in the home at night rather than at work. She recalled,

> My boss and my friends asked, "Why are you leaving?" I liked the job but I have
> [*sic*] to do it for my kids so I can be there for their homework and everything.
> . . . I did a lot of things with them about school. . . . I said, "I don't care, they

need me, they have to be in school. They have to be in college. I want a doctor or a teacher—something like that in my house!"

Parents like Alejandro's and Ron's explicitly encouraged their children to surpass their own achievements, making financial sacrifices to facilitate their children's progress in any way that they could. This was almost always expressed in relation to the hopes that their children would experience greater financial security and comfort than that which they themselves were experiencing and had experienced during their lifetimes. This dynamic was not exclusive to immigrant families; Sally (52 years old, White) spoke similarly about her hopes for her daughter Juliana's (19 years old, White) life to be different from her own, even as Juliana constructed her own trajectory as analogous to that of her parents'. For example, in explaining the abiding respect and affection that she holds for her parents, Juliana cited her father as an example to her of someone who has acquired expert knowledge in his chosen field through hard work, commenting that "certainly the way I think of it [is that] my father knows a trade, and I tell him I hope to learn about an academic subject as much as he knows about his trade." While Juliana understood her parents' desires for her to surpass their occupational status, her perception of their achievements was measured not in terms of their socioeconomic status, but rather in terms of the aspects of their examples that she would seek to emulate—albeit in a different context. On the other hand, referencing her own educational and occupational trajectory, Juliana's mother Sally lamented that she had graduated from high school and had simply gone directly to work full time. Speaking with palpable enthusiasm about how much Juliana had already experienced and grown as a result of her education, Sally commented, "I never had that higher education, or the social aspect of it. It is amazing." She then went on to speak in greater detail about Juliana's likely occupational choices as compared to her own, stating

> I think [her life] will be a lot different than mine. I think she will be working full time, I am sure, but I think it will be a totally different work. We got jobs wherever there was work; whoever was hiring. If there was an eyeglass place factory, you just got a job there. You did your forty hours and then went home. . . . I am hoping she will have a much better pick as far as a different lifestyle than we did.

Sally's enthusiasm for the variety of possibilities that lay ahead for her daughter's life was hopeful and proud, but nonetheless clearly conveyed the desire that her daughter would not have an occupational trajectory similar to hers or her husband's. This dynamic was salient in other families: parents' and students' orientation toward achievement was predominantly informed by direct knowledge—and fear—of the likely alternative outcomes for a student should their educational opportunities fall through. In these cases, the limited educational and occupational attainment levels of previous generations were invoked (by parents as well as students) as "cautionary tales," functioning as sources of motivation for greater educational achievement. However, this process did not foreclose all opportunities for students like Juliana to identify ways in which their parents had provided them with positive examples of personal attributes or orientations toward hard work and achievement that they might hope to imitate in their own lives.

Nonetheless, the impetus to pursue education was articulated in the form of specific urging to *not* follow in the footsteps of parents and family members, whose limited educational attainment levels were linked to the intergenerational transmission of socioeconomic vulnerabilities in the past. In another example of conscious differentiation from the circumstances of one's upbringing, when asked what kept her motivated to overcome obstacles, Katrina (22 years old, Black) became visibly emotional as she stated clearly, "What made me really start thinking about college was [that] I wanted something completely different than I had. I didn't like the things that I experienced coming up and I thought that college would be an escape from them."

At the time of her interview, Katrina was working between forty and fifty hours per week outside of school hours in order to pay for the housing, food, and books that her family was not in a financial position to assist her in financing. When I asked Katrina if she would feel comfortable explaining which specific aspects of her upbringing she was working so hard to escape from, her reply was strained: "Like . . . poverty. Excuse me . . . [pause] . . . if I get emotional. Poverty most of all, but like issues with my family, issues in education and the system I came up in . . . sometimes when I reflect on these things I get emotional about it." This kind of driving force for personal achievement posed a number of painful tensions for students who acutely feared that they could end up back "where they came from" should their educational aspirations fall through, while simultaneously bearing the burden of knowing that "where they came from" was where their loved ones remained. While these students might have experienced some degree of distance from the day-to-day hardships that their families' lives entailed during the time that they were away at school, the issues that plagued their families and communities were never entirely removed from their own experiences, nor disconnected from the sense of urgency that informed their own dispositions regarding education.

Similarly, Lydia (21 years old, Latina of Dominican descent) drew a direct connection between the prospects of her educational attainment and the likelihood that she would be able to escape the circumstances that she was exposed to during her own upbringing in both her mother's and her father's separate households. Her ongoing motivation to excel was fueled by the difficult realities of her family's experiences, and, implicitly, the fear that her own life experiences may be otherwise similar. Echoing Katrina's account, Lydia also characterized the meanings of her education as a pathway through which to "escape" the circumstances of her upbringing. She described this in the following way:

> My dad . . . he would come home really, really late, like 3 or 4 in the morning and have to leave to go back to work at 2 or 3 in the afternoon. My mom was in an abusive relationship for a long time. I saw the things that she was going through. She told me all the time, "If I had a career and could depend on myself I would leave him"; "This is why you need a career and why you have to go to school so you won't have to go through this." I knew I didn't want to be like them. I knew I didn't want to be in an abusive relationship like my mom was. Since [my family] told me that education was the only way I could do that, I knew. I tried my best in school, high school especially. I was going through a lot of issues and I knew that I wanted to do well in school. School was my escape and my outlet. I knew I wanted to go away to college.

This description of pursuing educational attainment as a means to the end of making one's own life circumstances as different as possible from those of one's parents was a common thread throughout the student interviews. Higher education was framed as the "one shot" at a better life that students like Lydia could hope for. Lydia's mother Mariana (38 years old, Latina immigrant of Dominican descent) explained that she had always held herself up to Lydia as an example of what *not* to be. As was the case in several other families, Mariana consciously used her own biographical narrative as a "cautionary tale" to encourage Lydia's educational persistence. She characterized her daughter's education as a means of protection against the struggles that she herself had faced:

> I told her that by not educating yourself, you expose yourself to embarrassment and humiliation and I don't want her to go through the things that I did. . . . I have been humiliated and I don't want her to go through that. [Her education] will protect her, because now when she is asked something, she will respond and nobody will think she has no knowledge and doesn't speak English. . . . Now that she has gone through college she has that advantage. [Education] is needed for independence. . . . if you do not have an education you receive the humiliation constantly.

While Mariana did not explicitly explain the "humiliation" that she refers to here in relation to her experiences of abuse (as referenced by Lydia in the previous excerpt), her tearful reference to education as a necessity for "independence" alludes to the dynamic of financial dependence on her abusive partner that Lydia had described. Lydia cites her mother's experience as one against which she, specifically "as a woman," wanted to be sure to protect herself.

While none of the parents indicated that they believed education to be more important for children of a particular gender, gendered implications were sometimes attached to parents' hopes in relation to what kind of security their children's education would provide. For example, both Romeo (21 years old, Arab of Egyptian descent) and Ron (19 years old, of Guyanese descent), faced expectations, as the eldest sons in their families, to provide for their siblings in the event that their parents were not able to do so in the future. As previously noted, Lydia's mother associated her daughter's education with the idea of independence, implicitly juxtaposing this hope with the circumstances under which she had previously been financially dependent on an abusive partner. Similarly, Sally (52 years old, White; mother of Juliana, 19 years old, White) and Corina (46 years old, Black immigrant of Jamaican descent; mother of Tara, 18 years old, Black immigrant of Jamaican descent) noted that they were glad to know that their daughters' educational achievements would "protect" them from ever being in the position of being financially dependent on a man. Corina noted, "No one will ever be able to take advantage of her." The implied vulnerability in these accounts is gendered, in the extent to which it reflects patriarchal and heteronormative expectations of female financial dependence upon male partners, even as they are expressed in terms of hoping to circumvent this dynamic. These efforts are reflective of strategies adopted by poor and working-class women described in previous scholarship, whose "hard-won independence makes them wary" (Silva 2013, 78) of dependency upon male partners and/or whose experiences of motherhood have—out of necessity—yielded a particularly vigilant orientation toward their children's economic well-being (see, e.g., Edin and Kefalas 2005). As with the previously described examples of conceptualizing education as a safeguard against social reproduction, the combined data from these student and parent interviews demonstrate how messages regarding the "protective" function of educational attainment for future well-being are transmitted intergenerationally and used to compel students' efforts at educational persistence.

DISCUSSION AND CONCLUSION

Data from this study demonstrate that while parents from low-income families were significantly constrained in their ability to support their children's capacities for success within educational institutions in some ways, they were also uniquely positioned to provide their children with compelling incentives for achievement in other ways. The low-income parents in this study exercised agency in their efforts to interrupt intergenerational patterns of social reproduction to an extent that has not been previously given due attention. Even while struggling in the face of the persistent financial obstacles of low-wage and often unstable employment, parents took advantage of opportunities to cite their own biographical narratives as "cautionary tales" for their children, explicitly pointing out the ways in which educational attainment would have alleviated the familial struggles that shaped their children's worldviews. While it is true that the families in this study lacked the kinds of financial capital necessary to provide children with tangible resources for academic success, aspects of familial habitus germane to the dimensions of students' worldviews regarding higher education, and the potential to interrupt patterns of social reproduction that it represented, were cultivated by parents with conscious intent. Children's high educational aspirations were often compellingly framed in terms of "necessity," "survival," and "basic needs" by parents who lacked assets with which to insure their children's future financial security and stability in other ways.

By intentionally fostering a perception of education as a "way out" of circumstances that mirror the struggles of past generations, low-income parents constructed the development of children's aspirations toward educational mobility as a parental responsibility—particularly in the absence of intergenerational assets to pass down to secure economic stability for children later in life. These parents may not have had been able finance private tutors or extracurricular activities, but their practical strategies aimed at cultivating high aspirations within their children's dispositions toward schooling nonetheless constituted a contribution toward their success. Cautionary tales (wherein parents' educational and occupational trajectories were cited by parents *and* their children as examples of what *not* to replicate) functioned within families to imbue students' educational pursuits with particular, intergenerational social meanings. While these more ideologically based efforts do not compensate for the kinds of structural inequities that advantage middle- and upper-class students in educational settings, they nonetheless constitute a cultural dimension of educational mobility that has been previously under-examined.

The in-depth interview design, and the specific sampling of a subpopulation of low-income families wherein students were enrolled at an elite university, has been particularly useful in revealing cultural dynamics of family life not otherwise accounted for in studies which have focused exclusively on the ways in which structural constraints inhibit achievement for socioeconomically disadvantaged youth. A potential hazard of this more typical framing is the assumption that low-income first-generation college students who achieve academic success at the college level do so only despite their family backgrounds, without taking into account the possibility that familial systems of meaning surrounding educational attainment may in some ways be helpful to or supportive of students' academic persistence. What emerged from the data was a set of practical strategies employed by parents who consciously utilized their own positions of low educational attainment and socioeconomic status to illustrate the importance of educational mobility to the children they hoped would surpass them.

Habitus comprising worldviews which frame education as necessary to the possibility of disrupting social reproduction processes thus indeed operates herein as, in Bourdieu's (1990) terms, "a system of acquired dispositions functioning on the practical level as categories of perception and assessment" employed by social agents as "organizing principles of action" (13). In this case, the principles of actions are those geared toward understanding education as a means through which to achieve intergenerational mobility. As a result of framing my sample around students *and* parents, my data illustrates the interactive familial dynamics through which this perspective has been purposefully cultivated. In these cases, what Bourdieu (1996) would term the "structured" constraints faced by families of LIFG students may be drawn upon to derive shared social meanings of higher education that encourage and support social mobility, rather than automatically translating into a structuring force for the transmission of cultural capital that can only inevitably inform processes of social reproduction.

It is, of course, true that—unlike middle- and upper-class parents—low-income parents contend with significant structural constraints in terms of their capacities to mobilize material resources to bolster children's academic performances. It is accurate to say that the students in the study were not able to draw directly from their parents' educational experiences or academic skills as significant sources of information and guidance regarding their college careers. However, in a pattern which emerged repeatedly in various forms, many of these students *were* able to draw upon their parents' lived examples of resilience in the face of limited access to inequitably distributed resources, determination to creatively survive trying circumstances, and orientation toward faith in deferred rewards for hard work. As demonstrated by previous study and supported by these findings, resilience and the capacity to endure and cope with adversity (see Reay, Crozier, and Clayton 2009, 1107) are traits that may be demonstrated through parental examples irrespective of whether or not the adversity in one's life has subsided, or the resilience that one has displayed has yielded distinctly identifiable rewards. In other words, whether or not an individual parent has "overcome" the structural constraints on mobility that they have faced, these particular attributes may serve to enhance the likelihood of success for their children when replicated in the context of educational opportunity. These parents' experiences of structural constraint are not, therefore, tantamount to a lack of agency or efficacy with which to encourage children's scholastic achievement.

Scholarship has considered the ways in which students may acquire cultural capital to "offset" the habitus of their familial environment through educational institutions, with the implication that there is a mutually exclusive and dualistic set of relations involved: the habitus of low-income families is presumed to be counterproductive and/or detrimental to academic achievement, while the habitus of middle- and upper-class families is presumed to be of value to one's academic success within higher educational institutions. Yet, Bourdieu's operationalization of habitus is multidimensional, comprising internalized tastes, beliefs, conduct, perceptions, worldviews, practical strategies, and dispositions (Bourdieu 1977, 1980, 1984) shaped by material conditions, albeit not in ways that are entirely deterministic or consistent across similarly situated populations. Bourdieu discusses "disposition" in *Outline of a Theory of Practice* (1977) as seeming "particularly well-suited to express what is covered by the concept of habitus (defined as a system of dispositions)" (214). He goes on to operationalize the concept of disposition as expressing "in particular, a *predisposition, tendency, propensity,* or *inclination*" (214). In other words, dispositions function as influences which "[dispose] actors to do certain things, orienting their actions and inclinations, without strictly determining them" (Jenkins 2002, 75). Habitus thus operates as a "strategy-generating principle enabling agents to cope with unforeseen and ever-changing situations" (Bourdieu 1977) rather than an entirely deterministic force.

The cautionary tales comprising, in part, the aspects of familial habitus that shaped these students' worldviews regarding the transformative potential of higher education—although squarely framed, and informed, by the structural constraints that their families had endured—were *not* reductively antithetical to academic success. Structural constraints, and the consequent "deficits" constituted by familial positioning within them, were still relevant to the challenges that these students faced, but they neither negated nor were negated by the tools that their parents *were* able to provide to them. Rather, these disadvantages and tools coexisted in multidimensional and intricately intertwined relationships to which overly deterministic analyses do not do justice.

Some of the cultural dimensions of family life for these students reinforced the necessity of their educational pursuits by motivating their persistence in connection to a deeper sense of purpose and accountability to other members of their families and communities, as well as to themselves. A central, driving force for the success of these students did not evolve *despite* the structural constraints that their families experience but, rather, *because* of the ways that those constraints created particular meanings and motivational frameworks for the purposeful pursuit of alternative outcomes through education.

This project extends insight from previous studies on the relationships between social reproduction, intergenerational mobility, and education. Further, in contrast to previous scholarship emphasizing only the experiences of "departure" (see, e.g., Langenkamp and Shifrer 2017), disconnection, and alienation that LIFG students may face in relation to their families and communities of origin in relation to their educational mobility, this study presents the possibility that "cautionary tales" within families of LIFG students may act as a mechanism through which students come to see their own education as particularly meaningful in the specific context of how they are connected to their families' intergenerational biographical narratives, including the struggles and sacrifices of previous generations. Meanings and motivations associated with educational attainment of LIFG students in the study were inextricably tied to the ways that they and their parents understood the structural barriers to mobility imposed by their familial socioeconomic status and formulated educational strategies to transcend them. While students did experience challenges in their communication with their parents as they undertook their educational careers, these challenges were not tantamount to total disconnection from their families of origin. In fact, students frequently cited reflections on their parents' struggles and sacrifices as a primary source of motivation and inspiration for their educational persistence.

Given that this study was based on in-depth qualitative data collection from a purposive sample, it is simultaneously limited in its lack of statistical generalizability and well positioned to make a conceptual contribution to the framing of future scholarship on this particular population. Future study should further investigate the ways in which differences amongst students on the basis of race, class, gender, and immigration differently intersect with low-income and first-generation status to inform experiences at elite institutions. In addition, given that the majority of low-income and first-generation students do not attend elite, private, four-year colleges and universities, the extent to which dynamics described in this study may or may not manifest similarly for students attending other types of educational institutions, such as community colleges, warrants further study. Finally, as the sample in this study overrepresents the experiences of academically successful low-income first-generation college students, further inquiry into the relevance of cautionary tales, and familial meaning-making processes more broadly, for students who do *not* persist in their studies is also merited.

Previous studies and reports have addressed the relationships between low-income first-generation college students and the institutional contexts within which their classed and racialized experiences are framed (Aries 2008; Engle, Bermeo, and O'Brien 2006; Engle and Tinto 2008; Lee and Kramer 2012; Wirt et al. 2004). Few, however, have turned an analytic lens toward the dynamics of familial relationships as they manifest in the specific processes of intergenerational meaning-making through which these students understand and experience their educational pursuits. My findings do not negate the importance of critically engaging the structural disparities that inform intergenerational patterns of social reproduction. However, they add an important dimension to our understandings of parental participation in the meaning-making processes related to educational mobility. Rather than passively contributing to the reproduction of intergenerational social reproduction patterns, parents of these successful LIFG college students consciously endeavored to encourage and support the disruption of these social patterns, despite the material constraints that framed their efforts. My data illustrate that significant meaning-making processes related to education occur at the level of familial contexts, as well as within the broader structural contexts of race-, gender-, immigration- and class-based stratification systems, and the educational institutions that they frame. The meanings attached to LIFG college students' educational pursuits are woven into the intergenerational, biographical narratives of their family systems, and vice versa. Even as these familial contexts are structurally situated at the intersections of broader structural inequities pertaining to racial, ethnic, gender, socioeconomic, immigration, and educational disparities, parents of LIFG college students used cautionary tales as one way to consciously participate in attempts to interrupt (rather than passively replicate) intergenerational processes of social reproduction, vis-à-vis conscious efforts to cultivate aspirational dispositions and encourage persistence in their children's pursuit of educational and occupational mobility.

REFERENCES

Adair, Vivyan C., and Sandra L. Dahlberg, eds. 2003. *Reclaiming Class: Women, Poverty, and the Promise of Higher Education in America*. Philadelphia: Temple University Press.

Aries, Elizabeth. 2008. *Race and Class Matters at an Elite College*. Philadelphia: Temple University Press.

Belley, Philippe, and Lance Lochner. 2007. "The Changing Role of Family Income and Ability in Determining Educational Achievement." *Journal of Human Capital* 1, no.1: 37–89.

Blau, Peter, and Otis Dudley Duncan. 1967. *The American Occupational Structure.* New York: The New Press.

Bourdieu, Pierre. 1977. *Outline of a Theory of Practice.* Oxford: Cambridge University Press.

Bourdieu, Pierre. 1980. *The Logic of Practice.* Cambridge, MA: Polity Press.

Bourdieu, Pierre. 1984. *Distinction: A Social Critique of the Judgment of Taste.* London: Routledge.

Bourdieu, Pierre. 1990. *In Other Words: Essays Towards a Reflexive Sociology.* Stanford: Stanford University Press.

Bourdieu, Pierre. 1996. "On the Family as a Realized Category." *Theory, Culture, and Society* 13, no. 3: 19–26.

Cabrera, Nolan L., and Adolfo Padilla. 2004. "Entering and Suceeding in the 'Culture of College': The story of Two Mexican Heritage Students." *Hispanic Journal of Behavioral Sciences* 26, no. 2: 15–70.

Charmaz, Kathy. 2006. *Constructing Grounded Theory: Practical Guide Through Qualitative Data Analysis.* Thousand Oaks, CA: Sage Publications.

Chen, Xiang Lei, and Dennis C. Carroll. 2005. "First Generation Students in Post-Secondary Education." *The Condition of Education.* National Center for Education Statistics. Washington, DC: U.S. Department of Education.

Cheng, Simon, and Brian Starks. 2002. "Racial Differences in the Effects of Significant Others on Students' Educational Expectations." *Sociology of Education* 75, no. 4: 306–27.

Conley, Dalton. 2009. *Being Black, Living in the Red: Race, Wealth, and Social Policy in America.* Berkeley: University of California Press.

Connell, Raewyn W. 2004. "Working Class Parents' Views of Secondary Education." *International Journal of Inclusive Education* 8, no. 3: 227–39.

Denzin, Norman K., and Yvonna S. Lincoln, eds. 2007. *The Sage Handbook of Qualitative Research.* New York: Sage Publications.

Dews, C.L. Barney, and Carolyn Leste Law, eds. 1995. *This Fine Place So Far From Home: Voices of Academics From the Working Class.* Philadelphia: Temple University Press.

Duncan, Otis D., and Robert Hodge. 1963. "Education and Occupational Mobility: A Regression Analysis." *American Journal of Sociology* 68, no. 6: 629–49.

Edin, Kathryn, and Maria Kefales. 2005. *Promises I Can Keep: Why Poor Women Put Motherhood Before Marriage.* Berkeley: University of California Press.

Engle, Jennifer, Adolfo Bermeo, and Colleen O'Brien. 2006. *Straight from the Source: What Works for First-Generation College Students.* Washington, DC: The Pell Institute for the Study of Opportunity in Higher Education.

Engle, Jennifer, and Vincent Tinto. 2008. *Moving Beyond Access: College Success for Low-Income, First Generation Students.* Washington, DC: Pell Institute for the Study of Opportunity in Higher Education.

Fainstein, Norman. 1993. "Race, Class, and Segregation: Discourses About African Americans." *International Journal of Urban and Regional Research* 17, no. 3: 384–403.

Feliciano, Cynthia. 2006. "Beyond the Family: The Influence of Premigration Group Status on the Educational Expectations of Immigrants' Children." *Sociology of Education* 79, no. 4: 281–303.

Filmer, Deon, and Lant Pritchett. 1999. "The Effect of Household Wealth on Educational Attainment: Evidence from 35 countries." *Population and Development Review* 25, no. 1: 85–120.

Fine, Michele. 2003. "Witnessing Whiteness, Gathering Intelligence." In *Off White: Readings on Power, Privilege, and Resistance*, edited by Michele Fine, Lois Weis, Linda Pruitt, and April Burns, 245–56. New York: Routledge.

Frankenberg, Ruth. 1997. *White Women, Race Matters*. Minneapolis: University of Minnesota Press.

Gándara, Patricia. 1995. *Over the Ivy Walls: The Educational Mobility of Low-Income Chicanos*. New York: State University of New York Press.

Glaser, Barney. 1965. "The Constant Comparative Method of Qualitative Analysis." *Social Problems* 12, no. 4: 436–45.

Glaser, Barney, and Anselm Strauss. 1967. *The Discovery of Grounded Theory*. Chicago: Aldine Publishing.

Goldsmith, Pat Antonio. 2003. "All Segregation is Not Equal: The Impact of Latino and Black School Composition." *Sociological Perspectives* 46, no. 1: 83–105.

Gofen, Anat. 2009. "Family Capital: How First-Generation Higher Education Students Break the Intergenerational Cycle." *Family Relations* 58, no. 1: 104–20.

Goyette, Kim, and Yu Xie. 2003. "Social Mobility and the Educational Choices of Asian Americans." *Social Science Research* 32: 467–98.

Grimes, Michael D., and Joan M. Morris. 1997. *Caught in the Middle: Contradictions in the Lives of Sociologists from Working Class Backgrounds*. Westport, CT: Praeger.

Guiffrida, Douglas A. 2006. "Toward a Cultural Advancement of Tinto's Theory." *The Review of Higher Education* 29: 451–72.

Hauser, R. M. 1978. "A Structural Model of the Mobility Table." *Social Forces* 56, no. 3: 919–53.

Hochschild, Jennifer. 1995. *Facing Up to the American Dream*. Princeton: Princeton University Press.

Hurst, Allison L. 2010. *The Burden of Academic Success: Loyalists, Renegades, and Double Agents*. Lanham, MD: Rowman & Littlefield.

Kao, Grace. 2004. "Parental Influences on the Educational Outcomes of Immigrant Youth." *International Migration Review* 38, no. 2: 427–50.

Kao, Grace, and Marta Tienda. 1998. "Educational Aspirations of Minority Youth." *American Journal of Education* 106, no. 3: 349–84.

Karagiannaki, Eleni. 2012. "The Effect of Parental Wealth on Children's Outcomes in Early Adulthood." Centre for Analysis of Social Exclusion paper no. 164. London: London School of Economics.

Kenny, Maureen E., and Sonia Stryker. 1996. "Social Network Characteristics and College Adjustment Among Racially and Ethnically Diverse First-Year Students." *Journal of College Student Development* 37, no. 6: 649–58.

Keister, Lisa A. 2000. *Wealth in America: Trends in Wealth Inequality.* Cambridge: Cambridge University Press.

Kim, Nadia. 2008. *Imperial Citizens: Koreans and Race from Seoul to L.A.* Stanford: Stanford University Press.

Lamont, Michele. 2002. *The Dignity of Working Men: Morality and the Boundaries of Race, Class, and Immigration.* Cambridge: Cambridge University Press.

Langenkamp, Amy G., and Dara Shifrer. 2017. "Family Legacy or Family Pioneer? Social Class Differences in the Way Adolescents Construct College-Going." Journal of Adolescent Research 32 (6). (Online First) doi: 10.1177/0743558416684951

Lareau, Annette. 2003. *Unequal Childhoods: Class, Race, and Family Life.* Berkeley: University of California Press.

Lee, Elizabeth. 2016. *Class and Campus Life: Managing and Experiencing Inequality at an Elite College.* New York: Cornell University Press.

Lee, Elizabeth M., and Rory Kramer. 2013. "Out with the Old, in with the New? Habitus and Social Mobility at Selective Colleges." *Sociology of Education* 86, no.1: 18–35.

Lehmann, Wolfgang. 2014. "Habitus Transformation and Hidden Injuries: Successful Working Class University Students." *Sociology of Education* 87, no. 1: 1–15.

Lewis, Amanda E. 2004. "Unequal Childhoods: Class, Race, and Family Life (Review)." *Journal of Marriage and the Family* 66, no. 3: 840–41.

London, Howard B. 1989. "Breaking Away: A Study of First-Generation College Students and Their Families." *American Journal of Education* 97, no. 2: 144–70.

London, Howard B. 1992. "Transformations: Cultural Challenges for First Generation Students." *New Directions for Community Colleges* 80: 5–11.

Louie, Vivian. 2006. "Second Generation Pessimism and Optimism: How Chinese and Dominicans Understand Education and Mobility through Ethnic and Transnational Orientations." *International Migration Review* 40, no. 3: 537–72.

Louie, Vivian. 2012. *Keeping the Immigrant Bargain: The Costs and Rewards of Success in America.* New York: The Russell Sage Foundation.

MacLeod, Jay. 2009. *Ain't No Makin' It: Aspirations and Attainment in a Low Income Neighborhood.* Boulder: Westview Press.

Mahony, Pat, and Christine Zmroczek, eds. 1997. *Class Matters: 'Working Class' Women's Perspectives on Social Class.* London: Taylor and Francis.

McSwain, Courtney, and Ryan Davis. 2007. *College Access for the Working Poor: Overcoming Burdens to Succeed in Higher Education.* Washington DC: The Institute for Higher Education Policy.

Melendez, Mickey C., and Nancy Blanco Melendez. 2010. "The Influence of Parental Attachment on the College Adjustment of White, Black, and Latina/Hispanic Women: A Cross–Cultural Investigation." *Journal of College Student Development* 51, no. 4: 419–35.

Mullen, Ann. 2010. *Degrees of Inequality: Culture, Class, and Gender in American Higher Education.* Baltimore: Johns Hopkins University Press.

Muraskin, Lana. 1997. *Best Practices in Student Support Services: A Study of Five Exemplary Sites.* Washington, DC: United States Department of Education.

Muzzatti, Stephen L., and C. Vincent Samarco, eds. 2005. *Reflections From the Wrong Side of the Tracks: Class, Identity, and the Working Class Experience in Academe.* Lanham, MD: Rowman & Littlefield.

Neckerman, Kathryn, Prudence Carter, and Jennifer Lee. 1999. "Segmented Assimilation and Minority Cultures of Mobility." *Ethnic and Racial Studies* 22, no. 6: 945–65.

Nora, Amaury and Alberto F. Cabrera. 1996. "The role of perception of prejudice and discrimination on the adjustment of minority students to college." *Journal of Higher Education* 67, no. 2: 119–48.

Ogbu, John. 1978. *Minority Education and Caste: The American System in Cross-Cultural Perspective.* New York: Academic Press.

Oliver, Melvin, and Thomas Shapiro. 1997. *Black Wealth/White Wealth: A New Perspective on Racial Inequality.* New York: Routledge.

Orfield, Gary. 2013. "Housing Segregation Produces Unequal Schools: Causes and Solutions." In *Closing the Opportunity Gap: What America Must Do to Give Every Child an Even Chance*, edited by Prudence L. Carter, and Kevin G. Welner, 40–60. Oxford: Oxford University Press.

Orfield, Gary, and Susan Eaton. 1997. *Dismantling Desegregation: The Quiet Reversal of Brown vs. Board of Education.* New York: The New Press.

Pearce, Lisa D. 2004. "Unequal Childhoods: Class, Race, and Family Life (Review)." *Social Forces* 82, no. 4: 1661–63.

Pfeffer, Fabian T., and Martin Hällsten. 2012. "Mobility Regimes and Parental Wealth: The United States, Germany, and Sweden in Comparison." In *Population Studies Center Research Report 12–766*, University of Michigan Institute of Social Research.

Portes, Alejandro, and Min Zhou. 1993. "The New Second Generation: Segmented Assimilation and Its Variants." *Annals of the American Academy of Political and Social Science* 530, no. 1: 74–96.

Portes, Alejandro, Samuel A. McLeod, and Robert N. Parker. 1978. "Immigrant Aspirations." *Sociology of Education* 51, no. 4: 241–60.

Qian, Zhenchou, and Sampson Lee Blair. 1999. "Racial/Ethnic Differences in Educational Aspirations of High School Seniors." *Sociological Perspectives* 42, no. 4: 605–25.

Reay, Diane, Gill Crozier, and John Clayton. 2009. "Strangers in Paradise? Working Class Students in Elite Universities." *Sociology* 43, no. 6: 1103–21.

Ryan, Jake, and Charles Sackrey, eds. 1984. *Strangers in Paradise: Academics from the Working Class.* Boston: South End Press.

Shapiro, Thomas M. 2005. *The Hidden Cost of Being African American.* Oxford: Oxford University Press.

Silva, Jennifer M. 2013. *Coming Up Short: Working Class Adulthood in an Age of Uncertainty.* Oxford: Oxford University Press.

Strage, Amy, and Tamara S. Brandt. 1999. "Authoritative Parenting and College Students' Academic Adjustment and Success." *Journal of Educational Psychology* 91, no. 1: 146–56.

Strayhorn, Terrell L. 2006. "Factors Influencing the Academic Achievement of First-Generation College Student." *NASPA Journal* 43, no. 4: 82–111.

Strauss, Anselm. 1998. *Basics of Qualitative Research: Techniques and Procedures for Developing Grounded Theory.* Thousand Oaks: Sage.

Streib, Jessi. 2017. "The Unbalanced Theoretical Toolkit: Problems and Partial Solutions to Studying Culture and Reproduction but Not Culture and Mobility." *American Journal of Cultural Sociology* 5: 127–53.

Stuber, Jenny M. 2006. "Talk of Class: Discursive Boundaries and Social Reproduction among Working- and Upper-Middle-Class College Students." *Journal of Contemporary Ethnography* 35: 285–318.

Tokarczyk, Michelle M., and Elizabeth A. Fay, eds. 1993. *Working Class Women in the Academy: Laborers in the Knowledge Factory.* Boston: University of Massachusetts Press.

Turner, Erlanger A., Megan Chandler, and Robert Heffer. 2009. "The Influence of Parenting Styles, Achievement Motivation, and Self-Efficacy on Academic Performance in College." *Journal of College Student Development* 50, no. 3: 337–46.

Weiss, Robert. 1995. *Learning from Strangers: The Art and Method of Qualitative Interview Studies.* New York: The Free Press.

Welsch, Kathleen A. 2005. *Those Winter Sundays: Female Academics and Their Working Class Parents.* New York: University Press of America

Wirt, John Choy Susan, Stephen Provasnik, Patrick Rooney, Anindata Sen, and Richard Tobin. 2004. *The Condition of Education 2004.* National Center for Education Statistics (NCES 2004–077). Washington, DC: Department of Education, Institute of Educational Sciences.

Zhou, Min. 1997. "Growing Up American: The Challenge Confronting Immigrant Children and Children of Immigrants." *Annual Review of Sociology* 23, no. 1: 63–95.

Zhou, Min. 1997. "Segmented Assimilation: Issues, Controversies, and Recent Research on the New Second Generation." *International Migration Review* 31, no. 4: 975–1008.

NOTES

1. In total, the racial breakdown of the sample was as follows: ten participants (six students and four parents) self-identified as Black, African American, African, or Afro-Caribbean; eleven participants (six students and five parents) self-identified as Latino/a, Hispanic, Mexican, or Mexican American; one student participant self-identified as Asian/Asian American; two participants (one student and one parent) self-identified as Arab/Arab American; two participants (one student, and one parent) self-identified as White; and three participants (one student and two parents) chose to self-identify as Guyanese. Within the sample, fifteen participants (six of the students

and nine of the parents) were women, and the other fifteen participants (ten of the students and five of the parents) were men.

2. According to the US Department of Education's National Postsecondary Student Aid Study data from 2009 (the year in which the data was collected), students of color comprised 54 percent of all college students from low-income *and* first-generation backgrounds, 35 percent of students who were from low-income *or* first-generation backgrounds, and only 26 percent of college students who were from neither low-income nor first-generation backgrounds. Students who were non-Native English speakers comprised 18 percent of all college students from low-income *and* first-generation backgrounds, 12 percent of students who were from low-income *or* first-generation backgrounds, and only 9 percent of college students who were from *neither* low-income *nor* first-generation backgrounds.

2

Interdependent Relationships and Family Responsibilities

How Socioeconomic Status and Immigrant Histories Shape Second-Generation Asian American Experiences

Fanny Yeung

Sociologists have documented the integral roles immigrants and immigrant labor have contributed to the physical and economic construction of the United States (Bean and Stevens 2003; Steinberg 2001). Immigrant communities have supplied abundant high- and low-skilled labor that bolstered the US economy and have significantly contributed to the formation of a multi-ethnic society (Kasinitz et al. 2006; Roediger 2006; Steinberg 2001). Early immigration patterns evolved as key immigration policies were introduced, most notably occurring in 1965 with the Hart-Celler Immigration and Nationality Act, which enabled adult immigrants to immigrate for work or political asylum (Portes and Zhou 1993). Most recently, the era of new immigration between 1990 and 2010 spurred demographic changes that have changed the face of the United States. The foreign-born population in the United States doubled to 40 million people, of which 11.2 million were from Asia (US Census Bureau 2010). Likewise, the population of children of recent immigrants has grown drastically; in 1995, one in five school-age children lived in immigrant households (Suárez-Orozco and Suárez-Orozco 1995; Zhou 1997). Second-generation immigrants are defined as children of first-generation immigrants (foreign-born individuals) and include first-generation immigrants who arrived to the United States prior to age five (Suárez-Orozco and Suárez-Orozco 1995).

Asian American experiences are often generalized in ways that overlook disparities based on socioeconomic status (SES) (Teranishi et al. 2004). Studies on Asian American students often utilize skewed samples comprising educated students from higher socioeconomic subgroups (Kao and Tienda 2005) and seldom explore the educational experiences of low socioeconomic Asian immigrants. Research disaggregated by SES has shown that Asian parents were actually the least likely to be proficient in English (Tseng 2004) and more likely to be low-income (Teranishi et al. 2004), complicating the experiences of Asian American students who are first in their families in college. Furthermore, prevailing assumptions related to the model minority myth disregard complex immigration experiences and the subsequent challenges for children of immigrants who pursue higher education (Chou and Feagin 2015).

The majority of scholarly research on Asian American undergraduate students has overlooked family contexts, socioeconomic statuses, and the effects of immigration and settlement conditions on subsequent generations. In contrast, this chapter explores the connection of students' immigrant histories that have been shaped directly by their families' socioeconomic status and parents' participation in the service-oriented employment industry in the United States. Furthermore, interdependent relationships between immigrant parents and their children are explored as an example of a direct survival strategy to navigate a foreign language and US policies and practices. This study was guided by the following research questions:

1. How do immigrant histories and socioeconomic contexts shape the family roles and responsibilities of children of Asian immigrants?
2. How do interdependent family dynamics shape immigrant family contexts?
3. What are the implications of students' immigrant histories and SES on students' postsecondary experiences?

Thus far, most research has lumped first- and second-generation immigrants together or has predominantly focused on first-generation, foreign-born immigrants (Suárez-Orozco 2005). While all immigrants have an immigrant history, this new second generation is the fastest growing, most ethnically diverse group in schools nationwide, yet the most neglected as well (Suárez-Orozco 2005). The intersection of immigrant generation with educational system, particularly among first-generation college students—those whose parents' highest degree is a high school diploma or less (Pascarella et al. 2004) or who were the first in their families to attend college (Terenzini et al. 1996)—is the distinguishing factor of this group of college students. Furthermore, recognizing that first-generation college students who are also ethnic minorities face additional challenges compared to their peers (Ting 2003), this chapter bridges the intersection of immigration histories and education to provide insight into the lived immigrant histories as well as the present realities for these students.

LITERATURE REVIEW OF API EXPERIENCES IN HIGHER EDUCATION AND FAMILY RELATIONSHIPS

This literature review begins with Asian and Pacific Islander (API) experiences in higher education by reviewing scholarship that highlights differences by SES, limited acknowledgment of familial factors, and the role of educational attainment in immigrant families. The next section considers SES and family relationships within Asian and Pacific Islander (API) immigrant groups given the complexity of immigrant family contexts, racialized immigrant experiences, and the lasting implications of one generation's struggles on those of the next generation.

API Experiences in Higher Education

Research has established that disparities exist in the college-going process as well as in degree attainment. According to the Chronicle of Higher Education *Almanac of Higher Education* (2009), in the 2006–2007 academic year, approximately 9 percent of Blacks, 7 percent of Hispanics, and 6 percent of Asians had obtained a bachelor's degree compared to 68 percent of Whites. Although, taken as a group, the percent of API students going to college has increased over three decades, it is important to acknowledge that that growth varies dramatically according to ethnicity and SES, with the greatest change among "Southeast Asians (43.3 percent) and Chinese Americans (29.0 percent) . . . with a combined income of less than $24,999 per year" (Teranishi et al. 2004, 532). In fact, significant differences in the college choice process were noted among Asian American students from different socioeconomic classes (Teranishi et al. 2004). Given disparities in college attendance, it is not surprising that among ethnic groups, Asian Americans and Pacific Islanders were awarded the fewest postsecondary degrees nationwide in 2009–2010: 7.3 percent Asians/Pacific Islanders, 10.3 percent Black, 8.8 percent Hispanics, and 72.9 percent White students (National Center for Education Statistics 2012).

While most researchers have documented that educational attainment is the strongest predictor of upward mobility (Kasinitz et al. 2009; Nuñez and Cuccaro-Alamin 1998), parents' education level is the single most important factor in determining the educational and economic success of the next generation, as much as four times stronger than any other family background characteristic (Kasinitz et al. 2009). Given that many second-generation youth are first-generation college students, particularly among immigrant families employed in the service sector, it is important to examine the progress of children of low-skilled immigrant groups in their educational pathway toward and in higher education (Alba and Nee 2003; Hirschman 2001). Similarly, it is also important to document the complex challenges that children of working-class immigrants face as they disrupt the process of social reproduction of the underclass to achieve social and educational mobility beyond the parameters previously established by their immigrant and family communities.

Research on ethnic minority first-generation college students often reported students with poorer academic achievement indicators and higher dropout rates. Despite research that indicates grim outcomes for students with poor educational preparation and matriculation to college, students of color generally aspire to higher levels of educational attainment than their White counterparts when socioeconomic status is held constant (Feliciano 2006; Kao 2004; Kao and Tienda 2005). To provide context for why this might be the case, Lopez (2001) found that education is often viewed as an avenue for social and economic mobility for students from low-SES backgrounds and their families. For first-generation college students from immigrant families, moreover, postsecondary attainment is often framed as an "immigrant bargain" in which students are expected to perform well in school in the face of their parents' sacrifices related to migration (Louie 2012; Smith 2006). As such, motivation for educational attainment is deeply rooted in collective advancement; however, students aspire to educational achievement while simultaneously trying to meet familial demands, which may become a challenging balance (Maramba 2008; Tseng 2004).

While their motivation is high, low-income first-generation college students often report feeling like academic imposters, with frequent experiences of insecurity and a low sense of belonging on their academic campuses (Rondini 2016). Additionally, students reported both feeling guilty about their success in relation to their family background and experiencing conflict because their educational institutions were disconnected and disregarded their communities and backgrounds as active components of their holistic lives (Piorkowski 1983; Rendón 1992; Rondini 2016). Rendón's (1992) scholarship on validation theories reinforced the notion that students' familial connections and community should not be disjointed identities for students, particularly if we want students of color to be successful.

For example, in Maramba's (2008) study of primarily second-generation Filipina American college students, students reported the following factors that challenged their college experiences: (1) parents' desire for students to stay close to home; (2) internalization of parents' immigrant struggles into motivation for college and pressure to excel; (3) strained family relationships due to home and college demands; and (4) difficulty balancing cultural identity across the home and college environment. Similarly, in her work with Chicana students, Delgado Bernal (2001) found that "pedagogies of the home . . . (or) communication, practices and learning that occur in the home and community" help students negotiate their education experiences (624). Other research on immigrant families and ethnic minorities in college has also documented a strong connection to family responsibilities and relationships (Hardway and Fuligni 2006).

Socioeconomic and Familial Considerations in API Research

Research on undergraduate experiences often overlooks students' relationships with their families. Most scholarship focuses on White, middle-class students; their college experiences are typically viewed as individualistic journeys, where successful transition to and retention within higher education is achieved by disconnecting from one's family and community (Tinto 1987). While numerous scholars have countered this perspective by critiquing its applicability to bicultural students of color (Cabrera, Nora, and Castaneda 1993; Rendón, Jalomo, and Nora 2000), more research is needed to understand how these dynamics work as well as resist the idea that API students' families are only a hindrance to their educational efforts—to focus, that is, on the strengths immigrant families and their histories can bring to students' academic pursuits. For example, Maramba (2008) documented how family and parental influences on Filipina Americans encourage students to stay close to home, focus on their academics as opposed to extracurricular activities, and maintain close relationships with their families. While familial factors often produced more nuanced and complicated postsecondary experiences, Filipina students often reported that their families also provided their greatest support during college (Maramba 2008).

As a unit, families are often overlooked when studying students' educational pathways and experiences. Zhou and Bankston (1998) observed: "To be an American, you may be able to do whatever you want. But to be a Vietnamese, you must think of your family first" (166). Previous studies have not explored actual obligatory behaviors and responsibilities within immigrant families (e.g., caregiving, household responsibilities, translating, negotiating social services, and so on) and how these responsibilities affect students' persistence in college (Fuligni and Witkow 2004). For example, children of Asian and Latin American immigrants have reported acute awareness of the sacrifices and demanding work of their parents (Suárez-Orozco and Suárez-Orozco 1995), and in return "possessed stronger values and greater expectations regarding their duty to assist, respect, and support their families than their peers with European backgrounds" (Fuligni, Tseng, and Lam 1999, 1030). By studying family responsibilities that extend from early childhood, we can begin to understand how students' own responsibilities and roles within their immigrant families then influenced their postsecondary experiences. Given that familial responsibilities are among the most significant sources of conflict between immigrant youth and their parents (Zhou 1997), further exploration of familial dynamics can provide valuable insight into a growing population of college students.

Scholars across academic disciplines have studied the repercussions of racialized settlement experiences and economic underemployment common among immigrant populations (Buenavista 2010; Ceja 2004; Suárez-Orozco 2005). Employment opportunities for immigrants often include long hours (and low pay that renders childcare unaffordable), leaving children unattended and placing them in positions with adult-like responsibilities and roles at an early age. Scholars have also documented the influence and impact of students' awareness of their parents' sacrifices and of their difficult lives as immigrants to a new country (Ceja 2004; Suárez-Orozco 2005). These responsibilities, in conjunction with the sense of obligation students feel to their parents as a result of parents' sacrifices and laborious occupations (Fuligni 2006; Suárez-Orozco and Suárez-Orozco 1995), are often internalized and transformed into desires to obtain postsecondary degrees and, subsequently, well-paying jobs to repay their parents (Fuligini, Tseng, and Lam 1999; Fuligini and Witkow 2004).

Many researchers have discussed the relationship between children's acculturation to the dominant society and parents' experiences with role reversals within the family (Alba and Nee 2003; Bean and Stevens 2003). Role reversals have conventionally been framed as a consequence of children adapting to the dominant culture at a faster rate than their parents (Portes and Rumbaut 2001). While the reversal of power dynamics often occurs, Orellana (2009) asserts that children and parents "can contribute, perhaps differently but in balanced ways, according to their needs and capacities" (123). She argues that roles are not reversed at all; instead, parents and children contribute differently based on their roles within the family. For example, children's translator roles within their families fill an important need out of necessity (Orellana 2009). While children may have taken the lead in translating and negotiating services for their families, they continued to be perceived as children and thus had limited power within their families. Orellana (2009) further stated that while some "intergenerational power shifting" (123) occurred, the rebalancing of power within conventional family roles did not.

Ultimately, despite racial, ethnic, and socioeconomic struggles common among immigrant populations, Asian Americans' experiences are often overgeneralized—namely through the model minority myth—to assume high educational achievement and a presumption that few, if any, challenges are encountered. Although rich research on immigrant family contexts is present in sociology and primary and secondary education, little research connects these complex family experiences to college students. This chapter builds on previous research with the intersection of complex socioeconomic and immigrant dynamics often invisible in the narrative of Asian American experiences in higher education and highlights strengths cultivated through sophisticated, interdependent family relationships.

INTERCONNECTED STRENGTHS OF COMMUNITY CULTURAL WEALTH AS THE THEORETICAL FRAMEWORK

This chapter is part of a larger research project and data collection grounded in a community cultural wealth framework (Yosso 2005) on children of immigrants in college. Community cultural wealth is rooted within critical race theory and challenges conventional notions of cultural capital with a critical analysis of whose knowledge is valued and counted (Bernal 1998, 2002; Ladson-Billings 2000). Yosso (2005) operationalizes community cultural wealth by outlining six forms of conventionally unrecognized capital that are prevalent in communities of color: aspirational, navigational, social, linguistic, familial, and resistance capital. A community cultural wealth framework serves to highlight the strengths inherent within immigrant families, particularly the "social or cultural capital provided by the ethnic community, and characteristics of an entire immigrant group [that] may influence the next generation's educational success" (Feliciano 2006, 95).

This chapter applies an interdependency theory to highlight how immigrant families resist structural and hierarchical barriers and, ultimately, explain how students negotiate college within this context. Elder (1998) described a phenomenon called "linked lives" in which lives are lived interdependently, and social and historical influences are expressed through this network of shared relationships. Interdependent relationships are mutually beneficial; each serves a purpose to help navigate processes and procedures (e.g., language barriers, health care, and education and employment systems) in the dominant society. For example, immigrant parents with no or low proficiency in English often rely on their children to assist with translating materials and negotiating interactions. Interdependent relationships can also be seen as a strategy to (1) maximize limited resources while simultaneously addressing needs, (2) counter historical and politicized patterns of exclusion of immigrants, and (3) address the social stigma associated with help-seeking behaviors among immigrant communities. Connecting interdependent relationships and SES contexts highlights the need to collectively contribute to achieving family goals. Taking into account environmental contexts enables a greater understanding of how individuals are interconnected and are accountable to others in their decision-making processes and actions.

METHODS AND SAMPLE

To examine how students' college experiences are built upon their immigrant histories, socioeconomic status, and family relationships, I conducted semi-structured interviews to explore how students' roles and responsibilities alleviated gaps in language proficiencies in their families and mediated social interactions with government agencies and schools. I asked students to reflect upon roles assumed inside and outside of their homes and how they negotiated these responsibilities along with the demands of college. Interviews ranged from 45 to 180 minutes. I recruited students through in-class announcements, email listservs, student organizations, student affairs staff members, and word of mouth.

Utilizing a community cultural wealth framework, interview questions explored students' immigrant histories, family contexts, and the ways in which their family roles and responsibilities influenced their postsecondary experiences. I coded emerging themes through an iterative process of an initial review of all 32 transcripts that produced 36 categories. Coding categories were further refined to create seven thematic codes for analysis: college choice, college experiences, family responsibilities, identity, immigration history, messages about education, and parental involvement in education. The final coding schema was validated with a colleague, producing 75 percent interrater reliability with 15 percent of the sample.

This chapter includes interviews from 32 Asian American students at a highly selective, public research university in California. Participants identified as the following: 16 as Chinese Americans (50 percent), 6 as multiethnic Asian American (Chinese and one other ethnicity (19 percent), and the remaining students, collectively identified in this chapter as Asian American, as Vietnamese (3), Cambodian (2), and Taiwanese (1), Hmong (1), Indian (1), Filipino (1), and Korean (1). There were 14 male participants, 18 female participants, and 19 students from low SES families. More than half of student participants (53 percent; n = 17) are first-generation college students whose parents did not obtain a postsecondary degree. Among the first-generation sample, 7 students identified as Chinese, 5 as Southeast Asian, and 1 as Korean. All but one was classified as low-income and there were 11 female and 6 male students. There appeared to be a connection between parents' educational attainment and the degree of manual labor and service associated with their employment. Additional characteristics that appeared to be related to manual and service occupations were the likelihood that parents held multiple jobs and worked beyond the typical nine-to-five timeframe of administrative or professional positions.

Socioeconomic status (SES) is a fluid concept that is often captured through measures of parents' educational attainment and annual income. Given that English language proficiency determines immigrants' ability to navigate interactions in dominant society (Bean and Stevens 2003), this study defined socioeconomic status based upon three characteristics: parents' educational attainment, English proficiency, and parents' employment experiences (e.g., service-oriented vs. office work). In other studies, English language proficiency has predicted income differentials among Hispanic men (McManus, Gould, and Welch 1983) and overall success post-arrival (Espenshade and Fu 1997). Low-SES students were categorized as such if they had two or more of the three characteristics (e.g., parents without a postsecondary degree, low English proficiency, or employment in service industry). Language proficiency was incorporated as an additional consideration to more accurately capture immigrant families' SES within an often anti-immigrant US context that functions to further marginalize immigrants within ethnic enclaves and service industries (Dustmann and Fabbri 2003; Espenshade and Fu 1997). The additional complexity of immigrant parents who may have obtained a postsecondary degree in their native country was not considered due to limited sample size; however, it may be worthwhile for future research to consider whether the value of their degree has not translated into commensurate economic opportunities or employment in the United States (Buenavista 2010). These students were coded in the non-first-generation college student group. Overall, more than half of student participants (n = 19) identified with the low-SES group, and the remaining 13 students were categorized as non-low-SES. The majority of the immigrant families (88 percent) included in this study lived in two-parent households. A third of students lived in multigenerational immigrant households, defined as living with extended family members, or had daily interactions with extended family members.

The majority of students in this study (91 percent) matriculated to college directly from high school. Three students transferred from a community college. At the time of the study, there were 2 students in their first year of college, 6 second-year students, 4 third-year students, and 20 students in their fourth and fifth year in school. Students' ages ranged from 18 to 22 years. Their grade point averages (GPAs) ranged from 2.7 to 3.95, while their majors spanned various disciplines and represented the following fields: sciences (13), social sciences (15), humanities (2), and other (2).

FINDINGS

The data revealed two distinct themes that provide perspective on how immigrant histories and socioeconomic context shape family roles and responsibilities for first-generation college students from immigrant families and their postsecondary experiences. First, this section discusses how low-SES contexts generated unique roles and responsibilities for children of immigrants, which in turn facilitated their development of strong educational aspirations. Second, it highlights how students negotiated their postsecondary demands with their family roles and responsibilities.

Given the limited attention to them thus far in the literature, this chapter primarily focuses on the experiences of low-SES second-generation immigrants. Since non-low-SES second-generation immigrant students' experiences in college generally resembled typical postsecondary experiences with little reference to family responsibilities, these points of view will be discussed only briefly. Instead, the findings from this study aim to contribute a perspective about how contemporary, working-class immigrant experiences, and the socioeconomic conditions in which they are rooted, impact the postsecondary experiences of API children of immigrants in this study.

Influence of Socioeconomics on Immigrant Family Contexts

> I can't ask my parents to help me out in English . . . When you think about
> it, it's like a really big factor having parents that can at least speak a little
> English. That would help out a lot and it would make a major difference.
>
> —Lisa, first-year, direct-entry Chinese American student,
> undeclared major

The most defining characteristic that determined the degree of participation that second-generation youth had in their families centered on their parents' English fluency. Every low-SES student recalled experiences negotiating language barriers for their parents and serving as intermediaries with employers, teachers, and companies. Given students' early socialization in US schools, participants from low-SES families were more proficient in English from an early age than their own parents. As a result, beginning when students were very young, parents asked them to assist with logistical and administrative tasks that were critical to daily family functions. As Lisa describes above, immigrant parents' proficiencies affected their ability to navigate society and help with students' schooling as well as the overall level of assistance parents needed from their children. Most students reported navigating the college application process and FAFSA on their own with assistance from school counselors and peers. Furthermore, in the event of administrative challenges (e.g., delays in financial aid, FAFSA audits, or registration holds) students did not have safety nets in the form of parental help in navigating these procedures.

Samantha, a fourth-year Chinese American student majoring in international economics, said, "I took on the responsibilities in setting up doctor's appointments for everybody in the family: brother, sister, mom, dad. . . . If there was ever a problem with any of the (bill) statements, I took care of that . . . (since) I was 10." In addition to reading mail or serving as an intermediary between credit card or utility companies within their homes, students such as Samantha were also asked to translate. Students also recalled experiences utilizing their bilingual proficiencies to navigate employment opportunities for their parents from a young age. Brian, a fourth-year, direct-entry Asian American student in a psychology/biology major, recalled those experiences vividly:

I guess her stadium job [as a concessions representative] came when I was seven. I just remember the boss was asking basic interview questions about past experiences that you have had, what are your strengths, weaknesses, etc. . . . I remember, I wouldn't be able to always translate directly to my mom. She would be really confused. . . . That was my first time . . . my first exposure to a job interview and I was 7 years old.

The notions of age-appropriate behaviors for children differed in immigrant households and were negotiated based on necessity. For many students, the role of translating started at a young age and continued into their present lives. In contrast, these roles were nonexistent among non-immigrant, middle- or upper-class college students. Jenny, a fourth-year, direct-entry Asian American student majoring in economics, recalled:

There was a lot of translating. I think I started in the third grade with my brother's permission slips and all his school papers. My parents weren't really around, so in the third grade, I started filling out all the permission slips, and paperwork, and forging their signatures. I practiced and I was really good at my mom's signature. I took on the motherly role for my brother . . . and I helped with homework since my parents couldn't help them.

While some government agencies now have translators available, participants vividly recalled serving as their families' resource as translators and mediators in stores, hospitals, and doctors' offices during their childhoods. Reflecting on their experiences in these settings, many now realized the risk of translating something incorrectly and were relieved that they had not made any major mistakes. As children participated in important family roles and responsibilities, these roles became a normal part of their lives—"something they just did"—in response to a direct need in their childhood and while in college.

An important component of students' roles within their families was their awareness of their parents' sacrifices in their immigration experience and settlement. Some students framed their perception of their parents' experiences as a compilation of missed opportunities and struggle. Low-SES students shared this sentiment of being able to recognize their parents' struggles connected to their settlement experiences in low-paying jobs and experiences with discrimination. For instance, Jenny (fourth-year, Asian American) reflected on how her parents' immigration experience began with violence and turmoil in their native country and how that information helped her gain appreciation for her family's immigration history. Jenny recalled her experience visiting the genocide camps in Vietnam with her parents:

> There were bloodstains everywhere and there were the little cells that my family stayed in. There were images and pictures of all the victims and the bodies they found. It was gruesome but for me, it matters where they came from and what they went through during those four years. It made me appreciate them even more.

Experiences with parents' earlier histories, along with the circumstances of parents' settlement experience, contextualized participants' understanding of their personal history and journey.

Immigrant parents also shared their sense of loss in terms of their own educational opportunities and attainment with their children. Participants reported that parents openly discussed their limited schooling and how educational opportunities could lead to future employment possibilities. Brian (fourth year, Asian American), explained:

> They [my parents] couldn't help me with the actual subject material. They would be . . . [the] inspirational sources just to make sure I stay in shape, make sure I keep [my] mind on school and would always remind me, "Look how tired I am from coming home from work. Make sure you don't have to go through all this with your family. So, just make sure you keep studying hard and you better go to college . . ." which they told me when I was seven.

Brian highlighted how his parents discussed the potential for economic mobility through higher education from an early age and provided reminders about their struggles as a result of their limited opportunities for formal education. Awareness of their parents' long hours and laborious positions often grounded students' motivation to go to college and then to complete their own college careers. In addition, the majority of low-SES participants indicated that their higher-education pursuits would help them provide financial stability for their families in the future. Aligned with established literature, a common theme among children of immigrants who are first in their families to attend college was that their motivation to succeed transcended individual gains and affirmed their family responsibilities.

Non-Low-SES Contexts

Non-low-SES Asian American students did not report any roles in and responsibilities to their families aside from occasional chores. In fact, non-low-SES students were more likely to describe their parents' immigrant experiences with more detached, distancing language. For example, these students were more likely to use phrases such as "the immigrant experience" and "they" instead of "my parents." Also, non-low-SES students did not connect their parents' immigrant experiences as a significant factor in their own personal experiences or development. Instead, some non-low-SES students reported that they did not know much about their parents' immigration or settlement experiences. Joseph, a non-low-SES Chinese American student who was in his fourth year and majoring in political science, summarized this disconnect:

> To me those phrases [*immigrant history* and *experience*] . . . don't really connect to me in the sense that I feel somewhat removed from them. To me those are phrases from a textbook or those are phrases from my parents' history and those are the things that inform my understanding of what they went through and how they got to where they are or how they've been able to raise me but I don't really consider them to be my own.

Although every student in this study identified as a child of immigrant parents, students' understanding of and connections to their immigrant history differed according to their families' SES contexts. Students from low-SES families were more likely to reflect on their parents' immigration and settlement experiences as points of reference about sacrifice. The absence of awareness of sacrifice for non-low-SES students appeared to disconnect and distance students from their immigrant histories.

Negotiating Higher Education within Family Roles and Responsibilities

> Sometimes, it's actually the same [as if I was at home]. My parents would call me . . . and I would ask my brother to just send me the paperwork and I'll look at it. So, even from a distance they're still here.
>
> —Jenny (fourth-year, direct-entry Asian American economics major)

Given the extensive family roles held by second-generation youth from an early age, it is not surprising that many students continued to assume such roles while in college. In this study, the roles assumed by the children addressed barriers related to language, finance, and limited experience and knowledge of US society. Low-SES second-generation immigrants understood that their roles and responsibilities would not likely cease when they moved away for college, even if they had siblings who still lived at home. Rather, low-SES students strategized to uphold their responsibilities while balancing their academic demands. These experiences differed greatly from the postsecondary experiences of non-low-SES second-generation immigrant students.

Postsecondary Experiences of Low-SES Second-Generation Immigrants

While balancing rigorous academic demands in college, children of low-SES immigrants also maintained active roles within their immigrant families. While in college, the distance between students' postsecondary institutions and their parents' homes mediated students' involvement with their family roles and responsibilities. On average, students who lived within a 100-mile radius of home visited their families at least once a month, yet students who moved greater distances returned home once a quarter or less. Approximately two-thirds of students (n = 21) chose to remain close to home and indicated on average that they returned home at least two weekends a month.

For example, Sherlock, a 5th year senior majoring in biology, perceived his trips home as a way to check on his mother and the things that needed his attention at home:

> My moms at home by herself now, so I . . . try to go home as much as I can. It's just nice to like get away from school for a while. But it's interesting: on one hand I don't want to be at home but on the other hand, I feel kind of an obligation or like a responsibility to go home and see my mom and make sure everything's okay [in terms of the tasks he assisted with at home].

Students' understanding of their roles and responsibilities was embedded within their conceptualization of spending time with their families. Most students did not explicitly differentiate between their leisure time and time helping their families, as evident in the ways students framed their home time as a place to recuperate from their academic lives and simultaneously talked about their family roles and responsibilities.

Although they were in a new environment and moved away from their families, low-SES students found that their home lives did not disappear when they went away for school. Rather, low-SES students continued to negotiate their family roles and responsibilities while enrolled in college. While a few students transferred their administrative responsibilities—for example, oversight of bills—to younger siblings (n = 2), others maintained them despite geographical distances. For these students, technological strategies were set in place by both students and parents to facilitate continuity of responsibilities. Lisa (first-year, Chinese American, undeclared major) described how before she left for college her family devised a system in which correspondence regarding her family's bills would be directed to her email account:

> All their accounts, like all the bank accounts, our cable account, our AT&T account, Amazon account, insurance . . . basically all their accounts, I keep in my email to read. Sometimes they send mail directly home, but since I'm not there anymore and my sister is not there, it would be a hassle for my mom to mail every single letter to me. I always have to read them and translate, so I would just send them directly to my email. So in case my mom does get a letter . . . I will refer back to my account and read it on online and try to explain it to them. [It's] kind of a system we worked out before I left [for college].

Contrary to typical perceptions of higher education experiences, second-generation youth from low-SES immigrant families maintained extensive family roles and responsibilities while in college. Despite moving away from home for college, Lisa managed her family's utility bills, insurance statements, and so on from a distance. The majority of low-SES students retained their family roles and responsibilities (n = 17) despite moving away to college. Jenny (fourth year, Asian American) described how she managed her family's affairs from such a distance:

> Sometimes, it's actually the same [as if I was at home]. My parents would call me, "Jenny, can you call the phone company, there's a weird charge on it and I don't really understand it." And I would ask my brother to just send me the paperwork and I'll look at it and I'll call them [the phone company]. So, even from a distance they're still here. Yeah, a lot of the times . . . [they physically mail the bills to me] or they'll call and give me the number and information and I'll just call and clarify or whatnot. It's just that since they don't know how to use the computer, a lot of the roles go to me. If my parents wanted a plane ticket, they would ask me to find it online for them. A lot of them [requests] are busywork, like if they wanted reservations, I would do that for them.

Considering students' academic responsibilities as full-time college students, students were essentially negotiating and balancing two commitments that can be equally demanding. Throughout these interviews, students were able to articulate the importance of both roles for their personal future and their families' future. This awareness challenged students to develop the skills to balance both types of requests in their daily lives.

Most students maintained levels of involvement within their families while in college; however, one student admitted to struggling because she felt additional pressure to contribute more. Mara, a third-year Asian American transfer student majoring in international development, described how she managed her family's expectations for her role as the only daughter in the family:

> At the time, I felt like it was the only way to survive because no one else could do it. There was a point where it was really overwhelming. I think because I was juggling a lot with family during my community college, I had to stay a little longer. And now, I have to extend my stay here at this [4-year institution]. They [her family] want me to be there [home] [more]. I have an aunt who always says, "You should be there Mara; why aren't you helping your mom? You should help her at home." I think what she means is [that she should] assist, like helping my mom with the errands because she had to do everything else for the entire family. She [her aunt] wants me to take on that role. I guess because I am a woman, I am the only daughter and because I'm the oldest, they still have an expectation.

While some families were able to adapt, low-SES families were less likely to have social resources and capital outside of their immediate family to provide alternative sources of help. In those cases, immigrant parents relied on their children to assist with family roles and responsibilities. As such, home responsibilities were frequently a constant presence in students' lives regardless of the transitions they had made in their lifetime, including college.

In addition to administrative tasks, low-SES students in this study (n = 19) also shouldered financial responsibilities while in college. As students pursued their postsecondary goals, they also acquired sizeable financial burdens and expenses through these opportunities. Depending upon students' socioeconomic status, moreover, the financial implications and circumstances surrounding low-SES children of immigrants differed significantly. Although students' enrollment in college did not alter existing financial responsibilities they had within their family, those family commitments were compounded by students' new college expenses, including tuition, room, board, textbooks, and more. Students' contributions to their families represented one of two types: some students contributed financially, and others exercised financial independence by removing any financial impositions on their families. Only four students (of nineteen low-SES participants) were categorized as financial contributors in their families (i.e., they occasionally made financial contributions to family expenses). Julie, a second-year, direct-entry, multiethnic Chinese American student majoring in sociology, summarized, "I don't think

I ever had a problem giving her money though. I think it was very natural and I think I almost felt bad if I didn't give the money. I think at some point, I wasn't working as much but was still giving her the same amount." Julie's contributions were possible through her part-time work; the majority of other students in this study utilized funds from their financial aid package, including loans.

Having been familiar with their families' finances and expenses, many students elected to take responsibility for their own expenses and/or made contributions to family expenses to help alleviate the additional burden associated with their postsecondary education. The remaining fifteen students strived to be financially self-reliant in college and did not seek or receive any significant financial support from their families. At a time when educational fees were steadily increasing, students resorted to resourceful strategies to compensate for diminished financial resources. Brian (fourth year, Asian American) discussed how he utilized course reserves at the library to minimize his college expenses when his funding for the term was insufficient:

> At any time, [if I] felt I was going to fall a little short, like I could tell that sometimes the grants weren't going to be enough, I would just not buy the books that I needed. Instead I would just go to . . . [the library], there were course reserves and I will just study there. [Most of the] time, the grants were just fine and perfect but when they fell short, I would just make adjustments on the side. I understand that my parents don't have that much money. When you see like how hard they work just to support you, like provide food for you, make sure you get good education and whatnot. Then, you really don't want to ask them for additional money. "I'm going to college and I understand it's going to be good for me in the future, but I'm being even more [of a] burden on you right now." So, when I saw that I wouldn't be required to use too much of their money, I was really, really relieved from that.

This was one example of the ways in which students employed a strategy of utilizing on-campus resources to balance financial constraints. Students reflected that they were in a unique position in which they had access to a substantial amount of money—through student aid and grants—for the first time in their lives. While the four students who were financial contributors utilized their aid and money earned through work, other students aimed to be financially independent.

Postsecondary Experiences of Non-Low-SES Second-Generation Students

All students were concerned with and prioritized their academics, but students from non-low-SES immigrant families perceived their responsibilities as a college student as their sole responsibilities to their families and were typically not placed in any roles otherwise. Sherman, a non-low-SES, second-year Chinese American student in English, explained, "I think my mom's comment was, 'You need to be a student, that's your job first.'" While family members encouraged students from non-low-SES families to prioritize college and focus solely on their academics, low-SES students placed their academics and family as simultaneously important demands.

Despite not having direct financial responsibilities to their families, non-low-SES students were nonetheless cognizant of the rising expenses associated with their postsecondary experiences and the added postsecondary expenses their family shouldered. Given how a succession of tuition increases and decreased campus resources has strained the economic climate of higher-education institutions, non-low-SES students emphasized graduating on time to help alleviate any additional costs. Furthermore, non-low-SES students' responses to their academic roles took into consideration economic factors but did not otherwise alter behaviors to contribute to their families. Non-low-SES students' ability to focus on their postsecondary experiences, a privilege many low-SES students did not have, meant that in many respects their experiences resembled the narratives presented of traditional college students.

DISCUSSION

As school-age second-generation immigrants matriculate into college, their educational trajectories have the potential to represent the "most consequential and lasting legacy of the new mass immigration to the United States" (Portes and Rumbaut 2001, 18). The impact of increased diversity is already evident in postsecondary settings; for example, within the University of California system, more than half of all undergraduate students (54 percent) in 2006 had at least one parent who is an immigrant (Douglass, Roebken, and Thomson 2007). In the United States, structural diversity, enriched by historical and contemporary immigration patterns, is a documented facet of this country's history. Less acknowledged, however, are political contexts that shape immigrant experiences and the long-term implications of the settlement experiences of a future generation of citizens and their integration into social systems who arguably have not adapted to welcome and include a diverse populace. As a society, it is too convenient to disassociate from these immigrant histories, particularly if they differ from the more visible and valued Anglo-Saxon values and experiences. However, the counter-narratives provided by the students in this study challenge the assumption (shaped in turn by model minority assumptions) that Asian and Asian American student experiences in higher education emulate White student experiences. Students with immigrant experiences—particularly the API students in this study—paint a more complex picture of those experiences, one dramatically shaped by immigration and socioeconomic class.

Previous research has alluded to the notion that role reversals within families affect interpersonal relationships, often detrimentally (Suárez-Orozco 2005). However, while the results of the present study reflected distinct challenges and a greater level of complexity due to dynamic, interdependent relationships, the majority of participants displayed positive connections among family members. Elder's (1998) linked lives theory provided the foundation for understanding how students' psychological and emotional connections to their families shaped their perceptions about their educational processes. Students' insights into their parents' service employment and family circumstances influenced their perception and understanding of the purpose of higher education, the value and role of financial interdependency, and mutually supportive roles in their families. This foundational component of interdependency is a constant presence throughout students' lives as they enter and progress through college. That students have complex lives shaped by broader societal factors, and not general adolescent apathy or disregard, is a critical fact that that educators and practitioners should recognize.

Many children of immigrants have integral roles within their families as a result of their class origins, their parents' English proficiency, and their families' economic constraints. While the associated tasks may have been onerous to some students, others were committed to these roles and responsibilities due to their acute awareness of their parents' sacrifices in the service-oriented labor force, parental aspirations for their children's social and economic mobility, and a sense of both accountability and gratitude for having educational opportunities that their parents did not. Students' educational opportunities and achievements became a responsibility in and of themselves, particularly as a way to repay parents for their support and to alleviate their families' economic struggles in the future. One key finding from this study is the acknowledgment that children's roles do not end when they matriculate into college; many shoulder family roles and responsibilities simultaneously. Additionally, this study recognizes students' complex family lives as a product of political, economic, and immigrant contexts that influence students' experiences in higher education.

As translators and social liaisons, second-generation youth were exposed to their parents' financial, emotional, and linguistic struggles associated with living in a foreign country. Participating in the processes necessary to coordinate basic necessities, ranging from utility bills and rent to schooling requirements, in addition to exposure to financial instability, forced students to gain a pragmatic awareness of these realities at a young age. Acknowledging these *interdependent family roles*, a unique distribution and exchange of leadership roles within immigrant families, challenges traditional notions of family life and has implications for how students approach and navigate their postsecondary educational trajectories. Having home responsibilities that include oversight of family accounts and financial contributions or independence impacts students' postsecondary experiences. These roles demonstrate a need to understand and recognize the complex student lives that accompany diverse characteristics and increasingly diverse undergraduate populations.

Given most institutions' commitment to recruiting low-income and low-SES students to diversify their undergraduate enrollment, consideration of complex family roles and responsibilities among low-SES children of immigrants is vital. It is equally important to balance the structural diversity desired and simultaneously address the needs of a more multifaceted student body. Institutions should be cautious of how campus politics, discussions, and practices contribute to the reproduction of the model minority stereotypes when Asian students are excluded from targeted student success initiatives and programs more purposefully geared towards African American and Latinx students. Additionally, staff and faculty development should promote culturally relevant programming that acknowledges students' families in the curriculum, conversation, and as significant roles in students' ongoing lives.

Furthermore, as the cost of postsecondary attendance continues to rise in an environment of declining state and federal support, financial aid (e.g., Pell grants, in-state aid, work-study opportunities) will be crucial funding sources. Additionally, student loans will likely have short-term implications on students' academic success as well as long-term financial implications of high debt. Financial aid advisors and financial literacy courses that can effective address both spectrums through culturally sensitive frameworks would be crucial services for first-generation college students. Furthermore, student services, including computer labs and printing support, library reserves, tutorial programs, and employment opportunities are essential to ensuring the success of low-SES students. Without these considerations, institutional initiatives to support diverse learning environments with diverse student populations will fall short.

This study highlights the need to incorporate two key student characteristics—socioeconomic status and immigrant history—that are often not taken into consideration as attributes of a growing, diverse student body. Individually and as they intersect, these demographic factors have direct influences on how postsecondary experiences are negotiated. While some immigrant parents in this study obtained postsecondary degrees abroad, as Buenavista (2010) acknowledged, advanced degrees from their country of origin does not necessarily translate into economic opportunities for immigrants. Future research can also explore the value and transferability of international post-secondary degrees and credentials within the US context and how those circumstances complicate our understanding of postsecondary experiences and preparation for children of immigrants. Additionally, it is worthwhile to note that for the majority of students in this study, this was the first time they had discussed these roles and responsibilities publicly. Many had internalized and normalized these roles and were keenly aware of how atypical their childhood and adolescence had been. Students' survival strategies included minimizing discussion of their home lives in order to assimilate and blend into their surroundings. Opportunities for students to explore and validate their experiences and unpack deeply held emotions—such as those sometimes available through ethnic studies courses and on-campus cultural ally programs—may be instrumental to these students' identity development. Postsecondary institutions, while rightfully focused on intellectual development and graduation, would also benefit from prioritizing more holistic personal development opportunities cultivated through semi-structured interactions and more formalized curricula within the humanities, social sciences, and student affairs divisions.

BIBLIOGRAPHY

Alba, Richard, and Victor Nee. 2003. *Remaking the American Mainstream: Immigration and Contemporary Immigration*. Cambridge: Harvard University Press.

Bean, Frank D., and Gillian Stevens. 2003. *America's Newcomers and the Dynamics of Diversity*. New York: Russell Sage Foundation.

Bernal, Dolores Delgado. "Using a Chicana Feminist Epistemology in Educational Research." *Harvard Educational Review* 68, no. 4 (1998): 555–583.

Buenavista, Tracy Lachica. 2010. "Issues Affecting US Filipino Student Access to Postsecondary Education: A Critical Race Theory Perspective." *Journal of Education for Students Placed at Risk* 15, no. 1–2: 114–26.

Cabrera, Alberto F., Amaury Nora, and Maria B. Castaneda. 1993. "College Persistence: Structural Equations Modeling Test of an Integrated Model of Student Retention." *Journal of Higher Education* 64, no. 2: 123–39.

Ceja, Miguel. 2004. "Chicana College Aspirations and the Role of Parents: Developing Educational Resiliency." *Journal of Hispanic Higher Education* 3, no. 4: 338–62.

Chou, Rosalind S., and Joe R. Feagin. 2015. *Myth of the Model Minority: Asian Americans Facing Racism*. New York: Routledge.

Chronicle of Higher Education. 2009. "Degrees Conferred by Racial and Ethnic Group, 2006–7." *Almanac of Higher Education.* http://chronicle.com/article/Degrees-Conferred-by-Racial/48039.

Delgado Bernal, Dolores. 2001. "Learning and Living Pedagogies of the Home: The Mestiza Consciousness of Chicana Students." *International Journal of Qualitative Studies in Education* 14, no. 5: 623–39.

Delgado Bernal, Dolores. 2002. "Critical Race Theory, Latino Critical Theory, and Critical Raced-Gendered Epistemologies: Recognizing Students of Color as Holders and Creators of Knowledge." *Qualitative Inquiry* 8, no. 1: 105–26.

Douglass, John Aubrey, Heinke Roebken, and Gregg Thomson. 2007. "The Immigrant University: Assessing the Dynamics of Race, Major and Socioeconomic Characteristics at the University of California." *Center for Studies in Higher Education* 19, no. 7 (November): 1–19.

Dustmann, Christian, and Francesca Fabbri. 2003. "Language Proficiency and Labour Market Performance of Immigrants in the UK." *The Economic Journal* 113, no. 489: 695–717.

Elder, Glen H. 1998. "The Life Course as Developmental Theory." *Child Development* 69, no. 1 (February): 1–12.

Espenshade, Thomas J., and Haishan Fu. 1997. "An Analysis of English-Language Proficiency Among US Immigrants." *American Sociological Review* 62, no. 2 (April): 288–305.

Feliciano, Cynthia. 2006. "Beyond the Family: The Influence of Premigration Group Status on the Educational Expectations of Immigrants' Children." *Sociology of Education* 79, no. 4: 281–303.

Fuligni, Andrew J. 2006. "Family Obligation among Children in Immigrant Families." *Migration Information Source.* http://www.migrationinformation.org/Feature/display.cfm.

Fuligni, Andrew J., Vivian Tseng, and May Lam. 1999. "Attitudes Toward Family Obligations among American Adolescents with Asian, Latin American, and European Backgrounds." *Child Development* 70, no. 4: 1030–44.

Fuligni, Andrew J., and Melissa Witkow. 2004. "The Postsecondary Educational Progress of Youth from Immigrant Families." *Journal of Research on Adolescence* 14, no. 2: 159–83.

Hardway, Christina, and Andrew J. Fuligni. 2006. "Dimensions of Family Connectedness among Adolescents with Mexican, Chinese, and European Backgrounds." *Developmental Psychology* 42, no. 6: 12–46.

Hirschman, Charles. 2001. "The Educational Enrollment of Immigrant Youth: A Test of the Segmented-Assimilation Hypothesis." *Demography* 38, no. 3: 317–36.

Kao, Grace. 2004. "Social Capital and its Relevance to Minority and Immigrant Populations." *Sociology of Education* 77, no. 2: 172–75.

Kao, Grace, and Marta Tienda. 2005. "Optimism and Achievement: The Educational Performance of Immigrant Youth." In *The New Immigration: An Interdisciplinary Reader*, edited by Carola Suárez-Orozco and Marcelo Suárez-Orozco, 331–43. New York: Brunner-Routledge.

Kasinitz, Philip, John H. Mollenkopf, Mary C. Waters, and Jennifer Holdaway. 2006. "Becoming American/Becoming New Yorkers: The Second Generation in a Majority Minority City." *Migration Information Source* (October 1). http://www.

migrationpolicy.org/article/becoming-americanbecoming-new-yorkers-second-generation-majority-minority-city

Kasinitz, Philip, John H. Mollenkopf, Mary C. Waters, and Jennifer Holdaway. 2009. *Inheriting the City: The Children of Immigrants Come of Age*. New York: Russell Sage Foundation.

Ladson-Billings, Gloria. 2000. "Fighting for our Lives: Preparing Teachers to Teach African American Students." *Journal of Teacher Education* 51, no. 3: 206–14.

Lopez, Gerardo. 2001. "The Value of Hard Work: Lessons on Parent Involvement from an (Im) Migrant Household." *Harvard Educational Review* 71, no. 3: 416–38.

Louie, Vivian. 2012. *Keeping the Immigrant Bargain: The Costs and Rewards of Success in America*. New York: Russell Sage Foundation.

Maramba, Dina C. 2008. "Immigrant Families and the College Experience: Perspectives of Filipina Americans." *Journal of College Student Development* 49, no. 4: 336–50.

McManus, Walter, William Gould, and Finis Welch. 1983. "Earnings of Hispanic Men: The Role of English Language Proficiency." *Journal of Labor Economics*: 101–30.

Nuñez, Anne-Marie, and Stephanie Cuccaro-Alamin. 1998. *First-Generation Students: Undergraduates Whose Parents Never Enrolled in Postsecondary Education*. Washington, DC: National Center for Education Statistics.

Orellana, Marjorie Faulstich. 2009. *Translating Childhoods: Immigrant Youth, Language, and Culture*. New Brunswick, NJ: Rutgers University Press.

Pascarella, Ernest T., Christopher T. Pierson, Gregory C. Wolniak, and Patrick T. Terenzini. 2004. "First-Generation College Students: Additional Evidence on College Experiences and Outcomes." *Journal of Higher Education* 75, no. 3 (May/June): 249–84.

Piorkowski, Geraldine K. 1983. "Survivor Guilt in the University Setting." *Personnel & Guidance Journal* 61, no. 10 (June): 620–22.

Portes, Alejandro, and Rubén G. Rumbaut. 2001. *Legacies: The Story of the Immigrant Second Generation*. Berkeley: University of California Press.

Portes, Alejandro, and Min Zhou. 1993. "The New Second Generation: Segmented Assimilation and its Variants." *The Annals of the American Academy of Political and Social Science* 530, no. 1: 74–96.

Rendón, Laura I. 1992. "From the Barrio to the Academy: Revelations of a Mexican American 'Scholarship Girl.'" *New Directions for Community Colleges* 1992, no. 80: 55–64.

Rendón, Laura I., Romero E. Jalomo, and Amaury Nora. 2000. "Theoretical Considerations in the Study of Minority Student Retention in Higher Education." In *Reworking the Student Departure Puzzle*, edited by John M. Braxton. Nashville: Vanderbilt University Press.

Roediger, David R. 2006. *Working Toward Whiteness: How America's Immigrants Became White: The Strange Journey from Ellis Island to the Suburbs*. New York: Basic Books.

Rondini, Ashley C. 2016. "Healing the Hidden Injuries of Class? Redemption Narratives, Aspirational Proxies, and Parents of Low-Income, First-Generation College Students." *Sociological Forum* 31, no. 1 (March): 96–116.

Smith, Robert C. 2006. *Mexican New York: Transnational Lives of New Immigrants.* Berkeley: University of California Press.

Steinberg, Stephen. 2001. *The Ethnic Myth: Race, Ethnicity, and Class in America.* Boston: Beacon Press.

Suárez-Orozco, Carola, and Marcelo M. Suárez-Orozco. 1995. *Transformations: Migration, Family Life, and Achievement Motivation Among Latino Adolescents.* Palo Alto, CA: Stanford University Press.

Suárez-Orozco, Marcelo M. 2005. *Right Moves? Immigration, Globalization, Utopia, and Dystopia.* New York: Routledge.

Teranishi, Robert T., Miguel Ceja, Anthony L. Antonio, Walter R. Allen, and Patricia M. McDonough. 2004. "The College-Choice Process for Asian Pacific Americans: Ethnicity and Socioeconomic Class in Context." *The Review of Higher Education* 27, no. 4 (Summer): 527–51.

Terenzini, Patrick T., Leonard Springer, Patricia M. Yaeger, Ernest T. Pascarella, and Amaury Nora. 1996. "First-Generation College Students: Characteristics, Experiences, and Cognitive Development." *Research in Higher Education* 37, no. 1 (February): 1–22.

Ting, Siu-Man R. 2003. "A Longitudinal Study of Non-Cognitive Variables in Predicting Academic Success of First-Generation College Students." *College and University* 78, no. 4 (Spring): 27–31.

Tinto, Vincent. 1987. *Leaving College: Rethinking the Causes and Cures of Student Attrition.* Chicago: University of Chicago Press.

Tseng, Vivian. 2004. "Family Interdependence and Academic Adjustment in College: Youth from Immigrant and US-Born Families." *Child Development* 75, no. 3: 966–83.

US Census Bureau. 2016. "2010 American Community Survey." http://www.census.gov/population/foreign/data/acs.html.

US Department of Education. 2012. "The Condition of Education 2012." NCES 2012–045, Indicator 47. Washington, DC: National Center for Education Statistics.

Yosso, Tara J. 2005. "Whose Culture Has Capital? A Critical Race Theory Discussion of Community Cultural Wealth." *Race, Ethnicity and Education* 8, no. 1: 69–91.

Zhou, Min. 1997. "Growing Up American: The Challenge Confronting Immigrant Children and Children of Immigrants." *Annual Review of Sociology* 23: 63–95.

Zhou, Min, and Carl Bankston. 1998. *Growing Up American: How Vietnamese Children Adapt to Life in the United States.* New York: Russell Sage Foundation.

3

Out With the Old, In With the New?

Habitus and Social Mobility at Selective Colleges

Elizabeth M. Lee

Rory Kramer

Social mobility through higher education is as much the process of learning elite mannerisms, behaviors, and "rules of the game" as it is the process of gaining credentials, knowledge, or wealth.[1] Scholars of mobility have documented the inherent clash between elite and nonelite ways of being that arises during that process, typically focusing on how upwardly mobile students fare on campus (e.g., Aries 2008; Aries and Seider 2005; Armstrong and Hamilton 2013; Goodwin 2002; Lee 2016; Ostrove 2003; Stuber 2006, 2009, 2011; Torres 2009). A corollary—student interaction with their nonelite home community—has received far less scholarly attention (for an exception, see Rondini 2016). While scholars have examined the price of mobility for racial and ethnic minorities (Bowen and Bok 1998; Carter 2003), consideration of rifts along class lines that consider what happens at home rather than on campus have largely been limited to memoir (Dews and Law 1995; Lubrano 2004; Ryan and Sackrey 1984). Here we focus on that understudied component of class mobility by examining how the transition into an elite habitus affects students' interactions with their home communities.

Habitus is Bourdieu's term for a person's worldview or disposition. Bourdieu argued that a person's internalized and often unconscious cultural understandings are developed over their lifetime through family and broader class position (Bourdieu 1977, 1990; Bourdieu and Wacquant 1992; Lamont and Lareau 1988). To Bourdieu, habitus is a critical component of the perpetuation of inequality: individuals internalize their class status into their tastes and worldviews, which then reinforce that very same social position because, as Stuber writes, they "structure[. . .] social action and serve[. . .] as the basis for perceiving one's experience" (2009, 881). Critics argue that the formulation of habitus is overly deterministic—if one's disposition cannot change over time, then there is no opportunity for mobility (e.g., King 2000). This criticism, we assert, is due to a misinterpretation of Bourdieu's concept of habitus. Indeed, Bourdieu writes that, rather than being static, "*habitus*, as the product of social conditionings, and thus of a history (unlike *character*), is endlessly transformed either in a direction that reinforces it . . . or in a direction that transforms it and, for instance, raises or lowers the levels of expectations and aspirations" (Bourdieu 1990, 116). Through one's accumulated experiences, then, the habitus may shift over time—as in, for example, upward social mobility. Bourdieu describes that experience of transitioning and holding two habitus at one time as a "cleft *habitus*" (2004, 111).

Like Bourdieu (1996), we believe the experience of nonelite students in elite colleges is a prime opportunity to explore the connection between habitus and social mobility. We pair qualitative and quantitative data to examine the habitus conflicts that result from enrollment in selective colleges. To emphasize this use of Bourdieu's less-static understanding of habitus, we reintroduce that terminology here in our analysis. We first examine which students report losing connections to their home communities within a national survey of students at selective campuses. If students' senses of loss are patterned by socioeconomic status (SES), this would suggest that socially mobile students do develop a new elite habitus at college and that the new habitus causes a "cleft" between the students' college identity and habitus and those of their home communities. We then use in-depth interviews with first-generation students from both low-income and working-class family backgrounds at one campus to more closely examine the nature of students' habitus cleavages. Rather than focusing on experiences on campus, we examine tensions between socially mobile students and nonmobile home communities. We show that these students struggle to maintain ties to home, often adopting interaction management strategies to navigate their relationships with parents, siblings, and high school friends. Our findings suggest both immediate and long-term consequences for students, which we discuss in the concluding section along with theoretical implications for the study of mobility through higher education. Quantitative data are drawn from the National Longitudinal Survey of Freshmen (NLSF), a national sample of students attending twenty-eight selective colleges and universities, and our interview data come from students at one of the campuses included in the NLSF, a women's liberal arts college; we discuss each in more depth below. First, we contextualize our arguments by considering the literatures of social mobility, habitus, and higher education in more depth.

LITERATURE

The Experience of Mobility through Education

Socially mobile students face a unique pressure to acclimate to the dominant elite culture. Nonelite students often perceive themselves to be less prepared academically (Aries and Seider 2005; Stewart and Ostrove 1993) and find little in common socially with higher-SES peers (Ostrove 2003; Stuber 2011). This experience is often quite visceral, memorable long into adulthood (Stewart and Ostrove 1993, as well as memoirs from formerly-working-class adults—see, e.g., Dews and Law 1995; Lubrano 2004; Ryan and Sackrey 1984; Tokarczyk and Fay 1993). Scholars examining the experiences of low-SES students at these institutions often analyze these difficulties as evidence of either a deficit of elite cultural capital or a devaluing of home culture by the organization (e.g., DiMaggio 1982; Hurst and Warnock 2015; Lee 2016; Stuber 2011; for a review, see Lamont and Lareau 1988). The analytical focus is on the processes and experiences that take place in the elite setting, rather than how students interact with their nonelite home communities after adjusting to an elite setting that requires a new disposition or habitus.

However, scholarship on race in elite educational institutions suggests that students may also experience challenges in encounters with friends and family from their home communities (Gaztambide-Fernandez and DiAquoi 2010). Work on racial and ethnic identity examines the complexities of shifting from a non-White home community into elite, predominantly White institutions through upward social mobility. Through these shifts, ties to hometown family and friends may become attenuated or cut off entirely (Carter 2003; Stanton-Salazar 1997; see also memoirs by Carey 1991; Rodriguez 1982)—losses which are also tied to negative outcomes in college acclimation (Cabrera, Nora, and Castaneda 1993; Guiffrida 2006; Melendez and Melendez 2010; Nora and Cabrera 1996; for a counterexample see Turley, Desmond, and Bruch 2010). As Carter's research (2003) illustrates, students moving between discrepant home and school communities must make substantial efforts to maintain successful ties with family members and friends from home while attending elite schools. These works exemplify a shift toward understanding seemingly static identities (such as race) as a fluid, contextual social process instead of a fixed social position. Race is a critical component to a person's habitus, and work problematizing racial identity as fluid also highlights the inadequacy of considering habitus as a static and deterministic concept (Horvat 2003).

Social Mobility, Habitus, and Its Discontents

Previous research has shown the difficulties caused by moving between "worlds" and the challenges of fitting existing relationships and personal beliefs into new status contexts. Those personal beliefs, preconceptions, and ways of being can be labeled as an individual's habitus, created and formed largely by that individual's class status and background. Traditionally in American sociology, habitus is seen as rarely or never changing and embedded into an individual's identity at an early age. However, in an overview of Bourdieu's work, Wacquant (2006) explicates habitus's dual role as supporting both continuity and change in social structures and stratification:

> Habitus is also a principle of both social continuity and discontinuity: continuity because it stores social forces into the individual organism and transports them across time and space; discontinuity because it can be modified through the acquisition of new dispositions and because it can trigger innovation whenever it encounters a social setting discrepant with the setting from which it issues. (268)

The correct conceptualization of habitus, then, is as a fluid set of dispositions that are constantly changing as individuals go through different experiences and interact within and with new fields. Following this line of thinking, we use a more nuanced interpretation of habitus that allows for the possibility of mobility as individuals are exposed to novel opportunities and definitions of personal possibility, which "either reinforces or modifies [the habitus's] structures." (Bourdieu and Wacquant 1992, 133).

In an empirical example that challenges the common static reading of habitus, Horvat and Davis (2011) show that educational programs can and do reshape individuals' habitus within the American social class hierarchy and note, importantly, that changes in habitus are not total. While an individual may experience social mobility and a related change in habitus, "the *habitus* formed by early childhood experiences (either positive or negative) is not washed away, but new experiences can be and are incorporated into it" (Horvat and Davis 2011, 166).

However, as noted above, most empirical examinations of mobility—including that of Horvat and Davis—focus on the mobile individual's experiences in the new, elite setting. Whether or not internalizing that new habitus led to problems with respondents' original social networks has largely gone unexamined. Baxter and Britton (2001) are a valuable exception here. In their study of working-class British returning adult students, they find that their respondents are "on a trajectory of class mobility, which is experienced as a painful dislocation between an old and newly developing *habitus*, which are ranked hierarchically and carry connotations of inferiority and superiority"

(2001, 99). Their work—with a different population in a different country—captures the difficulties we expect traditional-age first-generation students to report about their interactions with their home communities and habitus.

Although the process described above could be interpreted as one of changing identity, we argue that habitus change and potential dislocation reflects the experiences of these students more readily. Interpreting these moments as interactions between multiple social class experiences provides a more nuanced lens than as part of an identity change, a concept that implies a more total and self-reflective change within the individual. That is, one's habitus changes without conscious effort or knowledge. Just as it is first internalized unconsciously in early childhood, so too is its change an unconscious shift in one's dispositions. By contrast, identity change involves a shift in how one consciously thinks about one's self—a process that occurs in college for many students (Sidanius et al. 2008), but may not actually occur with regard to class identity for students. Mobile students may still identify as members of their home communities, but their "common sense" and predispositions have changed. That schism between their new, hybrid habitus and the home community's habitus does not mean those students no longer identify as low-SES, but rather that their new habitus changes how and what identifying low-SES means to them and to others. Bourdieu's term "cleft habitus" highlights that complex both/and (and neither/nor) nature of a socially mobile habitus.

Working to fit into the elite culture of selective colleges may help low-SES students gain the same benefits as their elite peers at college and is often cast as a positive process, perhaps even the goal of elite education, a broadening of horizons. Here, however, we challenge the notion that successful acclimation to elite cultural settings is uniformly positive by shifting the focus from *fitting in* to *going home*. We ask two questions: First, do upwardly mobile students experience conflict between nonelite home habitus and elite campus habitus? Second, if so, how are such conflicts managed? We examine this through nonelite (defined here as low-income, working-class, or lower-middle income) respondents' reports of contact with hometown friends and family after acclimating to life in an elite college setting. We focus on elite residential colleges where the development of a new habitus is likely to occur due to the near-total immersion required (c.f. Cookson and Persell 1987). Moreover, habitus plays an important role in the American tradition of educational privilege because elite education in the United States has historically focused on instilling students with a homogenous habitus along with cultural and social capital (Karabel 2005). These colleges are an important "rung" on the ladder of mobility, providing access to social capital and economic benefits. They also present an environment in which elite cultural capital is uniquely important. These aspects can simultaneously make elite colleges

especially valuable for low-SES students, who have the most to gain by completing college (Brand and Xie 2010), but also especially difficult spaces in
which to feel a sense of "belonging" (Ostrove and Long 2007).

Data and Methods

By pairing a large quantitative data set and in-depth interviews at one of the
campuses included in the NLSF, we are able to connect individual experiences and strategies with more generalized evidence about the prevalence of
habitus cleavages. A multimethods approach is important because habitus is
particularly difficult to operationalize (Lamont and Lareau 1988). We utilize
the survey data to examine whether or not any reported schism between
home and college communities is correlated to socioeconomic status or other
demographic factors. Quantitative analyses thus allow us to make broader
and more generalizable claims about the nature of the relationship between
class, habitus, and college. At the same time, these data can only tell us *that*
such a schism exists; it does not capture how and why that schism exists. If,
for example, that schism exists due only to difficulties traveling to and from
college, due to cost, or because the students' families are less supportive,
that would not be indicative of habitus dislocation. We use qualitative data to
add evidence that the schism is, in fact, a result of the development of a cleft
habitus for socially mobile students.[2]

The quantitative data come from the National Longitudinal Survey of
Freshmen (NLSF). The NLSF tracks the academic and social experiences
of roughly 4,000 undergraduates at twenty-eight selective colleges and universities, designed to survey equal numbers of White, Asian, Hispanic, and
Black students. During the first wave of the survey, students were surveyed
face-to-face as freshmen in the fall term of 1999. That wave was followed
by shorter telephone surveys administered during the spring terms of 2000,
2001, 2002, and 2003. The surveyed institutions range from private institutions like Princeton (the most selective institution in the sample, with an 11
percent acceptance rate) to large, public universities such as Penn State and
UC–Berkeley. The response rate for the baseline survey was 86 percent and
produced a sample of 1,051 Black, 959 White, 998 Asian, and 916 Hispanic
students. Sampling restrictions required that participants be US citizens or
legal residents.[3] First-generation immigrant students are those who identified
as being foreign-born themselves, while second-generation is defined as having reported at least one foreign-born parent. All racial categories are based
on student self-identification during the first wave of the survey. Table 3.1
provides the demographic makeup of the sample in greater detail.

Table 3.1. Descriptive statistics, NLSF.

Demographic Characteristics	
Race/Ethnicity/Nativity Status	
White	27.8%
Black	25.7%
Hispanic	12.2%
Asian	19.9%
Multiracial	14.4%
First Generation Immigrant	15.3%
Second Generation Immigrant	34.8%
Gender	
Female	59.8%
Male	40.2%
Socioeconomic Characteristics	
Parents' Education	
No College Degree	19.5%
One BA	12.9%
Two BAs	14.9%
One Advanced Degree	29.6%
Two Advanced Degrees	23.1%
Parents' Income	
> $100,000/year	40.7%
< $100,000/year	34.8%
< $50,000/year	16.2%
< $25,000/year	8.3%
Ever on Welfare	11.3%
Homeowner	84.8%
Educational Characteristics	
High School Segregation	
> 70% White	70.3%
Mixed	15.0%
> 70% non-White	14.7%
Public High School	72.5%
Private High school	14.5%

continued

Table 3.1. (continued)

Parochial High School	13.0%
Top 10 Selective College	36.8%
School Undergraduate Pop	13773 (10124)
Ever Transferred	7.6%
Lost Connections (0-10)	2.44 (2.18)
GPA (0-4)	3.06 (.53)
Satisfaction (0-10)	7.3 (2.19)
N	2394

Roughly 2,400 of the original 3,924 students completed the questions comprising our scale of satisfaction in the fifth wave of the NLSF. We use multiple imputation with the full sample before deleting any respondents with imputed values in the dependent variables (von Hippel 2007). Multiple imputation provides an improved statistical accuracy compared to listwise deletion in cases in which the missing data are not missing completely at random (Allison 2001).

Our qualitative data come from in-depth longitudinal interviews that were conducted with 26 students from low-SES backgrounds at "Linden College," an elite women's college. While this setting prevents us from discussing the relationship between gender and cleft habitus in a rich way, it still provides unique advantages for our study because the interviews include questions specifically focused on relationships between the college student and their home community. The interview data thus shine a crucial light on the students' understandings of habitus change and conflicts between home and college (i.e., elite) locations that would not otherwise have been available. For this study, we analyze responses from students who are first-generation (no parent with a four-year college degree during the respondents' upbringing). These respondents grew up in either low-income (family adjusted gross income below $40,000 per year)[4] or working-class households (family AGI above $40,000 per year, parents working in blue-collar job). (Two respondents were exceptions to the first-generation designation: each had fathers who obtained college degrees or beyond, but were unable to utilize them either because of medical disability or immigration. These two respondents therefore grew up in low-income households and are included in the low-income category.) We refer to these 26 respondents collectively as *low-SES*. Because all responses used here are from students in these categories which we aggregate as low-SES, we do not provide each respondent's individual socioeconomic status. Similarly, because we do not develop analyses of respondents' experiences by race or ethnicity, we do not indicate those positions here.

Interviews at Linden were conducted between 2008 and 2010. Linden students were recruited through emails sent to all students with family incomes below $80,000 per year. All students who volunteered to participate were interviewed; as noted above, interview data included here are from low-SES respondents only. Interviews took place in locations selected by the respondents, typically the student center or a café near campus. Interviews were semi-structured and open-ended so that a core of questions was asked of each respondent but follow-up questions were added in order to pursue topics that arose in individual interviews. Respondents were asked generally about relationships with friends and family from home, and how they managed these interactions. The themes included here were then developed from students' responses. All respondents were asked to select pseudonyms, and other personally identifying information has been changed or omitted by the authors.[5]

Linden College (LC) is located in a small city in the northeast of the United States. The cost of attending LC is on par with similar private institutions and was above $53,000 annually in estimated costs in 2009–2010. A large financial aid budget supports those students whose families cannot finance this cost, and the college frequently notes publicly that approximately 60 percent of the student body receives grant aid. While this figure is high, need-based grants may range from $500 to over $40,000 (during the interview years), and the average Linden student is likely to be middle class or upper-middle class. LC is selective, admitting fewer than half of its high-achieving applicants.[6]

FINDINGS

While sociologists frequently focus on the mismatch between the dominant habitus expectations of the college and the struggle of nonelite students to fit in, they neglect the corresponding struggle to fit newly acquired skill sets or outlooks, so helpful on campus, into home environments. In some cases, this new learning is in direct contradiction to familiar practices or beliefs, while in others it is simply strange or confusing. The acquisition of new habits, mannerisms, and knowledge—a new, college-educated habitus—differentiates the student from his or her family members and/or friends. Below, we explore in detail how that differentiation occurs and the difficulties that arise due to a cleft habitus.

Does Class Matter? Growing Apart while Growing Up

Sharing a habitus with one's community members makes it easier to connect: people with similar habitus have similar interests, similar reactions to events, and common presumptions about how the world works and should be. Thus, as low-SES students acclimate to elite college life, their comfort on campus may increase. However, we also anticipated that students from low-SES backgrounds would report higher levels of difficulty interacting with their home communities during college as the result of this acclimation, indicating a cleft habitus. We examined this possibility using data from the fifth and final wave of the NLSF, completed during students' fourth years on campus, in which students were asked to report how much they feel they have become "an outsider in my home community." Combined with similar questions about losing connection to old friends and family (Cronbach's alpha = .70), we use this measure of precollege loss as quantitative proxy for whether or not a student feels that schism between collegiate habitus and home habitus (0–10).[7]

In order to understand whether low-SES students were more likely to experience a loss of connection to home than other students and whether or not this loss might be patterned by other demographic variables, we first examined bivariate relationships between measures of socioeconomic background, race, gender, and perceived sense of loss. Overall, we saw that students report relatively low levels of perceived loss. In a scale from 0 to 10, students reported levels of loss that averaged between 2 and 3. This finding does not come as a surprise, as work on friendship homophily suggests that high achieving students' friends in high school will likely be similarly high achieving and thus likely to share the selective college experience with students in our sample (Kandel 1978). This low level of reported loss shows that going to college—even for socially mobile students—does not automatically lead to a large sense of social distance. Rather, in line with Bourdieu's idea of a cleft habitus, these low levels of loss highlight the subtle changes in predisposition that create seemingly "natural" class distinctions.

Even with low reported levels of loss, there were statistically significant differences by background showing a connection between class and sense of loss but not race. In regards to race and ethnicity, Black and Hispanic students reported the same level of loss as White students, while Asians reported slightly higher levels of loss (possibly due to the disproportionate number of students from immigrant families in the Asian population). On the other hand, we saw a significant linear effect of socioeconomic background on sense of loss via both our measure of income and parental education, with working-class students experiencing a greater sense of loss than middle-class students. As Bourdieu originally theorized, habitus is a class-based means of perpetuating inequality, not a race-based means of doing so. These descriptive findings mirror previous research showing that stigmatization based on intellect in school ("acting Black") is related to socioeconomic class and racial dynamics in schools rather than a widespread problem in all Black and Hispanic communities (Tyson, Darity, and Castellino 2005).

While the association between class and a heightened sense of loss is small and does not directly measure changes in habitus, it provides evidence that attending a selective college creates greater schisms between home culture and school culture for students from lower socioeconomic backgrounds. Although we can see that this sense of loss is patterned along class lines, we cannot yet say what informs it, and for that we turn to interview data, below.

Table 3.2. Sense of loss by race, class, and gender.

	Mean sense of loss	*N*
Parental Education		
No College Degree	3.04[abcd]	461
	(2.45)	
One College Degree	2.61[acd]	299
	(2.25)	
Two College Degrees	2.39[ad]	340
	(2.13)	
One Advanced Degree	2.27[ab]	693
	(2.02)	
Two Advanced Degrees	2.03[abc]	547
	(1.95)	
Race		
White	2.27[a]	644
	(2.13)	
Asian	2.61[a]	463
	(2.15)	
Black	2.43	584
	(2.29)	
Hispanic	2.52	279
	(2.25)	

continued

Table 3.2. (continued)

	Mean sense of loss	N
Multiracial	2.40	340
	(2.12)	
Income		
< 25,000	3.38[abc]	171
	(2.54)	
< 50,000	2.81[abc]	401
	(2.29)	
< 100,000	2.38[abc]	723
	(2.03)	
> 100,000	2.16[ab]	796
	(2.13)	
Gender		
Male	2.72[a]	990
	(2.24)	
Female	2.25[a]	1473
	(2.13)	

Notes: superscript letters indicate a statistically significant (p < .05) difference between groups with the same letters.

Table 3.3 shows the results of an OLS regression, controlling for possible clustering of results by college, modeling whether or not the bivariate relationships described in table 3.2 persist in a multivariate model. We expected that students from communities least like the selective institutions should feel the greatest sense of loss. To some extent, that was the case—but with important exceptions. First, our model's low r-squared value (.06) highlights the limited overall relationship between student demographic and socioeconomic background and perceiving a sense of loss. While this is an important rejoinder that individual demographic and socioeconomic characteristics do not guarantee an emotionally and culturally difficult experience in college, it does not negate the substantial and significant association between class and perceived loss.

This association was observable along both income and education lines. Students from highly educated families (i.e., families in which both parents have at least a bachelor's degree [-0.42, p < .05], or in which one parent [-0.52, p < .01] or both parents [-0.76, p < .001] hold an advanced degree) reported lower levels of loss of community than students whose parents who do not both hold BA degrees. This is likely due to the internalization of the elite collegiate habitus, while their parents lack any comparable dispositions with which to understand the collegiate experience and subsequent changes in their children. Similarly, those whose family incomes were below $25,000 per year during childhood or whose families were ever on welfare (0.63, p < .05 and 0.46, p < .001 respectively), and those whose high schools were more than 70 percent non-White (0.54, p < .001) were more likely to report a loss of precollege community. We also found that the bivariate relationship between gender and reporting lost connections persisted in our multivariate model.

Table 3.3 OLS regression coefficients with clustering control predicting a sense of loss of precollege community, friends, and family using multiple imputation then deletion.

	B
Intercept	2.61***
	(.57)
Demographic Characteristics	
Male (1 = yes)	.49***
	(.09)
Black	−.30*
	(.14)
Hispanic	−.23
	(.17)
Asian	.12
	(.16)
Multiracial	−.16
	(.15)
First-Generation Immigrant	.26[+]
	(.15)
Second-Generation Immigrant	.22[+]
	(.12)

continued

Table 3.3 (*continued*)

	B
Socioeconomic Characteristics	
Parents' Education	
One BA	−.20
	(.18)
Two BAs	−.42*
	(.18)
One Advanced Degree	−.52***
	(.15)
Two Advanced Degrees	−.76***
	(.16)
Parents' Income	
< $100,000/year	.08
	(.11)
< $50,000/year	.39*
	(.16)
< $25,000/year	.63*
	(.26)
Ever on Welfare	.46**
	(.17)
Homeowner	.11
	(.14)
High School Segregation	
Mixed	−.09
	(.13)
> 70% Non-White	.54***
	(.16)
College Experience	
Top 10 Selective College	.10
	(.10)
School Undergraduate Pop (log)	−.04
	(.06)
R-squared	.06
N	2394

Also notable are the statistically significant differences by race or ethnic group. Black students were, perhaps surprisingly, *less likely* than White students to perceive a loss of community (-0.30, p < .05), while Hispanic and Asian students did not differ from White students at a statistically significant level. As with our bivariate results, this runs counter to the "acting Black" theory. These results lend credence to the idea that cleft habitus is not a race-based problem.

The data suggest that some students frequently considered by sociologists to be disadvantaged in their pursuit of higher education accrue an additional stumbling block *during* their college years, namely the loss of connection to family and home-community peers (although this effect is not consistent across groups). Numerous studies have shown the link between supportive home communities and college success (usually academic), especially for those students who are statistically less likely to complete four-year degrees (see Cabrera, Nora, and Castaneda 1993; Charles et al. 2009; Guiffrida 2006; Melendez and Melendez 2010; Nora and Cabrera 1996). Low-SES students who perceive a loss of connection to their home communities or families through their college experiences may therefore be at even greater risk.

Our quantitative analysis can only suggest that socioeconomic background is related to perceived loss; it cannot identify that these perceptions of loss are themselves caused by the experience of attaining a cleft habitus. To answer that question, we turn to our interview data for more detailed evidence of how such a sense of loss is experienced and explained by nonelite students at a selective liberal arts college. The responses also provide evidence that the class differences in perception of loss is related to changes in habitus and not to preexisting differences between students and their communities or more mundane concerns such as ability to return home frequently or stay in touch with friends and family via telephone or email. The interviews expose how habitus changes are manifested and the difficulties these changes create for low-SES students in interactions with family and friends (i.e., cleft). We then discuss the ways that students manage their interactions with family and friends to minimize such conflicts.

Habitus Shift: On Becoming a Snob

The conflicts between home and college habitus are most clearly expressed in interaction, particularly conversation. Because habitus is cultural in nature, it encompasses even the most mundane aspects of life, meaning that even a seemingly safe conversational topic or style itself can become an area of contention or misunderstanding across two incompatible habitus. Respondents in these interviews describe mundane subjects such as new food preferences—for example, Lynne (White) talked of learning to enjoy sushi and "all these mother-fucking [kinds of] cheeses" and Rose (multiracial) of becoming vegetarian —as being tense topics with friends and family. Over time, respondents find that their conversational repertoires have shifted such that they have difficulty communicating with the friends and family members they left behind at home. For example, Violet (White) recalls with exasperation how difficult it is to talk with her mother over breaks: "It's not just avoiding conversations or talking to [my mom], it's feeling on a totally different place. We wouldn't even talk about the same things, much less try and talk about them in the same way." Amber (White) has similar difficulties trying to explain to her friends and father, whose outlook she shared more closely as a teenager, the reasons their offhand comments or jokes are not appropriate:

Amber: But it's really hard, because there are some people that are in my group of friends that just clearly, I mean, I don't claim to be informed at all but they just don't have an idea with what's going on, with things like health care. They're very opinionated despite not really knowing anything. It's really hard to have conversations like that with people when you already kind of feel you put on this air of superiority just because I go to a school like Linden. And I don't want to come across with someone who's like trying to enlighten everyone, but at the same time I think it's an important thing to talk about. I don't want to offend people, not make them defensive. I think it's hard to do with people that you're close to.

Interviewer: That must be tough. So how did you deal with that? Like with your dad, friends, and acquaintances.

Amber: Well, with my dad, I kind of, I just sort of tell him whatever, and I don't know if he even really. . . . Sometimes he listens to what I say but sometimes he just kind of writes me off like a college kid. So, like I'm going through a phase or something. But with my friends it's a little bit harder, and I have to deal with some things, more with humor. I have a couple of friends that's still, will say really homophobic things or stuff like that. I kind of got into this habit of using a Bruno voice.[8] Whatever they had to say something, like, "oh God, the guy is so gay" and then I say "oh yeah, he totally was. Like white after Labor Day." I don't even know if I get my point across, but it's better than not doing anything I guess.

Interestingly, her father assumes that her new ideology or habitus is skin deep: once she is out of her elite environment, he expects her to return to the "true" Amber, one who will agree with him once she passes her "college kid . . . phase." Amber interprets her new beliefs and attitudes as part of a permanent shift in her understanding of the world. Both Violet and Amber describe a new difficulty communicating with friends and family because their interests, ideologies, and expectations have changed. While the details of what has changed are different—Violet's more abstract daily conversations, Amber's new political sensitivities—the end result is the same: their changed habitus has led directly to a newfound social distance from their friends and families.

It is important to note that low-income or working-class students are not the only ones to return home from college with new habits that are unintelligible to their families or friends. However, for nonelite students who are frequently the only ones in their home communities to attend elite colleges, these changes are heavily weighted by the symbolism of cultural change and status transition. This differs from the experiences of middle-class children, whose parents may simply chalk changes up to maturation or steps towards independence. Similar to Lamont and colleagues' findings on moral judgments, we find that low-income or working-class students are more subject to moral comparisons, or to being seen as making those comparisons themselves (Lamont et al. 1996). For example, Lynne (White) worries that her parents will think she has become a "snob," as she describes below:

> Even when I go to visit my parents, [I am] so scared of them thinking Linden has turned me into an elitist snob, my brother said [that] and I just lost it . . . he constantly makes fun of me for going to Linden, this whole British accent like, signifying high class, asking me if I'm, like, going to marry someone from Harvard, you know.

Similarly, Brianna (White) describes how there is "a little bit of tension there" in her interactions with her siblings, who did not go to college and work low-wage jobs or are unemployed: "My sister . . . always sneaks something in under the surface, about, like, oh you're really proud to go to college aren't you, and not in a way that's nice. . . . I'm not a sellout. It's hard to make her see that." Allison (White) characterizes her relationship with her family as "semi-ugly" because of the clash between her choice to leave home and study at Linden, and her adult siblings' choices to not attend four-year colleges and live closer to their parents. She explains, "I'm very different from many of them [family members]. My older sister a lot of the time would give me a hard time about things that aren't under my control, like not being home all the time, things having to do with my being here [at Linden], and me going to school. Because she didn't do that, she doesn't get it." Whereas students such as Amber expressed difficulties based on novel interests or outlooks, Allison's problems show that there are also microaggressions from members of one's social class of origin that help create and perpetuate a class divide, even within students' own families.

Interaction Management: Hiding the New and Faking the Old

Because of the frictions described above, low-income and working-class students work hard to reconcile their mobility with their home communities. This requires significant effort via multiple impression-management strategies. Students attempt not only to manage their interactions with others in order to preserve a positive image (or to avoid a negative image), but also try to maintain a personal sense of identity in line with their earlier status, even as they understand that changes in this status are happening. Respondents describe avoiding certain topics or styles of speaking in order to present themselves in an unchanged light, similar to Granfield's (1991) concept of "faking it," albeit in this case "faking" their original habitus. For example, Lynne (White) avoids using big words that she would not have used before enrolling in college: "I'm so, like, constantly checking myself when I go home, I don't want to use these big academic jargony words that Linden demands you use here, [that I] never ever knew before coming to Linden." She also takes care to emphasize her pragmatic, financial reasons for enrolling at Linden, without which (she reminds her friends) she otherwise might not afford college: "I always say, if I can sort of sense that people are like, judging me a little bit, I say, the only reason I'm going there is because they give me a ton of money." Lynne's verbal strategies help her to show that she has not become "an elitist snob," and to remind friends from home that she is in the same financial boat they are. Ramona (White) avoids talking about her experiences at college, preferring to allow friends from home to simply think whatever they will about Linden rather than engage in a detailed conversation about college life: "Yeah, I think they don't really know what it's like here, kind of preconceived notions about what a woman's college . . . is supposed to be like, so I guess I end up giving into that stereotype just to make the conversation go a little faster, [rather than] to sit down and explain what's here." Anna (White) similarly opts to keep quiet in conversation with friends at home because she wants to avoid implicit comparison. She remembers, "when I came home [from study abroad, it was like], I gotta stop talking about going abroad and doing all these things because people were like, 'I'm never gonna have the opportunity [to do that,] stop rubbing it in my face that you [did].'" She describes the way she "[has had] to kind of teach yourself not to talk about [study abroad]" and other advantages not available to friends at other colleges or who are working.

The stress of staying attached to one's less privileged background also manifest on campus for students. For example, Rose (multiracial) makes an effort while on campus to "remind herself" of her own background so that she does not become too dissociated from her home community or her history. Keeping her parents' occupations in mind, for example, or that she "went to

Europe on scholarship" helps keep her working-class identity clear—important because as she comes closer to graduation, that identity seems to move further from view. She describes, "it's really the only way I can keep myself, like, in check to remind myself where I come from. If I meet someone and talk about my thesis, my experiences, you'd never know [that I grew up working class]—and that's just part of me. I know how much I've grown and everything, but I just want to keep a hold of that." While Rose has worked hard for her college achievements, she does not wish to replace her working-class self.

In sum, respondents struggled to balance new experiences with their home relationships—often, relationships with others who are not upwardly mobile. Low-SES students' descriptions of their efforts to actively manage those relationships give further indication of their worries about potentially losing connections.

In line with the work of other scholars of class in education, many of the students interviewed describe a cleft habitus in which their experiences in college have led to novel social difficulties with their families and friends. This cleave is not something for which these students felt prepared or which they embrace without struggle; students do not interpret their entrée into a new social status as an easy transformation. Not only do these students face unique burdens at school (Aries and Seider 2005), but they also experience social burdens at home that traditionally elite students likely do not experience. Next, we look at the ways respondents understand the effects of mobility in themselves.

Keeping the Old, Accepting the New?

The interview data thus far have highlighted the complications low-SES students encounter interacting with nonmobile friends and family. But Bourdieu's discussion of a cleft habitus (as opposed to one that is simply changing or being reformulated) suggests that socially mobile students will also encounter conflicts within their own worldviews as they attempt to understand their new position in the social structure without the ability to "unlearn" the lessons, dispositions, and common sense born of their previous positions. In line with that analytic framework, students in our sample do not express a sense of a completely changed self-identity, but rather one that has now become more complicated and hybridized—a cleft habitus is both working-class and elite, fitting into neither comfortably. As Violet (White) reflects, "Once you learn things, you can't really unlearn them. It's a choice but, I don't know, you can't unmake that choice to know what you know." She refers here not to her class mobility as a college student on track to graduate, but rather to a novel perception of herself as highly educated. Students like Violet will not be able to go back to sharing the same world as their hometown friends and family. For some respondents, this came as an unanticipated and uncomfortable realization, as suggested in Rose's (multiracial) words below:

> I thought I'd just kind of like learn things and just be like a . . . you know, a working-class person who, like, knows how to contend. I thought that's what it was all about, but especially this year for you know, maturity or whatever, I'm realizing, it's not about pretending. I've become this person. I have this experience, [and] growing up as a working-class student—nothing about me says that anymore.

Rose does not assert that she self-identifies differently and she explicitly explains that she does not want to do so. Instead, she asserts that her mannerisms and experiences—that is, her habitus—has changed and that change means that others do not see her as working class. On the other hand, Lynne (White) asserts that graduating from Linden will enforce a new "identity that I'm going to carry with me and all its connotations": "also graduating from Linden, that means I'm never going to, like, now this is really an identity that I'm going to carry with me and all its connotations and I can't deny that, I can't—it changes the way people look at you, even if you don't think it changes you. But it definitely changes the way people look at you." Again, however, Lynne does not lose her original socioeconomic background: she has instead added another identity to "carry," even as she sees herself as unchanged. These shifts do involve an identity change, but one that students do not necessarily internalize as total or all-encompassing. These students articulate the fact that a cleft habitus is both an internalized and externalized problem, shaped not only by their interactions with nonmobile family and friends but also within their own minds, their own assessments of their social positions, *and how those positions are interpreted by others.* Their presentations of mobility as a form of irrevocable personal change belie the idea that mobility is a seamlessly beneficial process. Each speaker's words are tinged with a sense of regret or loss about the ways they might be changed by their mobility. Students struggle with that mobility and its implications.

Moreover, respondents highlighted the ways that their cleft habitus caused them to judge their new advantages skeptically. Brianna (White), for example, worried that the "natural process" of changing at school and becoming "part of an educated middle class" may make her irrevocably different from her parents and siblings:

> In fact something I've been scared about before is not losing my roots, but I can feel myself becoming very different from my family in ways that I don't

think—I mean I can try and slow it down but it's gonna happen anyway. I mean, it's a natural process. I'm becoming different from them in the way that my siblings haven't, in just that I'm going to graduate and I'm gonna be part of an educated middle class. Okay, I might not be making that much money at first but you know like, I'm still part of [that group:] I've got a bachelor's degree. I'm probably gonna get my master's degree, and what does that mean? How am I different? So there's almost a feeling of selling out a little bit.

Brianna directly articulates a changed identity, but still distances herself from that change. At the same time, Brianna never articulates that change as internalized: she questions whether or not she has changed and expresses her social mobility as joining a group, not changing how she sees herself or her class background. Of our respondents, Briana was the most explicit in depicting herself as undergoing any sort of identity change. Even then, she linguistically distances herself from that change and cannot articulate how she is different from her previous experiences. That invisibility of the identity change fits well with Bourdieu's concept of habitus—habitus emphasizes the invisible "common sense" that guides individuals through social interactions in subconscious ways. Briana is experiencing a cleft habitus and recognizes that tension between her old and new social class locations but had much more difficulty explaining how and why she herself has actually changed. That difficulty born from the invisibility of habitus complicates efforts to sustain relationships that had previously been intraclass but are now cross-class relationships.

DISCUSSION

Previous research shows that many students, particularly low-income first-generation students (Carnevale and Rose 2004; Tinto 2006–2007) face additional hurdles over the course of their enrollment, indicating that researchers should focus more on the college experience and persistence as well as access to college. Academics and other professionals from poor or working-class backgrounds frequently recall college as a difficult transition period (e.g., Dews and Law 1995, Ryan and Sackrey 1984), marked by feelings of "wanting" rather than "belonging" (Ostrove 2003). This is complemented by the findings of sociologists arguing that students from these backgrounds—particularly those at elite campuses—find it difficult to connect with peers, feel at home, and make the most of academic opportunities because they lack cultural capital (Aries and Seider 2005; Armstrong and Hamilton 2013; Ostrove 2003; Stuber 2009, 2011). Sociologists typically focus on how cultural capital and habitus function within these elite settings; that is, they are concerned with the mechanisms and interactions that take place in the site of mobility. This article adds to that literature by illustrating how mobility also dramatically affects interactions with one's previous community as well as the new, elite educational environment. We find that students experience what Bourdieu termed a cleft habitus as they shift between a nonelite home environment and an elite school setting, demonstrating the ways that "*habitus* [can] be practically transformed by the effect of a social trajectory leading to conditions of living different from initial ones" (1990, 116).[9]

Our paper makes both theoretical and empirical contributions. We apply Bourdieu's concept of habitus in a novel way to examine the process and problems of mobility. Rather than focus on the enhanced cultural and social capital of the socially mobile student, we use Bourdieu's concept of a cleft habitus to understand how mobility affects the students' interactions with nonmobile friends and family. Our quantitative analysis demonstrates that not all students experience strains with their home communities equally. That sense of strain is associated with demographic, primarily class, differences. Class-disadvantaged students (i.e., those whose families have lower incomes or education levels) report higher senses of lost community, and our interview data indicate that this is likely because their dominant cultural frame shifts over their four years in college. This confirms our hypothesis that nonelite students experience a cleft habitus. In particular, students indicate that interactions with one's family and friends from home require attention and management, and reveal the kinds of moral questioning that arise through comparing habitus and cultural capital gains. In addition, the regression provides evidence that our interviews at a women's college may be a relatively conservative barometer of the levels and effects of cleft habitus because men report higher levels of loss than women. Our qualitative data demonstrate the ways that ties become attenuated over time. As interactions with friends and family become strained, communication and contact become more difficult to maintain.

Empirically, then, we find that nonelite students struggle to maintain ties to home, often adopting interaction management strategies to navigate their relationships with parents, siblings, and high school friends. In addition to increasing low-SES students' campus stress levels in ways that may be detrimental to students' academic achievement (Charles et al. 2004), these findings also have important implications for larger mobility processes. As we show, low-SES students decrease or curtail communication with nonmobile friends and family as they develop cleft habituses. This reduces their capacity for becoming (echoing Carter's 2003 terminology) multi-class navigators who might be instrumental in a long-term family or community process of mobility. That is, rather than passing along new class-particular knowledge, low-SES students instead deflect, obscure, and minimize their new habitus when interacting with their home community. This may limit mobility to the individual student, rather than supporting efforts to distribute the new elite cultural capital gains through family or community ties. Moreover, our interview data suggest that this is a two-pronged problem. Students in the process of attaining socioeconomic mobility both feel the conflict of cleft habitus within themselves and are also confronted with it by their friends and family from home.

Theoretically, this work joins with Horvat and Davis (2011) to reconsider how sociologists of mobility incorporate Bourdieu's concept of habitus. While others contend that the concept is overly deterministic, we show that habitus can and should be seen as fluid: the students in our qualitative sample demonstrated the effect of college on their habitus—changing their food preferences, their conversational style, and their expectations. That individual habitus can and does change—particularly via an institution like a residential college—is not a novel finding. What is novel is our exploration of how those changes affect individuals' abilities to reconnect with their home communities. Cleft habitus has the effect of constraining and weakening relationships between those socially mobile individuals and their home communities.

These findings should be considered in context of scholarship on higher education retention. As scholars of college retention make clear, support from home is important to college completion for students who are not in the demographic majority on campus (Cabrera, Nora, and Castaneda 1993; Guiffrida 2006; Melendez and Melendez 2010; Nora and Cabrera 1996). Forming bonds to campus, be they work-related, purely social, or otherwise extracurricular, is also important for retention. Juggling both, however, may be uniquely difficult for socially mobile students. Our findings also complement and extend those examinations of cultural capital that highlight students' attempts to hold multiple habitus simultaneously. For example, Carter's (2003) research shows how students develop strategies for moving between academic and home settings, adjusting accordingly to each. Carter's work shows that students moving between discrepant school and home cultures must make special efforts to maintain ties to home, a process only exaggerated at a residential college. Granfield's (1991) respondents similarly demonstrate a need to manage this contrast between home and school. However, while the law school students he interviewed generally avoided confrontation with their earlier lives, this strategy is less feasible for undergraduates who typically return home over school breaks and maintain ties of at least minimal emotional and economic support and care with family and friends from home.

Our findings expand on these earlier works by examining qualitatively the ways that a cleft habitus is experienced and by measuring quantitatively the schisms between home and school associated with a cleft habitus. Social mobility is not a tidy process and scholars should look not only at the difficulties upwardly mobile individuals experience in their new environment, but also how elite settings create a cleft habitus that complicates contact with nonmobile friends and family. Moreover, our findings are important to those scholars and administrators seeking to improve the collegiate experiences of low-SES students. Even at elite schools with extremely high retention and graduation rates, low-SES students lag behind middle- and upper-middle income classmates on these measures (Tinto 2006–2007). As colleges increasingly focus on managing low-SES students' continued enrollment (Tinto 2006–2007), understanding the dynamics of acclimation—including the tensions created at home—may help in implementing effective support programs. These might include outreach to families, or counseling students like this study's respondents in managing relationships, or creating peer support groups to compare experiences.

While we believe measuring a sense of loss (combined with key demographic variables) identifies which students notice a change in habitus, cleft habitus is difficult to quantify and our proxy is only a limited effort to do so. Some students may feel a similar loss for more psychological and individual reasons as well. It is possible that some students want to lose connections with their home communities; many students who did not enjoy high school, regardless of personal background, view college as a new start. Moreover, students may not have felt well supported by high school friends or family to begin with, and replacing them with college friends could be a welcome change. Nonetheless, few of our interviewees reported such a desire, and our regression results showed that class is associated with a loss of connections. In addition, previous literature suggests that middle and upper-middle income students are both better able to adjust to the culture of college life and supported by networks of similar peers (Kaufman 2005). Finally, some students may not feel that they have lost connections to home even when they have, or they may be able to switch between home and collegiate habitus depending on their situation. Nonetheless, while our measure is inexact, it is a significant step towards quantifying the experience of changing one's habitus and measuring the impact of such a change.

A second gap in our data is that the qualitative sample is too limited to draw distinctions along racial, ethnic, or gender lines. As Kramer's (2008) and Kuriloff and Reichert's (2003) work suggests, Black students in private high schools are already shifting their stores of cultural capital through their enrollment in private schools and contact with elite culture in that setting. This very likely has an impact upon their experiences in elite college settings and their ability to align habitus and increasing cultural capital, as Jack found in his analysis of the "privileged poor," low-income African American students attending an elite university after graduating from private high schools (2014). Results not shown here also suggest an interaction between race and ethnicity, cleft habitus, and class status. Unfortunately, there are too few non-White students in the sample to draw conclusions in this direction. Moreover, there are no male students in the qualitative sample, so the association between gender and feeling disconnected from home communities that existed in our regression models cannot be fleshed out through interview data. Male students reported higher "sense of loss" than female students across all of the NLSF schools. Although several interviews indicated that gender may be an important aspect of the classed experiences of low-SES students, for example through gendered expectations of family involvement, we are not positioned to qualitatively compare the connections between gender, class, and family. Future research should address in more detail how the intersections between race, class, and gender can affect the likelihood of experiencing a cleft habitus.

Overall, our results provide an important caveat to the standard narrative of mobility via higher education. Mobility is often treated as a universal good—that is, it is assumed that acquisition of middle- or upper-class habits or preferences leads to positive outcomes for the individual. Our data suggest that students find it difficult to balance the newly gained cultural capital needed for college (and beyond) with their habitus, and that these difficulties demand a potentially painful process of habitus cleavage. Our interview and survey data both show that social and cultural mobility does not come without unique sacrifices. As Stevens notes, studying both those with privilege and the process of learning to wield that privilege is important to understanding social stratification (2007, 3–4). Unfortunately, as our qualitative and quantitative data both show, learning to wield that privilege often causes personal strain and potentially negative academic consequences that warrants future exploration.

What can campuses do to lessen these effects for students? Many campuses already have become more attentive to how a first-generation background may shape not only a person's pathway into college, but also their subsequent experiences. A wide variety of colleges provide "bridge" or targeted orientation programs, focused advising services, organized peer groups of fellow first-gen students, and mentoring connections to faculty mentors who were first-generation. However, programs welcoming parents to campus and offering similar information for parents and guardians are far fewer in number. Indeed, such parents may be challenging to reach because of difficulties getting them to campus, accommodating language needs, and/or financial costs. Helping students help their parents or guardians to understand their experiences more clearly—expectations, for example, about the transition from high school to college-level work and course-taking patterns, or how financial aid and work-study employment function—may substantially reduce students' stress levels and ideally would lead to coordinated efforts by the college and parents or guardians to support students. Providing counseling and other forms of support for students who may be caregivers in their families and now must balance those responsibilities with college life, or simply aren't sure how to explain what they are taking on at school, could also relieve some of the tension we find amongst first-generation students. Notably, these supports may come both through institutional venues as well as through organized peer groups. Campus faculty and administrators would do well to support multiple avenues.

REFERENCES

Allison, Paul. 2001. *Missing Data*. Thousand Oaks, CA: Sage Publications.

Aries, Elizabeth. 2008. *Race and Class Matters at an Elite College*. Philadelphia: Temple University Press.

Aries, Elizabeth, and Maynard Seider. 2005. "The Interactive Relationship Between Class Identity and the College Experience: The Case of Lower Income Students." *Qualitative Sociology* 28, no. 4: 419–43.

Armstrong, Elizabeth A., and Laura T. Hamilton. 2013. *Paying for the Party: How College Maintains Inequality.* Cambridge, MA: Harvard University Press.

Baxter, Arthur, and Carolyn Britton. 2001. "Risk, Identity and Change: Becoming a Mature Student." *International Studies in Sociology of Education* 11, no. 1: 87–101.

Bourdieu, Pierre. 1977. *Outline of a Theory of Practice*. New York: Cambridge University Press.

Bourdieu, Pierre. 1990. *In Other Words: Essays Towards a Reflexive Sociology*. Translated by Matthew Adamson. Stanford: Stanford University Press.

Bourdieu, Pierre. 1996. *The State Nobility: Elite Schools in the Field of Power*. Translated by Lauretta C. Clough. Stanford: Stanford University Press.

Bourdieu, Pierre. 2001/2004. *The Science of Science and Reflexivity*. Chicago: University of Chicago Press.

Bourdieu, Pierre, and Loïc J. D. Wacquant. 1992. *An Invitation to Reflexive Sociology*. Chicago: University of Chicago Press.

Bowen, William G., and Derek Bok. 1998. *The Shape of the River: Long-term Consequences of Considering Race in College and University Admissions*. Princeton, NJ: Princeton University Press.

Brand, Jennie E., and Yu Xie. 2010. "Who Benefits Most From College? Evidence for Negative Selection in Heterogeneous Economic Returns to Higher Education." *American Sociological Review* 75, no. 2, 273–302.

Cabrera, Alberto F., Amaury Nora, and Maria B. Castaneda. 1993. "College Persistence: Structural Equations Modeling Test of An Integrated Model of Student Retention." *The Journal of Higher Education* 64, no. 2, 123–39.

Carnevale, Anthony P., and Stephen J. Rose. 2004. "Socioeconomic Status, Race/Ethnicity, and Selective College Admissions." In *America's Untapped Resource: Low-Income Students in Higher Education*, edited by Richard D. Kahlenberg, 101–156. New York: The Century Foundation.

Carter, Prudence. 2003. "'Black' Cultural Capital, Status Positioning, and Schooling Conflicts for Low Income African American Youth." *Social Problems* 50, no. 1: 136–55.

Charles, Camille Z., Gniesha Y. Dinwiddie, and Douglas S. Massey. 2004. "The Continuing Consequences of Segregation: Family Stress and College Academic Performance." *Social Science Quarterly* 85, no. 5: 1353–73.

Charles, Camille Z., Mary J. Fischer, Margarita Mooney, and Douglas S. Massey. 2009. *Taming the River: Negotiating the Academic, Financial, and Social Currents in Selective Colleges and Universities.* Princeton: Princeton University Press.

Cookson, Peter W. Jr., and Caroline Hodges Persell. 1987. *Preparing for Power: America's Elite Boarding Schools.* New York: Basic Books.

Dews, C.L. Barney, and Carolyn Leste Law, eds. 1995. *This Fine Place So Far from Home: Voices of Academics from the Working Class.* Philadelphia: Temple University.

DiMaggio, Paul. 1982. "Cultural Capital and School Success: The Impact of Status Culture Participation on the Grades of High School Students." *American Sociological Review* 47, no. 2: 189–201.

Gaztambide-Fernández, Rúben, and Raygine DiAquoi. 2010. "A Part and Apart: Students of Color Negotiating Boundaries at an Elite Boarding School." In *Educating Elites: Class Privilege and Educational Advantage*, edited by Rúben Gaztambide-Fernández and Adam Howard, 55–79. Lanham, MD: Rowman & Littlefield.

Goodwin, Latty Lee. 2002. *Resilient Spirits: Disadvantaged Students Making It at an Elite University.* New York: Routledge-Falmer.

Granfield, Robert. 1991. "Making it by Faking it: Working-Class Students in an Elite Academic Environment." *Journal of Contemporary Ethnography* 20, no. 3: 331–51.

Guiffrida, Douglas A. 2006. "Toward a Cultural Advancement of Tinto's Theory." *The Review of Higher Education* 29, no. 4: 451–72.

Horvat, Erin McNamara. 2003. "The Interactive Effects of Race and Class in Educational Research: Theoretical Insights from the Work of Pierre Bourdieu." *Penn GSE Perspectives on Urban Education* 2, no. 1: 1–25.

Horvat, Erin McNamara, and Anthony Lising Antonio. 1999. "'Hey, Those Shoes Are Out of Uniform': African American Girls in an Elite High School and the Importance of Habitus." *Anthropology and Education Quarterly* 30, no. 3: 317–42.

Horvat, Erin McNamara, and James Earl Davis. 2011. "Schools as Sites for Transformation: Exploring the Contribution of Habitus" *Youth and Society* 43, no. 1: 142–170.

Hurst, Allison L., and Deborah M. Warnock. 2015. "*Les Miraculés*: The Magical Image of the Permanent Miracle—Constructed Narratives of Self and Mobility from Working-Class Students at an Elite College." In *College Students' Experiences of Power and Marginality: Sharing Spaces and Negotiating Differences,* edited by Elizabeth M. Lee and Chaise LaDousa, 102–17. New York: Routledge.

Jack, Anthony Abraham. 2014. "Culture Shock Revisited: The Social and Cultural Contingencies to Class Marginality." *Sociological Forum* 29: 453–75.

Kandel, Denise B. 1978. "Homophily, Selection, and Socialization in Adolescent Friendships." *American Journal of Sociology* 84, no. 2: 427–36.

Karabel, Jerome. 2005. *The Chosen: The Hidden History of Admission and Exclusion at Harvard, Yale, and Princeton.* New York: Houghton, Mifflin.

Kaufman, Peter. 2005. "Middle-Class Social Reproduction: The Activation and Negotiation of Structural Advantages." *Sociological Forum* 20: 245–70.

King, Anthony. 2000. "Thinking with Bourdieu Against Bourdieu: A 'Practical' Critique of the Habitus." *Sociological Theory* 18: 417–33.

Kramer, Rory. 2008. "Diversifiers at Elite Schools." *Du Bois Review* 5: 287–307.

Kuriloff, Peter, and Michael C. Reichert. 2003. "Boys of Class, Boys of Color: Negotiating the Academic and Social Geography of an Elite Independent School." *Journal of Social Issues* 59, no. 4: 751–69.

Lamont, Michele, and Annette Lareau. 1988. "Cultural Capital: Allusions, Gaps andGlissandos in Recent Theoretical Developments." *Sociological Theory* 6, no. 2: 153–68.

Lamont, Michele, John Schmalzbauer, Maureen Waller, and Daniel Weber. 1996. "Cultural and Moral Boundaries in the United States: Structural Position, Geographic Location, and Lifestyle Explanations." *Poetics* 24, no. 1: 31–56.

Lee, Elizabeth M. 2016. *Class and Campus Life: Managing and Experiencing Inequality at an Elite College.* Ithaca: Cornell University Press.

Lehmann, Wolfgang. 2009. "Becoming Middle Class: How Working-Class University Students Draw and Transgress Moral Class Boundaries." *Sociology* 43, no. 4: 631–47.

Lubrano, Alfred. 2004. *Limbo: Blue Collar Roots, White Collar Dreams.* Hoboken: John Wiley and Sons.

Massey, Douglas S., Camille Z. Charles, Garvey F. Lundy, and Mary J. Fischer. 2003. *The Source of the River: The Social Origins of Freshmen at America's Selective Colleges and Universities.* Princeton: Princeton University Press.

Melendez, Mickey C., and Nancy Blanco Melendez. 2010. "The Influence of Parental Attachment on the College Adjustment of White, Black, and Latina/Hispanic Women: A Cross-Cultural Investigation." *Journal of College Student Development* 51, no. 4, 419–35.

Nora, Amaury, and Alberto F. Cabrera. 1996. "The Role of Perceptions of Prejudice and Discrimination on the Adjustment of Minority Students to College." *The Journal of Higher Education* 67, no. 2: 119–48.

Ostrove, Joan, and Susan Long. 2007. "Social Class and Belonging: Implications for College Adjustment." *The Review of Higher Education* 30, no. 4: 363–89.

Ostrove, Joan. 2003. "Belonging and Wanting: Meanings of Social Class Background for Women's Constructions of Their College Experiences." *Journal of Social Issues* 59, no. 4: 771–84.

Rodriguez, Richard. 1982. *Hunger of Memory: The Education of Richard Rodriguez.* New York: Bantam Dell.

Rondini, Ashley C. 2016. "Healing the Hidden Injuries of Class? Redemption Narratives, Aspirational Proxies, and Parents of Low-Income, First-Generation College Students." *Sociological Forum* 31, no. 1: 96–116.

Ryan, Jake, and Charles Sackrey, eds. 1984. *Strangers in Paradise: Academics from the Working Class.* Boston: South End Press.

Sidanius, Jim, Shana Levin, Colette Van Laar, and David Sears. 2008. *The Diversity Challenge: Social Identity and Intergroup Relations on the College Campus.* New York: Russell Sage.

Stanton-Salazar, Ricardo D. 1997. "A Social Capital Framework for Understanding the Socialization of Racial Minority Children." *Harvard Educational Review* 67, no. 1: 1–40.

Stewart, Abigail, and Joan Ostrove. 1993. "Social Class, Social Change, and Gender: Working-Class Women at Radcliffe and After." *Psychology of Women Quarterly* 17, no. 4: 475–97.

Stuber, Jenny. 2006. "Talk of Class: Discursive Repertoires of White Working- and Upper-Middle-Class Students." *Journal of Contemporary Ethnography* 35, no. 3: 285–318.

Stuber, Jenny. 2009. "Class, Culture, and Participation in the Collegiate Extra-Curriculum." *Social Forces* 24, no. 4: 877–900.

Stuber, Jenny. 2011. *Inside the College Gates: How Class and Culture Matter in Higher Education.* Lanham, MD: Rowman & Littlefield.

Tinto, Vincent. 2006–2007. "Research and Practice of Student Retention: What's Next?" *Journal of College Student Retention: Research, Theory and Practice* 8, no. 1: 1–19.

Tokarczyk, Michelle M., and Elizabeth A. Fay. 1993. *Working-Class Women in the Academy: Laborers in the Knowledge Factory.* Amherst: University of Massachusetts Press.

Torres, Kimberly. 2009. "'Culture shock': Black Students Account for Their Distinctiveness at an Elite College." *Ethnic and Racial Studies* 32, no. 5: 883–905.

Turley, Ruth N. Lopez, Matthew Desmond, and Sarah Bruch. 2010. "Unanticipated Educational Consequences of a Positive Parent-Child Relationship." *Journal of Marriage and Family* 72, no. 5: 1377–90.

Tyson, Karolyn, William Darity Jr., and Domini R. Castellino. 2005. "It's Not 'a Black Thing': Understanding the Burden of Acting White and Other Dilemmas of High Achievement." *American Sociological Review* 70, no. 4: 582–605.

von Hippel, Paul T. 2007. "Regression with Missing Ys: An Improved Strategy for Analyzing Multiply Imputed Data." *Sociological Methodology* 37, no. 1: 83–117.

Wacquant, Loïc. 2006. "Pierre Bourdieu." In *Key Sociological Thinkers*, edited by Rob Stones, 267–78. Houndsmill, Basingstoke, Hampshire: Palgrave Macmillan.

Zweigenhaft, Richard L. 1993. "The Application of Cultural and Social Capital: A Study of the 25th Year Reunion Entries of Prep School and Public School Graduates of Yale College." *Higher Education* 23, no. 3: 311–20.

NOTES

1. This chapter was previously published as Elizabeth M. Lee and Rory Kramer. 2013. "Out With the Old, In With the New? Habitus and Social Mobility at Selective Colleges." *Sociology of Education* 86, no. 1: 18–35.

2. Several years passed between the data collection for each sample. The NLSF is unique in its sampling of students at (primarily) selective colleges, which made it ideal for our purposes: examining low- and middle-income students' experiences at elite colleges. Moreover, although some years passed between completion of the NLSF survey and our interviews, respondents in each sample are within the same generation and share many of the same cultural reference points and class-based habitus.

3. For a more detailed description of the overall NLSF institutions, sampling methodology and individual characteristics, see Massey et al. (2003).

4. The $40,000 marker was selected because of its accordance with the approximate income level below which Pell grants—federal financial grants awarded to students with the highest financial need—are awarded, making it a relevant marker when studying higher education and class.

5. Between the original publication of this article and the publication of this chapter, several respondents requested a change to their pseudonyms. This version reflects those changes.

6. For full discussion of the qualitative data, see Lee 2016.

7. The three attributes used to create our scale are responses to the question "To what extent do you agree with the following statements about the relative benefits of a college education?": "1) My going to college has led to the loss of some of my friends, 2) My going to college has made me feel less a part of my family, 3) My going to college has made me an outsider in my home community."

8. Bruno is a satirically flamboyant gay fashion designer character created by Sacha Baron Cohen.

9. We thank an anonymous reviewer for directing us to this passage from Bourdieu.

4

Moving Between Classes

Loyalists, Renegades, and Double Agents

Allison L. Hurst

Carolyn Chute, a novelist from the working class, tells this story of herself at a cocktail party. When a professional disparages his workers as "*just a pair of hands*" she reminisces about working at a poultry plant and thinks about how workers are always put down for their lack of ambition (and educational attainment):

> "Raise your aspirations," said others. Educators especially. They love that word. ASPIRATIONS. All over the state you can hear that long word rolling off their tongues. It's something the low-income people don't have enough of, they say . . . doesn't he realize that the higher the white-shirt pastel-people raise their aspirations for us who are already failing their idea of success, the more we lose sight of our own true aspirations and the deeper into complete failure they leave us? . . . "Low-income people have got to escape," they say. Escape what? Do they mean *leave home*? Leave town? Like they did? Do they mean escape that life we have here in Maine without family ties and hometown ties and go to . . . to . . . Harvard or Yale, like they did? Live in a faraway city? Be a yuppie? Is that the only acceptable choice? Why was it so easy for *them* to leave *their* homes, these leaders, these experts, these professionals? Were their homes dysfunctional in a way social workers aren't trained to recognize? (Carolyn Chute 2001, 41–43)

This passage highlights the dilemma of choice facing children from the working class—damned by society if you stay in your home community, but potentially seen as a traitor if you "escape."

From 2004 to 2006 I interviewed twenty-one working class students attending a large public university in the Northwest. All students were in their third or final year at the university, so expectations for the future were on most of their minds. They also had all been in college long enough to have experienced its highs and lows. I was interested in finding out how they experienced college and whether they recognized class differences on campus. In particular, I wondered how students whose parents hadn't completed college dealt with being "between classes," potentially moving "up" into the middle class. The whole story of what I discovered can be found in *The Burden of*

Academic Success, published in 2010. The part of the story I am retelling here comes from that book and focuses on the divided loyalties experienced by working-class students.[1]

I am not the first to point out that the culture of college is often perceived as markedly different from home cultures for many first-generation, low-income, and working-class college students. There is actually a long history of such studies, stretching from Jackson and Marsden (1962) in the UK to Matthys (2014) in the Netherlands. The United States has seen a sizeable growth of ethnographies highlighting class cultural conflict at college today (Aries 2008; Hurst 2010; Mullen 2011; Stuber 2012; Armstrong and Hamilton 2013) and edited volumes focused on the lived experience of class and inequality on college campuses (Stich and Freie 2015; Lee and LaDousa 2015; Hurst and Nenga 2016). Recently, a group of researchers in the UK have begun publishing results from the Paired Peers project, a study that compared students of different class origins attending two very differently situated colleges (Bathmaker et al. 2016; Bradley and Ingram 2012; Ingram and Abrahams 2016;); There is also a strong literature of accounts by working-class academics (faculty who were the first in their family to attend college), from the original contribution by Ryan and Sackrey (1984) to the collections by Tokarczyk and Fay (1993), Dews and Law (1995), Mahony and Zmroczek (1997), Grimes and Morris (1997), Adair and Dahlberg (2003), Welsch (2005), Samarco and Muzzatti (2005), and Oldfield and Johnson (2008). To this list we could include the recent collections of Thatcher et al. (2016) and Hurst and Nenga (2016), whose contributors include many working-class academics.

My own small contribution to this literature is to note that working-class students make choices when confronted with opposing class cultures. That is what this chapter will be about. All working-class students recognize (and most speak in) the discourse of loyalty and betrayal. Too often material success and social prestige for the working-class person are premised on betrayal of one's class. Put differently, our meritocratic system rewards individual strivers, not collective loyalists. Working-class college students must learn to navigate the opposing cultures of home and school. They sometimes feel they must choose between assimilation and resistance.

Previous literature that seeks to explain academic failure as a result of an "oppositional culture" (Everhart 1983; Fordham 1996; Fordham and Ogbu 1986; Solomon 1992; Ogbu 1974, 1978, 1986, 2003; Valenzuela 1999; Willis 1977) often stops short of questioning the roots of the opposition. Willis's study comes closest, in my mind, to questioning the value of the normative culture to which this "oppositional culture" is counterposed. However, even here the overall focus is on how working-class kids harm themselves by their adoption of a masculinist, working-class identity and set of values. This is not simply a matter of "friends holding you back," but a larger question about the nature of class and power in society and how one responds to this.

YOU CAN'T GO HOME AGAIN?

Ever since scholarships were first granted in the medieval academies (Rashdall 1958; Stone 1974; de Ridder-Symoens 1992), academically able working-class students have told twin stories of despair and promise, both semibiographically through fictions, journal entries, and letters. Social theorist and working-class academic bell hooks speaks impassionedly of the "psychic turmoil" created by demands that working-class students and students of color "surrender all vestiges of their past" (hooks 1994, 182). Zandy (1995, 65) refers to "the old working-class story" of feeling more separate from her parents with the more schooling she received. For some, this separation is viewed as betrayal (Clancy 1997). The biggest theme Dews and Law (1995) discovered among the contributors to their collection of working-class academics was *ambivalence*. Far from viewing education as an unmitigated good, working-class academics were deeply ambivalent about both their decision to go to college and their subsequent upward mobility. Dahlberg (2003, 75) argues that it is a false assumption to believe that all students attending college desire to transcend class boundaries, that there is a concomitant denial of a distinctive social existence outside of middle-class culture or academe. In reality, wanting "a better life" can mean desiring "safe, justly compensated work, work with possibility for autonomy and craft, work that does not exhaust and dehumanize" *rather than* "a better life that extracted as its cost familial and historic memory" (Zandy 1995, 1).

RESPONSES TO THE DILEMMA

In my research, I found three sharply delineated responses to the dilemma of divided class loyalties. These responses came out of multiple in-depth interviews with college students of various ages, racial identifications, and gender identities. About half of the students interviewed were White, and the others Latinx, Black, and Native American. Two-thirds of the students identified as female, with White women making up the largest single group (no surprise as I am myself a White woman). I asked the students questions ranging from how they got to college to what it was like growing up as they did, what they wanted for their future selves, and how they saw themselves presently. When I began the interviews I was unprepared for the stark differences in identification I discovered. Although all students shared similar stories of obstacles to achievement, they told very different stories about who they were, how they related to their families, and what they wanted in the future. I was also surprised at how little gender and race mattered in terms of who was telling which kind of story, as I will explain further throughout the chapter.

Loyalists

Almost half of the students I interviewed could be classified as Loyalists, and neither gender nor racial identification was associated with adoption of this strategy. Students adopting a Loyalist position draw sharp moral boundaries between themselves and middle-class people. When asked to describe the working class they use positive adjectives such as "strong" and "able" and discuss the value of hard work, the ability to keep a family together, the importance of working together as a community, and the sense of humor so essential to survival in an unequal world. Loyalists have structural understandings of inequality. Loyalists of color have a relatively sophisticated understanding of race as a system of oppression and its connections to class and the labor system. No Loyalist expressed feelings of embarrassment or shame for being working class or for having working-class family members. You could say Loyalists were adopting a "resisting" coping strategy (Jensen 2012, 169) or that they sought a "reconfirmed habitus" (Ingram and Abrahams 2016), in the words of more recent researchers whose research echoes my own.

Loyalists tend to wear their working-class-ness proudly, as a badge of honor. Most began the interviews speaking slang, dropping the ending "g" on words, using many connectives such as "like" and "you know." They did not dress up for the interview. Many slouched noticeably when they first sat down. They typically engaged in all the outward practices and demeanors that would have marked them as a "bad kid" in so many primary and secondary schools (Ferguson 2000; Valenzuela 1999). But they are decidedly not, and never were, "bad kids." They were always able to do schoolwork well, even if they didn't like it. In fact, three dropped out of high school—the only high school dropouts in the entire study. Over the course of the interview, the slang and the slouches disappeared. Once they realized that I was "on their side," so to speak, the performance of their working-class identity was no longer necessary (Bettie 2003).

They spoke passionately about the pain they felt toward social injustices and class inequality. They often described close (if sometimes troubled) relationships with family members and how they fought to ensure that college would not alienate them from the working class. They rejected the idea that college would make them middle class. Although they hoped for better jobs, they defined these in terms of job security and safe working conditions, not prestige. Often frustrated with the college culture, they felt they had little choice but to earn a degree if they wanted a decent job (and this before the Great Recession).

Renegades

In contrast to Loyalists, students adopting a Renegade position draw sharp moral boundaries between themselves and other working-class people (Lamont 2003). When asked to describe the working class they use negative adjectives such as "weak," "stupid," "ignorant," and "inferior." They raise the issue of fatalism among the working class, blaming their parents and other working-class people for not working hard enough or not adequately planning for the future. On the other hand, middle-class people were described quite positively. Middle-class people were "smart," "together," and had the "right" attitudes. Renegades spoke in an individualized discourse. There was little structural awareness of inequalities such as race and class. Students of color often believed they could avoid or mitigate the effects of racism by becoming rich. All Renegades expressed feelings of embarrassment and shame for being working class and for having working-class family members. You could say Renegades were adopting a "distancing" coping strategy (Jensen 2012, 167), or that they operated with an "abandoned habitus" (Ingram and Abrahams 2016).

The Renegade narrative sits quite comfortably with dominant understandings of social mobility. Renegades "escape" not just poverty but a morally bankrupt way of living in pursuit of a "better" place among "smart" people who are "together" and make proper plans for the future. Talia, a White woman, spoke incessantly of wanting to "access middle-class culture." Because Renegades lack a structural understanding, they understand poverty to be largely a matter of choice. They are determined to make the right choices in their lives in order to be better people. They evidence the "individualized aspirations" within neoliberal space that Diane Reay (2016) has so well described.

In contrast to the Loyalist slang and slouch, Renegades did dress up for the interviews (although this was college, so dressing up was relative). I often caught attempts at overenunciation and strange grammatical constructions in their conversation. They were so obviously *trying* to fit in, to speak "correctly," to wear the right clothes, to be the right person. They were not comfortable in this role either; often by the end of particularly long interviews they relaxed back into working-class speech patterns.

Renegades were often *hyperaware* of class differences around them, at least insofar as they were manifested in outward appearances. They described instances of acute embarrassment, shame, and discomfort being around middle-class people. They never wanted to be taken for working class. Given that, it was perhaps surprising that I had any volunteers for these interviews at all. Certainly, their reticence about identifying as working class limited the number of Renegades that came forward and partially explains, I believe, the higher proportion of Loyalists in this study. The Renegades I interviewed were comfortable with me, however, and I think they enjoyed telling someone who would understand all the progress they have made so far in their lives. They were proud of their achievements. They valued college as an experience that would make them middle class. They wanted to be professionals, managers, people with clout. They were tired of being afraid and small.

Double Agents

In contrast to Renegades and Loyalists who represent the twin poles of class identification among working-class college students, Double Agents occupy an unusual middle ground. Although some are more or less working-class-identified or middle-class-identified, Double Agents are a unique group in that certain special characteristics define them. Among these, the ability to blend in with several groups is key. Double Agents are not just good at playing the field between the working class and the middle class but are equally adept at moving between social groups and cliques of various kinds. All of the Double Agents spontaneously used words like "chameleon" and "blender" to describe themselves. All gave early examples of their unusual ability to fit in with several different social groups. You could say Double Agents were able to "build bridges" between middle- and working-class cultures (Jensen 2012, 173) or that they had successfully created a "reconciled habitus" (Ingram and Abrahams 2016).

Double Agents can be defined by their stark refusal to draw moral boundaries between themselves and another group. So far, they have not been compelled to make a choice between the working class and the middle class. I wondered why this was so, and whether they would be forced to make a decision at some point. As a group, they were younger than the Loyalists and Renegades. In addition, each of the students I identified as being a Double Agent was personally charismatic, and there were more White female students here than in any other group. Like Loyalists, Double Agents tend to have a structural understanding of inequalities, although it is not so clearly defined nor as salient to their life stories. For now, they are more concerned with "getting along" than "getting on." Many perform the role of peacemakers among their friends. They find value in both the working class and the middle class, although some stress working-class solidarity and some stress middle-class ambition as more important. Many are hopeful that they can find good jobs (well-paid and well-respected) that will also allow them to do well.

Double Agents are not embarrassed or ashamed of their families. They are proud of them. But they also are interested in going beyond them. They do not reject success, or fear it, as Loyalists do. They do not believe that success will contaminate them, or alienate them from their families. In many ways, the Double Agents were the most hopeful, and perhaps also the most naïve of the students. None of them disclosed any dysfunctions in their families. All had parents who were still married, or at least "together." Thus, in addition to unusual personal charisma, these students had so far led relatively simple and harmonious lives. This is why I do not believe that the Double Agents' strategy is one available to everyone. The fact that most Double Agents were women is also instructive, and mostly *White women* especially so. These are exactly the people who are least likely to be sanctioned for moving between groups. None of them had ever been disciplined or sanctioned at school.

UNDERSTANDING ONE'S PLACE: AMONG THE WORKING CLASS

This section will describe the strains of family relationships and analyze how working-class college students respond to the pressures they feel when at home. Because I did not interview the parents of these students, nor did I visit their homes, my focus is on *how the students described their family lives.* In other words, I am concerned with the students' interpretations of their home lives, and not their objective realities.

Most parents were described as "supportive" but "clueless" regarding their children's college attendance. Renegades often expressed resentment over their parents' lack of understanding (and their concomitant inability to be of much help). Talia, a White woman in her late twenties, claimed that talking about college with her parents was "a sore spot" because they seemed to take so little interest. She was particularly annoyed that, even after three years, they could not remember the name of the university she attended, or its mascot: "It's all this big college world to them and they don't really do much to . . . [laughs] put it into perspective."

About half of the students also brought up the issue of being accused of being pretentious or "uppity" now that they were in college. Bethany, whose father was part of a labor union, was very concerned about betrayal:

I also think maybe it was a sense of betrayal? You know, they worked their bones to the ground putting food on our table and keeping us, you know, clothed, healthy, and everything and so it's really . . . that's what a good family does, and that there is great character in that, and you should be proud of that, so it might have felt almost like betrayal of that for me to say, no, I'm going to go to college.

Betrayal also arose for different reasons among some students of color, whose communities were concerned about cultural assimilation. The accusation of being "uppity" because one succeeds academically often begins before college, and may affect success in high school as well as the decision whether to apply to college at all. The students I interviewed were similar in that they did not allow such accusations to stop them from seeking higher education. This may not be the case for many members of the working class, however. It is probable that many highly competent working-class children decide not to go to college because to do so would be experienced as a betrayal or as pretentiousness.

Isabel's story is instructive here. Problems for Isabel, Latina, began in tenth grade when she made the very conscious decision to do well in school. For this, many in her community considered her a *vendido*, or sellout—"They thought just because I wanted to do everything made me less of a person. Under their eyes, and they didn't want to be like me, there's this mentality, there's this resentment and they start talking, 'Oh, she thinks she's better than us!' And that happened a lot." To deal with this, Isabel isolated herself from many Chicano/a students. She knew that, if she were to succeed, she had to concentrate on herself—"I was always too worried about myself. I started not caring, that was a decision I made for myself the year I started [at the new high school]. That's why I didn't want to join a group. There weren't people who were welcoming at all. There were all these people who wanted me to be part of their group but, no, I didn't want to fall into that trap." This conscious rejection of her community left her socially isolated, as she was never fully accepted by the White middle-class students either. To deal with this, Isabel threw herself into schoolwork and extracurricular activities, building up an impressive resume that included internships with both the State Department of Justice and the Office of the Governor (working for minority affairs). Her hard work assuaged feelings of social isolation. "So, yes, I felt it [the rejection], and I still feel it now with those same friends—I lost contact with 90 percent of them. But it doesn't bother me because I am too busy. I have learned to be more selfish and care more about what I want for myself than to care about what others think."

Isabel prefers to "go it alone." She is uncomfortable and self-conscious when she has to share the classroom with other Chicano/a students, afraid that they will be judging her. In particular, she is afraid they will call her "a white girl," or, even worse, say that she thinks she is better than everybody else. Isabel draws much of her support from her new husband, a Mexican citizen. She continues to succeed academically and wants to go on to law school. Much of her motivation is to help those in her community make better decisions and lead better lives, as she has done.

Some working-class students report deeper problems maintaining closeness with their families. While Loyalists tend to downplay problems with their families, Renegades have well-articulated and substantial grievances. It important to remember, once again, that I am not necessarily discussing *the objective reality* of these relationships. Rather, the focus is on the students' *understanding* of their relationships with family members.

By definition, Loyalists are trying to maintain as close as ties as possible to their working-class roots—education is considered *supplemental* and is rejected to the extent that it contradicts working-class values. Double Agents see education as *additive*, and they struggle to balance both working-class values and new middle-class knowledges. They really do not want to reject either set. In other words, they like to keep their options open. It is for this reason they often come across as "neutral" about issues, and only truly become concerned when they feel they are being forced to make exclusive choices. By definition, Renegades are trying to acquire a new mindset and set of values—one they believe will improve their lives both materially *and* culturally. Education is meant to *replace* older, inefficient and unsuccessful values and behaviors. This does not mean that all Renegades reject their families—far from it. But they *do* reject the paths their families are on, the choices they have made, and the values that they espouse. Many times, as will be demonstrated below, they see themselves as the *patrons* of their families and the *role models* of a better way of life. In this, most middle-class society would agree.

Family relationships are fraught with difficulties and pitfalls for students adopting Renegade strategies. For most of the Renegades I interviewed, problems with family took up the bulk of our discussion time. I want to provide two sets of stories to show the contrast between Loyalists and Renegades in this regard. The first pairing includes one White woman, Talia, who narrates a Renegade account, and one Latina, Amy, who narrates a Loyalist account. In the second pairing, I have kept the same racial and gender configuration but the strategic orientations are switched—here I compare Bethany, a White woman adopting a Loyalist account, to Isabel, a Latina, adopting a Renegade account. These two sets of stories highlight the key differences in the ways that Loyalists and Renegades understand and respond to the working class. They also highlight the ways in which race and gender intersect with class to create a particular narrative. The first paired set highlights the different ways students explain subordinate class location and inequality, while the second paired set highlights the different ways students respond to families in need.

"It's Not That People Are Lazy. It's That They're Oppressed!"

The quote that opens this section was Amy's explanation for subordinate class location and inequality. She was particularly moved to combat assertions that Mexicans were lazy and therefore poor. In contrast, Talia explained poverty as being a result of poor choices and poor planning—dysfunctionality. Working-class people lack the cultural capital to succeed. In this explanation, working-class people must assimilate to the norms and behaviors of the middle class. In Amy's explanation, in contrast, there is, first, no call for assimilation and second, no recognition that assimilation would do much to "cure" the problem anyway. These are radically different stories.

Talia and Amy are both the first in their families to attend college. They both experienced sharp poverty while growing up. Talia's father worked at a gas station for several years, and then at an auto parts store. Her mother, as most of the mothers in this study, cleaned houses and provided childcare in addition to being the "homemaker" of the family. Talia began cleaning houses with her mother as a youngster. When Talia was fifteen, she left home and "adopted" a middle-class family, whose father was her high school track coach. Her understanding of cultural capital and the differences between working-class culture and middle-class culture were, I think, heightened during this period.

Throughout the interview, Talia expressed a great deal of hostility toward her biological family. She was bitter that her parents had not been able to afford Christmas presents for her and her siblings and resentful that they had, in fact, given presents to the even less fortunate instead. She was frustrated at what she perceived as her family's religiosity, and could not understand why they couldn't have "succeeded" in the more conventional sense. Throughout the interview, Talia made frequent references to the fact that her family, and the working class in general, did not plan for the future. For example, when describing her adoptive family, she said, "It was just interesting to join that family when I did and it was definitely different conversations—the conversations were more intelligent, they talked about what the future held, they talked about the possibilities that life has to offer, and that was never something that we talked about in the other household."

The middle class, according to Talia, had earned their privileged position because they made plans and followed through. They did not allow themselves to be diverted by poor neighbors or friends. Talia believes she can become part of this middle class through imitation. Jettisoning her family, not allowing them to pull her down with them, is both a priority and a moral imperative. This is key to the Renegade strategy. In addition, Talia believes she must adopt the behaviors and speech patterns of the middle class if she wants to be successful. She avidly read books about improving one's diction and self-presentation. Her life story becomes a quest to "access the middle class" and to drop old habits and the working-class "mindset" that would keep her from achieving this. In response to a question about what is *valuable* about the working class and her family in particular, she grew very confused: "That's really hard. I pride myself on divorcing a lot of the ideologies of that family. . . . *I am just so proud to be away from them!*"

The story Talia tells is one of shame at her roots and a constant movement away from the source of that shame. Angry and frustrated at fundamental inequalities she saw at school, she directed this anger toward her family rather than any sense of a social structure. In elementary school, she reports wanting to be like the middle-class kids because "they could focus on things like school. They didn't have to go home and take care of their brothers and sisters because the babysitter was there. I always wanted to access that and I always wanted to be part of that . . . for a long time I felt ashamed of myself like there was something wrong with me . . . so I just have to work it through and to make myself take on a different mindset." Talia's understanding of what it takes to "access the middle class," having to do exclusively with issues of cultural capital, does not allow her to feel any sympathy towards working-class people. On the contrary, the Renegade story of success is predicated on moving away from working-class people and their ways of life.

The life story Amy tells is quite different. Amy is the youngest of three, daughter of immigrants from Mexico, and, like Talia, the first in her family to go to college. Also like Talia, Amy experienced sharp poverty in her childhood. She began working at age ten, picking strawberries along with other family members. At age fifteen, she worked a full-time job at a grocery store in addition to going to high school. She has continued to work full-time ever since. At one point she had to drop out of college so that she could help her mother make the rent payments. She never really planned on going to college, but both her mother and her older sister encouraged her to think about it. One of Amy's biggest issues, she explains, is dealing with the fact that she has chosen a life path that is different from others in her community—"I try to stay real to where I came from. We've all come from the same struggle, and I try to say that their life path is not worse, and no *better* than my life path."

Whereas Talia struggled to distinguish herself from her family and home community, Amy struggles to "keep it real." She directs her frustrations not at her family, but at her middle-class peers. She is keenly aware of how her class and race mark her as different at college. After a bad experience with a more privileged roommate, Amy is very cautious about getting too close to her peers. She does not want to waste time on people who do not share her political and cultural understandings. "If you're uncomfortable with racial issues, if you're not even open to hear about them, we're not going to work out!" When asked why this was so important to her, Amy explained, "Because it makes me more comfortable with myself. I'm able to be myself, you know. . . . I don't want to have to explain everything, like why I can't afford to go to the movies." Notice that Amy's real "self" is rooted in her home community, and is not reflected by her college participation.

Amy's purpose in going to college is not to "get away" or "access the middle class." Rather, "the purpose for me to get through school is, I think, by bettering myself I'm able to bring back something to my family." This is a common theme of the Loyalist story. Going to school is another way of continuing the struggle against oppression; it is not a way to reinvent the self. Amy also has a fairly sophisticated understanding of the intersectionality of her class and race identities, and how they operate in a nexus of inequality. First and foremost, she argues, she identifies as Chicana, but she concedes that she cannot separate race and class in practice, only in theory because "on a day to day basis, my class has so much to do with what I identify with. They kind of go hand in hand, you know." Rather than feeling shame, Amy is "deeply appreciative" of her working-class Chicana identity. "I appreciate the struggle, you know. Some people I know get disempowered by how *hard* it is, but I gain strength from that. . . . You just keep fighting. And that has so much to do with class! Not just race, or anything else."

Like Talia, Amy suffered bias and ostracism in elementary school because of her subaltern position: "If you don't have the nice shoes, if you don't have the nice clothes, and the cute hair, then you're gonna be made fun of and ostracized." In her case, she got the brunt of the double stigma of being "a poor Mexican." She refused to let this affect her identity, however. Rather than internalize these classist and racist biases, Amy ignored them. She knew that these are biases and she knew where they came from—they are attacks in an ongoing war between the haves and the have-nots ("it's not that people are lazy, it's that they are oppressed"). She also knew where she stands, where she wants to stand, in this war. "It's always a fine line to walk. I'm always remembering where I stand and, you know? I'm just constantly questioned. But that's the best thing about school; it keeps me humble." Thus, rather than using school as a way to climb out of the working class, Amy uses school to remind her of the fault lines of US society, and to keep her cognizant of where she needs to be. As for her future, Amy does not want to become part of the middle class and she does not want a middle-class job. She would like to teach in her home community or be a coordinator at a nonprofit organization.

Responding to Families in Trouble

Renegades may want to climb out of the working class, and they may hold unflattering pictures of their families and their home communities, but this does not mean that they sever all ties with their families. Talia, for example, kept in close contact with her younger brother and sister. In fact, the issue of younger siblings sheds further light on these accounts. Whereas Loyalists like Amy, and Miriam below, were careful to use college as a way to bring back specific knowledge and material resources to their home communities and families, Renegades like Talia, and Isabel below, were more likely to engage in a form of cultural patronage (to which their families were often greatly resistant). Both Miriam and Isabel had younger siblings in need. How they dealt with these brothers and sisters is instructive.

Like Talia and Amy, Miriam and Isabel faced both relative and absolute poverty in their childhoods, although the particular form of the experience operated in a racial field. I have chosen to compare Miriam and Isabel to tease out the racial component in what are otherwise remarkably similar stories. Miriam, who is White, grew up in the country in a very patriarchal family, with eight younger siblings. Isabel, who is Latina, grew up in the city in a family with strong traditional gender norms, the oldest of four children. Both families went through incredibly difficult times. Both families were very religious. Miriam's father, a boilermaker by trade and sometime salvage man, held very strict rules about the proper place of women in society. Miriam and her sisters were expected to do all of the domestic work alongside their mother. Since they often lived off the grid, without electricity or running water, these domestic chores were onerous and time-consuming. They were awakened by the sounding of a bell at daybreak, at which time their "chores" began, ending only at nightfall. For most of this time, Miriam was not allowed to go to school, as her father believed women did not need an education. Miriam left home when she was sixteen when a neighbor notified Child Protective Services of the ways in which the children were being raised. The youngest siblings were all in foster care at the time of the interview; Miriam's oldest sister, now an adult, chose to return to her parents.

Isabel's father was not a strong presence in her family, although she too grew up among traditional gendered expectations (which she understands as reflecting Mexican culture). Her parents both came to the United States as seasonal laborers. Isabel herself began working at a very young age, under the table when necessary. Isabel at first rebelled against the strict morality of her family, joining a Latina gang while in junior high. But she turned her life around when she began a new school and made a decision to become a success. She had always known she was poor and felt like a second-class citizen (because of her race), and wanted to erase the feelings of shame and embarrassment that had haunted her throughout her childhood. In this sense, she is strikingly similar to Talia. Isabel's Renegade story is different than Talia's, however, in that she must deal with the contradiction of wanting to leave behind people whom she finds dysfunctional (for the same reasons as Talia) but without "acting White" or leaving behind her cultural heritage. She often blames the *machismo* of Mexican culture for her mother's subordinate status, deftly linking dysfunctionality to race without seeming to embrace Whiteness. Sometimes, she ascribes her family's continuing struggles with their adoption of a hedonistic present-oriented American value system.

Both Miriam and Isabel have younger siblings. How do Loyalist and Renegade narratives explain the proper relationship between the upwardly mobile and those that are still living the life that has now become the past? Loyalists tend to reject the way I framed this issue in the first place. Although Miriam has "left" her family for the moment, she has surely not "left them behind," although she struggles on a daily basis with the guilt of her good fortune. Renegades, on the other hand, have a peculiar narrative of patronage. Having discovered the key to success, they are eager to pass this knowledge on to younger siblings, who often resist being cast as the returning native's charity case.

The most frustrating aspect of Isabel's life, as narrated, was this resistance. At an early age, Isabel defied gender expectations (her rejection of *machismo* culture) and took on a leading role in the household, shepherding her mother through relief agencies and confrontations with English-speaking authorities. Despite her brief adolescent rebellion, Isabel saw herself as the backbone, counselor, and moral exemplar to her family. Isabel was sad that her younger siblings did not share her ambitions. "They don't have that in them, they have nothing in them, that little seed I always had." She understood that her going away to college may appear as betrayal, but she insisted that that type of "selfishness" is admirable. Sometimes she wondered if she should even continue trying to help "if every time I try to help they end up stepping on me—they don't care about my happiness at all." Extremely self-disciplined (Isabel juggles not only a full-time education and full-time job, but plans for law school and a new husband), Isabel sometimes feared she may have to move away from all those who have a bad influence on her, including her mother and siblings. "I guess college has made me a better person—not one that my family necessarily likes, but I like it, I love it."

Miriam did not see herself as a role model. She struggled with the decision to stay in college or work enough so that she could "adopt" her four youngest siblings, currently in foster care. She understood that, by going to college now, she may be in a better position to take care of them in the long run. This was not an easy decision to make, however, and she continued to struggle with it. The fact that the foster mother is kind and allowed Miriam frequent visits allayed some of her fears.

Although Miriam suffered many of the same embarrassments as a child as Isabel (remembering the shame of using food stamps, for example), and she harbored resentment towards her father for his bullying ways, she did not read dysfunction into the script. She was proud of the fact that she knew how to survive with few resources. "I really like the fact that I can do the dirty jobs. Does that make sense? I'm really proud of that. I cut firewood, and we made a living from it! That fact that I've washed clothes in a creek . . . the fact that I can do that, even though I know a lot of other people would look down on that." Because Miriam had not adopted the dominant society's value system, she could retain pride in aspects of her culture in ways that Isabel could not. There was no discussion in Miriam's story of encouraging her siblings to go to college. That decision was not tied up with one's moral worth, and so it was not something Miriam found essential in the same way Isabel did. Besides, she acknowledged, she was lucky to have gone. Very bright, and a great autodidact (having read all the greats of English literature as a teenager when she found a stack of discarded books), Miriam knew that not everyone (younger siblings included) would have the same chances as she did. The fact that there are still people out there who must live without indoor plumbing bothered Miriam on a societal level, not a personal one. Like all Loyalists, Miriam understood this as an issue of social stratification, inequality, and oppression, not individual choice or dysfunction.

UNDERSTANDING ONE'S PLACE:
AMONG THE MIDDLE CLASS

If working-class college students must rethink and sometimes reframe their relationships with family and friends, they must also find their place among the middle class. In this final section I want to take a closer look at how these students manage the burden of "success." I argue that the lack of a structural understanding of poverty and inequality leads Renegades to see the move from working class to middle class in moral terms while the more structuralist Loyalists question the very idea of "moving up." I begin with two stories (Loyalist and Renegade) about race and racism.

Responding to Racial Oppression and the Politics of Skin

John and Calder are both charming, courteous young men. They come from
very large families—John was the middle of seven children, Calder had
three siblings and several very close cousins. John's parents emigrated from
Mexico in the 1970s, while Calder is both Native American and Mexican, and
he strongly identifies as Indian. Both young men were acutely aware of racial
oppression in the United States, but they handled it quite differently. John,
a Renegade, and "the darkest-skinned" of his "mother's children," believed
that moving up in class would erase the impact of racism. He believed that
becoming middle class would act as a whitener, giving examples of popular
and powerful men of color whom he believed have literally escaped their
skin by becoming successful. Calder, a Loyalist, was fiercely proud of his
ethnic heritage and had the greatest resistance to the hidden curriculum of assimilation operating in the educational system. Their contrasting stories give
us insight into the dilemmas of education for the working class, as played
out in the politics of skin. They point to the ways in which individualist and
structuralist explanations for poverty and inequality impact the stories we tell
ourselves about who we are and where we are going.

A constant theme for John was overcoming racial stigma through social
and financial success. This appeared to be a long-standing story in his personal development. For example, he stressed that he was to be called by the
Anglo name of John, not the Spanish *Juan*. His grandfather gave him the
name John, specifically to distinguish him from the many *Juans* of his community. As the darkest-skinned of his many siblings, John felt the internalized
racism of his mother, believing that she held the lowest expectations for him.
John's dark skin marked him from an early age, "and so my whole thing was
to prove to my mom that I was smarter than her children." Note that John did
not say "her other children," but rather "her children." John often stressed
how isolated and overlooked he felt in his family. Perhaps some of this has to
do with being a middle child, but the account given by John used skin color
as an explanation. At another point, he goes further:

> I wanted to prove to my mom that, and it's stupid, but to prove to her that I was
> better than her other kids, that I was smarter than them, that I could do more
> things than they could, you know, because, I don't know, they were always like,
> like my older brother he always got everything, he's lighter than me, he's very
> light skinned, he's almost white, you know? He always got everything—so for
> me it was always to prove myself to people. Of my worth, you know? And now,
> now my brother tries to give me words of wisdom and it's just like, it goes in
> one ear and out the other, because a lot of stuff he tells me—it's almost sad.
> Now a lot of people are proud of me and I think that's cool but I really don't,
> it's almost like, I don't know, it's kinda frustrating to hear them, they're always

like, well, if you ever need anything just tell us, you know, we are so proud of you and I was so rejected when I was younger so it's like where were you when I needed you? And I don't really need you now.

John was angry and bitter towards his family when I interviewed him. He was angry that his mother claimed pride in him once he began college: "My mom used to tell her friends, 'my kid is in college.' Like she was putting me through school. Like she had helped me get here and all that! I used to tell her not to tell anyone I was her son. Tell them about your other kids, huh? Tell them [that one] is over their smoking weed with his friends." It is impossible to tell, without much more extensive interviewing with parents and siblings, whether Renegades reject their families in reaction, or whether family rejection of Renegades results from prior attitudes of Renegades. Many Renegades I encountered have felt rejected by their families, but it is likely that rejection, if this is not too strong a word, is mutually reinforcing, as well as the result of many misunderstandings. Having this feeling, however, makes it much easier to "get educated out" of one's class and community.

Throughout the interview John expressed disdain and contempt for the working class, adopting as his motto, "Tell me who you hang out with and I'll tell you who you are." In college, John was quick to pledge a fraternity. The particular fraternity that he joined was predominantly White and affluent. John preferred hanging out with his brothers, even though they engaged in a great deal of racist stereotyping and offensive behavior, because these were scions of the elite. Although comments about "dumb Mexicans" and illegal immigrants bothered him, he was happy to play the token minority if it would help him climb up the social ladder.

How John dealt with the racism he experienced at college and among his fraternity brothers is enlightening. For John, any amount of discomfort he experienced now was offset by his expectations of future gain. John believed in the American Dream. He believed very strongly that he would eventually surpass (financially and socially) his fraternity brothers in the same way he had already surpassed his brothers by blood. In the process of achieving social mobility, his dark skin would lose its meaning. This was, in many ways, the entire point of social mobility for John. Note the consonance of color and class in the following narration: "See, the way I talk to my friends—'Yeah, White boy, you are wealthier than I am, you have more money than I do, but I guarantee you that I will make more money than you'—you know, like, what I am saying? I will have made more than they will and that is just a matter of fact and they know it."

John did not expect this success to come easy—he was willing to work at it, as he had been doing ever since he could remember. John blamed his parents and other working-class people, especially working-class Latino/as, for not getting ahead. Like Talia, he understood poverty to be a result of indecision, fatalism, and simply "not wanting it enough." Like Isabel, he saw himself as a role model for younger siblings, even as he simultaneously viewed them in a condescending and patronizing manner. For John, the politics of class and social mobility were inextricably tied up with the politics of skin. The only way to overcome racial stereotypes, to make his dark skin *not matter*, was to become part of the establishment.

If John does succeed, he will be cut off from his roots. Whether White society will ever fully recognize him as one of its own remains an open question. Calder's story illustrates the opposite pitfall for working-class college students—the possible dangers inherent in choosing *not to succeed.* Calder, a Loyalist, is most concerned with resisting assimilation. The very path that John eagerly embraces is the path Calder fears the most.

From the very beginning of our interview, Calder identified as poor and Indian, and expressed a great deal of pride in both. Within the first five minutes, Calder had managed to raise issues of race, class, government policies of genocide, and the criminal justice system (Calder's father died of a heroin overdose). He was also quick to give a reason why he was in college—because he was good in sports, happened to be smart, and figured he could keep playing sports if he stayed in school. Besides, he had firsthand experience of the types of bad jobs available to him otherwise. The determined linearity of John's story had no parallel in Calder's account. Nor was there any parallel with John's story of moving out and away from family and community. On the contrary, Calder had managed to pull in several relatives with him—although only one, a younger brother, was also attending college, five brothers and cousins were living on the same street (or in the same house) in the town in which his college was located. Unlike John, who eschewed Latino/a clubs and joined a White fraternity instead, Calder remained aloof from everyone except members of the Native American Students' Alliance.

Calder tried to present college as "no big deal." It was, in some ways, just another job, another way to pass the time until something better came along. When he first went away his mother drove him to campus, dropped him off along with his mattress, and quickly left. There were no emotional farewells because, in many ways, Calder never really left. Even though he acknowledges that several of his friends from before college are in jail, working bad jobs, "in the ghetto or on crack," he seemed to pass no judgments on them, nor did he see himself as doing anything special or more admirable than they. In this, he is very similar to Amy and Miriam who made the same point. Where people end up is as much a matter of luck (especially in evading the disciplinary side of the class/race system) than it is a result of hard work or desire.

In no way did Calder try to deny any of his identities. His biggest criticism of college was the lack of diversity and the silence around issues of race and class. "I was just thinking it would be better if everybody could at least just put it out there because if higher education isn't going to confront racism then what is?" he asks. Calder would prefer to hear people's racist comments and stereotypes rather than pretend they don't exist. He continued,

> If you're going to lead, then lead! If people don't want to talk about race, make them talk about it! Grab one of them and ask them, "What do you think of this?" Don't just ask a Black guy about slavery or me about, you know, reservations, or the *barrio* because they think I'm Mexican or something like that—everyone thinks that only these three people can answer those questions, but you need to hear everything from everyone. If illusions are going to be broken then they need to be addressed. We need people to talk about them. Ain't no other way around it.

Notice that Calder, like Amy and Miriam before him, has a systemic understanding of race and class and the connections between the two. I wondered where this came from. Calder told me his grandfather sat him down when he was a young child and explained to him the facts about White expansionism and genocide. He realized that the stories he learned at home were not the stories he was told in school and this has made him deeply suspicious ever since of official knowledge. Calder's school career, as he presented it, was one long struggle balancing the need for education with the need to remain skeptical and aloof. At one point he considered dropping out because he felt to continue would be a betrayal:

> I was getting all this history about westward expansion and it was eating at me and eating at me, and I was just thinking, "why am I even part of this institution? Why do I even want to be a part of it?" Part of it is just like me joining in and being a traitor and I just wanted to go back and be among my people, and drink some beer.

The question about the function and necessity of college continued to plague Calder throughout his educational career. He adamantly rejected training for any type of managerial position, as did all of the Loyalists I encountered. He did not want to become better than anyone else, he rejected the idea of "being educated out" of his class, and he certainly did not want to erase his racial identity. Thus, although he participated in college, Calder, like other Loyalists, may end up not benefiting materially from his college degree. In point of fact, Calder chose to work with Native Americans as a teacher's aide on a reservation—a job with little prestige or recompense, but inwardly gratifying.

The Burden of Academic Success

The stories of John and Calder were repeated, with variations, among Renegades and Loyalists. Renegades viewed ambition as a sign of moral character whereas Loyalists feared becoming traitors. Renegades believed that success would erase the stigma of being poor, erase racism, and certify them as morally deserving people. Loyalists feared success if it meant being the boss of anyone else. Renegades blamed their families and working-class people for being too stupid, ignorant, and too lazy to succeed. Loyalists recognized a system that produced winners and losers and wanted nothing more than to subvert the rules of the game. Academic success thus brought with it dilemmas of class and identity that all working-class students must work through.

For Renegades like Talia, Isabel, and John, becoming middle class was intimately tied up with escaping the stigma of poverty/race. Because they did not see a social structure holding their families back, they believed that joining the middle class was a relatively straightforward matter of choice. Making wise choices certified one as middle class. Making "stupid" choices meant you remained working class. Middle-class people were thus morally superior to working-class people. By becoming middle class, you could become a moral person. Being a middle-class person was less about what job you held and more about what clothes you wore, how you spoke, the choices you made, and your overall commitment to an individualist ethos.

As has been said elsewhere, students adopting Renegade strategies are very concerned that their working-class patterns of speech, appearance, mannerisms, and behaviors will somehow "mark" them as inferior—even, perhaps, "stupid." Isabel's biggest fear was to be stereotyped as "low class" and therefore "gross" and less than others. To overcome these stigmas, Renegades actively sought out middle-class role models, both on and off campus, so that they could learn the middle-class mentality. John's strategy at campus involved learning as much as he could about "the other side." That is why he joined a wealthy White fraternity and also why he had no time for clubs like MEChA (which he described as counter-productive).

Another student endorsed the idea that success entailed great sacrifice, arguing, for example, that poor people should not have children and endorsing personal abstention, for life if necessary. They were not going to have any children until they were financially stable. It was simply impossible not to get ahead if you had the proper willpower and were willing to work, save, and live in self-denial. Happiness should not be a consideration. Poor people should be willing to sacrifice their happiness for the future. Success is a grim taskmaster in these Renegade accounts. Everything—family, happiness, community—must be sacrificed to it. This is not a discourse of selfishness. It is a discourse of pain, and of *proving* oneself worthy.

Loyalists understand things quite differently. They have little to say about conforming to fit in with other middle-class students—that is not their primary concern. Instead, they have a much more focused critique of college and the labor market. Statistically, having a college degree generally means having a higher income later in life. But some types of jobs pay more than others, regardless of level of education. Bosses get paid more than workers, managers get paid more than assistants. Loyalists do not want to be the boss, and this often made them suspicious of the economic value of their college degree. Calder refused to work in a profession in which he would be required to disrespect members of his community. Similarly, Bethany rejected the idea of a job in management. The paradox is that, like other Loyalist students in this study, Calder and Bethany came to college with the expectation that a college degree would enable them to have a more economically secure future—but as what? They were confused about what jobs college was actually preparing them for.

Like Renegades, Double Agents are masters at learning about "the other side" as much as possible for emulative purposes. Most have close personal friends and mentors from the middle class. However, unlike Renegades, they are not doing this in the spirit of rejection of a working-class identity. Nor do they feel the same anxiety about being "marked" as inferior. Double Agents are social chameleons, and they take pleasure in adapting to different social circumstances. There are some indications that, among students adopting this strategy, they had earlier successes adapting to different social scenes that may have had nothing to do with class. Thus, this is not a class-specific strategy. It certainly comes in handy when a working-class student goes to college, however. Double Agents often put themselves in situations where they will meet many different types of people. They also refuse to adopt an exclusive identity or group affiliation.

Angela epitomizes the Double Agent strategy. She was proud of her working-class heritage, yet able and willing to move across class borders. She always put herself in positions where she would be forced to interact with many different social groups. In high school, Angela took a few honors classes where she mingled with the socially affluent students of her community. She was also a "band geek" and a "redneck." "So, yeah, like I was in everything," she told me. In addition, Angela "plays the middle" politically and acts as mediator between different social factions. She portrays herself as a "redneck" to her middle-class peers in college because she wants to educate them about what life is like for different kinds of people. "They see that and they, it's really all about making it OK to be who you are. If I can get them to accept people who come from maybe my background, then they will be a little bit more open-minded about people who are lower class and I definitely

am not ashamed of my upbringing or where I lived, I didn't like it, but whatever, when people ask me I will tell them all about it." She tried to bridge
the gap politically as well, frequently helping working-class and middle-class
friends understand each other's positions. "I do like to be the middleman a
lot. I like to make people understand things they don't get."

Double Agents were natural adepts at learning speech and behavior patterns
of social groups and classes. This was easy for them. Unlike Renegades, they
were not looking for a permanent makeover. They did not believe the middle
class was morally superior to the working class. Unlike Loyalists, however,
they did not reject ambition either. Having always been able to have their
cake and eat it, too, the burden of academic success weighed the lightest on
them. In a more egalitarian society, where prestige and moral worth are not
measured by the job one does or the language with which one speaks, Double
Agents may be the best role models. For now, given the odds against success
and the very measurements of such success, the Double Agent strategy is a
rather narrow, perhaps even temporary one. Beyond college, the strains of
managing two worlds equally effectively may become overwhelming.

THE CONSEQUENCES OF CHOOSING SIDES

A few points can be drawn from the preceding accounts. First, the stories
confirm the "divided loyalties" and "dilemmas of class" that pervade the accounts of working-class academics and the findings of educational researchers. Second, the stories reflect fundamentally different strategies for dealing
with the dilemmas of class.

Renegades, as typified by Talia, Isabel, and John, tell stories that mirror
society's prejudices and beliefs about the poor. "We live, in America, with so
many platitudes about motivation and self-reliance and individualism—and
myths spun from them, like those of Horatio Alger—that we find it hard to
accept the fact that they are serious nonsense" (Rose 1989, 47). Like the students in Brantlinger's (1993) study, Renegades blame their own families and
communities for being "dysfunctional"—that is, for not clearly embracing
middle-class values, norms, and behaviors. This does not make them "traitors" to their class, however. As Isabel's story illustrates, Renegades very
much want their families to succeed; they just believe the best way to do this
is to become something else. In a sense, Renegades are idealists. They are
more likely to believe in the reality of the American Dream.

Without a structural understanding of class, Renegades blamed the poor for
their circumstances. "Unable to relate analytically the macropolitical to the
micropolitical, I, like many young people, blamed my family for everything,

believing that they were deliberately holding me back in life" (Morley 1997, 110). The invisibility of a class discourse, particularly in the United States, makes personal problems, like family "dysfunction," much more salient (Jensen 2004, 172). This salience means that dysfunction is *relatable*—it can be told as a convincing story that most people, including middle-class people, will understand. Furthermore, the studied linearity of these narratives mirrors the types of stories middle-class people tell about their own occupational choices and careers (Linde 1993, 129).

Interestingly, even though Renegades lack a discourse of class (in a political sense), they may be more likely to recognize (even overrecognize?) the existence of other structural barriers like racism. Indeed, John's story hints that Renegade strategies may be an immediately effective means of responding to racism ("the only way I can succeed is to become like them"). In Price's (2000) study, a young Black man named Jeff seems engaged in a very similar response: "If it takes me to change my culture, to change my speech, to get ahead in life, to get that big house with that white picket fence, I'm going to do it" (186).

How do we evaluate these stories of desired assimilation? We might call them "bad stories" if we measure them against a standard of political viability—if, that is, we are looking for organic intellectuals from the working class (Villanueva 1993). But they may also be "bad stories" from a nonpolitical, individual standpoint. Renegade stories fail to provide a convincing explanation for inequality, they lead the narrator to uproot him or herself (psychologically, emotionally, and physically), and they provide no basis for understanding future "failures." In other words, Renegades who succeed often lose their families in the process, and Renegades who fail (believe they) have only themselves to blame. This is exactly what comes through in accounts of other working-class academics. This is why Peckham (in Jensen 2004, 179) called the price of success "erasure."

This would not be true for Loyalists, however. Loyalists tell a fundamentally different story that is rooted in a systemic understanding of class oppression and its connections with race. Loyalists embrace a working-class identity as a matter of pride and political defiance. Theirs is a "good" story if measured for political viability, working-class solidarity, and individual cohesion, although it is arguably a tough story to maintain in the light of the dominant ideology of social mobility and American classlessness. It is also a story unlikely to yield worldly success.

The Loyalist story requires a delicate balancing act—how do you stay true to your roots at the same time you are going to college, a recognized path of upward social mobility? How to reconcile the two? One way is to disentangle cultural values from occupation and class position. "My family, my friends who are poor, and my children and I are families of love and support. It is hunger and exhaustion and pain that I want to leave behind, not the people I treasure so much" (Mitchell 2003, 118). But how is this possible over time, and over generations? At some point, the educated working-class person either will have to face the fact that he or she has entered the middle class or will have had to willfully choose working-class jobs, in spite of educational credentials. A great deal of concern among working-class academics today is the disconnect their children feel from the working class. In some ways, then, the Loyalist story may only be a postponement of a larger political question. Namely, what side are you on in the class struggle? And where does the middle class fit in? Historically, members of the middle class have been supportive agents of capital. But this need not be true. There is no reason that the more privileged cadre of workers we call the middle class cannot align with the working class. So here is the second option for working-class college students. Loyalist stories may be the beginning of this realignment.

What needs to be recognized by educators, theorists, and policymakers is the dilemma success poses for some working-class students. Not only are they in danger of becoming alienated from their roots but they must also deal with the possibility of being perceived as "tokenistic proof of meritocracy" (Reay 1997, 25) and the American Dream, the fact that their academic success "serves to underscore the unworthiness of those who fail" (Reay 1997, 25). On the other hand, there is potential for radical realignments. If Loyalists can succeed academically and socially, and at the same time continue to tell stories that enact working-class identities and politics, academia itself has the potential to be transformed from a training ground for capital's agents to a true "practice of freedom" (hooks 1994).

Listening to the different accounts working-class people tell of their experiences in and reactions to college and the promise of upward social mobility tells us a great deal about how the trope of meritocracy functions in our society as well as how class continues to matter. The different accounts mark out the importance of stories and meaning-making to the project of class formation and reconstruction. They show us that working-class people are under great pressure to assimilate in order to succeed, and that this assimilation in practice means conforming to certain bourgeois cultural norms, behaviors, and expectations, as well as "leaving behind" those who do not share these norms, behaviors, and expectations. Assimilation also requires a particular kind of story, one in which the working class is vilified as a dysfunctional other and education is understood as a path *out* of one's original class location. Poverty and class inequality generally are then justified as the results of a properly functioning meritocratic system, whereby all those with the "right stuff" (right values, right commitment to hard work and planning for the future, right level of intelligence) get ahead and those without do not. Those who do not get ahead have only themselves to blame and should be properly ashamed. This is the dominant story told of those who "pulled themselves up by their bootstraps." If it sounds uncharitable, it is. Retelling this story to explain their own lives and those of their families, as Renegades do, is an act of internalized classism. But we should not fault those who tell this story. It is hard to resist, it is everywhere, it is in every aspirational poster proclaiming "anyone can be president!" and every exhortation to "not be a dummy; stay in school!" It is in every show depicting the "ignorant redneck," every story of the "welfare queen," every "rags to riches" film about the kid who made it out of the ghetto. It is our American story. Generally, we do not pause to look at what effect this story has on those who get left behind. Listening to Renegade accounts gives us a good glimpse of the psychic costs of this story.

Against the weight of this cultural juggernaut we call the story of the American Dream, there is an alternative story being told. Loyalist accounts also acknowledge the call to assimilation, but they strenuously reject it. Their stories describe the obstacles placed in the way of poor people and people of color. Their stories celebrate working-class values of solidarity and acknowledge that the middle class does not have a monopoly on intelligence. Although educationally successful themselves, Loyalists resist the siren call of believing themselves somehow "special" and gifted, more intelligent, and thus more deserving of success than their families and communities. Instead, they describe themselves as lucky, the few that the system overlooked and who were let through. Along with this luck comes a special responsibility to those who were not so fortunate. In that spirit, I leave this chapter with the words spoken by Tillie Olsen (Edwards 1995, 357) to a first-generation Chicana professor who voiced regret over no longer being working class:

> You are the working class that your working-class parents fought into being, believed could be. To call education a privilege, to call development of self, of capacity—to call those the province of the middle class is a distortion of history. You are the first generation of your family to be able to claim this birthright. You have not left your family behind, you carry them with you. You are committed to the true potentiality of your students. You are doing your work serving and honoring the working class.

REFERENCES

Adair, Vivyan Campbell, and Sandra L. Dahlberg. 2003. *Reclaiming Class: Women, Poverty, and the Promise of Higher Education in America.* Philadelphia: Temple University Press.

Aries, Elizabeth. 2008. *Race and Class Matters at an Elite College.* Philadelphia: Temple University Press.

Armstrong, Elizabeth A., and Laura T. Hamilton. 2013, *Paying for the Party: How College Maintains Inequality.* Cambridge: Harvard University Press.

Bathmaker, Ann-Marie, Nicola Ingram, Jessie Abrahams, Anthony Hoare, Richard Waller, and Harriet Bradley. 2016. *Higher Education, Social Class and Social Mobility: The Degree Generation.* London: Palgrave Macmillan.

Bettie, Julie. 2003. *Women without Class: Girls, Race, and Identity.* Berkeley: University of California Press.

Bradley, Harriet, and Nicola Ingram. 2012. "Banking on the Future: Choices, Aspirations and Economic Hardship in Working-Class Student Experience." In *Class Inequality in Austerity Britain: Power, Difference and Suffering*, edited by Will Atkinson, Steven Roberts, and Mike Savage, 51–69. London: Palgrave Macmillan.

Brantlinger, Ellen A. 1993. *The Politics of Social Class in Secondary School: Views of Affluent and Impoverished Youth.* New York: Teachers College Press, Columbia University.

Chute, Carolyn. 2001. "Faces in the Hands." In *What We Hold in Common*, edited by J. Zandy, 34–36. New York: Feminist Press.

Dahlberg, Sandra L. 2003. "Families First—but Not in Higher Education: Poor, Independent Students and the Impact of Financial Aid." In *Reclaiming Class*, edited by V. C. Adair and S. L. Dahlberg, 169–195. Philadelphia: Temple University Press.

de Ridder-Symoens, Hilde. 1992. *A History of the University in Europe.* Cambridge, UK: Cambridge University Press.

Dews, C. L. Barney, and Carolyn Leste Law. 1995. *This Fine Place So Far from Home: Voices of Academics from the Working Class.* Philadelphia: Temple University Press.

Edwards, Julie Olson. 1995. "Class Notes from the Lecture Hall." In *Liberating Memory*, edited by J. Zandy, 338–358. New Brunswick, NJ: Rutgers University Press.

Everhart, Robert B. 1983. *Reading, Writing, and Resistance: Adolescence and Labor in a Junior High School.* Boston: Routledge & Kegan Paul.

Ferguson, Ann Arnett. 2000. *Bad Boys: Public Schools in the Making of Black Masculinity.* Ann Arbor: University of Michigan Press.

Fordham, Signithia. 1996. *Blacked Out: Dilemmas of Race, Identity, and Success at Capital High.* Chicago: University of Chicago Press.

Fordham, Signithia, and John U. Ogbu. 1986. "Black Students' School Success: Coping with the 'Burden of "Acting White."'" *The Urban Review* 18: 176–206.

Grimes, Michael D., and Joan Morris, eds. 1997. *Caught in the Middle: Contradictions in the Lives of Sociologists from Working-Class Backgrounds.* Westport, CT: Praeger Press.

hooks, bell. 1994. *Teaching to Transgress: Education as the Practice of Freedom*. New York: Routledge.

Hurst, Allison L. 2010. *The Burden of Academic Success: Managing Working-Class Identities in College*. Lanham, MD: Lexington Books.

Hurst, Allison L., and Sandi Kawecka Nenga, eds. 2016. *Working in Class: Recognizing How Social Class Shapes our Academic Work*. Lanham, MD: Rowman & Littlefield.

Ingram, Nicola, and Jessie Abrahams. 2016. "Stepping Outside of Oneself: How a Cleft-Habitus Can Lead to Greater Reflexivity Through Occupying 'The Third Space.'" In *Bourdieu: The Next Generation*, edited by Jenny Thatcher, Nicola Ingram, Ciaran Burke, and Jessie Abrahams, 140–156. London: Routledge, Taylor & Francis Group.

Jackson, Brian, and Dennis Marsden. 1962. *Education and the Working Class; Some General Themes Raised by a Study of 88 Working-Class Children in a Northern Industrial City*. London: Routledge & Kegan Paul.

Jensen, Barbara. 2004. "Across the Great Divide: Crossing Classes and Clashing Cultures." In *What's Class Got to Do with It?* edited by M. Zweig, 168–184. Ithaca: Cornell University Press.

Jensen, Barbara. 2012. *Reading Classes: On Culture and Classism in America*. Ithaca: Cornell University Press.

Lee, Elizabeth M., and Chaise LaDousa. 2015. *College Students' Experiences of Power and Marginality: Sharing Spaces and Negotiating Differences*. New York: Routledge.

Linde, Charlotte. 1993. *Life Stories: The Creation of Coherence*. New York: Oxford University Press.

Mahony, Pat, and Christine Zmroczek. 1997. *Class Matters: Working-Class Women's Perspectives on Social Class*. London: Taylor & Francis

Matthys, Mick. 2013. *Cultural Capital Identity and Social Mobility: The Life Course of Working-Class University Graduates*. New York: Routledge.

Morley, Louisa. 1997. "A Class of One's Own: Women, Social Class, and the Academy." In *Class Matters: Working-Class Women's Perspectives on Social Class*, edited by P. Mahony and C. Zmroczek, 109–122. Bristol, PA: Taylor & Francis.

Mullen, Ann L. 2011. *Degrees of Inequality: Culture, Class, and Gender in American Higher Education*. Baltimore: Johns Hopkins University Press.

Ogbu, John U. 1974. *The Next Generation: An Ethnography of Education in an Urban Neighborhood*. New York: Academic Press.

Ogbu, John U. 1978. *Minority Education and Caste: The American System in Cross-Cultural Perspective*. New York: Academic Press.

Ogbu, John U. 1986. "Stockton, California, Revisited: Joining the Labor Force." In *Becoming a Worker*, edited by L. Valli, 29–56. Norwood: ABLEX Publishing Corp.

Ogbu, John U. 2003. *Black American Students in an Affluent Suburb: A Study of Academic Disengagement*. Mahwah, NJ: L. Erlbaum Associates.

Oldfield, Kenneth, and Richard Gregory Johnson III. 2008. *Resilience: Queer Professors from the Working Class*. Albany: SUNY Press.

Rashdall, Hastings, ed. 1958. *The Universities of Europe in the Middle Ages*. Cambridge: Cambridge University Press.

Reay, Diane. 1997. "The Double-Bind of the 'Working-Class' Feminist Academic: The Success of Failure or the Failure of Success?" In *Class Matters: Working-Class Women's Perspectives on Social Class,* edited by Pat Mahony and Christine Zmroczek, 18–29. London: Taylor & Francis.

Reay, Diane. 2016. "'We never get a fair chance' Working-Class Experiences of Education in the Twenty-First Century." In *Class Inequality in Austerity Britain: Power, Difference and Suffering,* edited by Will Atkinson, Steven Roberts, and Mike Savage, 33–50. London: Palgrave Macmillan.

Rose, Mike. 1989. *Lives on the Boundary: The Struggles and Achievements of America's Underprepared*. New York: Free Press, Collier Macmillan Publishers.

Ryan, Jake, and Charles Sackrey. 1984. *Strangers in Paradise: Academics from the Working Class*. Boston: South End Press.

Samarco, C. Vincent, and Stephen L. Muzzatti. 2005. *Reflections from the Wrong Side of the Tracks: Class Identity and the Working Class Experience in Academe*. Lanham, MD: Rowman & Littlefield.

Solomon, Rovell Patrick. 1992. *Black Resistance in High School: Forging a Separatist Culture*. Albany: State University of New York Press.

Stich, Amy, and Carrie Freie, eds. 2015. *The Working Classes and Higher Education: Inequality of Access, Opportunity and Outcome*. New York: Routledge.

Stone, Lawrence. 1974. *The University in Society*. Oxford: Oxford University Press.

Stuber, Jenny M. 2012. *Inside the College Gates: How Class and Culture Matter in Higher Education*. Lanham, MD: Lexington Books.

Thatcher, Jenny, Nicola Ingram, Ciaran Burke, and Jessie Abrahams. 2016. *Bourdieu: The Next Generation: The Development of Bourdieu's Intellectual Heritage in Contemporary UK Sociology*. London: Routledge, Taylor & Francis Group.

Tokarczyk, Michelle M., and Elizabeth A. Fay. 1993. *Working-Class Women in the Academy: Laborers in the Knowledge Factory*. Amherst: University of Massachusetts Press.

Valenzuela, Angela. 1999. *Subtractive Schooling: US-Mexican Youth and the Politics of Caring*. Albany: State University of New York Press.

Villanueva, Victor. 1993. *Bootstraps: from an American Academic of Color*. Urbana, IL: National Council of Teachers of English.

Welsch, Kathleen A. 2005. *Those Winter Sundays: Female Academics and their Working-Class Parents*. Lanham, MD: University Press of America.

Willis, Paul E. 1977. *Learning to Labour: How Working Class Kids Get Working Class Jobs*. Farnborough, England: Saxon House.

Zandy, Janet. 1995. *Liberating Memory: Our Work and our Working-Class Consciousness*. New Brunswick, NJ: Rutgers University Press.

NOTES

1. This chapter has been reprinted from *The Burden of Academic Success* (2010), permissions granted by Rowman & Littlefield Publishing. Substantial revisions have been made to clarify and shorten the original text.

I use working-class purposefully here, for both intellectual and political reasons. The students I interviewed were the children of adults with working-class jobs, defined as primarily manual/service, without autonomy, with pay below the national average (at the time $35,000 per year), and not requiring a college degree. In reality, all but one were also first-generation (one had a mother who had earned a BA from a local college and was currently working a manual labor job), and most were low-income. Although "first-generation," "working-class," and "low-income" do not always equate, there are large overlaps among these students in colleges, and my study was no different in that regard.

5

Seeking Out Support

Looking Beyond Socioeconomic Status to Explain Academic Engagement Strategies at an Elite College

Anthony Abraham Jack and Véronique Irwin

The old saying goes, "It's not just what you know. It's who you know." Social science research aligns with folk knowledge (Granovetter 1973; Zweigenhaft 1993). Availing oneself of relationships with those in positions of authority or power, however, does not come easily to everyone (Lareau 2003). In academic arenas, this process is particularly important (Calarco 2011; Holland 2015; Stanton-Salazar and Dornbusch 1995; Tinto 1987). Relationships with teachers and faculty affect youth's access to institutional resources, which can enhance not only their academic experiences but also their mobility prospects thereafter (Calarco 2014; Crosnoe, Johnson, and Elder 2004; Erickson, McDonald, and Elder 2009; Rivera 2015; Stanton-Salazar 1997; Stuber 2011; McDonough 1997; Holland 2015). Scholars argue that compared to undergraduates from working-class families, many of whom are first-generation college students, those from middle-class backgrounds are rewarded by colleges and universities as these institutions privilege a narrow set of orientations, styles, and skillsets that those from privileged backgrounds are more likely to bring with them to college (Armstrong and Hamilton 2013; Bergerson 2007; Stephens, Fryberg, et al. 2012; Stuber 2009; Torres 2009; Walpole 2003).

Answering the call by Lareau and Weininger (2003, 569) for research on culture and inequality to focus on "micro-interaction processes whereby individuals' strategic use of knowledge, skills, and competence come into contact with institutional standards of evaluation," this chapter explores the "experiential core of college life," the overlooked moments between college entry and exit when students employ different cultural competencies to navigate relationships with peers and professors as well as the larger college culture (Lamont, Beljean, and Clair 2014; Stevens 2008; Stevens, Armstrong, and Arum 2008, 131). Previous investigations that connect familial class origins with strategies for engaging college officials treat these behavioral patterns as essentially set by the time youth enter college. These studies, however, downplay how student experiences in academic institutions prior to college shape their approaches to life therein. Consequently, extant research on first-generation college students affords insufficient attention to the influence of interactions outside the family on individuals' cultural endowments (Jack 2014). We fill this gap by examining how lower-income, Black undergraduates with disparate precollege experiences—principally during high school—adopt different orientations and strategies toward help-seeking and engaging with college officials. In so doing, we show that class origins alone are inadequate to explain the cultural competencies of undergraduates entering elite postsecondary education.

Ascribing appropriate gravity to this heterogeneity of precollege experiences is critical to understanding how precollege exposure to poverty, segregation, and other structural inequalities may contribute to the uneven accumulation of cultural and social capital in college (Massey et al. 2003; Charles et al. 2009), which has implications for mobility after college (Stuber 2011; Rivera 2015). We examine the disparate college experiences of two groups of Black lower-income undergraduates who share similar social origins but travel different paths to college: the *Doubly Disadvantaged*, lower-income students who enter college from local, typically distressed public high schools, and the *Privileged Poor*, lower-income students who come from similarly impoverished communities but attend boarding, day, and preparatory high schools through pipeline programs like A Better Chance or scholarship initiatives at private schools aimed at increasing diversity.[1]

We document variation in the engagement strategies of lower-income, first-generation Black undergraduates and show how their precollege experiences shape these interactional skills and preferences. We show that the Privileged Poor enter college with cultural resources and skills akin to those of their Black peers from middle-class backgrounds. The Privileged Poor report being more comfortable forming close relationships with faculty and college officials. Additionally, they view such interactions as integral to a successful Midtown experience. By contrast, the Doubly Disadvantaged generally report withdrawing from college officials and feeling uncomfortable when prompted to engage. Consequently, the Privileged Poor potentially secure greater benefits than the Doubly Disadvantaged in college due to the relatively high alignment between their preferred modes of interaction and implicit expectations about how to engage college officials.

To understand the experiences and address the needs of first-generation college students, it is important to study the gamut of their experiences. One approach to accomplishing this breadth would be to study first-generation students with similar secondary experiences as they navigate different kinds of postsecondary contexts. This chapter takes the converse approach and contributes to a nuanced understanding of first-generation college experiences by studying students in a single institutional context, but who arrived there through disparate trajectories. We conclude with implications and questions for policies and practice.

CULTURE AND ACADEMIC INTEGRATION

Different engagement strategies lead to unequal returns. Engagement with adults in academic settings (e.g., teachers, professors)—a dominant form of cultural capital—provides a mechanism through which youth gain access to valuable resources like mentoring, referrals, and recommendation letters, which affect students' academic and social standing (Calarco 2011; Stanton-Salazar and Dornbusch 1995; Kim and Sax 2009; Pascarella and Terenzini 2005; Holland 2015; Gast 2016). Moreover, unequal access to institutional supports also affects post-graduation mobility (Rivera 2015; Stuber 2011; see also Binder, Davis, and Bloom 2015). Some students feel comfortable answering the social mandate to proactively engage faculty inside and outside of class, while others experience increased anxiety when forced to interact with authority figures.

Scholars argue that this process is highly classed. Building on the social reproduction framework put forth by Bourdieu (1984, 1986), scholars focus on how parents impart cultural resources to their children, especially how to navigate mainstream institutions and how to engage authority (Lareau and Weininger 2003). Scholars argue that given their higher levels of education, greater access to resources, and varied experiences navigating mainstream institutions themselves, middle-class families teach their children to be more self-directed, confident when engaging adults, and willing to advocate for themselves (Calarco 2014; Lareau 2003; Streib 2011). They also argue that such a classed disposition, or *habitus*, persists into adulthood (Lareau and Weininger 2003; Lee and Kramer 2013; Lehmann 2014). Consequently, by the time children enter college—an environment where they are expected to proactively engage faculty without explicit rules telling them when or how they should do so (Collier and Morgan 2008; Stephens, Fryberg, et al. 2012)—youth from middle-class families are disproportionately more likely to be rewarded than their working-class and poor counterparts, who tend not to adopt such behaviors (Armstrong and Hamilton 2013; Kim and Sax 2009; Stephens, Townsend, et al. 2012).

Examining the pathways through which social class shapes behavior later in life is important, but present investigations focus too narrowly on primary socialization—the preferences and interactional styles that parents instill in their children when they are young. As Erikson (1996, 222) argues, however, the Bourdieusian understanding of class transmission "overestimates the lifelong influence of parents' class" (see also Jack 2014; Lamont and Lareau 1988; DiMaggio 1982; Kisida, Greene, and Bowen 2014). As children age, the primacy of familial influences wanes to a host of ecological factors found in children's neighborhoods and schools (Furstenberg 2007; Stephens, Markus, and Phillips 2013; Young 1999; see also Bronfenbrenner 1993). To fully understand how inequality shapes students' integration into college, we must acknowledge how these precollege institutions and environments shape the development of their stocks of cultural capital (Markus and Hamedani 2007; Massey et al. 2003). To account for these extrafamilial influences, we give ample attention to how immersion and orienting experiences in different milieus shape students' integration strategies once they arrive in college, especially for youth from similarly disadvantaged socioeconomic backgrounds.

The Path Less Studied

Access to valued cultural resources—orientations and skills that enable youth to successfully navigate mainstream institutions—does not fall evenly across the populace (Putnam 2015; Stephens, Markus, and Phillips 2013). In addition to having more formally-educated parents, youth from middle-class backgrounds have greater access to safer neighborhoods and higher-resourced schools (Calarco 2011; Cookson and Persell 1985; Lareau 2003; Logan, Minca, and Adar 2012; Massey 1996; McDonough 1997). In contrast, youth from disadvantaged families are more likely to reside in troubled communities, attend underresourced schools, and are often the first in their families to attend college, limiting their access to specific advice about applying to, enrolling in, and navigating college (Kozol 1992; Massey et al. 2003; Pascarella and Terenzini 2005; Orfield et al. 1994; Perna et al. 2008). These differences are made even more stark for lower-income Black and Latino youth who are disproportionately more likely to attend hypersegregated or "apartheid" schools, both historically and today (Orfield, Kucsera, and Siegel-Hawley 2012; Reardon and Owens 2014; Massey and Denton 1993).

Undergraduates rely on skillsets that they develop before college—most immediately in high school, where youth craft their academic identities—to chart their paths through college (Tyson 2011; Nunn 2014). Newer research shows that in addition to the class-stratified path to college that separates middle-class youth from their working-class and poor counterparts, a significant minority of lower-income undergraduates at elite colleges are alumni of boarding, day, and preparatory high schools (Jack 2015a, 2016). Through academic pipeline programs like A Better Chance and Prep for Prep that place students in boarding, day, and preparatory schools as well as through scholarship initiatives at individual private schools (Cox 2017; Zweigenhaft and Domhoff 1991), the Privileged Poor enter private high schools, where independent thought and close contact with teachers is encouraged (Gaztambide-Fernandez 2009; Kane 1992; Khan 2011). In contrast, the Doubly Disadvantaged share similar social origins but attend their local public high schools. In these schools, close contact with faculty is not always encouraged or even possible, as many teachers must focus on maintaining order rather than encouraging independent thought (Kozol 2005; Paulle 2013; Ryan 2010).[2] The shared beginning but divergent path to college between the Doubly Disadvantaged and the Privileged Poor—and the disparate experiences they have along the way—leads them to adopt different strategies of action in college (Swidler 1986; Jack 2016).

We contend that the divergent precollege experiences between the Doubly Disadvantaged and Privileged Poor account for the greatest differences among lower-income undergraduates (Jack 2014). Thus, rather than comparing first-generation to non-first-generation lower-income students, we focus on differences in engagement with faculty *among* lower-income students. Both the Doubly Disadvantaged and Privileged Poor in the full interview sample are overwhelmingly first-generation college students.[3] In the qualitative data reported here from lower-income students, we draw exclusively from those who are the first in their family to attend college. By showing that variation exists in orientations toward and strategies for engaging faculty within this apparently homogenous group of "students at risk" (Terenzini et al. 1996), we draw attention to the importance of examining youth's trajectory to college.

DATA AND METHODS

The People

We draw on thirty-five semi-structured, in-depth interviews with native-born, Black undergraduates who were enrolled full-time at Midtown College. We limited the study to native-born undergraduates to highlight how structural inequalities in the United States shape students' paths to college and their experiences therein. We specifically examined the everyday experiences of Black undergraduates because they are exposed to higher levels of segregation, poverty, crime/violence, and other social dislocations in both their neighborhoods and schools over the life course than other racial groups in the United States (Massey et al. 2003; Charles, Dinwiddie, and Massey

2004; Sampson and Wilson 1995) The majority of students in our sample come from large urban areas. This is not to say that students from rural communities do not aspire to attend colleges like Midtown or that the needs of rural students are not equally important in establishing an elite college environment that is conducive to the success of all students.

One author, who is Black, recruited participants by email and snowball sampling. The email lists of the Black Student Association and the Black Cultural House at Midtown College, which has the contact information for currently and formerly active undergraduates, served as initial points of recruitment. He conducted all but two interviews on campus in meeting rooms in the campus library. Two students opted for interviews off campus because it fit their schedules better. One was at a local eatery and the other was in an office. Eleven students are from middle-class families (MC), defined as having college-educated parents with professional careers. Twenty-four are from lower-income backgrounds, defined as either having non-degree-holding parents with nonprofessional careers or receiving significant financial aid (> $40,000).[4] Many lower-income students discussed receiving Section 8, food stamps, and other forms of government assistance before coming to Midtown. Additionally, while all but one middle-class student came from two-parent homes, lower-income students disproportionately came from single-parent households.

Ten Doubly Disadvantaged and fourteen Privileged Poor constitute the full lower-income sample. Importantly, students were not sampled based on the type of high school they attended. Rather, students were recruited based on race (identified as Black or African American) and attendance at Midtown. Doubly Disadvantaged and Privileged Poor emerged inductively as analytical concepts from the data and are used to capture lower-income students' divergent precollege and college experiences (Charmaz 2006).

The interview guide was divided into two sections. The first component of the interview guide followed a targeted life history approach to investigate students' depictions of and experiences in their homes, neighborhoods, and schools, as well as their participation in precollege enrichment and pipeline organizations such as Questbridge and A Better Chance (see Young 1999). For example, questions aimed at understanding students' trajectories to college included directed prompts like "How was your family involved in your education?" and questions that prompted comparisons, like "How would you compare your high school to Midtown?" The second component of the interview guide focused on academic and social life at Midtown. Questions explored students' transition to college, sense of belonging, and day-to-day interactions with peers, professors, and the larger college community. For example, the questions focused on daily life included "To what extent do you agree with this statement: I feel that I fit in well with the college environment" and "What has been the most important to you at Midtown?" Questions were purposefully general and open-ended to permit students to discuss their modal experiences as they acclimated to social and academic life at Midtown without predetermining what specific responses were important, which could then be probed with follow-up questions (see Hirsch and Jack 2012 for a similar methodology).

For this analysis, we draw on data specifically from moments when students reflected on their engagement with faculty and college officials. The experiences of undergraduates from middle-class backgrounds serve as a theoretical yardstick to highlight how the divergent path to college between the Doubly Disadvantaged and the Privileged Poor influences their integration into college. Comparing both groups to this yardstick brings renewed attention to the varied ways precollege experiences shape academic and social life therein. Furthermore, this two-way comparison not only deepens our understanding of the social processes that shape the reproduction of inequality in college, but also provides opportunities to think about different aspects of the college experience in which engagement matters, both for social and academic well-being in college and for mobility upon graduation.

We used the qualitative data analysis software ATLAS.ti to tag segments of transcript where students discuss engagement with faculty and college officials. This allowed for comparisons across and within groups. Each interview was coded by one author and a research assistant. Additionally, one author and a research assistant read each transcript in its entirety to assess students' general behavior towards engaging adults and comfort in elite academic environments over the life course and in college as well as their sense of belonging at Midtown more generally. Interviews lasted, on average, 1.5 hours and were recorded with a digital recorder and later transcribed verbatim.

The Place

Midtown is a highly ranked, academically rigorous, private college in the United States with a long history of educating youth from wealthy, White families. More than half the undergraduates at Midtown identify as White, and more than 40 percent of those who matriculate do not qualify for any need-based financial aid. Midtown is highly competitive: the college accepts less than 15 percent of applicants, and of those admitted, the middle 50 percent of admits' SAT scores are between 2250 and 2350. Demographically, Black undergraduates make up roughly 10 percent of the undergraduate student body.[5]

In addition to its elite status within the larger ecology of colleges, Midtown expanded its financial aid initiatives to support lower-income admits and actively engages in aggressive outreach and recruitment efforts. As a result, nearly 20 percent of Midtown undergraduates are Pell-eligible. An equal share of the students is the first in their families to attend college. Such policies at Midtown and similar institutions opened these bastions of privilege to an increasing number of students who traditionally have been excluded because of an inability and/or reluctance to pay their lofty tuition prices (Avery et al. 2006; Karabel 2005; Jack 2015b; Hillman 2013). Although fewer undergraduates attend small, elite colleges than large public universities, attendance at elite colleges increases chances of retention, graduation, and upward mobility more than other institutions, especially for lower-income and minority undergraduates (Bowen and Bok 1998; Carnevale and Strohl 2010; Small and Winship 2007; see also Brand and Xie 2010; Brewer, Eide, and Ehrenberg 1999). Furthermore, such financial aid policies lower the need for undergraduates from economically disadvantaged backgrounds to seek off-campus and/or full-time employment, both of which are associated with academic and social disengagement in college (Bergerson 2007; Pascarella and Terenzini 2005; Phinney and Haas 2003). Lastly, Midtown is almost exclusively residential, which places campus life and students' acclimation to the cultural norms that dominate it front and center.

FINDINGS

Privileged Poor and Doubly Disadvantaged: Demographics and Discernable Differences

Before examining how undergraduates integrate into academic life, we provide a demographic snapshot of native-born, lower-income undergraduates at Midtown to show how prevalent poor students from private school are among them.[6] Using administrative data from Midtown from 2003 to 2009, we show that, on average, 50 percent of lower-income Black undergraduates at Midtown graduated from private high schools (figure 5.1). This private school pathway, however, is not limited to Black students. The Privileged Poor, for example, constitute, on average, 36 percent of lower-income Latinos, 29 percent of lower-income Whites, and 11 percent of lower-income Asians at Midtown across this seven-year period.[7]

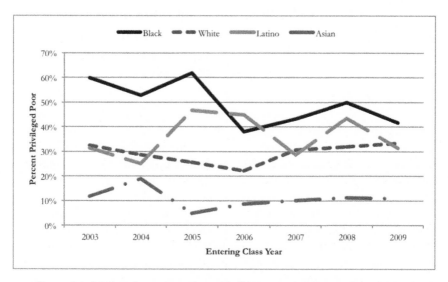

Figure 5.1. Privileged poor at Midtown College, entering classes of 2003–2009.

Beyond the numbers, undergraduates at Midtown are keenly aware of differences among them, and they connect these differences to their pathways to college. Walking around campus, Marilyn (DD), a first-generation college student from a single-parent home, recalls pointing at her lower-income peers and saying, "You went to a prep school. You went to Prep for Prep." She continues, "A bunch of kids have that established foundation with Midtown. But me, it was a draw. I'm the only person from my school to go here." In addition to attributing her admission to Midtown to luck, Marilyn experienced a heightened sense of difference from her peers and isolated herself from both professors and the larger college community throughout college and up until graduation. By contrast, Sahara (PP), who was also brought up by her mother who did not go to college and who made ends meet while receiving government aid, was ready for Midtown, especially when comparing herself to lower-income peers. "Coming to Midtown, I feel pretty prepared," she began. "Even academic-wise, I felt . . . I just wasn't fazed by a lot of things, whereas some of my other friends who didn't go to prep schools had issues." Rather than sharing similar perspectives about college due to their similar social origins, as social reproduction theory would predict, Marilyn and Sahara differentiated themselves and their college experiences on the basis of their exposure to elite academic settings prior to enrolling at Midtown.

Daily Life at Midtown College: Engaging with College Officials

Before turning to discussing implications of the findings, we outline in this section how middle-class students, the Doubly Disadvantaged, and the Privileged Poor report engaging with faculty in college.

Middle-Class Students

Students from middle-class families highlight continuities between their lives before college and what they faced at Midtown. Such similarities, they assert, bolstered their sense of belonging and prompted them to integrate into the life of the college. Describing her transition to Midtown as "very easy," having long been "used to living in a dorm, sharing showers" at both her posh, private Northeast middle and high schools, where multiday trips were part of the curriculum, Claire (MC) feels particularly fortunate to be at Midtown, stressing "the genuine concern that I feel teachers in my major have for their students. They have high expectations; it encourages me to work hard." Tellingly, she continues to say that she values how these expectations exist "inside and outside of school." Smiling, Regina (MC) calls Midtown the "next step" from high school before offering that she really values "the professor-student relationships that you're able to form here" because they are "really unique." In fact, when prompted to reflect on the most important aspects of being a student at Midtown, she immediately identified the relationships she has built with advisors.

Some middle-class students develop relationships with faculty that extend beyond material covered in the classroom. In almost comedic fashion, Adam (MC), a legacy student whose parents are lawyers, recounts an interaction in one of his math classes during his freshman year that subsequently developed into a great relationship with the professor. On what seemed like just another day, Adam wore a shirt that read "Make Tea Not War." Upon entering the class, the professor, noticing his shirt, stopped by Adam's desk, asking, "Do you like tea?" Adam replied "sure," thinking of his shirt more as a piece of clothing than a culinary or political statement. From that day forward, Adam recalls with a smile, the professor brought two cups of tea to class, one for himself and one for Adam. After a semester of early morning conversations over tea and right before administering the final exam, the professor offered the mug in which he had been bringing the daily tea—gift-wrapped with a personalized note—to Adam as a parting gift. Chuckling, Adam admits that he did not do terribly well in the course (or as well as he would have liked to do). Yet in the same breath, he speaks of the encounters positively and recalls vowing to nurture that tie throughout his time at Midtown. For Adam,

Midtown presents opportunities for informal yet still personal mentoring and support for his future endeavors both in college and beyond.

In addition to outlining how the relationship formed, this example showcases the ease with which Adam engaged adults and how receptive he was to informal interactions with his professor. Like Claire and Regina, and his other middle-class peers, Adam saw connecting with faculty as part of college life. The more personal nature of those connections—a hallmark of a liberal arts education at a small college—did not make him uneasy. In fact, this style of engagement made Adam feel at home as a freshman. In line with extant literature, students from middle-class backgrounds at Midtown generally enter college ready and willing to engage authority figures, which matches what is expected and rewarded by elite academic institutions. Middle-class students typically hit the ground running when they arrive at Midtown and work to take full advantage of relationships with authority figures.

Doubly Disadvantaged Students

Most of the Doubly Disadvantaged frame the expected norms of academic engagement at Midtown as stressful or anxiety-inducing and generally report withdrawing from interactions with professors and other college officials.[8] Unlike their middle-class peers, the Doubly Disadvantaged typically do not feel at home at Midtown and they describe being uneasy adjusting to college life. Midtown is so different and alienating for Robin (DD), who attended a socioeconomically and racially segregated high school where academics were not stressed, that she equates going home to lifting a "weight off my shoulders. I can be me; I don't have to worry about acting in a certain way." Instead of embracing informal personal relationships with faculty like the one Adam (MC) describes, Amy (DD), who grew up in a lower-income Black community with her single mother and attended large, public schools where poor Blacks were overrepresented among the student body, finds such interactions "too touchy-feely." She says,

> I feel like no one needs to know about my private life. Alright, if I have a personal relationship with you and we see eye to eye and we are on an even playing field. . . . I feel that way with my peers. I'll tell them things. I don't feel that way about any outside person who I'm not on an even playing field with. When you deal with faculty and administrators, I'm down here and you're up here. I feel like they don't keep their distance, their professional distance.

Amy draws boundaries between herself and college officials. She prefers for personal relationships to be between herself and those she sees as equals, her peers, and not those she sees as authorities. The intimate advisory relationships that small liberal arts colleges pride themselves on are not only foreign to her; they are also undesirable and off-putting.

Like Robin (DD), many Doubly Disadvantaged students report having rough transitions to Midtown, both socially and academically. Rose (DD) lamented how her high school, where resources were severely limited and teachers focused on maintaining order as gang disputes and prostitution disrupted academic life, could not prepare her for what she encountered at Midtown. From the demographics of her classmates to the expected style of faculty engagement, Midtown was beyond what her community could expose her to. When asked about interacting with faculty at Midtown, Rose says she limits her engagement because she always leaves the conversations feeling unsatisfied.

> They're not really. . . . I don't want to say sympathetic because that's not really what's needed. They're not understanding of what kids from [disadvantaged] backgrounds need. One administrator in particular here, any time a minority— whether it's a socioeconomic minority or a racial—any time they have a hard problem with their education or what professors expect of us, the first thing [she] tells us is, "Oh, maybe you should leave." Weird thing, it's like, I thought you guys were here to teach me something. I was supposed to learn from this and every time there's a bump in the road the question is, "Maybe you should leave." That goes against what the diversity thing was trying to do for Midtown. It's essentially assimilate and become like these rich kids or get out. That defeats the purpose. What's diversity if everybody's the same?

For Rose, engaging college officials at Midtown—something she intimates is a common experience among her peers—increases her anxiety rather than alleviates it. She feels that administrators are not prepared to deal with the issues faced by undergraduates like her, from underprivileged backgrounds. Moreover, she laments how such issues are brushed to the side or how quickly college officials offer voluntary withdrawal as a solution to their problems.

Together, Amy's and Rose's testimonies suggest that the Doubly Disadvantaged find themselves between a rock and an uncomfortable place. On the one hand, the more personable nature of many informal relationships, particularly between students and faculty, makes many students uneasy (the uncomfortable place); on the other, students' interactions with university personnel can be outright callous or unhelpful (the rock). Perhaps fearing such treatment, many students seek no help at all (Jack 2016). For example, Steven (DD), who also feels that Midtown mishandles the diversity it proclaims to invest in, elected not to seek help from his professor or the math center on campus when he was struggling in his freshman psychology course. He recalled how he eventually "gave up," especially after his professor told him,

"This isn't your thing." He explains, "I didn't like it, someone telling me I can't do something. I did give up at that point." This negative interaction reinforced his belief that the gap between himself and those at Midtown was real and insurmountable.

The Doubly Disadvantaged have a tendency to withdraw from faculty and other college officials. And they do so early on in their undergraduate careers. They are also more likely to report negative encounters with faculty. Unable to find the help that they want in a style they are accustomed to, and uncomfortable with the help Midtown tells them they need, the Doubly Disadvantaged may face a heightened risk of waiting too long to seek support or slipping through the cracks altogether.

Privileged Poor Students

By contrast, the Privileged Poor feel more at home at Midtown. They attribute their smooth transitions to years of navigating culturally, demographically, and structurally similar academic institutions. Like Doubly Disadvantaged students, Monica (PP) comes from a predominantly Black, lower-income neighborhood with a high unemployment rate and other problems that made walking around streets at night less than safe. Things changed in high school, however. A diversity scholarship program allowed her to attend one of the most elite, wealthiest private schools in the country, where many teachers had terminal degrees and class sizes were small. After calling her transition from her poor, segregated middle school to her private high school the biggest change in her life, she likened coming to Midtown to an academic and social "next step." Going further, she reports feeling supported by faculty and administration in all her endeavors at Midtown. For example, not one to sit idly by, Monica worked on different college committees with college deans and built strong ties with them through their work together. After serving on one committee, she was invited to continue the work by one of the deans at Midtown. These positive experiences prompt her to call Midtown "a place that can be very nurturing . . . a place that is very forgiving."

The Privileged Poor were introduced to much of what they saw at Midtown four to six years prior to their matriculation (Jack 2014). Accustomed in high school to close contact with teachers that extended beyond the classroom, Privileged Poor students generally are at ease with faculty and report being proactive in engaging with faculty at Midtown. In fact, Sarah (PP), who participated in a pipeline program, offered that Midtown and her high school "held the same values," especially small classes, to promote close "relationships with faculty." Office hours were one particular way students engaged faculty. When Veronica (PP) discussed office hours, she explained that she had been familiar with this process since the ninth grade. Her high school im-

pressed upon her that office hours were as much as part of her academic training as class time. In contrast to Steven (DD) who did not seek help when he
struggled academically, Veronica reported attending office hours frequently
for both academic and social matters. In fact, after her interview she ventured
across the commons to the science building for last-minute advice. Laughing,
she noted, "Actually, I have to go today for my test."

Sahara (PP) is similar in how proactive she is with respect to reaching out.
She attended a small boarding school where the student/teacher ratio was less
than ten to one and contact with faculty outside of class was high. Faculty
served as dorm parents, academic advisors, and coaches for teams and clubs.
After years of connecting with teachers in different roles and reaping the benefits, from earning summer internships to seeking guidance and recommendations for college, she focused on making connections with faculty beginning
when she arrived at Midtown. She reported feeling comfortable doing so,
especially as she saw so many parallels between the expected style of engagement with faculty at her boarding school and those at Midtown. Although
sometimes Sahara likes to just "chill," integrating herself into academic life
at Midtown is of paramount concern. She says,

> In terms of trying to be a part of Midtown and using it for what I can, I definitely
> get involved academically. Of course! I definitely go to classes but I make rela-
> tionships with teachers outside of class just so that those relationships are there
> if I ever needed them.

Sahara has no qualms with developing ties to professors that can be acti-
vated when she needs an introduction for an internship or a recommendation
letter for a job, let alone for help and extra time on assignments (extensions)
while enrolled in a class. She does not see it as opportunistic or shallow to
build relationships that may—or that are intended to—benefit her down the
line. The Privileged Poor see connecting with faculty as an important and
necessary part of their college education. More generally, like Sahara, their
orientation toward and approach to engagement more closely resembles those
of their middle-class counterparts than the Doubly Disadvantaged. They are
more at ease in interacting with faculty and college officials and are more
proactive in doing so.

DISCUSSION AND FUTURE DIRECTIONS

Proactive help-seeking and engagement with school and college officials
represent mechanisms through which students gain access to valuable
resources and institutional support, which influences both college life

and postbaccalaureate mobility (Calarco 2011; Collier and Morgan 2008; Stanton-Salazar and Dornbusch 1995; Stephens, Townsend, et al. 2012; Rivera 2015; Binder, Davis, and Bloom 2015). Extending previous theories of the relationship between social class and academic engagement, we provide evidence that it is not just family background that drives academic engagement behavior in college. Rather, it is important to examine how one's precollege experiences shape one's orientation toward college and the strategies undergraduates pursue inside college walls. We engage this line of inquiry specifically by focusing on the overlooked divergence in high school experiences among lower-income undergraduates. This approach is in line with recent research focusing on the accumulation of capital and the types of interactions or settings that provide youth with cultural resources outside of the family (Kisida, Greene, and Bowen 2014; see also DiMaggio 1982; Young 1999). However, it extends this research beyond cultural participation to focus on how immersion in and exposure to different social milieus affects youth's acquisition of capital.

The divergent and contrasting experiences between the Privileged Poor and Doubly Disadvantaged show how disparate precollege experiences have a lasting influence on students' cultural repertoires (Swidler 1986). Lower-income Black undergraduates who socialized in culturally, socially, and structurally similar academic settings before college feel confident engaging with college officials and report doing so earlier on and more often. Given colleges' bias towards helping those who make themselves known to officials (see Collier and Morgan 2008; Stephens, Fryberg, et al. 2012), these students may find more doors opened to them over the course of their college careers than their low-income, first-generation college student peers who enter college with less exposure to elite academic environments. Examining the social processes that undergird the hidden curriculum sheds new light on how inequality is reproduced in institutions of higher education (Anyon 1980; Smith 2013), especially as colleges increase access for those previously left outside of their gates (Jack 2015b; Hillman 2013).

Colleges must account for the cultural resources undergraduates bring with them to college (Armstrong and Hamilton 2013; Jack 2014; see also Nee and Sanders 2001). We highlight three possible arenas, of which there are likely many more, in which being uneasy with authority may hamper the outcomes of students during and after college. First, many fellowship, grant, and internship opportunities flow through employment or career service offices on college campus. Beyond general advertising and mailings, these offices typically wait for students to enter their doors, operating on the principle that if students need or want help they will ask for it (Collier and Morgan 2008). Such practices may limit the resources that reach the Doubly Disadvantaged. For example, elite universities place undergraduates in "elite" jobs like consulting and investment banking—a process facilitated by on-campus career offices (Binder, Davis, and Bloom 2015; Rivera 2015). Undergraduates who do not go to these offices or who go late for help with resumes or interview preparation may be left behind more than their proactive peers. Although few people would argue that elite colleges *should* funnel all students into consulting and finance careers, they are nevertheless extremely lucrative fields and may be an important realm for understanding the reproduction of income inequality.

Alternatively, it is conceivable that career services actually level the playing field *most* for high profile and/or lucrative careers in consulting and finance because these jobs are widely recruited and advertised on elite college campuses through these offices (Rivera 2015; Binder, Davis, and Bloom 2015). Therefore, even if students are unlikely to seek help with applications and interviews for these jobs, they at least know they *could*. More generally, given the prevalence of on-campus recruiting and interviews, access to career services helps with access to a host of career paths. If the Doubly Disadvantaged are already less likely to seek help on everyday matters like difficulties in their classes, we may presume that they are even less likely to seek specialized help that occurs in auxiliary university offices, and *especially* unlikely to seek help that is not well advertised (as with careers that are not heavily recruited). Because these students are also less likely to have made informal network connections in college that might help with job placement, this lack of alternative information may exacerbate inequality. Thus, understanding (1) how precollege experiences shape the utilization of career services as well as (2) the centrality of career services to success in various fields may be important for research concerning the degree of occupational stratification that is maintained by elite institutions between students who are accustomed to engaging with adults and advocating on their own behalf and students who are not.

Second, access to mental health resources is incredibly important, as depression, anxiety, and other mental health issues disrupt academic and social life (Eisenberg, Golberstein, and Gollust 2007; Stephens, Townsend, et al. 2012). Studies show that lower-income students have lower uptake than their middle-class peers. Consequently, they are less likely to get help and their problems tend to go untreated, often until there is a serious psychotic break or they are forced into treatment (Pescosolido, Gardner, and Lubell 1998). The present chapter offers no direct hypotheses as to how use of mental health services might differ between the Privileged Poor and Doubly Disadvantaged, if at all. It is reasonable to wonder, however, whether Amy's (DD) disdain for "touchy-feely" interactions with superiors and overall tendency to keep adults at arm's length might translate into a reluctance to seek mental health support from professionals. We must understand the cultural and social barriers to access that go beyond socioeconomic status (Cauce et al. 2002), especially for mental health practitioners on college campuses whose diversifying student bodies are facing a new set of academic and interpersonal challenges.

Finally, for students who are less likely to seek formal help within the institution, colleges must understand if and where advice *is* sought. The notion of college as isolated environments where, once within the gates, home and neighborhood problems cease to affect undergraduates is a false one. However, little research explores how parents of first-generation college students impart lessons about how to navigate college and how students must negotiate between mandates from home and expectations in college (Rondini 2016; Engle, Bermeo, and O'Brien 2006). For example, Jack (2016) showed that while the Privileged Poor focus on lessons learned about navigating relationships in elite spaces while in high school, the Doubly Disadvantaged referenced their parents' suggestions, even if those parental lessons contradicted what their college expected and/or required of them. Moreover, the Doubly Disadvantaged experienced heightened anxiety coming to terms with opposing directives because they felt like they were being pulled in different directions.

More research on how the families of lower-income undergraduates navigate the college transition process, beyond the moment when they drop their children off at college, is greatly needed. In particular, research should investigate (1) whether parental advice, or the manner in which parents offer advice, differs between the Privileged Poor and the Doubly Disadvantaged, and (2) how students' ability to navigate this advice impacts the strain of maintaining family ties as lower-income youth transition to adulthood. Due to their children's divergent experiences before college, lower-income parents may also be differentially prepared not only to face the college transition themselves but also to help their children through the process. Colleges can work to reduce the tension between family and school, especially for the Doubly Disadvantaged, by making explicit what is expected of students (Wang 2014; López et al. 2012; Vasquez-Salgado, Greenfield, and Burgos-Cienfuegos 2014). Without conveying or advocating a shift in values, this explicit communication might allow parents to better understand and support their children as they navigate this very specific social context.

CONCLUSION

College is tough. Academically, it is supposed to be. But many students face added roadblocks, especially first-generation college students. Unfortunately, the students who are most likely to arrive socially underprepared, the Doubly Disadvantaged, may also be the least likely to forge the important connections necessary to navigate the social side of academic life. This may strain their mental health, their relationships with family, and their mobility after college. On the one hand, elite institutions are designed to train students for continued participation in elite milieus after graduation, for which the confidence and ease of interaction with superiors is a valuable asset. On the other, elite institutions have added to this academic and career training the mission of increased diversity. In order to fulfill this mission, as some of our students have pointed out, colleges must recognize and value the wide range of interactional skills and preferences that students bring with them. This is a fine balance to strike. Understanding how students' interactional preferences and competencies are shaped throughout the entire precollege trajectory, rather than treating them as static class characteristics, should therefore be an important part of the research agenda to close the achievement and persistence gaps for first-generation students and to inform policies that can lead to their greater integration into the academic and social community at their colleges.

REFERENCES

Anderson, Elijah. 1999. *Code of the Street: Decency, Violence, and the Moral Life of the Inner City*. W. W. Norton & Company.

Anyon, Jean. 1980. "Social Class and the Hidden Curriculum of Work." *Journal of Education* 162, no. 1: 67–92.

Armstrong, Elizabeth, and Laura Hamilton. 2013. *Paying for the Party: How College Maintains Inequality*. Harvard University Press.

Avery, Christopher, Caroline Hoxby, Clement Jackson, Kaitlin Burek, Glenn Pope, and Mridula Raman. 2006. "Cost Should Be No Barrier: An Evaluation of the First Year of Harvard's Financial Aid Initiative." Working Paper 12029. National Bureau of Economic Research. http://www.nber.org/papers/w12029.

Bergerson, Amy. 2007. "Exploring the Impact of Social Class on Adjustment to College: Anna's Story." *International Journal of Qualitative Studies in Education* 20, no. 1: 99–119.

Binder, Amy J., Daniel B. Davis, and Nick Bloom. 2015. "Career Funneling: How Elite Students Learn to Define and Desire 'Prestigious' Jobs." *Sociology of Education* 89, no. 1: 20–39.

Bourdieu, Pierre. 1984. *Distinction: A Social Critique of the Judgment of Taste*. Harvard University Press.

Bourdieu, Pierre. 1986. "The Forms of Capital." In *Handbook for Theory and Research for the Sociology of Education*, edited by J. G. Richardson, 241–58. Greenwood Press.

Bowen, William, and Derek Bok. 1998. *The Shape of the River: Long-Term Consequences of Considering Race in College and University Admissions.* Princeton, NJ: Princeton University Press.

Brand, Jennie E., and Yu Xie. 2010. "Who Benefits Most from College? Evidence for Negative Selection in Heterogeneous Economic Returns to Higher Education." *American Sociological Review* 75, no. 2: 273–302. doi:10.1177/0003122410363567.

Brewer, Dominic J., Eric R. Eide, and Ronald G. Ehrenberg. 1999. "Does It Pay to Attend an Elite Private College? Cross-Cohort Evidence on the Effects of College Type on Earnings." *The Journal of Human Resources* 34, no. 1: 104–23. doi:10.2307/146304.

Bronfenbrenner, Urie. 1993. "Ecological Models of Human Development." In *Readings On the Development of Children*, edited by M Gauvain and M Cole, 2nd edition, 37–43. New York: Freeman.

Calarco, Jessica McCrory. 2011. "'I Need Help!': Social Class and Children's Help-Seeking in Elementary School." *American Sociological Review* 76, no. 6: 862–82.

Calarco, Jessica McCrory. 2014. "Coached for the Classroom: Parents' Cultural Transmission and Children's Reproduction of Educational Inequalities." *American Sociological Review* 79, no. 5: 1015–37.

Carnevale, Anthony, and Jeff Strohl. 2010. "How Increasing College Access Is Increasing Inequality." In *Rewarding Strivers: Helping Low-Income Students Succeed in College*, edited by Richard Kahlenberg, 71–190. New York: The Century Foundation Press.

Cauce, Ana Mari, Melanie Domenech-Rodríguez, Matthew Paradise, Bryan N. Cochran, Jennifer Munyi Shea, Debra Srebnik, and Nazli Baydar. 2002. "Cultural and Contextual Influences in Mental Health Help Seeking: A Focus on Ethnic Minority Youth." *Journal of Consulting and Clinical Psychology* 70, no. 1: 44–55. doi:10.1037/0022-006X.70.1.44.

Charles, Camille, Gniesha Dinwiddie, and Douglas Massey. 2004. "The Continuing Consequences of Segregation: Family Stress and College Academic Performance." *Social Science Quarterly* 85, no. 5: 53–1373. doi:10.1111/j.0038-4941.2004.00280.x.

Charles, Camille, Mary Fischer, Margarita Mooney, and Douglas Massey. 2009. *Taming the River: Negotiating the Academic, Financial, and Social Currents in Selective Colleges and Universities.* Princeton, NJ: Princeton University Press.

Charmaz, Kathy. 2006. *Constructing Grounded Theory: A Practical Guide through Qualitative Analysis.* Thousand Oaks, CA: Sage Publications.

Collier, Peter J., and David L. Morgan. 2008. "'Is That Paper Really Due Today?': Differences in First-Generation and Traditional College Students' Understandings of Faculty Expectations." *Higher Education* 55, no. 4: 425–46. doi:10.1007/s10734-007-9065-5.

Cookson, Peter, and Caroline Persell. 1985. *Preparing for Power: America's Elite Boarding Schools.* Basic Books.

Cox, Amanda Barrett. 2017. "Cohorts, 'Siblings,' and Mentors: Organizational Structures and the Creation of Social Capital." *Sociology of Education* 90, no. 1: 47–63. doi:10.1177/0038040716681053.

Crosnoe, Robert, Monica Kirkpatrick Johnson, and Glen H. Elder. 2004. "Intergenerational Bonding in School: The Behavioral and Contextual Correlates of Student-Teacher Relationships." *Sociology of Education* 77, no. 1: 60–81. doi:10.1177/003804070407700103.

Diamond, John, and Amanda E. Lewis. 2015. *Despite the Best Intentions: How Racial Inequality Thrives in Good Schools.* Transgressing Boundaries. New York: Oxford University Pres.

DiMaggio, Paul. 1982. "Cultural Capital and School Success: The Impact of Status Culture Participation on the Grades of US High School Students." *American Sociological Review* 47, no. 2: 189–201.

Eisenberg, Daniel, Ezra Golberstein, and Sarah E. Gollust. 2007. "Help-Seeking and Access to Mental Health Care in a University Student Population." *Medical Care* 45, no. 7: 594–601.

Engle, Jennifer, Adolfo Bermeo, and Colleen O'Brien. 2006. "Straight from the Source: What Works for First-Generation College Students." *Pell Institute for the Study of Opportunity in Higher Education.* https://eric.ed.gov/?id=ED501693.

Erikson, B. 1996. "Culture, Class and Connections." *American Journal of Sociology* 102, no. 1: 217–51.

Erickson, Lance, Steve McDonald, and Glen H. Elder. 2009. "Informal Mentors and Education: Complementary or Compensatory Resources?" *Sociology of Education* 82, no. 4: 344–67.

Furstenberg, Frank F. 2007. "The Making of the Black Family: Race and Class in Qualitative Studies in the Twentieth Century." *Annual Review of Sociology* 33, no. 1: 429–48. doi:10.1146/annurev.soc.33.040406.131727.

Gast, Melanie Jones. 2016. "'You're Supposed to Help Me': The Perils of Mass Counseling Norms for Working-Class Black Students." *Urban Education* (June): 1–27. doi:10.1177/0042085916652178.

Gaztambide-Fernandez, Rubén. 2009. *The Best of the Best: Becoming Elite at an American Boarding School.* Cambridge, MA: Harvard University Press.

Granovetter, Mark S. 1973. "The Strength of Weak Ties." *American Journal of Sociology* 78, no. 6: 1360–80. doi:10.2307/2776392.

Hillman, Nicholas. 2013. "Economic Diversity in Elite Higher Education: Do No-Loan Programs Impact Pell Enrollments?" *The Journal of Higher Education* 84, no. 6: 806–33.

Hirsch, Nicole Arlette, and Anthony Abraham Jack. 2012. "What We Face: Framing Problems in the Black Community." *Du Bois Review: Social Science Research on Race* 9, no. 1: 133–48.

Holland, Megan. 2015. "Trusting Each Other: Student-Counselor Relationships in Diverse High Schools." *Sociology of Education* 88, no. 3: 244–62. doi:10.1177/0038040715591347.

Jack, Anthony Abraham. 2014. "Culture Shock Revisited: The Social and Cultural Contingencies to Class Marginality." *Sociological Forum* 29, no. 2: 453–75.

Jack, Anthony Abraham. 2015a. "Crisscrossing Boundaries: Variation in Experiences with Class Marginality among Lower-Income, Black Undergraduates at an Elite College." In *College Students' Experiences of Power and Marginality: Sharing*

Spaces and Negotiating Differences, edited by Elizabeth Lee and Chaise LaDousa, 83–101. New York: Routledge.

Jack, Anthony Abraham. 2015b. "What the Privileged Poor Can Teach Us." *The New York Times*, September 12. http://www.nytimes.com/2015/09/13/opinion/sunday/what-the-privileged-poor-can-teach-us.html.

Jack, Anthony Abraham. 2016. "(No) Harm In Asking: Class, Acquired Cultural Capital, and Academic Engagement at an Elite University." *Sociology of Education* 89, no. 1: 1–19.

Kane, Pearl Rock. 1992. *Independent Schools, Independent Thinkers*. San Francisco: Jossey-Bass.

Karabel, Jerome. 2005. *The Chosen: The Hidden History of Admission and Exclusion at Harvard, Yale, and Princeton*. Boston: Houghton Mifflin.

Khan, Shamus. 2011. *Privilege: The Making of an Adolescent Elite at St. Paul's School*. Princeton, NJ: Princeton University Press.

Kim, Young K., and Linda J. Sax. 2009. "Student–Faculty Interaction in Research Universities: Differences by Student Gender, Race, Social Class, and First-Generation Status." *Research in Higher Education* 50, no. 5: 437–59. doi:10.1007/s11162–009–9127-x.

Kisida, Brian, Jay P. Greene, and Daniel H. Bowen. 2014. "Creating Cultural Consumers The Dynamics of Cultural Capital Acquisition." *Sociology of Education* 87, no. 4: 281–95. doi:10.1177/0038040714549076.

Kozol, Jonathan. 1992. *Savage Inequalities: Children in America's Schools*. New York: HarperPerennial.

Kozol, Jonathan. 2005. *The Shame of the Nation: The Restoration of Apartheid Schooling in America*. New York: Three Rivers Press.

Lamont, Michèle, Stefan Beljean, and Matthew Clair. 2014. "What Is Missing?: Cultural Processes and Causal Pathways to Inequality." *Socio-Economic Review* 12, no. 3: 573–608.

Lamont, Michèle, and Annette Lareau. 1988. "Cultural Capital: Allusions, Gaps and Glissandos in Recent Theoretical Developments." *Sociological Theory* 6, no. 2: 153–68. doi:10.2307/202113.

Lareau, Annette. 2003. *Unequal Childhoods: Class, Race, and Family Life*. Berkeley: University of California Press.

Lareau, Annette, and Elliot Weininger. 2003. "Cultural Capital in Educational Research: A Critical Assessment." *Theory and Society* 32, no. 5/6: 567–606. doi:10.2307/3649652.

Lee, Elizabeth, and Rory Kramer. 2013. "Out with the Old, In with the New? Habitus and Social Mobility at Selective Colleges." *Sociology of Education* 86, no. 1: 18–35.

Lehmann, Wolfgang. 2014. "Habitus Transformation and Hidden Injuries Successful Working-Class University Students." *Sociology of Education* 87, no. 1: 1–15. doi:10.1177/0038040713498777.

Lewis-McCoy, R. 2014. *Inequality in the Promised Land: Race, Resources, and Suburban Schooling*. Stanford, CA: Stanford University Press.

Logan, John, Elisabeta Minca, and Sinem Adar. 2012. "The Geography of Inequality Why Separate Means Unequal in American Public Schools." *Sociology of Education* 85, no. 3: 287–301.

López, Steven R., Concepcion Barrio, Alex Kopelowicz, and William A. Vega. 2012. "From Documenting to Eliminating Disparities in Mental Health Care for Latinos." *The American Psychologist* 67, no. 7: 511–23. doi:10.1037/a0029737.

Markus, Hazel Rose, and MarYam G. Hamedani. 2007. "Sociocultural Psychology: The Dynamic Interdependence among Self Systems and Social Systems." In *Handbook of Cultural Psychology*, edited by Shinobu Kitayama and Dov Cohen, 3–39. New York, NY: Guilford Press.

Massey, Douglas. 1996. "The Age of Extremes: Concentrated Affluence and Poverty in the Twenty-First Century." *Demography* 33, no. 4: 395–412. doi:10.2307/2061773.

Massey, Douglas, Camille Charles, Garvey Lundy, and Mary Fischer. 2003. *The Source of the River: The Social Origins of Freshmen at America's Selective Colleges and Universities*. Princeton, NJ: Princeton University Press.

Massey, Douglas, and Nancy Denton. 1993. *American Apartheid: Segregation and the Making of the Underclass*. Cambridge, MA: Harvard University Press.

McDonough, Patricia. 1997. *Choosing Colleges: How Social Class and Schools Structure Opportunity*. Albany: State University of New York Press.

National Academy of Independent Schools. 2013a. "NAIS Facts at a Glance: Independent School Facts at a Glance for All Non-Member Schools." http://www.nais.org/Articles/Documents/NAISNonMembersFactsAtAGlance201213.pdf.

National Academy of Independent Schools. 2013b. "NAIS Facts at a Glance: Independent School Facts at a Glance for the National Association of Independent Schools (NAIS)." http://www.nais.org/Articles/Documents/NAISFactsAtAGlance201213.pdf.

Nee, Victor, and Jimy Sanders. 2001. "Understanding the Diversity of Immigrant Incorporation: A Forms-of-Capital Model." *Ethnic and Racial Studies* 24, no. 3: 386–411.

Nunn, Lisa. 2014. *Defining Student Success: The Role of School and Culture*. New Brunswick, NJ: Rutgers University Press.

Orfield, Gary, John Kucsera, and Genevieve Siegel-Hawley. 2012. "E Pluribus . . . Separation: Deepening Double Segregation for More Students." Los Angeles, CA: Civil Rights Project.

Orfield, Gary, Sara Schley, Diane Glass, and Sean Reardon. 1994. "The Growth of Segregation in American Schools: Changing Patterns of Separation and Poverty Since 1968." *Equity & Excellence in Education* 27, no. 1: 5–8.

Pascarella, Ernest T., and Patrick T. Terenzini. 2005. *How College Affects Students: A Third Decade Of Research*. San Francisco: Jossey-Bass.

Paulle, Bowen. 2013. *Toxic Schools: High-Poverty Education in New York and Amsterdam*. Chicago: University Of Chicago Press.

Perna, Laura W., Heather T. Rowan-Kenyon, Scott Loring Thomas, Angela Bell, Robert Anderson, and Chunyan Li. 2008. "The Role of College Counseling in Shaping College Opportunity: Variations across High Schools." *The Review of Higher Education* 31, no. 2: 131–59. doi:10.1353/rhe.2007.0073.

Pescosolido, Bernice A., Carol Brooks Gardner, and Keri M. Lubell. 1998. "How People Get into Mental Health Services: Stories of Choice, Coercion and 'Muddling Through' from 'First-Timers.'" *Social Science & Medicine* 46, no. 2: 275–86.

Phinney, Jean S., and Kumiko Haas. 2003. "The Process of Coping Among Ethnic Minority First-Generation College Freshmen: A Narrative Approach." *The Journal of Social Psychology* 143, no. 6: 707–26. doi:10.1080/00224540309600426.

Putnam, Robert D. 2015. *Our Kids: The American Dream in Crisis*. New York: Simon & Schuster.

Reardon, Sean F., and Ann Owens. 2014. "60 Years After Brown: Trends and Consequences of School Segregation." *Annual Review of Sociology* 40, no. 1: 199–218. doi:10.1146/annurev-soc-071913–043152.

Rivera, Lauren. 2015. *Pedigree: How Elite Students Get Elite Jobs*. Princeton, NJ: Princeton University Press.

Rondini, Ashley C. 2016. "Healing the Hidden Injuries of Class? Redemption Narratives, Aspirational Proxies, and Parents of Low-Income, First-Generation College Students." *Sociological Forum* 31, no. 1: 96–116. doi:10.1111/socf.12228.

Ryan, James. 2010. *Five Miles Away, A World Apart: One City, Two Schools, and the Story of Educational Opportunity in Modern America*. Oxford: Oxford University Press.

Sampson, Robert, and William Julius Wilson. 1995. "Toward a Theory of Race, Crime, and Urban Inequality." In *Crime and Inequality*, by John Hagan and Ruth Peterson, 37–56. Stanford, CA: Stanford University Press.

Small, Mario Luis, and Christopher Winship. 2007. "Black Students' Graduation from Elite Colleges: Institutional Characteristics and between-Institution Differences." *Social Science Research* 36, no. 3: 1257–75.

Smith, Buffy. 2013. *Mentoring At-Risk Students through the Hidden Curriculum of Higher Education*. Lanham, MD: Lexington Books.

Stanton-Salazar, Ricardo. 1997. "A Social Capital Framework for Understanding the Socialization of Racial Minority Children and Youths." *Harvard Educational Review* 67, no. 1: 1–40.

Stanton-Salazar, Ricardo, and Sanford Dornbusch. 1995. "Social Capital and the Reproduction of Inequality: Information Networks among Mexican-Origin High School Students." *Sociology of Education* 68, no. 2: 116–35.

Stephens, Nicole M., Stephanie A. Fryberg, Hazel Rose Markus, Camille Johnson, and Rebecca Covarrubias. 2012. "Unseen Disadvantage: How American Universities' Focus on Independence Undermines the Academic Performance of First-Generation College Students." *Journal of Personality and Social Psychology* 102, no. 6: 1178–97. doi:10.1037/a0027143.

Stephens, Nicole M., Hazel Rose Markus, and L Taylor Phillips. 2013. "Social Class Culture Cycles: How Three Gateway Contexts Shape Selves and Fuel Inequality." *Annual Review of Psychology* 65, no. 1: 611–34. doi:10.1146/annurev-psych-010213–115143.

Stephens, Nicole M., Sarah Townsend, Hazel Rose Markus, and Taylor Phillips. 2012. "A Cultural Mismatch: Independent Cultural Norms Produce Greater Increases in Cortisol and More Negative Emotions among First-Generation College Students." *Journal of Experimental Social Psychology* 48, no. 6: 1389–93. doi:10.1016/j.jesp.2012.07.008.

Stevens, Mitchell. 2007. *Creating a Class: College Admissions and the Education of Elites.* Cambridge, MA.: Harvard University Press.

Stevens, Mitchell. 2008. "Culture and Education." *The ANNALS of the American Academy of Political and Social Science* 619, no. 1: 97–113. doi:10.1177/0002716208320043.

Stevens, Mitchell, Elizabeth Armstrong, and Richard Arum. 2008. "Sieve, Incubator, Temple, Hub: Empirical and Theoretical Advances in the Sociology of Higher Education." *Annual Review of Sociology* 34, no. 1: 127–51.

Streib, Jessi. 2011. "Class Reproduction by Four Year Olds." *Qualitative Sociology* 34, no. 2: 337–52. doi:10.1007/s11133–011–9193–1.

Stuber, Jenny. 2009. "Class, Culture, and Participation in the Collegiate Extra-Curriculum." *Sociological Forum* 24, no 4: 877–900.

Stuber, Jenny. 2011. *Inside the College Gates: How Class and Culture Matter in Higher Education.* Lanham, MD: Lexington Books.

Swail, W. Scott, and Laura W. Perna. 2002. "Pre-College Outreach Programs: A National Perspective." In *Increasing Access to College: Extending Possibilities for All Students*, edited by William G. Tierney and Linda Serra Hagedorn, 15–34. Albany: SUNY Press.

Swidler, Ann. 1986. "Culture in Action: Symbols and Strategies." *American Sociological Review* 51, no. 2: 273–86. doi:10.2307/2095521.

Terenzini, Patrick, Leonard Springer, Patricia M. Yaeger, Ernest Pascarella, and Amaury Nora. 1996. "First-Generation College Students: Characteristics, Experiences, and Cognitive Development." *Research in Higher Education* 37, no. 1: 1–22.

Tinto, Vincent. 1987. *Leaving College: Rethinking the Causes and Cures of Student Attrition.* Chicago: University Of Chicago Press.

Torres, Kimberly. 2009. "'Culture Shock': Black Students Account for Their Distinctiveness at an Elite College." *Ethnic and Racial Studies* 32, no. 5: 883–905.

Tyson, Karolyn. 2011. *Integration Interrupted: Tracking, Black Students, and Acting White after Brown.* New York: Oxford University Press.

Vasquez-Salgado, Yolanda, Patricia M. Greenfield, and Rocio Burgos-Cienfuegos. 2014. "Exploring Home-School Value Conflicts Implications for Academic Achievement and Well-Being Among Latino First-Generation College Students." *Journal of Adolescent Research* 30, no. 3: 271–305.

Walpole, Mary Beth. 2003. "Socioeconomic Status and College: How SES Affects College Experiences and Outcomes." *The Review of Higher Education* 27, no. 1: 45–73.

Wang, Tiffany R. 2014. "'I'm the Only Person From Where I'm From to Go to College': Understanding the Memorable Messages First-Generation College Students Receive From Parents." *Journal of Family Communication* 14, no. 3: 270–90. doi: 10.1080/15267431.2014.908195.

Weber, Max. 1978. *Economy and Society: An Outline of Interpretive Sociology.* Edited by Guenther Roth and Claus Wittich. Fourth edition. Berkeley: University of California Press.

Young, Alford. 1999. "The (Non)Accumulation of Capital: Explicating the Relationship of Structure and Agency in the Lives of Poor Black Men." *Sociological Theory* 17, no. 2: 201–27.

Zweigenhaft, Richard. 1993. "Prep School and Public School Graduates of Harvard: A Longitudinal Study of the Accumulation of Social and Cultural Capital." *The Journal of Higher Education* 64, no. 2: 211–25. doi:10.2307/2960030.

Zweigenhaft, Richard, and G. William Domhoff. 1991. *Blacks in the White Establishment?: A Study of Race and Class in America.* New Haven, CT: Yale University Press.

NOTES

1. Doubly Disadvantaged and Privileged Poor terms represent Weberian ideal types (Weber 1978; see also Anderson 1999), theoretically informed, analytic concepts used to outline the overlooked the heterogeneity among lower-income undergraduates. For an extended discussion of selection bias see scholar.harvard.edu/files/anthonyjack/files/culture_shock_revisited_online_appendices.pdf.

2. Attendance at underresourced, distressed public schools is a general pattern for lower-income minority youth, especially those who are Black and Latino. It is true that suburban busing programs exist and some students attend more integrated schools. Newer research investigating these schools highlight how racial inequalities are reproduced even in these schools (Lewis-McCoy 2014; Diamond and Lewis 2015).

3. One Privileged Poor and one Doubly Disadvantaged student noted that a parent had some college education but that exposure came later in life (i.e., while the student was in middle school or later). Another Doubly Disadvantaged student noted that his stepfather had a bachelor's degree but he did not live with him (the stepfather lived in a different state).

4. This figure, $40,000, is roughly one standard deviation above the average financial aid package for undergraduates at Midtown between 2003 and 2009. We use it as a proxy for family income as it serves as a relative measure of economic position at Midtown and an absolute measure in that for these students, more than 75 percent of their tuition is covered by the college.

5. The faculty demographics are similar. Greater than two-thirds of the faculty identify as White.

6. We created an economic disadvantage scale that consists of first-generation status, Pell grant receipt, institutional classification of familial disadvantage ($\leq$ $40,000 annual household income), and financial aid award ($\geq$ $40,395) (Chronbach's alpha = 0.81) to capture students' relative and absolute disadvantage. Students were given a score of 0 to 1. If a student met no economic disadvantage marker, they received a 0. If they met one criterion, they received a score of .25. Given the overlap between those on high financial aid, receipt of Pell grant, and first-generation college students status, we dichotomized the scale, and any student meeting one or more of the eco-

nomic disadvantage markets was given a 1 and classified as lower-income. We use private school attendance for Privileged Poor classification.

7. Documenting lower-income students at private schools, often through programs like Prep for Prep, aligns with findings by Stevens (2007), who observed that many minority and lower-income applicants arrived in college having participated in what he calls academic "roadside assistance programs" that serve as informational bridges between high school students and colleges. Our analysis expands our thinking about the range of programs available to students from underprivileged backgrounds (Swail and Perna 2002). Furthermore, the prevalence of the Privileged Poor at Midtown is striking given that fewer students attend private schools than public schools in the United States and that recent annual reports compiled by the National Association of Independent Schools (2013b, 2013a) show that roughly 28 percent of all private school students are students of color (e.g., Black, Latino, and Asian) and 23 percent of students receive financial aid, which is roughly an 8 percent increase over the past decade in the proportion of both students of color and students who receive financial aid at independent schools in the United States.

8. Natalie (DD), who felt comfortable engaging adults, also entered Midtown through a nontraditional path but still attended a public high school. Her parent served as a domestic worker for wealthy clients who rented a modest home to them. As a result, Natalie attended a resource-rich, racially mixed (though mostly White) high school, where classes were small and teachers invested in each student individually.

6

Rethinking First-Generation College Status among Undocumented Immigrant Students

Thomas Piñeros Shields

In recent years, there has been a surge of scholarly interest in the structural barriers to college faced by the almost two million undocumented immigrants who entered the United States as children, referred to as the "1.5 generation" (Rumbaut 2004; Rincon 2008; Gonzales 2009a; Kasinitz et al. 2009; Perez et al. 2009; Rocha-Tracy 2009; Chen 2010; Gonzales 2010; Menjívar 2010; Jefferies 2014). Undocumented students face barriers such as unaffordability due to lack of access to in-state tuition rates and financial aid (Gonzales 2009b; Rincon 2008), fear of deportation for themselves or their families that can disrupt school enrollment and attendance (Jefferies 2014), and primary and secondary school opportunity structures that shape and limit their ability to attend and complete college (Gonzales 2010). An understudied barrier to college attendance for undocumented immigrant students is that a high proportion of their parents did not attend college, especially colleges in the United States, and so they cannot provide guidance to their children through the college application and attendance process. The reasoning underlying how parent educational attainment affects undocumented immigrant student college access and completion has been described by Gonzales (2010):

> Rising levels of immigration and accompanying complexities brought about by immigrant legal status issues have generated new problems, as greater numbers of Latino immigrant students move through school with little assistance. Because an overwhelming majority of these children outpace their parents in educational attainment, many are left without proper guidance about school. Particularly for students whose parents never went to college, knowing what it takes to successfully finish high school and get to college requires outside support and assistance. For undocumented immigrant students, the need for such assistance is compounded by the barriers erected by non-legal status. (471)

The large number of immigrant students in schools, combined with low rates of college-educated parents among the undocumented student population, surfaces multiple challenges for college completion. In addition to school structures, fears of deportation, and financial barriers faced by undocumented students, some also lack the support, guidance, and advocacy of parents who understand the US educational system, similar to other first-generation college students.

First-generation college student status can be understood as a constructed status within larger structures of opportunity and belonging through an intersectional lens that stands in relationship to these students' liminal or unauthorized immigration status (Crenshaw 1991; Collins 2000; Nunez 2014). The analytic frame of intersectionality addresses how life opportunities are shaped and constrained by multiple and simultaneous systems of oppression in a "matrix of domination" (Collins 2000). An intersectional approach to understanding educational opportunities for undocumented immigrant students incorporates an analysis of social locations defined by class, panethnicities and race, nationality, first-generation college status, and immigration status to reveal co-occurring systems of power and structural opportunity. As Collins (2000) notes, an intersectional approach notes that persons simultaneously hold marginalized and privileged positions. In this chapter, an intersectional approach reveals a dimension of privilege/marginalization among undocumented 1.5-generation immigrants by focusing on a distinction between those whose parents completed college and those whose parents did not, referred to as *first-generation students*.

Scholarship on first-generation college-going (including other chapters in this volume) helps reveal the intergenerational mechanisms that support college success while also surfacing unique challenges that first-generation college students face in postsecondary education institutions. First-generation college students face unique challenges as they access and complete postsecondary education without the guidance of parents who attended college themselves. First-generation students who graduate from high school are more likely than their peers to not enroll in college and to not complete their degree (Engle, Bermeo, and O'Brien 2006).

While the effects of first-generation college-going have been well documented, there has been ambiguity in the definition of *first-generation college student* (Toutkoushian, Stollberg, and Slaton 2015). A first-generation college student refers to someone whose parents did not attend college; however, there is variation in how this definition has been interpreted among policies that target first-generation students. For instance, some definitions of first-generation require that only one parent did not attend college, or in other cases both parents; and yet others have different requirements about how to account for whether nonbiological step- and foster parents attended college (Toutkoushian, Stollberg, and Slaton 2015). Such categorical confusion may be exacerbated when we look at cases of undocumented immigrant students whose parents attended and/or graduated college in another country before migrating to the United States (Feliciano 2006). For many migrants to the United States, the college credential system within the labor market can delegitimize college degrees earned in other countries (Arbeit and Warren 2013).[1] Furthermore, as parents of adult children entering the US college system, these parents may have little experience with various college and university programs, the application process and timeline, or financial aid. This dilemma opens up an interesting question for analysis that brings scholarship about undocumented immigrant status into conversation with scholarship about first-generation status: How does premigration college completion by first-generation undocumented immigrant parents shape college preparation and completion of their 1.5-generation children?

In this chapter, I examine how premigration parent college completion shapes college preparation and completion among undocumented immigrant students. To address this question, I compare undocumented immigrant students whose parents completed college with those whose parents did not complete college. For the purposes of this analysis, I refer to only to those for whom neither parent completed college as a *first-generation* college student. My analysis seeks to surface how undocumented students' parents' college attainment might shape postsecondary education attainment among undocumented immigrant students. Although all undocumented immigrant students face structural barriers to accessing and completing postsecondary education in the United States, this chapter suggests that those whose parents attended college (premigration) fare better than those undocumented immigrant students who are first-generation college students in their families. This current chapter breaks new ground by considering first-generation college status among undocumented immigrant students by recognizing transnational college credentials, and thereby providing sharper analytic clarity to the definition of first-generation college-going. Furthermore, this chapter sheds light on the intergenerational dynamics that shape the processes by which undocumented immigrant students access postsecondary education.

The data for this analysis is drawn from a longer ethnographic study of undocumented immigrant students. In a secondary analysis of this data, I analyzed the college access and completion of six undocumented immigrant students: three whose parents completed college and three whose parents did not. In the next section, I provide further background about challenges to higher education faced by undocumented immigrant students. I then describe my methodological approach and sample. The bulk of this chapter presents analysis organized longitudinally around three stages of development—early childhood, primary school, and secondary school—with a final, fourth stage when undocumented students graduate high school and come to terms with barriers to postsecondary education due to their immigration status. The chapter's conclusions include recommendations for future research and policy-making.

UNDOCUMENTED IMMIGRANT STUDENTS
AND COLLEGE ACCESS

Overall, the children of immigrants, documented and undocumented, represent the fastest growing portion of the US population. The proportion of immigrant children grew by 51 percent in the twenty-year period between1995 and 2015 to reach a total of 18.4 million children (Child_Trends 2014). Children with one or more immigrant parent represent one-quarter of all US children today. Significantly, new immigrants are overrepresented in comparison to native-born families at both the high and low ends of the socioeconomic spectrum, suggesting that scholarship about college access needs to examine immigrant status intersectionally, in relation to class and racial hierarchies (Suarez-Orozco, Suarez-Orozco, and Todorova 2008; Jaffe-Walter and Lee 2011). One study found, for instance, that 90 percent of Asian immigrants entered the United States with a college degree, while over 60 percent of Latino immigrants entered the United States without a high school degree, suggesting that level of college attainment among immigrant parents not only varies, but is racialized (Rumbaut and Komaie 2010; Williams and Ferrari 2015). While racial hierarchies continue to shape college access among immigrant groups, critical scholars have asserted that panethnic and racial categories fall short of capturing the experiences of specific ethnic groups of immigrant students as they navigate college (Rumbaut 2009; Ryan and Ream 2016).

Several studies have pointed to how parent social capital helps immigrant students navigate college attainment (Rumbaut and Komaie 2010; Jaffe-Walter and Lee 2011; Ryan and Ream 2016). For instance, Jaffe-Walter and Lee (2011) explore the intersection of class and race among immigrant high school students, documenting how schools prepare students for college through the development of academic skills and social capital to resist racial hierarchies, noting that all parents tend to have high aspirations for their children's education, but middle-class immigrant families' knowledge of the educational system and how to advocate within it allow their children to better navigate the college entry process in ways that newcomer and poorer immigrant parents cannot (Jaffe-Walter and Lee 2011). Furthermore, research has identified class differences among immigrant parents that include how newcomer and poorer immigrant parents tend to face more cultural and linguistic barriers to supporting their children's education (Portes and Zhou 1993; Jaffe-Walter and Lee 2011; Vasquez-Salgado, Greenfield, and Burgos-

Cienfuegos 2015) and the tendency of less well-educated families to have a more collectivist culture that requires more obligations of those students (Vasquez-Salgado, Greenfield, and Burgos-Cienfuegos 2015).

Despite scholarly recognition that immigrant students face similar challenges to first-generation college students, there has been little scholarship that analyzes premigration educational attainment by parents of immigrants. In one unique exception that deserves careful consideration, Feliciano (2006) analyzed how premigration educational status of parents affected children's educational attainment. She conducted logistic regression analysis on a unique data set that combined international data and US census data for 30 immigrant groups with data from the Children of Immigrants Longitudinal Survey of an initial 5,262 second-generation students.

> The main finding of this article is that group-level premigration educational status influences educational expectations among the second generation. Some of this effect works through the influence of parents, or at least the students' perceptions of their parents' desires for them. That is, the respondents' perceptions of their parents' aspirations were partly influenced by the prior relative class standing of the entire immigrant generation who migrated to the United States from their country (295).

Importantly, Feliciano's large-scale quantitative study concurs with findings in this chapter that parents' expectations were shaped by class standing, and that partly influenced their children's college attainment. The current chapter differs from and builds upon the previous study methodologically, with an in-depth qualitative approach that sheds light on children's perceptions of parent college attainment, and specifically focusing on undocumented immigrants, who face structural barriers to education and full incorporation in society (Gonzales 2016).

On top of challenges stemming from first-generation and immigrant status, many undocumented immigrant children also experience the barriers of unauthorized status (Gonzales 2010; Gonzales and Chavez 2012; Olivas 2012; Jefferies 2014; Gonzales 2016). According to research at the Pew Research Center for Hispanic Trends (2014), among the roughly 40 million immigrants living in the United States today, about 11.3 million are undocumented (Passel and Cohn 2010; Passel et al. 2014, 26). For the past ten years, the size of the undocumented immigrant population in the United States has remained relatively stable (Passel et al. 2014, 26) About 61 percent of undocumented immigrants are long-term US residents, and about 38 percent (about 4 million) live with US-born children (Passel et al. 2014, 26). There were approximately 775,000 undocumented children (under age eighteen) living in the United States in 2012, a decrease from about 1.6 million in 2005 due to a slowdown of immigration and the aging out of many undocumented immigrant youth from child to adult status (Passel et al. 2014, 26).

When it comes to the education of undocumented students, US policies create experiences of uncertainty, inconsistency, and contradiction. Although the 1982 *Plyler v. Doe* US Supreme Court decision gives children access to public education, regardless of immigration status, upon graduating from a US high school, college access remains elusive for many qualified undocumented students. Undocumented immigrant students face structural challenges when applying to college, and some colleges and universities prohibit admission by undocumented students altogether. Once accepted, financial barriers make attending an impossibility for many, since undocumented students cannot, by law, apply for or receive any federal financial aid (Olivas 2012; Gonzales 2016). Furthermore, most public state aid follows federal guidelines as well and is thus unavailable to undocumented immigrant students. This experience of partial inclusion and partial exclusion in the education system of the United States has been referred to as "legal liminality" (Menjívar 2006). On the one hand, undocumented students are prepared through the K-12 school system to enter US society, and on the other hand, when they reach graduation, they are denied the college admissions or "merit-based" scholarships that they earned through grades or test scores. To explain this experience, Gonzalez and Chavez (2012) adopt Butler's (1999) definition of *abjectivity* to explain the lived experiences of undocumented immigrant students who are incorporated into K-12 education in the United States before being "cast out" once they graduate: "The 'abject' designates that which has been expelled from the body, discharged as excrement, literally rendered 'Other.' This appears as an expulsion of alien elements, but the alien is effectively established through this expulsion" (Butler 1999, 5).

More recently, in his book *Lives in Limbo: Undocumented and Coming of Age in America*, Roberto Gonzales (2016) applies a longitudinal analysis to undocumented student lives who face a transition, not to adult privileges and autonomy, but to "illegality" as a master status that excludes them from full participation in society (Willen 2012; De Genova 2013).[2] This experience of "illegality" shapes job, housing, and transportation options for undocumented adults as well as a pervasive awareness of these young people's contingent and deportable status (Gonzales 2016, 184). Comparing undocumented immigrant students who were college educated with "early exiters" who did not attend college, Gonzales (2016) notes that as they enter adulthood, the undocumented immigrant "early exiters" seemed better adjusted, having settled into the routine of illegality in their late teens (180). The undocumented college graduates were "still trying to cope with the staggering mismatch between the new reality and their high educational attainment and aspirations for the future" (181).

These sobering outcomes for undocumented college graduates were partially mollified by the enactment of Deferred Action for Childhood Arrivals (DACA), an executive order by President Obama in June 2012 that provides a temporary and contingent reprieve from deportation for those undocumented immigrants who attended college and provides legal access to work permits (Gonzales 2016, 25). As of March 2016, 728,285 immigrants had been approved for DACA by US Citizenship and Immigration Services (USCIS) (Hipsman, Gomez-Aguinaga, and Capps 2016, 19). Although DACA does not confer the right to vote, travel freely, or obtain federal financial aid, it has led to benefits for undocumented immigrant students. One survey of DACA recipients found a marked increase in economic opportunities for undocumented immigrants, including finding new jobs, obtaining driver's licenses, opening bank accounts, and access to credit cards (Gonzales and Terriquez 2013). Another survey, conducted in September 2016, found that wages for DACA recipients increased by 40 percent and that 60 percent of respondents reported moving to a job that offered better pay (Wong et al. 2016). That same survey found that 46 percent of DACA recipients were enrolled in school, among whom 92 percent reported that because of DACA "I pursued educational opportunities that I previously could not" (Wong et al. 2016). It seems clear that DACA expanded college access overall for undocumented immigrant students, though only 48 percent of those who are estimated to be eligible for DACA actually applied, a figure that varied considerably by states (Hipsman, Gomez-Aguinaga, and Capps 2016, 19). For instance, in Massachusetts, there are an estimated 21,000 DACA-eligible undocumented immigrant youth and young adults, of whom only 38 percent applied for DACA (Hipsman, Gomez-Aguinaga, and Capps 2016, 19).[3] Furthermore, DACA provides no pathway to permanent legal residency or citizenship and may be modified or rescinded by the president without an act of Congress. Indeed, as of this writing, the Trump administration has ended the DACA program, and the future status of these young adults remains uncertain.

METHODS AND SAMPLE

As other scholars have noted, the vulnerability of undocumented immigrant students suggests that research requires long-term, trusting relationships (Gonzales 2016, 16). The analysis in this chapter is drawn from a nine-year (2008–present) ethnographic research project conducted with a social movement organization comprised of undocumented immigrant students in Massachusetts.

As a site for this research, Massachusetts represents a relatively understudied region in the study of the undocumented immigrant student population in the United States. Most of the research about undocumented students has concentrated on the largest immigrant destination states: California (Perez et al. 2009, Gonzales 2016), New York (Kasinitz et al. 2009), and Texas (Rincon 2008). Unlike those regions, in Massachusetts the largest portion of immigrants do not migrate from Mexico, but (in declining order of frequency) from Brazil, the Dominican Republic, China, Haiti, Portugal, India, Vietnam, Canada, Italy, El Salvador, Guatemala, and Russia (Clayton-Matthews, Karp, and Watanabe 2009). The geography of these sending countries suggests that the majority of Massachusetts immigrants entered through airports and therefore held visas, rather than crossing the border on foot to work as farm laborers.

In 2007, there were 912,310 immigrants in Massachusetts, representing about 14 percent of the total population (Clayton-Matthews, Karp, and Watanabe 2009). Despite its widespread reputation as liberal state, Massachusetts policy has lagged behind other states when it comes to promoting the integration of new immigrants—so while eighteen states have passed legislation offering in-state tuition to undocumented students, six states provide financial aid to them, and twelve states and the District of Columbia provide driver's licenses to them, none of these policies has been passed in Massachusetts (Morse et al. 2016).

For this ethnography, I participated in hundreds of individual and group meetings, travelled with participants to national meetings, and attended public events that focused on the political mobilization of undocumented immigrant students. In addition, as part of this longer study, between 2010 and 2011, I conducted life course interviews with fifteen undocumented immigrant student leaders in their late teens to early twenties. The interview protocol included questions about early life experiences and family, school, and involvement in political activism. The interviews ranged from just under forty-five minutes to almost three hours in length. Among these interviews, six interviewees revealed information about their parents' college completion status and were thereby selected into the current analysis to compare undocumented first-generation college students with those undocumented students whose parents completed college in their country of origin or (in one case) in the United States. Basic background about these six participants is presented in table 6.1. As the table shows, three of the six participants identity as female and the remainder as male. Three were born in Brazil, and the others were from Colombia, the Dominican Republic, and Guatemala. Also, three completed their earliest education in private school in their home countries, while the other three began formal elementary education in the United States. All but one (Victor) entered the United States on a legal visa, but at some point overstayed or were denied renewal.

Table 6.1. Summary of interviewees in alphabetical order of pseudonym.

Pseudonym	Country of birth	Parents completed college premigration?	Early experiences	Status	Postsecondary education (2016)
Alejandra (F)	Colombia	Parents completed college	Private school; entered US at age 12 via tourist visa	Undocumented	Finished college; seeking advanced degree
Eliza (F)	Dominican Republic	Parents completed college	Entered US before age 8: K-12 in US via tourist visa	Undocumented	Finished college; seeking advanced degree
Neil (M)	Brazil	Parents completed college; father entered US on education visa	Private school; entered US at age 8 via father's education visa	Visa expired senior year	Finished college; seeking advanced degree
Paula (F)	Dominican Republic	Mother and father did not complete college	Entered US before age 5; K-12 in US via tourist visa	Undocumented, grandmother is US citizen	Started college; not clear if finished
Tiago (M)	Brazil	Parents started but did not complete college	Private school; entered US at age 13 via tourist visa	Undocumented	Not finished college (8+ years)
Victor (M)	Guatemala	Parents did not complete college	Entered US at age 12 by crossing border	Undocumented; family deported	Not started college; entering trade

In 2016, I followed up with this sample and inquired about their college experiences. Central to the thesis of this chapter is the observation that *all* of the undocumented students whose parents attended college have subsequently completed college. Of the three first-generation college students in 2010–2011, two have not yet finished college. The third's (Paula's) completion is unknown, since she left the organization and has not remained in contact with its members. One caveat in interpreting these observations is that the purpose of this chapter is not to prove, nor even to suggest, a robust empirical causal relationship between first-generation college status and college completion, although such a relationship is consistent with other scholarship about first-generation students (Engle, Bermeo, and O'Brien 2006). Instead, as a qualitative study, this chapter seeks to reveal the dynamics within the lives of these six undocumented immigrant students to better understand how their parents' education status may have shaped their future postsecondary college aspirations, access, and completion, with the intention of building theory (Charmaz 2000).

For this analysis, transcripts of the six interviews were entered into NVIVO software. I read each text thoroughly to identify emergent themes about these young people's education, schooling, and postsecondary education plans (Corbin and Strauss 2008). Using an inductive approach of grounded theory with a longitudinal framework, I grouped these codes and their corresponding text into an initial set of five data families: (1) early family influences on education, (2) transitions to the US school system; (3) primary and middle school experiences, (4) high school experiences, and (5) access and barriers to postsecondary education related to undocumented status (Charmaz 2000, Corbin and Strauss 2008). Within each of these five data families, themes were identified to explain how college attainment among undocumented immigrants is shaped by first-generation college status or by a parent's college completion, and then those themes were regrouped into the theoretical propositions in this paper.

Prior to discussing the data and themes, I have presented short biographies of the six undocumented immigrant students below. Note that all names are pseudonyms, and details (e.g., school names) that might be used for identification have been altered or deleted.

Alejandra. Alejandra's parents were both college educated in Colombia and placed a very high value on education. In Colombia, Alejandra was enrolled in a private school until age twelve, when she moved to the United States in response to growing fear of violence and worsening economic conditions. Upon arriving in the United States, Alejandra moved through ESOL classes in two years. She excelled in school, participating in clubs and extracurricular activities as well as honor society. Upon graduation, she attended a community college. Eventually, with DACA, Alejandra completed her bachelor's degree and is enrolled in a graduate degree program in the health care field. In 2015, Alejandra married a US citizen and a year later, she received her citizenship.

Eliza. Both of Eliza's parents completed college in the Dominican Republic, where Eliza was born. When her parents moved to the United States, she lived on a farm with her grandparents for two years. At age eight, she moved to the United States to be reunited with her parents and began school. Her early school experiences were difficult as she learned English and faced discrimination by peers. She found support from her family, peers, and mentors through the years. Eliza attended and graduated college. She is now planning to attend graduate school for an advanced degree.

Neil. After Neil's father enrolled in graduate school in the Boston area, Neil's family moved to the United States from Brazil five days before his ninth birthday. For the next nine years Neil obtained dependent child visas status since his father held an F-1 student visa and, later, his R-1 religious visa. Neil attended school and excelled in school academics and extracurricular activities. His legal documentation allowed him to obtain a driver's license and make plans to apply to elite colleges and universities. During his senior year in high school, his father's green card application was denied and Neil's access to college aid evaporated as he became undocumented. Neil attended community college and later a public university part-time while working to pay out-of-state tuition rates without access to financial aid. After several years, Neil was accepted for admission into an Ivy League university on a scholarship, where he completed his bachelor's degree. He is now enrolled in a STEM-related doctoral program at another elite university.

Paula. Neither of Paula's parents completed college. Paula was born in the Dominican Republic and moved to the United States at age five, where she was raised by her grandmother, a legal permanent resident of the United States. At the time of this interview, at age 22, after years of unstable and unsatisfactory work, Paula had enrolled in community college. She attended intermittently. Soon after this interview, Paula left the student organization. It is not clear whether she finished college.

Tiago. Tiago's parents both began college in Brazil, but dropped out. His father was a successful entrepreneur in a family business in São Paolo, where they lived in relative comfort as a middle-class family with a car, a nice apartment, and private school education. Global competition led his family's business to fail, so his father moved to the United States. At age twelve, Tiago joined his family in the United States. Tiago attended middle and high school in an urban school district. He was recognized as smart, but his performance in class was inconsistent. With the encouragement of caring teachers and other adults, Tiago applied to and enrolled in a public university. He has attended intermittently over the past eight years but has had to repeatedly leave school for financial reasons and has not finished.

Victor. Victor migrated to the United States in sixth grade from a rural area of Guatemala, where he spoke a regional Mayan dialect. Neither of his parents attended college, and his own schooling in Guatemala ended before he became proficient in the Spanish language. In school, he moved from the bilingual program to a vocational high school, where he did well and planned to attend college. His educational plans were interrupted when his mother was detained as part of an immigration raid, and one year later, a few months after Victor's high school graduation, his father was deported in a follow-up home raid. Victor did not go to college and instead went to work to support his mother and siblings.

ANALYSIS

The remainder of this chapter explores how parent college completion shaped the college preparation and completion among undocumented immigrant students. The chapter is organized around three meta-themes that emerged from analysis of the interview data: (1) parent influences on education; (2) differential experiences in school among first-generation and children of college-educated parents; and (3) different responses to illegality and being denied college access.

Theme #1: Parental Influence on Education

The first theme, parental influence on education, can be split into two subthemes: direct parental influences on education to form a college-going identity and indirect parent interventions in the form of advocating and choosing quality schools.

Direct Parental Influences to form a College-going Identity

The influence of parents on their children's future college-going begins early in life. Both groups of undocumented immigrant students saw their parents as valuing education; however, how those young people reported hearing and interpreting that value as they developed literacy in English revealed different parenting practices. When the children of college-educated parents described their parents' messages that education mattered, they used concrete and specific examples and actions. For example, Alejandra, whose parents had both attended college in Colombia, understood the value of education through clear and concrete memories of her father reading to her: "I always had [studied] since I was little; my parents read to me." As she got older, she recalls her own reading being encouraged as a way to earn social freedom and privileges: "My dad was always like, if you want to go out, you have to read a book. Like you cannot go out if you do not tell me what you read in a book." Alejandra's father established his daughter's reading as a part of her life.

Such practice became such a part of Alejandra's identity that later in life, when faced with despair about her undocumented status, Alejandra continues the practice of studying and taking classes for herself.

> Alejandra: I was going through a phase where I was like, even if I have my papers, why am I studying? What am I doing? I'm just going to go and have fun and wait until I get deported. Y'know, nothing was going on in the state house. Nothing was going on law-wise. It was like, nothing. But like, I guess, like, old habits die hard, so like, I kept studying. I feel weird if I don't study. I feel weird if I don't take a class.
>
> TPS: Okay. Being a student is part of who you are.
>
> Alejandra: Yeah! I was like, it's so weird to not do well in school. My dad was like, my parents also pushed me to do well; my parents went to college. They are school graduates, they know. So, they, like—so they know.

In the above passage, the routine and habit of studying seems to provide security or comfort that reaffirms Alejandra's identity as a college student. Alejandra clearly makes the connection between her own established habit of studying and enrolling in classes, despite the apparent lack of opportunity to ever normalize her immigration status. Further, Alejandra acknowledges the intergenerational origin of her own college-going habit by referencing her parents' college experiences: "My parents pushed me to do well, my parents went to college."

In a similar fashion, Neil, whose father attended a graduate program in the United States, sees his father's decision to seek advanced education in the United States as an exciting opportunity, and an opportunity for himself.

> The whole decision to come here was my dad wanted to get his master's degree in theology. And the year before, he came here for a summer semester at [a private university in Boston] and he did one class in theology and he got to go around Connecticut. . . . And then he came back home and he spoke some English, and I was like "oh my God, my dad is speaking English, that's really cool!" [laugh] So I got enticed into going—he kind of swayed the whole family, I started taking English lessons, and we got ready to go.

As in Neil's case, parents who had attended college led these immigrant students to be excited about learning in school, but in some cases, they also helped to model English language learning and inspired them to get excited about moving to the US for a period of time.

Eliza also experienced a concrete intervention by her father to help her learn English upon arriving to the United States at age eight. She tells the story of getting off the plane and seeing her father and mother for the first time in two years. "I was Daddy's little girl," she admits. Later, when I asked her how she learned English, she explained:

> Eliza: When I came here my dad gave me like crayons and a notebook and he gave me a dictionary and he told me that he wanted me to learn five words every day.
>
> TPS: Five words.
>
> Eliza: Five words. And I would have to tell them and repeated them and have a conversation by. And so that is how I learned English.

Eliza's memory of the five-word daily ritual that her father initiated suggests that her parents not only stated the importance of education at a young age, but actively took responsibility for Eliza's learning.

In contrast to Eliza, who arrived in the United States without English fluency, Tiago had learned English in Brazil in manner that was more entrepreneurial. When I asked him about his English upon arrival to the United States, he explained:

> I could read English, and turns out I could speak, like I had never spoken English with anybody, but I could read English okay, because I did take classes in Brazil from a young age. And I've always had an ease with language since I was young. I always liked playing video games, and stuff where it is in English. If you want to link to save Zog, then you have to know where to go. So I learned from a young age how to read a lot of stuff in English. And then when I came here, I was pretty solid and my mom didn't speak a word. My dad spoke, but he was at work all the time.

The above passage reveals a difference between Tiago's learning and that of the children of college-educated undocumented immigrants. As he notes, Tiago supplemented what he learned at school with teaching himself to read English in order to play video games. Furthermore, his mother did not speak any English and he recalls that his father worked long hours. As a result, Tiago often found himself travelling with his mother to provide translation as she navigated the landscape of school registration for her two children; shopped for food, clothing, and other needed household items; and managed the household.

Although the students whose parents completed college were reported to employ concrete strategies for language acquisition, one first-generation student's experiences also revealed such strategies in her household. Paula's grandmother, who had lived in the United States for many years, raised her. Halfway through our interview, Paula explained that she refers to her grandmother as her "mom." Paula shared a story about her grandmother's tutoring in English and math.

TPS: How important was it for you to get good grades, both to you and your family?

Paula: It has always been very important. My mom has always been very. . . . Grades have always been very important. My mom, I remember when, I was making the transition from like bilingual classes to English classes, we had to like learn like certain spelling words or whatever, and my mom would make sure that I would rehearse them all the time. So she would put those, like the list, right in front of my bed, so every day, I would have to like see everything.

TPS: What grade were you in?

Paula: I was in third grade. Also my multiplication tables. [Laugh]

TPS: She would post it so it was the first thing you would see in them morning.

Paula: Yes. I always had to like, every day if I would stop by, if she was there, she would be like, "oh, you have to go through them." I would say it was very important.

Like Alejandra and Eliza, Paula's "mom" encouraged her to learn English and math through directly intervening in her learning. As did parents who had attended college, Paula's grandmother encouraged her to seek education by engaging her in concrete ways. Despite the importance that her grandmother placed on school, Paula struggled to stay engaged when she entered high school, and later, she postponed college for many years. This suggests that even when first-generation parents (or grandparents, in this case) send concrete and clear messages to undocumented students about the importance of education, students whose parents did not themselves attend and complete college may continue to struggle for a variety of reasons.

Parent Influences on Education through Advocating and Intervening in School

Unlike the direct support that parents provide in their children's educational lives, the intergenerational and transnational process that privileges undocumented students with college-educated parents over their first-generation peers operates in less direct and sometimes unexpected ways. The educational trajectory of immigrant students is shaped by the educational systems and opportunities for these students in their home country as well as those they are met with upon arriving in the United States, reflecting social, political, and economic differences between sending countries as well as differences in wealth among immigrant families (Portes and Rumbaut 2001, Feliciano 2006). Contrary to some common expectations about the quality of education in developing nations compared to the United States, three interviewees described private schools that they attended in their home country, and the shock of transitioning to an urban school system in the United States. This observation about the experience of private education does not imply that all immigrants experienced higher educational quality in their home country than in the United States; rather, it is meant to challenge sometimes mistaken assumptions about the superiority of US education and is consistent with segmented assimilation theory, which recognizes that many new immigrant children are channeled into low-income public schools (Portes and Zhou 1993). For example, Alejandra, one of the students with college-educated parents, described her shock when she encountered the behavior of classmates in Boston Public Schools:

I was sheltered in Colombia. Y'know, Colombia is very violent, yeah, you hear all about this, but I was very sheltered in a way, so I didn't hear it. But my experiences in [US] public school, I toughened up. I guess that's the word like, I toughened up. I learned about that kids would do drugs. I learned that kids who don't go to school, they could drop out at 16. I never thought that. . . . And oh!—what shocked me the most was like, when kids would yell at the teachers. Like, in Colombia you don't do that. You respect your teachers. You're supposed to respect your elders. Y'know, but you don't hear them yelling, be like "bitch! You're such a bitch." I never heard that in Colombia until I came here. I never thought that kids my age would be yelling at their professors, saying like "bitch!" Or "you're such an asshole." Y'know, all those bad words. That was really a shock, a cultural shock for me because kids were like very "out there." I don't know what kind of "out there" but they were out there. I went to [a competitive public school] because my experience was like, too much for me, I couldn't take it.

TPS: That was here in Boston?

Alejandra: Yeah, in [another neighborhood]. So, then I went there, but I was in shock, because I thought that [my neighborhood public school] was tough... but that was so much tougher than [the public school]. Like they had no mirrors inside the bathrooms. Because they knew that they would fight, the girls, and y'know they would hurt them with the mirrors. I remember that I learned the word "pussy" there. I didn't know what "pussy" was until I was like 15 because

I heard it at [the competitive public school] [laughing]. . . . So I went back to [neighborhood public school].

In the above passage, Alejandra describes her shock at the behavior of students toward teachers, the drug use, students dropping out, the foul language, and threats of violence. She contrasts these experiences with Colombia, which as a nation has faced decades of civil war and has a reputation for drug cartel-related violence. For Alejandra, though, the US school experience was far more violent and dangerous. In the end, Alejandra's parents moved her out of the highly competitive public school and into a neighborhood public school.

Like Alejandra, Tiago, who is a first-generation college student, also experienced private education in his birth country of Brazil. Upon arriving to an urban public school in Massachusetts, Tiago felt well prepared, even overprepared, for the academic challenges that he faced in the United States. In the following excerpt, he describes his experience with math.

I went to private school in Brazil and the education was much further ahead. Like in eighth grade, most of my peers were learning pre-algebra and some of them were learning Algebra 1, but in Brazil in seventh grade, I was already doing Algebra 2. So, when I got to school here, they didn't have a book that could teach me something I couldn't do. So me and this other girl that was at the same level, like that whole year, the teacher would say, "I don't have any work for you." He would give us these little standardized tests that he had, but that was like just busy work. So she and I would just talk the whole class. I did well in his class, but it set me up for failure in math in the future, because I just totally disconnected from the material so when I got to high school, I was in math class and I had like no class work ethic, like I forgot a lot of these concepts because I wasn't actively studying. He totally set me up for failure. I mean it wasn't his fault, it was more of a systemic issue, but it kind of messed me up.

Like Alejandra, Tiago transitioned from a strong private school education in his home country to a public school that represented the type of "downward assimilation" that sociology of immigration scholars identify as a threat to the integration of the children of immigrants (Portes and Zhou 1993). In this case, Tiago described how his educational advantage evaporated, and even "set me up for failure," because he had allowed his study habits to wither and forgotten material in math.

Finally, while Alejandra and her parents exerted agency to remove her from an unsatisfactory secondary education environment, Tiago's parents did not. This is understandable, given that his mother was also newly arrived in the United States, did not speak English, and relied on him to translate his own school registration, while his father was forced to work long hours to support the family. Such dynamics may also be explained by gendered, cultured, or idiosyncratic choices, but they follow a class-based pattern that suggests that one possible factor in the educational trajectory of first-generation college students among this undocumented immigrant sample may include active involvement by college-educated parents in their children's school experience.

Theme #2: Differential Experiences with School Sorting Among First-Generation and Children of College-Educated Parents

Schools at all levels organize students into groups based on age, educational needs, and perceived potential for learning. Two systems for this are described: (1) bilingual programs in primary and middle school, and (2) high school ability-based grouping or tracks. Among the undocumented immigrant students in this sample, those whose parents completed college experienced these groupings differently from those whose parents did not.

Bilingual Program Contexts in Primary and Middle School

Tiago's narrative about middle school experiences in the United States is striking for how independently he navigated the school system. An extended narrative about Tiago's first day of school demonstrates his independent encounters with the school system:

TPS: What was it like to start school in a new country?

Tiago: Well, it was actually really funny. So, I came to school and it was like the fourth or fifth day and I was expecting it to be all American kids. But then I came in and they were like, we are putting you in the bilingual school, because you are from Brazil and you just got here, and I didn't know what that meant. So, they put me in a class and it was a low-level Portuguese class, and the teacher was Portuguese, and the kids were a mixture of Cape Verdean, Brazilian, and some Hispanic kids, but not a single American kid in sight. And the class was like complete chaos. Just chaos. Like no one was doing anything, just throwing stuff and like the teacher had no control. And then he started doing the work in class of dictation. And he was like "okay, write the dictation." I hadn't done dictation since like the second grade, and this is the eighth grade, and it was like two-syllable words, and I was like, "what is going on? Like what is this? Are you serious? Like, this is the work we are doing in class?" To me it was like total, like I couldn't believe it. This is the work we are doing in class? And I had no context for what was going on, so I was like, "What the fuck is going on?" And the class got so out of control that the teacher was like "c'mon we are getting out of here," so he like rescued me. [Tiago gestures as if the teacher is taking his arm.] And he said, "let's go, let's go, I'm going to take you to Portuguese 4," since this was Portuguese 2. And so, I'm walking with him, and I'm like totally confused, following this really funny and chubby Portuguese guy. It's like cartoonish what's going on. And I follow him. And he's like "no, we are taking you to a different class. Those kids are idiots. Those kids are idiots."

TPS: What were they doing?

Tiago: They were just like arguing and screaming. He had like no control over the class at all. Like he had no authority over the kids. It was like chaos and he couldn't control so he was like, "we are getting out of here." And then he is referring to them as idiots, and I was like, *"what the?* The teacher is referring to them as idiots." And he follows me and is bringing me to the Portuguese 4 class. And it was a totally different, the kids are quiet. And then it was the end of the period so they brought me to the English class. And I went to the English class and I sat down, just because they didn't know where to put me. It was the highest-level bilingual class. And, I'm sitting there while the guidance counselors and two of the teachers in the bilingual program are talking about where to put me. And I'm sitting there and I'm listening and I'm following what they are saying. But then, like the three of them are like "I think he is understanding what we are saying?" And then, they look around and ask, "do you understand what we are saying?" And I say "yeah" and they are like oh, okay. And then they like asked me some questions that I don't remember—

TPS: In English?

Tiago: In English and they ask, "Do you want to just stay in this class?" And I'm like, "I don't know. Okay, sure." I don't have any context. So I just stayed in that class. I started making my friends and stuff. . . . But yeah, that was my first day of school.

The above narrative once again describes a chaotic scene that Tiago's experience at a private school in Brazil did not fully prepare him for. His story reflects how the stereotypes and assumptions of school officials initially resulted in him being placed into a low-level bilingual classroom. In the chaos, the teacher, referring to the other students as "idiots," took notice of him and reassigned him to an upper level class. Unbeknownst to the teachers, Tiago speaks English and follows their conversation about what classroom he should be in. In many ways, this narrative demonstrates Tiago's sense of himself as an agent who can shape the world around him. Despite the structural barriers to his parents' engagement in school at this point, and despite his not "hav[ing] any context" at the time, Tiago played an active and direct role in determining, with his teachers, his classroom.

In contrast, when I asked Alejandra about starting school in the United States, she describe how "my parents pushed me to go into regular classes so soon because they were planning on leaving after two years of being here." She notes almost ruefully that "plans changed and we stayed here." Her narrative of placement in and movement from bilingual classes is driven by her college-educated parents' plans.

The positioning of students either in a bilingual class environment with other non-English speakers or into a mainstream classroom environment has been a source of public policy attention, especially in Massachusetts, where voters chose to eliminate bilingual education as part of a 2002 ballot initiative in favor of a more immersive "Sheltered English" educational model (Quinn 2013). Five of the six participants described participating in the bilingual program. Only Eliza entered mainstream classrooms early in her US education experience. She described her difficulties:

> It was hard. I didn't know English. The first of school it was really hard, because I didn't know anyone; it was a new language, new people, new weather. People would ask me questions in English and I didn't know it, and so people would make fun of me when I was young. I would get really upset but I wouldn't tell anyone. My mom would say, "How was your day?" I would say, "It was great!"

Eliza performed her role as the dutiful daughter, doing the emotional labor of protecting her mother from the loneliness that she felt at school.

The three first-generation college undocumented immigrant students also described, in some detail, very positive experiences in their bilingual classrooms. Paula, who tended to answer questions with short, direct replies, summarized her experience in the bilingual program as follows:

> TPS: At school in general, did you find the teacher was friendly? Did you make friends easily?

> Paula: Yeah, but within the bilingual class, not within the school overall. I would say, we were in the same situation as we were learning English, so I don't know we could relate more I guess. I mean I still have plenty of those friends still.

As Paula notes—and the other students echo these comments—new immigrant students often felt supported in bilingual programs. Victor, especially, points to his positive experiences in the bilingual program. In his case, he had grown up speaking a mixture of Spanish with a native Guatemalan language—a situation that might have caused him to feel alienated. Instead, his teachers found a way to help him feel special:

> And when I got here, I forgot to mention that in Guatemala that I knew Spanish as a first language, but then I was also learning the native language, which is . . . like I guess there are 26 in Guatemala, or 23, dialects. So, I already knew it where I could understand it [Spanish] 100 percent and I could speak it a little bit. I just needed a little bit more and then I would be fluent, I would have been. But

then I came here and, even my Spanish, like all that I knew was my dialect. It just like ah, stopped and halted. And when I came here, nobody taught me Spanish because there's no Spanish classes. So then from there it's just English. So I was placed like in a bilingual class. . . . I remember being in the class, and this one teacher would always put me on the spot, whenever I had some answers. She would point me out that I was the best in her class. So she would always ask me questions like "oh, where are the Incas located?" Y'know, "what part?" Or "where were the Mayans?" So I remember it got to the point and she would ask me, "oh, you also know some dialect." She was like "teach us." I was teaching the class, but I was like nervous, so I said the word like *orange*, y'know the fruit, in the dialect is called *lan sheesh*. And then from there, everyone was like "ooh, ahh!" So I never felt out of place I guess, because I felt like everybody that I was with was like Spanish and Latino.

In the above example Victor describes being "put on the spot" and singled out to demonstrate his native Mayan K'iche' language, for which he received admiration from his peers and acknowledgment from his teacher. This example also demonstrates how culturally competent teachers in the bilingual program might respond to a student who is fluent in neither Spanish nor English.

One puzzling pattern emerged in these six interviews: although all participated in bilingual education, none of the undocumented immigrant students whose parents had attended college shared stories about their bilingual program experiences. In contrast, all three of the first-generation college students spoke with affection about the friendship and support that they received in their bilingual education program. Furthermore, as the next section will discuss, all three students with college-educated parents were all able to transition from these bilingual programs in primary and middle schools to more mainstream honors programs in secondary school. None of the first-generation students effectively transitioned to their schools' honors programs.

High School Ability Grouping and Obstacles to Inclusion

Ability grouping, sometimes called *tracking*, is a system in which schools sort students into high-, middle-, or low-performance-based cohorts that direct some students and not others towards college. Tracking has been widely criticized for its inherent racial discrimination that segregates white students from students of color (Kohli 2014). Among these cases of undocumented students, two of the first-generation college students, Victor and Paula, both entered vocational education programs in high school. Tiago explained cultural challenges that he faced when he entered the honors program:

I went straight from bilingual into the honors program in high school. The honors program had a couple of like Brazilians that had been living here forever, who were very acclimated. But the rest were all Americans. Up until that point, I had been living here for more than a year, but I had had no contact with American kids. Even in elementary school it was, y'know, not to say it was segregated because I don't want to put a negative implication on it, but it was just like, y'know we were the bilingual kids and they were the mainstream kids and that is what it was called and that is that. And, so I got to the honors program and that's when I really got lost, because I was like *Wow!* Like I couldn't relate to any of the kids. The teachers were so odd. They felt so different because they didn't know how to approach a bilingual kid, whereas the elementary school teachers were trained in approaching different cultures and using that as a teaching tool. These teacher were like, to them, it didn't cross their mind. I was just another honors kid who happened to be Brazilian. So that was a hard transition for me into high school, and all of my kids, all of my friends who I was close with were not honors kids.

Tiago's insights here about the indifference of the honors teachers stands in sharp contrast to Victor's teacher in the previous section, who saw cultural differences as a learning opportunity for her entire class. Here, Tiago describes a cultural, not academic, barrier to participating in the honors program. As Tiago notes, he was one of only two Brazilians in the program at a school with a larger Brazilian and Latino population. Further, he had made his close friends as part of the bilingual program, but they were not invited into the honors program in high school. Finally, Tiago describes teachers in the honors program who were insensitive to his sense of alienation as a Brazilian student. Such a situation reflects the color-blindness that allows the dominant society to ignore and minimize cultural differences through a "new racism" (Bonilla-Silva 2014).

Despite these cultural barriers inherent in tracking immigrant students, for the three undocumented immigrant students with college-educated parents, small, sheltered educational programs provided resources and a means for preparing themselves for postsecondary education. Gonzales (2016) identifies these types of settings as "specialized smaller learning environments" that were designed to boost academic achievement and provide additional resources to students (77).

While both Alejandra and Neil seemed to embrace honors programs in their public high schools, Eliza attended a private girls' high school on a scholarship, where she was captain of the cross-country team as well as a member of the track team, Spanish club, God club and "lots of other clubs." Despite her active involvement, when I asked her about her high school experience, she told me it was very hard due to the racism of her classmates.

I went to a private high school and that was really really hard, because that was like the first time that I experienced like racism in my life. I didn't even know what it was. People would make fun of me because I had an accent and I was really really ashamed. I was ashamed that I was in this country and that my parents put me through that, and that my parents didn't know English. Like when we would go out to a restaurant I would always have to order for them, and I was like, this is really embarrassing, y'know? And I was ashamed of that for the longest time and for the fact that I wasn't born here.

I asked her to share an example of this racism.

It was one time that a teacher gave homework . . . assignment and I was the only one that wrote it down. And the next morning people were asking each other [what the assignment was), so I stepped in and I said, "this is the homework, I wrote it down." The girl told me, "Well, how would you know? You don't even know English?" Right? And I was already in the country for like six years, and I thought I knew English. Y'know, I was really, really confused. So after that day I never really spoke to anyone. I would only speak to people that were from like the country that I was from, or like I wouldn't want to talk to my teachers. It was a just a really hard time for me, high school. And then on top of that it was like, "you're undocumented."

The above peer conflict reflects some of the patterns of relational social aggression among teen girls, but with the additional dynamics of exclusion through the deployment of dominant cultural and racial group membership, resulting in exclusion and abject status for 1.5-generation immigrant students (Butler 1999; Gonzales and Chavez 2012). As an undocumented immigrant student, Eliza internalized these slights, allowing them to silence her and uncover shame that she felt about herself and her family. Eliza's experience parallels that of all of six undocumented immigrant students, and others, as they encounter the structural barriers of their immigration status that constitute the system of "illegality." For most, they come to terms with this reality in high school.

Theme #3: Responses to Illegality Related to College-Going

As they discuss their experiences with undocumented status, differences between those who were first-generation college students and those whose parents completed college seemed to be suppressed. Being undocumented was seen by these young people as a "master status," thereby subsuming any alternative identity that these undocumented students had developed for themselves through their success in academic work, extracurricular activities, or work (Gonzales 2016, 176). At the same time, there were two differences in how the first-generation college students responded to being denied college when compared to those whose parents completed college. First, the three first-generation students expressed less overt outrage at being denied college opportunities due to their undocumented status. It seems at least plausible that perhaps something about their identity as first-generation college students shaped and prepared them for the realities of their undocumented immigrant status. Second, these same first-generation students (Tiago, Victor, and Paula) dropped out of college at various times—being, perhaps, less likely to persist in their college plans when confronted with difficulties.

Reactions to Being Denied Education

Among the six interviewees, the three children of college-educated parents seemed to have expressed greater emotional outrage and shock when coming to terms with illegality through their lack of access to college. Neil, Alejandra, and Eliza all expressed strong emotions of betrayal and even tears about being denied college. In contrast, Tiago, Paula, and Victor described this disappointment with less outward emotional outrage, suggesting that perhaps they were more mentally prepared for the limitations that come with a lack of official immigration status. That is not to say that they did not see this as unfair, but for them, there was less sense of indignation at not attending college and more of a seeming acceptance of their status as undocumented.

The one case that was particularly different from the others was Neil, who did not become undocumented until his senior year in high school. Under the protection of his father's legal visa, Neil saw himself as a college-bound student. By the time Neil entered high school, he was ready to participate in honors classes and prepared for advance placement college exams:

> I wasn't a popular kid at school, but I made friends and I started doing sports. I picked up the trumpet. And, my whole life just began as a regular American boy, because I fell into the crowd and I wanted to fit in. And, so I went through middle school and high school, and I did everything I could as a normal boy in America.

During his senior year, Neil applied to six prestigious colleges across the country.

> Neil: I didn't even bother applying to any schools in Massachusetts. My guidance counselor didn't suggest it and I didn't think about it. To me, y'know, senior year, I was doing really well in school. I knew that I was going to be in the top 10 (class rank), and y'know, why go to an in-state school when I can go to a school that I really wanted, like Cal Tech.
>
> TPS: So your father had a visa. You had a visa at that point.

N: Yeah. To me it seemed like, we were, we were just waiting for that final decision for our papers to come in. And then I applied, and that was the whole application process was in the fall of my senior year, and then you are just kind of waiting in limbo for the decision after January first, because most applications are due January 1st, but then I found out that we got denied on January 6th I believe.

When his father's green card application was denied, Neil came to terms with the system of immigration laws that define inclusion and exclusion for undocumented immigrant students.

Neil: I remember that day . . . I came home at like 5pm after [track] practice. And I see my mom in the kitchen, she is trying to cook, but she keeps slowing down, and she's crying, and I am going halfway up the stairs and I ask her, "what's wrong?" And she is like, "Dad got a call. We got denied." And I was halfway up the stairs and I just freeze there and I'm like [sigh]. And then, I just walked up to my room. I put my bag down . . . my desk was facing the wall, and I just sat at my desk, nothing on the table, and I just stared at the wall. I just wanted to break everything. And then, 20 minutes of this, I called my friend. My best friend . . . and I just basically told him what happened. I was in tears. And I was like, I don't know what to do man! I was like, now, I want to go here, and I want to go there, and I want to get a job and I want to do this and that and I want to, y'know, there are a lot of things I want to do, but everything is closed on me. And I don't care about this homework right now, because what does it matter?

For Neil, the juxtaposition of his life as a "normal American boy" and his loss of legal status were shocking. Prior to that day, he was an excellent student who was active in school clubs and sports. As a high school senior, he had applied to a list of highly competitive colleges. He had friends. He did homework. Then suddenly, he was cast out of that life and faced the prospect of returning to a country that was unfamiliar to him, with no option of applying to stay in the United States. In that state, when he considered his work, he asked, "what does it matter?"

Alejandra described her feelings of anger as she watched her friends go to college, not knowing the real reason that she would not be joining them:

I felt so full of anger and frustrations because all my friends were going to college—all of them! Because I was part of I guess the elite group of students in my high school. And they were like, y'know. . . . And what angered me most was that [audible sigh] I never told them my situation. I couldn't say y'know, "oh, I can't go to school." I was also afraid of what they would think.

Further fueling her anguish at not going to college was the enforced secrecy of not being able to tell her peers or teachers about why she was not going. This thought brought visible emotion and tears to her eyes as she described the isolation of not attending the college of her choice, in contrast to her friends. For Alejandra, coming to terms with her undocumented status meant letting go of the plans that she had developed as part of the honors course track at her high school:

Mario graduated a year before me from Public High. He told everyone that he was going to have one [cough] he was going to have one year of rest, just not to tell people that he could not go to college. And I thought about it, because that's what Maria said too. Maria graduated in '04 and she said to her friends the same thing too. She said, "oh, I'm going to take a break." I mean it's believable but, at the same time, all of us were in the honor society and all from AP classes, I mean, like, what kind of student like that is "going to take a break." Like, I don't hear of students like that saying, "I'm going to take a break." Like, in my mind, I say, "No one is going to believe me that I am going to take a break."

In the above, Alejandra mocks herself and her fellow undocumented students who made up unbelievable stories about wanting to take time off from college. Alejandra's experience of not telling friends about her college plans was common to many undocumented immigrant students in this study, and is consistent with scholarship about undocumented students (Menjívar 2006, Rincon 2008, Gonzales 2009a, Gonzales and Chavez 2012, Gonzales 2016).

Among the six students, Victor seemed to have accepted his undocumented status earliest in his high school career. As a child, he "knew that there was something about my situation that I wasn't supposed to be here." His mom cautioned him to not get into trouble or conflict with others and instead to focus on school, which he did. Early in his high school career, however, he adopted an approach to presenting his undocumented status as a way to gain popularity.

Victor: I remember in high school it was all English. And my English was like good, but it needed a little bit of help, I guess. And then as time continued, y'know, I guess, I got more interested in my status. Throughout the whole time I knew, how it was, how everything was. So I accepted my status as being undocumented. So when I started high school, y'know, I was telling people, it's like oh, I'm undocumented. But then I thought of it as like a good thing, in a sense, that I'm undocumented, but I didn't know that you wouldn't get anything if you're undocumented. [Laughs]

TPS: You just came up with this on your own, that you thought of this as a good thing?

Victor: Yeah, because y'know a lot of people, they see me and are like "oh, where are you from," and I'd say, oh I'm undocumented, and they would be

like "oh you're this bad person." Y'know "bad" in a "cool" way, you know it's
like "cool bad"?

In high school, Victor "accepted [his] status as being undocumented." He
then began telling people about his undocumented status to seek status, to
seem "cool." It is interesting to consider how Victor was, at this point, positioned in a vocational education program and attended a school with a high
concentration of immigrants.

His attitude toward being undocumented was very different from other
undocumented students who kept their immigration status secret, even from
close friends. Paula had grown up knowing that she was undocumented. Her
mother warned her repeatedly not to tell anyone. In high school, as her friends
got jobs and then driving permits, Paula described how "it hit me." Despite
support from her mom, who continued to encourage her to study, Paula felt
alone. Here she describes her feelings of isolation:

> Paula: I never told anyone. It was really hard, like, I kind of felt isolated, be-
> cause I was in this situation, and I thought I was by myself, alone in this situa-
> tion. So, I couldn't tell anyone. Well, I felt like I couldn't tell any of my friends.
>
> TPS: It sounds pretty isolating.
>
> Paula: Yeah. And it was really bad because, it was like you have to like make
> up things in order, well I felt like I had to make up things in order to like justify
> why I am not getting my permit, or why I am not working. Or why, I mean until
> this day, there are certain people that know. Just a handful of people that know
> out there that know that I am undocumented but not everyone.

Paula felt that keeping her secret about being undocumented forced her to
"make things up" to justify why she was not getting a permit or not working.
She saw herself as an honest and empathic person, but as she matured into
adulthood, it became increasingly difficult to not tell friends. She thought that
sharing her undocumented status would be a "burden" to her friends:

> Being undocumented was like shameful to me, in some ways. It's not something
> that I want to be. I don't want people to feel awkward around me, or to think
> like, so today, for instance, for some friends I don't want them to think, like,
> "Oh, we can't go here with you, because if we get stopped by cops or some-
> thing." I don't want them to feel uncomfortable. So, I guess that is why I haven't
> said that I am undocumented to certain people.

The type of isolation caused by undocumented status can be a barrier to
college entry and completion. Peer networks are an effective means for sup-

porting college access for first-generation peers.[4] Of course, peer networks can also hinder college aspirations for students, as Tiago explains:

> Tiago: I got into my senior year knowing that I wouldn't go to college.
>
> TPS: How did you become sure you weren't going to go to college?
>
> Tiago: First it's like there is this mythology that exists, that to this day still exists, that you can even get to college, but they won't give you your diploma. Like, just tons of people who say that and they believe that. When, in my years of doing this and being involved in SIM and doing this kind of work, I have never heard of this happening to anybody, but it is like this mythology that is pervasive. And, oh, you can go, but you won't get a degree. And that was the thing, it wasn't an aspiration of any of my peers. Like no one in my group of friends felt like, oh, I'm going to go to college, like that wasn't a thing for people. There was like no support network for kids. And half were dropping out already and getting GEDs. They were like "why am I going to do another year, I could just drop out and get my GED" because that was like the end of the line so if you could get to the end of the line now, why would you do another year?

As the above quote shows, the types of rumors and myths that circulate among undocumented immigrant students through peer networks lead some students to drop out of high school altogether, or at least to not pursue a GED. In Tiago's case, however, an adult reached out to him and changed his mind in his senior year.

Dropping Out or Persisting

As Paula finished high school, she had already convinced herself that she could not go to college.

> TPS: So when you finished high school. What were your plans, where were you planning to go next?
>
> Paula: I would say when junior year came around, I was starting to look at schools, I was starting to visit schools with my friends. I mean, everyone thought that I was going to go on to college. I mean, they were like, there are many scholarships. My teachers were like, "oh you should apply for this or you should apply for that." Even my friends, but, I knew that I had a limitation. I knew that I was undocumented and I couldn't go to college. Well, at least, at that point I thought I couldn't.

In her senior year, despite encouragement from her teachers and friends, Paula did not apply to college. Instead she went to work, but she began attending classes at a community college a few years later. When she did attempt to enroll in school, Paula found a system that was unwelcoming and unable to help her:

> Three years or four years after I had graduated high school. Went to this school, and I went to apply, but I guess the, the person I was speaking to didn't understand. I was trying to explain that "yes I am here to apply, I have everything and I know what I have to bring, ready to apply," and they were like, "oh no you are an international student." And then I went up over there (to the international student office). And they would say, "no you are not an international student, so you have to go back." Then, like I went back and the guy was not helpful at all. So I pretty much like, gave up. And it took me a while to actually go back. And when I did go back, I realized that there was another office that I could have gone to where I had gone and applied, and nothing was asked, but it has been a struggle.

Paula's story is not unique. Many undocumented immigrant students tell similar stories of getting a runaround and of being misidentified as international students, despite having attended US schools from a young age and graduated from high school in the United States. Although, in recent years, college and university personnel have begun to be more aware of the situation of undocumented immigrant students, such barriers can and do cause capable first-generation young people like Paula to postpone their college entry.

In contrast, Eliza, whose college-educated parents supported her education by applying for scholarships to send her to private high school, continued to seek opportunities for her education. During our interview, Eliza told me that she had only told her closest friends about her immigration status. I wondered if she had been able to speak to any teachers about her situation.

> Eliza: I told one of my teachers when I was a senior, in the bathroom. Aah, It's funny, because sometimes you don't think. I was like washing my hands and she asked me about college. It was senior year. And I said, well, I don't know if I can, my paperwork is not alright. And she was from Lebanon. And she's like, y'know what? She knew what I was talking about. She said everything will be okay. And she said, "When I first here to this country I didn't have a green card, and my kids couldn't go to college and now they are professionals." And I thought of that. I didn't really tell her my story, and she pretty much kind of knew.
>
> TPS: She had a similar story?
>
> Eliza: Yeah.
>
> TPS: She had been undocumented. Wow.
>
> Eliza: Yeah and that was my favorite teacher, my math teacher.

Eliza's experience of finding a teacher who had once been undocumented, though, did little to help her apply to college at the time. But she remained motivated to apply to college:

> I told my counselor since I was like a freshman. I told her I was like "I don't have my papers." She was like, she didn't know what it was, but we talked about it. The school wanted to help in some way but they never did anything. It was really confusing. But my counselor told me that I couldn't do anything pretty much about it and not to apply anywhere and that it was going to be hard for me. She didn't know what to do so she couldn't tell me what to do. So, I gave up for few months; but then I decided to apply to schools anyway because, I knew that there were things that I could do in life and that it wasn't gonna stop me.

Eliza researched schools and got in touch with a friend who had become involved with politics. The friend had just obtained a job at the office of a member of Congress. That friend helped put her in touch with other students across the state who were organizing a political campaign for the rights of undocumented immigrant students. As already noted, Eliza worked to raise money for her college degree. She also found support from friends who helped raise money on her behalf. When Eliza graduated with her undergraduate degree, she was the valedictorian, and gave a speech to the classmates of her college.

Factors That Help Equalize Differences Between First-Generation and Those with College-Educated Parents among Undocumented Immigrant Students

The previous three emerging theories help to explain differences between the undocumented immigrant students who were first-generation and those whose parents had attended college. I want to point to two factors from the data that seem to have the potential to lessen the difference between first-generation and children of college-educated parents. First, the role of adults who intervened in the lives of these students seemed to have a positive effect on first-generation college students. Second, the threat of deportation also tended to equalize differences between those undocumented immigrant students who were first-generation college-bound and those whose parents completed college.

Finding Support of Teachers and Other Adults

Tiago's parents started college but did not finish. Throughout his trajectory, he has been on the most circuitous and inconsistent path toward college completion. Recall that he went to a private school and entered the US school system with advantages, but watched those advantages disappear. He then entered the honors program in high school, but found himself inconsistently engaged in his academic work. Tiago's profile seemed to be one of underachieving relative to his academic potential. At the start of his junior year, he thought that he might drop out of school, but by his senior year, was, in his word, a "turnaround." He attributes this turnaround to something that a teacher told him.

> But my senior year was kind of a turnaround. I was like "maybe I need to salvage things here." So I argued and I managed to get into English honors, which was a blessing for me because I had a teacher there, who, indirectly she put me in college. The thing is that even in her class I was disengaged. But she, instead of like, like blaming me or punishing me for being disengaged, she would always tell me, she was like, "y'know what, like I understand why you are disengaged." She was like, "you should be in college now. You are like ready to be in college right now. Like, I understand why you feel you are wasting your time here, because you are ready to go do college work, I totally get it." And that was like, "well maybe I am. Maybe I am. Maybe that's why I don't do well in school, and don't succeed, because I know that I am a smart kid and like could do stuff," but I didn't and I couldn't pinpoint why, at least at that point. She was like, "y'know you should be in college, like, you can do it!" She was like "you should take the SATs." Because I took the PSATs and I did like really well, so she was like, "you should take the SATs." And I was like "okay." And I got a waiver so I didn't have to pay for it and I took the SATs and I did wonderful on the SATs. I did very well.

Tiago credits his teacher with motivating him to take the SATs. Both her class and her support led him to apply. He began college the following year; however, eight years later, he still has not finished, maintaining his on-again, off-again academic record. His lack of college completion is the result of a complex web of factors, including his parents' financial precariousness, which led Tiago to go to work at low-wage jobs at a catering company, in a law office, and for low-paying jobs as a community organizer for various campaigns for immigration- and non-immigration-related issues for eight years. In addition to trying to save for college, he helped support his family. The financial struggle led him to repeatedly step away from his college coursework, and his success as a community organizer eventually led him to decide that college would no longer teach him what he wanted and needed to know. "Realistically, it's a bad deal," Tiago recently told me.

The Threat of Deportation

One aspect of "illegality" that was omnipresent among all of the undocumented immigrant students that I spoke with was the threat of deportation of themselves or their family members. For Victor, this threat became a reality for his family when his mother was arrested as part of a workplace immigration raid and faced possible deportation. Victor described coming hope to an empty home.

Victor: I was just coming from high school, just a regular day, when ah, y'know asking "where's my mom?" y'know, and then she wasn't there. Usually she's there from work because she leaves [work] at three and then she gets home at 3:15. I get home at 3:30. So y'know I'm just waiting there, and then I get a phone call from my aunt saying "did you hear what happened?" And I said "no what happened?" And then she said "There was a raid at the company," and that my mom was there. It was a big shock to me. I didn't want to believe it. The whole situation happened so quickly because people were actually being deported. They wanted to send everybody they caught to Texas. Every family would talk to each other. I would hear from my aunts or my cousins. "Oh, y'know this is what they are doing. Like they are sending people here and making them sign this paper." You hear from everybody what's going on, and then everything is happening too quick. So, it was very, very tough. And then as time continued, I remember my mom just being in jail. And we couldn't actually visit her, like I couldn't or my father couldn't visit her. Nobody could visit her. Only my little brothers or my aunt.

TPS: Your little brother who was born here [which implies they had citizenship]?

Victor: Yes. So, so it was really tough situation. We could only talk on the phone, and just hearing the sadness. It [felt] just helpless. And it was very tough for me because I didn't know what to do. I didn't know how to help her, or what to do. So the only thing I could do was take care of my brothers. And that whole week we spent at my aunt's house. As time progressed, I wanted to know what was going on. There was this situation where my mom was about to be sent to Texas. So when you hear, like all the people saying that the people who sent to Texas that, once they are there, then their case is lost and they are going to be deported. So my mother was going to be sent there and then I was like "oh I'm going to lose my mother." But my father acted quick in getting a lawyer. This lawyer fought for her, and then he got her out and then she won her case. And now she has her work permit, so I guess in the end it was a good thing with a really positive turn out.

The trauma of the above ordeal, which lasted only three weeks, had repercussions for a long time afterward. Several months later, Victor began to question the value of his own education.

So everything was good, but for me, I guess it was not. And the next year, like in school, I started thinking more about this, like what happened, and my situation was that, well, what's going to happen to me after I'm graduated? That's when it hit me. After graduation, I'm still not going to be able to do anything. So it's not going to be worth it.

As Victor wrestled with these questions, his family experienced another trauma at the hands of Immigration and Custom Enforcement (ICE) officers. Almost a year after his mother's detention, ICE officers arrived at his home and woke him. Victor described the scene vividly:

Around 6:30 in the morning, there was no school. Y'know I was in like thinking I could sleep in. And then I remember in my room some person opened the door and then they checked inside and then they closed it back up. And I was like whoa, who is this?

TPS: So you didn't know who was opening your bedroom door! Wow.

Victor: And then I heard people talking and I was like who is this so early in the morning? There was like a lot of people. So I was like cleaning my eyes, and opening the door, and I was like boom! I see six ICE officers in the living room. And there was two on the couch, one looking around, one sitting talking to my mom, one was just standing there like intimidating. They would not leave unless we give them a lead on where my father was. We were saying that he is not here anymore, but they wouldn't believe it. They were like, "oh it's a lie." And then my father, because he worked like 25 hours each day, [laughs] I don't know how he gets that extra hour in. And he like works really hard, so he had this "worker of the month" thingy in the living room. I remember when he got it, he was like "oh look that I got this," he put it on the wall, and they saw it and were like "oh who is this person?" And it had his full name. [laugh] And then I was like "oh it's me" because my name, is kind of mixed with his. They wouldn't believe me. And I saw, because my mom goes through panic attacks, so my mom was about to go into a panic attack. She was getting very, her breathing was very weird. And at this moment who am I going to call? They are supposed to be the good people, y'know. And they are not going to be helpful.

TPS: So you would ordinarily want to call the police. But you can't.

Victor: To me they were like the police. I didn't know there like was a separate branch from ICE. So, I was like, what should I do? So that's when I took the decision of telling them where my father was working. So, after I told them, they wanted more information. And they were like "where exactly is it?" And, I was like "I don't know," I gave them a different address. And they left. And then my mother was mad at me, she said, "ah, why did you do that?" After they left, she calmed down, and we called him and asked him to leave. So he left. And then an hour later they came there and then they missed him. By then, he couldn't work there anymore. So y'know he was like, "this is a really bad situation," because it's like being hunted down.

The above extended narrative is both dramatic and sad. In this scene, six armed officers pressured a woman and her 16-year-old son to reveal their father's whereabouts. Although Victor's father did not get arrested that day, the threat of his deportation hurt his employment prospects and instilled fear in his family. Victor's father decided to turn himself in to Immigration and Customs Enforcement (ICE), leaving Victor to take on more responsibility for the family.

> I was the one who knows English really fluently, so I was doing all of the translating and appointments and doing all of these bad news telling. I don't know, it's just like ah, this bad thing to carry around with you. So, like all of my school work just started going down, and then, like I couldn't concentrate anymore, and then, like in my head, it's like what am I doing this for?

Predictably, Victor's schoolwork continued to deteriorate after this second trauma. After this incident, Victor's father began a series of court appearances to consider his case. Each time, for a little over a year, his father's case was postponed for three months more. As Victor describes it, his father's case was being considered in Spring 2009, two weeks before Victor's high school graduation.

> He was about to get deported and in 2009 when I was graduating, they do it in May, I forget the month, but . . . his court date was a week before my graduation. So each court date that he went to was like either stay or he would go. Yeah, every year they would kick it for three more months. It got to the point where it was my graduation day and then a week before my graduation day, was his court date. And I was very nervous, because throughout that whole time I didn't know if he was going to stay or not. I really wanted him to see my graduation. I was really happy when he got two more months. But then I was nervous that he had two more months and they usually give him three. But y'know I didn't put much into it. He saw my graduation, and I graduated, and I walked. Y'know I stayed home and tried to do what I could and then the two months came up and it was his court date, and then I hear like a phone call saying that he was detained and that he can't leave, and, it was like a really tough situation because I guess the hardest part was the accepting part, rather than the whole process, I thought that it wasn't real. I was like "oh he is going to come back, he is just working and then at midnight I am going to hear the door." I didn't want to believe it. And then as time passed, and then on August 15th or something, he got deported. So at the end of 2009, it was all of this bad situation and I didn't know what to do anymore because I had just graduated high school.

As the above quote describes, the impending deportation of his father served as a motivation for Victor to continue his schoolwork. His father's desire to see him graduate high school became a rallying point for him to improve his grades and even obtain awards and scholarships that made him eligible for college. A few months after Victor's graduation, however, his father was deported. Instead of college, Victor went to work to support his mother and younger siblings in the absence of his father. Years later, Victor enrolled in community college courses, but he eventually abandoned them for an apprenticeship in a professional trade.

CONCLUSION

This study reveals the way first-generation college status intersects with undocumented immigration status. In many ways, this study challenges commonly held notions that attempt to paint undocumented immigrant students with a broad brush. Instead, as the cases here suggest, undocumented immigrant students' college access and completion may be, in part, shaped by a set of dynamics put into play by their parents' educational completion years before. Three such dynamics are presented here as "emergent theories" to explain differences between those undocumented students whose parents completed college and those with parents that did not.

The first emergent theory is that *college-educated undocumented immigrant parents play a direct role in the early education of their children in ways that are, at least, less common for non-college-educated parents.* This occurs in two ways: First, by influencing the college-going identity of undocumented immigrant students through direct interventions and, second, by advocating for and intervening in problematic educational settings.

Parents influence the college-going identity of undocumented immigrant students through direct intervention. Alejandra, Eliza, and Neil described how their parents' college-educated status served to shape expectations for their own identity and educational goals. While both first-generation parents and college-educated parents cared about and sought to support their children's early English learning, interviews with children of non-college-educated parents revealed parents who themselves had less English language literacy or had to work longer hours and were unable to support their children's schoolwork. While Paula's grandmother provided her with strategies to support her English and academic lessons, Victor and Tiago needed to make more entrepreneurial efforts to learn English and navigate their schooling. One possible explanation is that direct parental support for learning may, in some ways, be gendered. That said, any such conclusions depend on future research.

Many undocumented immigrant students who transition to US schools face poor educational environments. Alejandra, Neil, and Tiago were shocked to find chaotic classrooms and low academic standards, in comparison to the education in their home countries. First-generation parents may find it more difficult to support and advocate for their children's education in US K-12 schools, especially if they face long work schedules and language barriers. As noted above, Alejandra's parents moved her to a new school when she encountered a difficult school environment.

The second emergent theory is that *first-generation undocumented immigrant students experience school structures very differently.* Bilingual education programs and high school ability grouping provide two systems that structure the populations of students. According to the first-generation students, bilingual education programs played an important role in providing support as they integrated into the US school system. Victor, for instance, was able to build his sense of inclusion, despite his lack of either English or Spanish literacy, as a result of culturally competent teachers. While these bilingual programs worked well for early integration among these students, and helped them to establish strong peer networks, the children of college-educated parents did not refer to them. As we saw, Tiago was unique among his bilingual program peers in the honors program, and that was only after the intervention of one teacher late in his high school career.

In another example of sorting students, high school ability groups tend to sort students who are college-bound into preparatory programs, and tend to benefit those students whose parents completed college (Gonzales 2010). At the same time, Eliza's experience reminds us that the high-performance mainstream classroom can be a site in which immigrant students experience discrimination from peers. Among this sample, ability grouping tended to exclude the first-generation undocumented immigrant students from college preparatory groups, despite their college potential.

A third emergent theory about the importance of college-educated parents for the college completion of undocumented immigrant students is that *first-generation college students responded to illegality less acutely, but also with a greater willingness to opt out or give up on their college plans.* As Gonzales (2016, 180) notes, those who had expectations of college success felt the loss of those plans perhaps more acutely as they encountered structural barriers related to their undocumented status. As noted above, Neil, Alejandra, and Eliza experienced "being cast out" as profoundly painful disappointments. In contrast, Victor, Tiago, and Paula had come to terms with their undocumented status, even if that meant delaying or opting out of plans for college.

The above three theories point to ways that first-generation students differ from undocumented students whose parents completed college prior to migration. That said, a final emergent theory suggests that there are *two experiences that serve as equalizers between undocumented immigrants with college-educated parents and undocumented first-generation college students.* The first experience involves adults, especially teachers, who cared and intervened in the lives of these students, having a positive effect on first-generation college students, helping to equalize factors that may have undermined the college plans of these young people. The second factor to equalize the differences between those undocumented immigrant students who were first-generation college-bound and those whose parents completed college is the threat of deportation. As Victor's story reveals, the deportation of his parents was the factor that led him to leave college. Although Victor would have been a first-generation college student, it is unlikely that his parents' college experience would have buffered the effects of deportations that required him to return to work.

Limitations and Implications for Research and Policy

The current study is designed to suggest the potential dynamics at the nexus of first-generation college status and undocumented immigration status. This study is intended to surface the dynamics of this small sample of undocumented immigrant students in Massachusetts. At the same time, firm conclusions should be considered with caution. It is, of course, impossible to generalize from six cases about the implications of a family's college experience on an undocumented student's college prospects. Instead, this study serves to develop hypotheses for future research on a larger sample.

In addition, most of the data collection for this study took place prior to DACA and in a state that does not allow access to in-state tuition for undocumented students. Both DACA and in-state tuition policies provide structural supports that have the potential to increase college access for undocumented students. It may be that differences between family college-going for undocumented students with DACA or in states with in-state tuition policies disappear.

Future research might better consider whether and how parent college education holds explanatory power for understanding the dynamics among undocumented immigrant students. Another dimension of analysis that deserves more attention is the role of gender among parents and children, within schools, and even in how undocumented students experience threats of deportation, to better understand how gender shapes interactions between college-educated parents or non-college-educated parents with male, female, or transgender children differently.

This study also suggests implications for education policies to undocumented immigrant students in US schools. First, K-12 teachers in honors programs could benefit from a greater awareness of cultural bias, just as the teachers in bilingual programs might benefit from greater attention to college goal-setting. Likewise, Paula's experience reveals ways that colleges and universities might better guide admissions staff about opportunities for which undocumented immigrant students do and do not qualify. Finally, the context of college-going for undocumented immigrant students who entered as children depends upon an immigration system that provides opportunities for these young people to normalize their status as legal residents, if not citizens, in the United States.

REFERENCES

Arbeit, Caren A., and John Robert Warren. 2013. "Labor Market Penalties for Foreign Degrees Among College Educated Immigrants." *Social Science Research* 42: 852–71.

Bonilla-Silva, Eduardo. 2014. *Racism without Racists: Color-Blind Racism and the Persistence of Racial Inequality in America.* Lanham, MD: Rowman and Littlefield Publishers.

Butler, Judith. 1999. Gender Trouble: Feminism and the Subversion of Identity. New York: Routledge.

Charmaz, Kathy. 2000. *Constructing Grounded Theory: A Practical Guide Through Qualitative Analysis.* Thousand Oaks, CA: Sage Publications.

Chen, Ping. 2010. *Assimilation of Immigrants and Their Adult Children: College Education, Cohabitation and Work.* El Paso, TX: LFB Scholarly Publishing.

Child_Trends. 2014. *Immigrant Children: Indicators for Children and Youth.* KIDS Count Data Center (16 pages). Report accesssed on October 13, 2017 at: https://www.childtrends.org/wp-content/uploads/2012/07/110_Immigrant_Children.pdf.

Clayton-Matthews, Alan, Faye Karp, and Paul Watanabe. 2009. *Massachusetts Immigrants by the Numbers: Demographic Characteristics and Economic Footprint.* Malden, MA: Immigrant Learning Center.

Collins, Patricia Hill. 2000. *Black Feminist Thought: Knowledge, Consciousness and the Politics of Empowerment.* New York: Routledge.

Corbin, Juliet, and Anselm L. Strauss. 2008. *Basics of Qualitative Research.* Thousand Oaks, CA: Sage Publications.

Crenshaw, Katherine. 1991. "Mapping the Margins: Intersectionality, identity politics, and violence against women of color." *Stanford Law Review* 43, no. 6: 1241–99.

De Genova, Nicholas. 2013. "Spectacles of Migrant 'Illegality': the Scene of Exclusion, the Obscene of Inclusion." *Ethnic and Racial Studies* 36, no. 7: 1180–98.

Engle, Jennifer, Adolfo Bermeo, and Colleen O'Brien. 2006. *Straight from the Source: What Works for First-Generation College Students.* Washington, DC: Pell Institute for the Study of Opportunity in Higher Education.

Feliciano, Cynthia. 2006. "Beyond the Family: The Influence of Premigration Status on the Educational Expectations of Immigrant Children." *Sociology of Education* 79, no. 4: 281–303.

Gonzales, Roberto G. 2009a. "On the Rights of Undocumented Children." *Society* 46, no. 5: 419–22.

Gonzales, Roberto G. 2009b. *Young Lives on Hold: The College Dreams of Undocumented Students.* Washington, DC: College Board. 28.

Gonzales, Roberto G. 2010. "On the Wrong Side of the Tracks: Understanding the Effects of School Structure and Social Capital in the Educational Pursuits of Undocumented Immigrant Students." *Peabody Journal of Education* 85, no. 4: 469–85.

Gonzales, Roberto G. 2016. *Lives in Limbo: Undocumented and Coming of Age in America.* Oakland: University of California Press.

Gonzales, Roberto G., and Leo R. Chavez. 2012. "Awakening to a Nightmare." *Current Anthropology* 53, no. 3: 255–81.

Gonzales, Roberto G., and Veronica Terriquez. 2013. "How DACA is Impacting the Lives of Those Who Are Now DACAmented: Prelimininary Findings from the National UnDACAmented Research Project." Migration Policy Institute and the Center for the Study of Immigrant Integration. www.americanimmigrationcouncil. org/sites/default/files/research/daca_final_ipc_csii_1.pdf.

Hipsman, Faye, Barbara Gomez-Aguinaga, and Randy Capps. 2016. *DACA at Four: Participation in the Deferred Action Program and Impacts on Recipients.* Policy Briefs. Washington, DC: Migration Policy Institute. www.migrationpolicy.org/ research/daca-four-participation-deferred-action-program-and-impacts-recipients.

Jaffe-Walter, Reva, and Stacey J. Lee. 2011. "'To Trust in My Root and to Take That to Go Forward': Supporting College Access for Immigrant Youth in the Global City." *Anthropology and Education Quarterly* 42, no. 3: 281–96.

Jefferies, Julian. 2014. "Fear of Deportation in High School: Implications for Breaking the Circle of Silence Surrounding Migration Status." *Journal of Latinos and Education* 13, no. 4: 278–95.

Kasinitz, Philip, John H. Mollenkopf, Mary C. Waters, and Jennifer Holdaway. 2009. *Inheriting the City: Children of Immigrants Come of Age.* New York: Russell Sage Foundation.

Kohli, Sonali. 2014. "Modern-Day Segregation in Public Schools." *The Atlantic*, Nov. 18, 2014. www.theatlantic.com/education/archive/2014/11/modern-day-segregation-in-public-schools/382846/.

Menjívar, Cecilia. 2006. "Liminal Legality: Salvadoran and Guatemalan Immigrants' Lives in the United States." *American Journal of Sociology* 111, no. 4: 999–1037.

Menjívar, Cecilia. 2010. "Immigrants, Immigration, and Sociology: Reflecting on the State of the Discipline." *Sociological Inquiry* 80, no. 1: 3–27.

Morse, Ann, Gilberto Soria Mendoza, Connor Jackson, and Joana Leung. 2016. "Immigrant Policy Project: 2016 Report on State Immigration Laws (January–June)." National Conference of State Legislatures. www.ncsl.org/documents/immig/ImmigrationReport_Sept2016_Final.pdf.

Nunez, Anne-Marie. 2014. "Employing Multilevel Intersectionality in Educational Research: Latino Identities, Contexts and College Access." *Educational Researcher* 43, no. 2: 85–92.

Olivas, Michael A. 2012. *Citizenship and Migration in the Americas: No Undocumented Child Left Behind : Plyler v. Doe and the Education of Undocumented Schoolchildren.* New York, NY: NYU Press.

Passel, Jeffrey, and D'Vera Cohn. 2010. *US Unauthorized Immigration Flows are Down Sharpley Since Mid-Decade.* Washington DC: Pew Hispanic Center.

Passel, Jeffrey S., D'Vera Cohn, Jens Manuel Krogstad, and Ana Gonzalez-Barrera. 2014. *As Growth Stalls, Unauthorized Immigrant Population Becomes More Settled.* Sept. 3, 2014. Washington, DC: Pew Research Center Hispanic Trends. www.pewhispanic.org/2014/09/03/as-growth-stalls-unauthorized-immigrant-population-becomes-more-settled/

Perez, William, Roberto Espinoza, Karina Ramos, Heidi M. Coronado, and Richard Cortes. 2009. "Academic Resilience Among Undocumented Latino Students." *Hispanic Journal of Behavioral Sciences* 31, no. 2: 149–81.

Portes, Alejandro, and Ruben G. Rumbaut. 2001. *Legacies: The Story of the Immigrant Second Generation.* Berkeley: University of California Press.

Portes, Alejandro, and Min Zhou. 1993. "The New Second Generation: Segmented Assimilation and Its Variants." *The Annals of the American Academy of Political and Social Science* 530, no. 1: 74–96.

Quinn, Colleen. 2013. "Students Languishing Under Massachusetts' Bilingual Education Law, Critics Say." State House New Service, April 9, 2013. www.masslive.com/politics/index.ssf/2013/04/students_languising_under_mass.html

Rincon, Alejandra. 2008. *Undocumented Immigrants and Higher Education: Si Se Puede!* El Paso, TX: LFB Scholarly Publishing.

Rocha-Tracy, Maria Natalicia. 2009. "Encounters Between Immigrant Students and US Urban Universities." *Human Architecture: Journal of Sociology of Self-Knowledge* 7, no. 1: 23–34.

Rumbaut, Ruben G. 2004. "Ages, Life Stages, and Generational Cohorts: Decomposing the Immigrant First and Second Generations in the United States." *International Migration Review* 38, no. 3: 46.

Rumbaut, Ruben G. 2009. "Pigments of Our Imagination: On the Racialization and Racial Identities of 'Hispanics' and 'Latinos.' In *How the U.S. Racializes Latinos: White Hegemony and its Consequences*, edited by Jose A. Cobas, Jorge Duany, and Joe. R. Feagin, 15–36. Boulder, CO, Paradigm Publishers.

Rumbaut, Ruben G., and Golnaz Komaie. 2010. "Immigration and Adult Transitions." *Future of the Children* 20, no. 1: 43–65.

Ryan, Sarah, and Robert K. Ream. 2016. "Variation Across Immigrant Generations in Parent Social Capital, College-Aligned Actions and Four-Year College Enrollment." *American Educational Research Journal* 53, no. 4: 953–86.

Suarez-Orozco, Carola, Marcelo Suarez-Orozco, and Irine Todorova. 2008. *Learning in a New Land: Immigrant Students in American Society.* Cambridge, MA: Harvard University Press.

Toutkoushian, Robert K, Robert S. Stollberg, and Kelly A. Slaton. 2015. "Talking 'Bout My Generation: Defining 'First-Generation Students' in Higher Education Research." Paper presented at the Association for the Study of Higher Education.

Vasquez-Salgado, Yolanda, Patricia M. Greenfield, and Rocio Burgos-Cienfuegos. 2015. "Exploring Home-School Value Conflicts: Implications for Academic Achievement and Well-Being Among Latino First-Generation College Students." *Journal of Adolescent Research* 30, no. 3: 271–305.

Willen, S. S. 2012. "Migration, 'Illegality,' and Health: Mapping Embodied Vulnerability and Debating Health-Related Deservingness." *Social Science and Medicine* 74, no. 6: 805–11.

Williams, Shannon M., and Joseph R. Ferrari. 2015. "Identification Among First-Generation Citizen Students and First-Generation College Students: An Exploration of School Sense of Community." *Journal of Community Psychology* 43, no. 3: 377–87.

Wong, Tom K., Greisa Martinez Rosas, Adrian Reyna, Ignacia Rodriguez, Patrick O'Shea, Tom Jawetz, and Philip E. Wolgin. 2016. "New Study of DACA Beneficiaries Shows Positive Economic and Educational Outcomes." Center for American Progress, October 18, 2016. www.americanprogress.org/issues/immigration/news/2016/10/18/146290/new-study-of-daca-beneficiaries-shows-positive-economic-and-educational-outcomes/

NOTES

1. The recognition of credentials earned in developing nations is shaped by systemic transnational racial, class, and gendered constructions and evaluations of knowledge. Economic and political barriers deny the knowledge and experiences of non-Western institutions of education and, when employed, enact a penalty of 17 percent in wages for females and 11 percent for males (see Arbeit and Warren 2013).

2. Recent attention to "illegality" as an object of study attempts to shift the analytic lens away from the subjects of unauthorized migrants and towards the judicial and sociopolitical condition of unauthorized status (Willen 2007; DeGenova 2002, 2013; Gonzales and Chavez 2012). Discourses of "illegality" when deployed by the state, but also by cultural and social institutions, including academic scholars, come with risks of reifying subjects (Willen 2012, 2007; DeGenova 2002, 2013). Most importantly, "illegality" suggests a holistic appropriation of these subjects, thereby defining subjects through a lens of the "other." The "illegal" stain becomes fully defining of subjects, leaving invisible the spheres of discourses not recognized as "illegal," whether they be cultural, social, physical, or organizational "counterpublics" that provide opportunities for resistance and social movement mobilization (De Genova 2013).

3. According to the report, this figure includes 21,000 total eligible and those who would be eligible, but for the education requirements of DACA. Eight thousand DACA applications have been accepted by USCIS from Massachusetts residents (Hipsman et al. 2016).

4. For an example of this, see the Posse Program, described in Kim Godsoe's chapter in this volume. The Posse Program is built around a model of peer-supported college-going and completion.

7

First-Generation Students and Their Families

Examining Institutional Responsibility during College Access and Transition

Judy Marquez Kiyama, Casandra E. Harper, and Delma Ramos

Parental involvement in children's education has been consistently encouraged and is widely accepted as a positive form of support, particularly during the precollegiate years (Auerbach 2004; Berzin 2010; Ishimaru et al. 2016; Jun and Colyar 2002; Tierney 2002; Tekleselassie, Mallery, and Choi 2013). The role that parents should have during the transition to and throughout college is less certain. Characterizations of family engagement at the college level are often depicted as negative (Carney-Hall 2008; LeMoyne and Buchanan 2011; López Turley, Desmond, and Bruch 2010; Taub 2008) and tend to reflect the engagement of upper- and middle-class White families (Wartman and Savage 2008). Some argue that active family engagement during the college transition is undesirable for student well-being and socialization (LeMoyne and Buchanan 2011). Missing from much of the discussion on family engagement during the college transition process is a conversation inclusive of first-generation college students and their families. First-generation students and their families must be part of our understanding of familial engagement when we consider the educational opportunities and long-term educational attainment for these students. Research indicates that there is a degree-attainment gap for first-generation college students. The US Department of Education reported that only 24 percent of first-generation students earn a bachelor's degree compared to 68 percent of non-first-generation students (Chen 2005; Digest of Education Statistics 2011). Students of color comprise 36 percent of the first-generation population (Chen 2005). Thus, we must pay attention to both the attainment gap affecting first-generation students and the negative messaging regarding their families' engagement.

Within the larger societal landscape, it is imperative for institutions to recognize the multitude of factors that shape the level and degree to which families participate in higher education; such factors include race, ethnicity, poverty, and parental educational attainment (Lee and Bowen 2006). Communication patterns between students and their families are particularly noteworthy as families can influence students' alcohol use (Labrie and Cail 2011; Wood et al. 2010), intimacy and relationships in college (Morgan, Thorne, and Zurbriggen 2010), college success (Wang 2014) and well-being (Sax and Weintraub 2014). Although literature on the role of families in higher education offers a somewhat narrow view of their engagement by focusing on communication patterns, such research nonetheless offers some evidence of the important role families play in the college experience of their children.

Research on the role of families in higher education emphasizes their participation during the precollegiate years in developing expectations and aspirations for college access, enrollment, and success. Regarding college aspirations, social familial support is key in the formation of such aspirations and ideologies in young children (Auerbach 2004; Berzin 2010; Jun and Coylar 2002; Tekleselassie, Mallery, and Choi 2013; Tierney 2002). Historically, teachers and other educators have assessed the academic preparation and family support of students from underrepresented backgrounds as less than adequate (Corbett 2004; Martinez 2003). This argument has been countered by others (Auerbach 2004; Berzin 2010; Jun and Coylar, 2002; Kiyama 2010; Perna 2000; Tierney 2002), who assert that the role of families from underserved groups is important not only for the development of college-going aspirations but also for college access and enrollment. This argument is supported by scholars who encourage families from underrepresented backgrounds to have a more pronounced role within the college-going process, as higher involvement can translate directly into college enrollment (Tekleselassie, Mallery, and Choi 2013; Tierney and Auerbach 2002). Family engagement during the precollegiate years can result in emotional, social, and logistical support for college-bound students (Tekleselassie, Mallery, and Choi 2013; Tierney and Auerbach 2002).

The involvement of families of first-generation college students has received limited attention in research and practice, as their support can often go unnoticed. Drawing on qualitative findings, this chapter examines the role that institutions play in engaging and valuing first-generation families, particularly low-income and families of color. Our research also reveals many instances of oblivious or overtly dismissive practices targeted toward or affecting this population. Thus, a significant contribution of this chapter is an exploration of the institutional ideologies and practices of engagement when working with first-generation students and their families.

LITERATURE REVIEW

The Role of First-Generation Families

One area of emerging literature on the role of first-generation families emphasizes the experiences of Latinx first-generation families, focusing on specific areas in which they support the college experience of their children, including lending emotional, moral, and spiritual support (Auerbach 2006, 2007; Castellanos et al. 2013; Hernández 2000; Terenzini et al. 1994). This support is accessible to students via family visits and engagement in family rituals and functions. First-generation families of Mexican descent, for example, offer emotional support to their students through *consejos* (advice) as a way to motivate their children to attend and succeed in college (Castellanos et al. 2013). The approaches these families take to support their children speak to their desire for them to build a promising future. It also alludes to roles that are crucial in supporting student motivation to succeed in college but that are not easily visible, such as offering emotional and moral support. These studies collectively stress the importance of familial support for students from first-generation families and a need for institutions to better understand and foster their engagement in college.

Depictions of First-Generation Families

Some research on first-generation families takes a deficit perspective, suggesting, for example, that students from first-generation families experience more difficulties accessing college primarily due to the close ties they maintain with their families. López Turley, Desmond, and Bruch (2010) argue that students who are closer to their families choose not to attend college in locations that would physically separate them from their loved ones. Such a claim supports the continuity of deficit views of first-generation families and blames students' restricted college enrollment decisions on family cultural values without taking into consideration larger structural systems that influence college access for students from underrepresented communities. Similarly, Smith and Zhang (2010) argue that students who come from first-generation families find themselves at a disadvantage in college, as they receive less familial support than students from highly educated families. Dennis, Phinney, and Chuateco (2005) argue that first-generation family involvement in their children's college transition does not contribute to student success in college, including academic achievement, adjustment, or commitment to persist. Others suggest that students from these families experience competing responsibilities, which in turn become barriers to their academic success in college (Soris and Stebleton 2012) because of having to balance two different contexts: that of their first-generation family and that of the institutions of higher learning they attend (Jehangir 2010). With the exception of work that outlines positive implications of family engagement in terms of psychological well-being and socialization (Sax and Weintraub 2014; Melendez and Melendez 2010), the extant literature positions this group in a place of disadvantage, where they are seen as less supportive of and less resourceful for their college children. This deficit focus ingrained in the literature is largely fueled by historical, perennial negative perceptions about underrepresented, less economically advantaged groups in the United States (Solorzano and Yosso 2001).

Current Practices of Engaging Families

The deficit ideologies presented in the literature related to family engagement are a call for institutions to reconsider the ways in which they can support families throughout students' college transition. Of particular interest are the engagement and inclusion of first-generation families, who are often absent not only from the literature but also from the college landscape as perceived by college personnel. Researchers recommend not only revising current programming efforts but also strategies through which they can build bridges to connect familial engagement and support to student retention and success in college (Sax and Wartman 2010).

Guidelines on engaging families for institutions of higher learning are commonly developed by professional associations and consortiums in the field. In the field of higher education, the Council for the Advancement of Standards in Higher Education (CAS) formulates and develops professional standards that inform the creation, implementation, and assessment of policies, programs, and services on college campuses. With regard to family engagement, CAS standards frame parents and families as key institutional partners in the retention and success of students in college (CAS 2012). To these ends, CAS standards encourage and guide the creation of parent and family programs, with the goal of engaging parents and families through education, communication, and collaboration. CAS standards for parent and family programs include the following: programs must help families maintain a connection to the institution; programs must be located in an organizational structure that can best provide for effective programming and services for achievement of their mission; and programs must be staffed adequately by individuals qualified to accomplish their mission (CAS 2012, 1–19).

The influence of standards and guidelines offered by entities such as CAS is reflected in the ways in which higher education institutions choose to engage parents and families and in their interest to identify best practices for engagement. A portrayal of these efforts is found in the work of Daniel et al. (2009), which explored intentional communication between student affairs professionals and parents and families of first-year students. Findings revealed that traditional forms of communication, such as paper mailings, were an effective approach to maintain a connection with families regarding campus activities and resources to support student success. Similar work has investigated other forms of parent and family engagement, including orientation programming (Gassiot 2012; Granholm 2009). Insights from these inquiries suggest that parents and families are compelled to attend orientation because they see it as a sign of continued affiliation with the institution upon student enrollment. For these parents and families, orientation provides a comfortable environment where they are supported in developing a relationship with the institution and a setting where they can learn more about ways to remain involved, such as campus events and local parent groups sponsored by the institution.

Ward-Roof, Heaton, and Coburn (2008) support this idea by postulating that orientation programs are an opportunity for institutions of higher education to partner with parents and families to foster student success in college. Important factors to keep in mind, as institutions move toward designing orientation programming inclusive of families, are the varying structures that embody the familial institution and the language used when naming these types of programs, with the goal of making them as inclusive as possible (Mayer 2011).

Orientation programming provides an opportunity to offer inclusive and relevant information for families, including information on life in college and potential changes that students might experience, an explanation of campus services, and a discussion of expectations regarding the characteristics of the family-student relationship while in college (Budny and Paul 2003). These components are geared toward equipping families to better lend support to their students. Three main pieces of advice that emerge from Budny and Paul's (2003) suggestions are (1) information about fundamental changes in the lifestyle of college students can help families better understand and communicate during the transition process, (2) knowledge of campus resources can help families be more effective in advocating for their college-bound children, and (3) information about potential changes in the family-student relationship can help mitigate misunderstandings and strengthen the ways in which families can better support their children socially and emotionally.

Although much of the literature on how institutions can engage families revolves around orientation programming, scholars have begun to look at alternative opportunities for engagement (Apprey et al. 2014). Among these endeavors are mentoring efforts that include the participation of parents and families. These programs provide support to parents so that they can engage in literacy activities with other families and play advisory roles in the program on topics including diversity and retention.

Other forms of institutional engagement of parents and families include parent/family weekends and events for younger siblings. Parent/family weekends offer opportunities for institutions to showcase aspects relevant to the student experience, including academic and nonacademic accomplishments, campus resources, and important updates that concern the success of students at that institution. In the same vein, events that engage other family members including younger siblings serve as a way for institutions to demonstrate their interest and continued commitment to the college access and success of other members of the family (Ward-Roof, Heaton, and Coburn 2008). Other programming to encourage parent and family involvement might include convocation and graduation and the development of parent associations.

Literature on how institutions are currently engaging families remains scarce. Further research is needed to expand our understanding of how colleges and universities can successfully partner with first-generation families (Guiffrida et al. 2012; Harper, Sax, and Wolf 2012; Wartman and Savage 2008; Wolf, Sax, and Harper 2009). Acknowledging that the transition to college is not only lived by students but also by their families is fundamental as institutions of higher education begin their journey toward the establishment of long-lasting, effective partnerships with families (Kiyama and Harper, 2018).

AN EMERGING CONCEPTUAL MODEL

The role of parents and families in the college transition process represents an emerging area in both research and practice. There currently does not exist a conceptual model that depicts the role and influence of first-generation, low-income, and families of color in the college transition process. Thus, we have begun to develop a conceptual model, *Model of Parent and Family Characteristics, Engagement, and Support*, as part of our larger research agenda on this topic. We believe that developing a more inclusive model of family engagement will better inform research, theory, and practice. Figure 7.1 illustrates a visual representation of this emerging model and includes the multiple factors that might be included in the model. Our forthcoming article "Beyond Hovering: A Conceptual Argument for an Inclusive Model of Family Engagement in Higher Education" includes a full discussion of the development of this emerging model. The model represents a complex portrayal of parents and families, their characteristics, and various ways they are engaged with their college-going students (Kiyama and Harper 2018).

The emerging model of family engagement identifies the pre-college and college contributions of parents and families and can be linked to college student outcomes (i.e., academic, social, emotional, etc.). We share the following in our forthcoming article,

> The center of the model identifies important pre-college and college dimensions of parent and family characteristics, engagement, and support that add complexity to our understanding of the full nature of contributions made by parents and family members. The spiral shape conveys the lack of temporal order or hierarchy to these factors. The model's pre-college characteristics offer an understanding of the personal characteristics of the parents and family, their involvement with schools, the aspirations they have for their child(ren), the various forms of support they might provide, their own self-efficacy related to navigating the educational system, and their social network of resources and information. (Kiyama and Harper 2018)

The model offers utility when considering the larger context of the family and community, as well as institutional responsibility to engage and serve first-generation college students and their families.

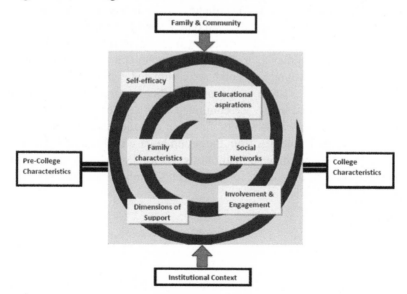

Figure 7.1 Model of parent and family characteristics, engagement, and support.

For the purposes of this chapter, we focus specifically on the "Institutional Context" within the model. By focusing on the institutional context, we are better able to consider the messages conveyed, forms of engagement encouraged, and responsibilities institutions have when working with first-generation families. Likewise, special focus on the institutional context provides an analysis of how this part of the model is informed by and informs family and community contexts with respect to family engagement in postsecondary education.

OUR STUDY

We entered into our broader research study, "Parents and Families in Transition," with the assumption that diverse families are engaged in multiple forms of support as they participate in the college transition process with their college-aged children. Yet, we found little evidence in the literature documenting the ways in which first-generation, low-income, and/or families of color are engaged with their students and with the institutions their students attend. We found even less in the literature about the ways in which institutions work with and engage families from an organizational or programmatic frame. Thus, we designed a multiple case study (Yin 2013) research project that would allow for examining the experiences and roles of parents and families during the college transition process. We specifically focused on institutional practices and commitment to engaging low-income, first-generation, and/or families of color, and did so through three distinct phases. First, we conducted a descriptive content analysis of orientation programs across the country. Second, we completed a multiple case study of parent and family orientation programs, including program observations and interviews with staff. Finally, we continued with a series of interviews with parents and families during students' first year of college. For the purposes of this chapter, we pull findings from the second phase of this study. The cases are comprised of nine diverse institutions, each of which offers orientation and/or year-long programming for parents and family members.

Sample

Institutions

The nine institutions included in this study were intentionally sampled using multiple approaches in an effort to assemble a diverse group of institutions. First, staff members associated with orientation programs requested that their institutions be selected for participation in the study after learning about the project during national conference presentations about the study. Second, we included institutions based on recommendations from individuals; this was the case for one institution that we noted as having an exemplary parent and family orientation program. Third, we included institutions that offered varied programming, for example Spanish and English orientation sessions, differences in the length of programming during orientation, and year-long programming. Both public and private institutions are represented. Student enrollment at these institutions ranged from approximately 1,000 to over 38,000 students. Table 7.1 represents a summary profile for each institution.

Table 7.1: Institution profile.

Institution	Overview	Student Population	Parent/Family Programs
Mountain Public Flagship	4-year and above More selective Very high research activity	First-year enrollment over 6,000 students	Includes office of parent/family relations. Does not offer programs specific to first-gen families.
SW Public Land Grant	4-year and above Selective Very high research activity	Total undergraduate enrollment over 32,000	Includes a parent association. Orientation programs offered Does not offer programs specific to first-gen families.
Mountain Exemplar Public	4-year and above Selective Very high research activity	First-year enrollment over 4,000 students	Includes office of parent/family relations. Does not offer programs specific to first-gen families.
Open-Access Public	4-year and above Selective Baccalaureate college	Total undergraduate enrollment over 20,000	Included both English & Spanish orientations. Does not offer year-long programming. Does not offer programs specific to first-gen families.

(continued)

Chapter 7

Table 7.1 (continued)

Institution	Overview	Student Population	Parent/Family Programs
Prestigious Private	4-year and above More selective High research activity	Total enrollment over 11,000	Includes office of parent/family relations. Parents officially recognized as part of campus community. Does not offer programs specific to first-gen families.
Liberal Arts Private	4-year and above More selective Baccalaureate college	Total enrollment over 2,000	Includes a first-gen family session during orientation. Includes office of parent/family relations.
Midwest Public Land Grant	4-year and above Selective Very high research activity	Total enrollment over 35,000	Includes office of parent/family relations & parent association. Included first-gen family session in past but has broadened it.
Christian Private	2-year and above Moderately selective Baccalaureate college with some masters degrees offered	Approx 2,000 on-campus students	No parent/family office. Family day during the year. Does not offer programs specific to parent/family relations.
Liberal Arts Private	4-year or above Selective Baccalaureate college	Total enrollment under 1,000	Includes a parent association & family weekend.

Participants

For the second phase of data collection, we interviewed at least one orientation staff member and one parent-/family-liaison staff member at six of the participating institutions. Our goal was to understand how families were perceived, engaged, and communicated with during the period beginning with orientation and continuing through academic-year programming. In total, we interviewed seven orientation staff members (coordinator, assistant director, and director levels), six parent and family staff members (assistant director and director levels), and three staff members who oversaw academic-year family engagement programs. Participants included twelve women and 4 men; their time at their respective institutions ranged from two to over fifteen years. All participants, institutions, and institutional mascots have been given pseudonyms.

Data Collection

Case study research requires that multiple points of data are collected (Yin 2013). Data collection began in June 2014 and continued through the 2016 spring term. With respect to the second phase of the study, three points of data were collected for each institutional case. Research team members attended a parent/family orientation at each institution. Team members were participant–observers and took detailed observation notes about the programs, sessions, and the ways in which personnel communicated with parents and families. We focused on the presence or absence of (1) inclusive language, (2) attention devoted to diverse families, and (3) sessions offered for first-generation families. We collected documents related to communication with parent/family members from each institution. Within this phase of the study we also conducted semistructured interviews with parent/family programming staff at each institution. The interview protocol focused on the types of programming offered (specifically for diverse families), frameworks informing parent and family programming, the evolution of parent and families programs at the institution, and the types of families served by the institution. For this phase of the research, we conducted over two hundred hours of observations and interviewed sixteen parent/family staff members.

Data Analysis

Data analysis occurred through a multistep process. First, all members of a five-member research team read the same two interview transcripts and all of the orientation observation notes to generate a list of codes to use for analysis in NVivo10. The coding process was established both inductively, as informed by the initial read of the transcripts, and deductively, as informed by the literature. We aimed to create consistency and intercoder agreement through that initial process (Merriam 1998). Next, two members of the research team were assigned to each point of data (i.e., observations and interviews). We were then able to begin with a code like *first-generation* and further analyze related secondary terms like *families* or *scholarship*.

For example, if we follow the coding process through *first-generation* as a primary code, to *families* as a secondary code, NVivo allows us to further isolate specific data within that code, highlighting *low income families, minority families, families of color.* These terms were all used either during observations or in interviews. A strength of this type of analysis is that it allowed us to highlight the intersectionality of identities associated with first-generation families. Our use of the emerging Model of Parent and Family Characteristics, Engagement, and Support allowed us to situate the primary and secondary codes against (and sometimes within) the broader context of the institution. As an example, the framework provided the lens through which we could understand the role of scholarships (a secondary code noted above) as a "dimension of support" in the model and how the institution interacted with this specific dimension of support to either dismiss or engage first-generation students and their families.

Trustworthiness

In an effort to establish trustworthiness, we drew on multiple techniques. Our research team consists of two teams, one at the University of Denver and one at the University of Missouri. The two teams have met regularly to offer an "external check of the research process" (Creswell 2007, 208). We also drew on peer debriefing as a validating strategy. Peer debriefing occurred through regular Skype research meetings and writing retreats where we discussed data collection and analysis procedures, emerging themes, and preliminary findings. The process of peer debriefing and external checks has also occurred with campus colleagues. For example, preliminary findings have been shared with campus life administrators working directly with first-generation families. These meetings have been instrumental in developing further analysis questions for the data. Finally, we drew upon triangulation in data collection and analysis by including multiple points of data. This triangulation method helped to establish reliability in our findings.

FINDINGS

This section provides an overview of the findings of our research regarding the transition and adjustment of first-generation students and their families to college. Our emphasis within this presentation of findings was on themes that expose the juxtaposition around inclusive and exclusive institutional practices of engagement when working with families of first-generation students. We first present the institutional practices that emerged that demonstrate inclusive engaging of first-generation students and their families. We open this section with a summary table of some of the most inclusive practices observed across the institutions in our study. As noted, many of the inclusive practices of the institutions honor family characteristics, engagement practices, and dimensions of support highlighted in our emerging conceptual model. We then move to a discussion of the ideologies and practices that were overtly dismissive or oblivious to the needs of and resources offered by first-generation populations present on campus. What is demonstrated, then, is a complex illustration of how first-generation families can be both engaged and alienated by postsecondary institutions.

Table 7.2: Forms of first-generation family support.

Events & Programs	Financial	Designated Session at Orientation	Emotional
First-generation welcome reception at orientation	Academic year scholarships for first-generation students	Workshop at orientation specifically focused on addressing questions of first-generation families	Acknowledged emotions parents and families of first-generation students may be feeling during orientation
First-generation families welcomed into advising labs during academic year. Coffee served.	Exceptions or waivers for orientation fees	Panel at orientation with other first-generation students, staff, faculty, and/or parents	Presenters acknowledged their own first-generation identities during orientation sessions
Dinner for first-generation students with first-generation faculty and staff		Intentionally defining terms that may be unfamiliar for first-generation families (in multiple sessions)	Stickers of support that first-generation faculty and staff placed on office doors and windows
Academic year retention programs for first-generation students			Using humor and storytelling to personalize the information, reduce anxiety, and connect with families

Inclusive Practices and Ideologies

Events for first-generation families took many forms during both orientation and the academic year. Two institutions offered a welcome event during orientation that was coordinated by the multicultural affairs offices at the two respective campuses. One was a luncheon for first-generation, low-income, and families of color, and the other was a dessert reception for first-generation families. Both welcome events felt more informal than the structure presented throughout the rest of the orientation schedule, and both included eating and mingling directly with the families. Recognizing and congratulating the families were key components of the two events, and staff went out of their way to ensure that families knew who staff members were and that they would serve as sources of support throughout the academic experience. In essence, the sponsoring offices created extensions of family and a broadening of the social networks seen in our Model of Parent and Family Characteristics, Engagement, and Support.

Another way in which the notion of extensions of family was cultivated was through academic-year programming, as noted by a staff member:

> For example, a college of agriculture—it serves more first-generation students. Well, in their advising they openly invite families to come in, in fact, they have coffee for them for the advisement lab. Now that's because they recognize the population they serve.

What is unique in this quote is that the efforts were coordinated outside of traditional orientation programming and from an academic unit. The general sentiment observed during orientation was that parents and families should not be present during academic advising sessions and that students must now make independent decisions regarding their course selection, majors, and the like. It is refreshing, then, to see that first-generation family members can be brought into the academic advising process while still developing independent thinkers in their students.

Staff members were also very honest in revealing that they still had work to do when it came to serving first-generation families. A liberal arts private institution was experimenting with programs that took the staff, and the event itself, out to where the families resided. The staff member shared:

> Folks were very appreciative that we would take the time to meet them where their family is as opposed to expect them to come here, and some of that is shifting in how to do—how to best reach all of our families. We're grappling with those things, there's talk of should our office be located more with orientation and transition programs and advancement and development, and different campuses for different reasons have parent family programs located where it is.

Although this particular institution was still working out the details, it was encouraging to see the recognition that first-generation, low-income, and families of color might benefit from the institution welcoming them in a space and community context that was already familiar to them. What is distinctive about this initiative is that it draws on Family and Community contexts in an effort to welcome families into the Institutional Context noted in our emerging model.

Finally, many institutions offered academic-year retention programs for first-generation, low-income, and students of color. These programs include TRiO programs (or similar initiatives), ongoing peer and tutoring support, student success strategy workshops, and sometimes an association with a living-learning community in the residence halls.

Financial support in the form of waivers or scholarships represented a concrete way that institutions recognized and supported first-generation college students. The cost of attending orientation often created a barrier for first-generation and low-income students. However, as the orientation director from Mountain Public Flagship University conveyed,

> The people who asked for exceptions are almost never low-income or first-generation. [First-generation and low-income families] say the institution says this so we do that, that's what's required and the people who do this, ask for exceptions, are privileged and they have all kinds of resources and very often they're going to get their exception and at times I wanna beg people to ask for an exception. . . . I really actually want people to ask for exceptions when they need them in that way.

Although fee waivers or exceptions were available for orientation, the orientation director was struggling with communicating that information, noting that relatively few low-income and first-generation families took advantage of the exception. It becomes important to partner with other offices on campus that have more open lines of communication with these families and who have established trusting relationships so that information about financial resources can be more readily conveyed. Doing so builds on an important element of Dimensions of Support, that of financial support.

While academic-year scholarships were not a common practice, we did note that scholarships for first-generation students were available at two of the participating institutions. An administrator at one public institution, Mountain Exemplar Public University, linked this commitment back to their land-grant status, suggesting they have a "long-standing history of supporting this population" and that focusing on "first-generation college students fulfills their land-grant mission." This particular administrator linked the commitment back to an institutional charter and, one could argue, a moral imperative for the institution rather than solely a need to meet the individual needs of students and their families. He went on to proudly report that their institution was a national leader for supporting this population, indicating, "we just celebrated 30 years of having a significant amount of scholarship money available for first-gen identified students." The institution offered fifty-five scholarships annually to first-generation students.

A staff member at Open-Access Public, who worked with first-generation students during the academic year, recognized that many first-generation families may not be able to attend orientation because of the fact that they are also high financial need. She expressed, "Especially with our program, first-generation students that are in our specific program, also have high financial need. And a lot of times, parents aren't able to come because they have to work. . . . we always intentionally invite [parents], and it's open to them, but it's obviously not required." In response, the program worked to ensure that parents and family members were regularly contacted during the academic-year programming. Creating multiple opportunities for contact during the academic year is important across all institutional types when serving large numbers of first-generation families who are also high financial need since taking time off of work for a multiple-day orientation may not be an option.

Perhaps the most specific and intentional form of Dimensions of [Institutional] Support during orientation was designated workshops or sessions for first-generation students and their families. Oftentimes, these sessions were tied to a specific program like TRiO or a similar initiative that served as the starting point from which to welcome the families into the session. Other times, the sessions were more general and consisted of a panel of first-generation faculty, staff, and other parents or an open session where the purpose was to address many of the questions or concerns that families might have. Important during these sessions was the attention paid to defining higher-education terminology and institution-specific acronyms, abbreviations, and processes. Many of these sessions worked intentionally to engage families in community-building activities and incorporated family members into the session. The following observation notes were taken at the Mountain Public Flagship University orientation session:

> After filling out paperwork on test scores, we were all moved into an icebreaker. Using a ball of yarn, we all stood in a circle and everyone participated in introducing themselves, including parents, staff, students, and me. It created a web. The support of family was noted. Then we moved into an activity where students read and answered questions around the room. Parents and families were similarly engaged in this process.

What was powerful about this session was that traditional forms of presentation—PowerPoint slides, lecturing, and auditorium-style seating—were not used. The staff members instead drew upon icebreakers and community-building activities to establish rapport while also addressing families' common questions and concerns.

The most frequently used form of support occurred within the category of what we have termed *emotional support*. Some of the institutions in our sample did offer specific workshops or panels for first-generation families at orientation events; however, more often than not, support came in the form of acknowledging the questions, concerns, and/or emotions that first-generation families were experiencing within the context of the general sessions. Many staff members acknowledged that families may be feeling both excited and nervous at the same time. Other staff members shared their own personal experiences being a first-generation college student. One institution in particular was able to identify that one-fourth of their current student population identified as first-generation. The institution was able to weave in both more emotional support and more academic-year programming for first-generation college students and their families.

While observing orientation sessions, we noted that another strategy used to build community and establish rapport was to incorporate humor and storytelling as a way to introduce a new topic and ease tensions. The orientation experience at some of the observed institutions involved multiple days and long hours. Being able to capture and hold the attention of the families attending seemed to be facilitated by making the information more personal and accessible. When working from an ideology of inclusivity, an integrative effort is imperative. Programming efforts cannot be left to one sponsoring department or program. Positive messaging and personal stories for first-generation families must come from various actors within both orientation sessions and academic-year efforts. Institutional commitment in the form of scholarships, human resources, and retention efforts must be in place to build first-generation student success. When considering these efforts through the lens of the Model of Parent and Family Characteristics, Engagement, and Support, findings demonstrate that the Institutional Context has an opportunity to nurture Dimensions of Support, forms of Involvement and Engagement, and Social Networks. We turn now to a review of practices and ideologies of exclusion. These exclusionary practices of first-generation families emerged from our analysis of on-campus observations during orientation sessions and individual interviews with staff.

Exclusion of First-Generation Families

While many supportive institutional practices for first-generation families exist, there are also areas requiring further growth and development for colleges and universities to consider. We group these areas of growth under the broader ideological understanding of excluding first-generation families by either being intentionally dismissive of or unintentionally oblivious to their needs. Our data reveal that on some college campuses administrators were not aware of the needs of first-generation families or chose not to address the specific needs and resources that these families might need. The following quote by a parent/family coordinator illustrates exclusive ideologies and practices:

> What I will tell you is that's honestly not our area of focus. We don't basi-cally—first off, we don't know if somebody comes from a first generation, or a student or parents are first-generation, low-income. We don't know. We treat all of the parents exactly the same. So we really don't—we don't tailor our services to any particular group. Now there are probably other organization on campus that might be involved in that type of activity. They may have programs on their own. But we don't really—we don't run those, and honestly, I don't know a heck of a lot about what they might do.

As is illustrated in table 7.1, which summarizes each participating institu-tion, only one institution (Private Liberal Arts College) offered a session specifically focused on first-generation students and their families during orientation. This was an informal dessert reception coordinated by the mul-ticultural affairs office. Thus, two important points are noted. First, there is a significant lack of focused programming among participating institutions for first-generation families during orientation. Second, when programming was offered, it was coordinated outside of the orientation department or the office of parent/family relations. When multicultural affairs offices become the only form of first-generation programming, it reaffirms the message that the staff member firmly stated above: that programming for specific groups is not part of the activities coordinated through parent/family or orientation offices. Such practices also reaffirm to first-generation families that they are excluded from the process and the culture of the college.

One institution, Midwest Public Land Grant, had included a first-genera-tion student and family session during orientation in the past but broadened it into a general "frequently asked questions" session. Staff members conveyed that families either did not identify with the term, did not know what the term meant, or felt offended that they might be viewed as having less understand-ing as a result of the label. Although the intentions of this particular institu-tion reflect steps to create inclusive spaces, the result of changing the session to a general FAQ, rather than finding ways to proactively explain the role and assets of first-generation families, may have further excluded these families in the process.

Exclusionary ideologies manifested when applications and registration materials did not ask specifically about first-generation status and when orientation programming failed to define and/or acknowledge first-generation students and families. In many cases, all parents and families were treated under the same umbrella without recognition that there may be differences in needs, concerns, and knowledge amongst first-generation, low-income, and/or families of color. Family Characteristics, found within the Model of Parent and Family Characteristics, Engagement, and Support, are an integral element to building more inclusive Institutional Contexts. When all parents and families are treated the same, without recognition of distinct family characteristics, assumptions are made about the types of knowledge and experience—of college in particular, but also broader knowledge and experience—that parents and families may have. Our observation notes indicate that blanket statements were made about "when you [parents] were in college," perpetuating the assumption that everyone in the room had previously attended college. A common sentiment noted during observations was that it was time for parents and families to step aside and "let the student experience responsibility"—presuming that families need to remove themselves, but also that students have not previously experienced responsibility. The same institution, Prestigious Private, went so far as to say, "let go or get out of the way." Undoubtedly, students are experiencing a new phase in their developmental process into adulthood. However, if the message to families is to get out of the way, institutions are not acknowledging that family engagement can be integral to student success.

The Case of "First-Generation Family University"

Up to this point we have demonstrated the juxtaposition in practices and ideologies of first-generation family engagement that were present in our participating institutions. To further elaborate on our key findings, particularly the forms of support, we have written a case of a "composite institution" that illustrates best practices of institutional support that was created for first-generation students and families. We offer the case from the perspective of a first-generation family. This composite institution includes examples that were present in different forms at each of the institutions we observed. However, as is the case with composite characters or cases, no one institution included every form of support mentioned within the case.

It was an exciting day. Our daughter was about begin her college education and today marked the start of a new adventure. We walked up to the registration line at orientation and noticed that there was a line for new students and another line for "family and support members." "Support members" felt like a nice way to welcome the other individuals who might accompany a student to orientation. In our case, our daughter had asked if her best friend could attend orientation with her since she had been through the process with her older sister. That felt like a good idea given that we had never gone through this type of experience before.

Once we checked in, the staff reviewed the schedule with us and pointed out that there was a workshop for first-generation college families. They explained that the workshop was meant to introduce us to resources that could help our daughter transition successfully to campus and help us navigate that college environment as well. We also noticed that there was a reception for first-generation families where we would be welcomed by staff and faculty.

The opening welcome session began, and various administrators introduced themselves and welcomed us to campus. We were surprised when many of them shared that they were the first in their families to attend college. They actually thanked family members for coming with our sons and daughters and commented on how important the role of the family is in helping students with their transition into college. Many shared their own personal stories about how scared they and their families were to enter into a new, unknown space. It felt nice to realize that we were not the only ones who had experienced being the first. All of the administrators offered to speak with us if we ever had questions or concerns.

After going through a few academic sessions, it was time for the first-generation family workshop. Here we learned about multiple resources that are available during the academic year. For example, there is a retention program that our daughter can sign up for that will provide her with a peer advisor and a tutor that she can meet with weekly. The program is specifically for first-generation college students. We also learned that the university has a separate pool of scholarship money just for first-generation college students. It is available for students to apply at any point during their time on campus.

Finally, we were told about the various events that are open to parents and family members during the year. Of course, we knew about family weekend, but we also learned that there are some departments on campus that have walk-in times when parents and families can come visit and ask questions. The session also included information about college lingo. We never realized there is a whole new language when it comes to college, but we were able to see a sample syllabus, learn about office hours, and look through the websites where all of the professors post readings and assignments. Overall, we learned a lot about the support offered to first-generation families. The session ended with a panel presentation that included staff, faculty, and parents who all identified as first-generation. It was great to hear their stories and ask specific questions about how we can support our daughter.

The whole day went by very fast but ended with a great dessert reception for first-generation families. After spending much of the day together, it was fun to talk to other families in a more relaxed setting and be recognized for the support we give to our children. The faculty and staff actually applauded all of us as parents and family members. The director of the department reiterated that going to college is a family affair and that they want to work in partnership with us to best support students. As we left the reception we were able to pick up contact information for all of the people we had heard from throughout the day. They helped to make us feel welcomed rather than scared about the information we do not know.

DISCUSSION, RECOMMENDATIONS, AND IMPLICATIONS

First-generation family members play an important role for their sons and daughters entering and transitioning through postsecondary education. First-generation students often report the desire to remain close to their parents and family members, in terms of emotional support, opportunities for advice, and geographic proximity (Bradbury and Mather 2009). With this in mind, we wrote this chapter with the purpose of highlighting the role that institutions play in engaging and valuing first-generation families. We were informed by the emerging Model of Parent and Family Characteristics, Engagement, and Support, which helped us to situate the Institutional Context in our analysis and presentation of findings. We hope this will begin to highlight how first-generation families can help to facilitate successful college access and transition for their college-aged children.

We recognize that it can be difficult to identify first-generation families, especially when the term itself is not familiar to many families. One strategy that was used was to ask specifically about first-generation status on students' admissions applications and ask again during their registration for orientation. This allows institutions to track first-generation applicants and develop specific programming targeted at this population. In order to gather the cleanest data possible, institutions should define *first-generation* when asking this question of prospective and admitted students.

The findings that emerged illustrate both the inclusive and exclusive nature of family engagement demonstrated at the institutions in this study. The inclusive ideologies and practices illustrated asset-based resources and programs that institutions offer to welcome and engage first-generation families. These asset-based resources include specific events or workshops during orientation, financial support for first-generation students in the form of academic-year scholarships, drop-in times for first-generation families to come to campus, and networks of first-generation faculty and staff to support first-generation students and families. Findings also revealed areas in which institutions demonstrated exclusive ideologies and practices around the engagement of first-generation families. For example, treating all families as if they enter into postsecondary spaces with the same college knowledge, experiences, or cultural histories can further isolate first-generation families. Failing to identify first-generation families will result in lack of opportunity to generate unique resources for this particular group.

The findings also offer some promising potential practices regarding the roles that parents and families can serve in as resources for other families. The structure of programs like orientation can offer times and spaces for more informal interactions with other families. Given the focus on institutional responsibility and perspectives of family members, we turn next to a set of questions that we hope will help institutions think through their efforts when working with first-generation families.

Institutional Context Considerations When Working with First-Generation Families

We return to the role of the Institutional Context within the emerging Model of Parent and Family Characteristics, Engagement, and Support and the influence of the context on family engagement. It is important that higher education institutions consider the diverse students and families they will be serving. Thus, we encourage institutional representatives to examine their assumptions, biases, and engagement practices regarding diverse families, and specifically regarding first-generation families. We have adapted the following sets of questions and subquestions posed to administrators and practitioners as a reflection tool for thinking through how first-generation families are engaged by the institution.

Assumptions

What assumptions do you have regarding first-generation parents and families? What assumptions exist regarding the responsibility of the institution to serve the full range of students, parents, and families in higher education today? When envisioning first-generation families, what pictures emerge? How do institutional practices, costs, or assumptions influence and reinforce attendance patterns for first-generation families at campus programs or events? What assumptions are made about the parents not present? Does your institution collect data on first-generation students and families? What data is collected to better understand first-generation participation patterns and needs? How might current programs and communication strategies limit the engagement of first-generation families?

Relationships

How can institutions engage first-generation families much earlier than orientation sessions to create meaningful and effective relationships? In what ways can earlier outreach build trust and participation by first-generation families over time? Developing strategies to begin building relationships with parents and families can provide opportunities to engage first-generation families in more inclusive ways over time, thus developing a culture of inclusivity upon college entry. How can cross-departmental collaborations (e.g., among Admissions, Early Academic Outreach, Multicultural Affairs, Orientation, Campus Life) tap into existing programs and resources to offer engagement opportunities to families much earlier in college-going processes? Are there opportunities to offer programs and resources in the communities in which first-generation families reside? If so, can collaborations be created with local K-12 school districts and/or local community organizations to provide a familiar space for first-generation families?

Policies and Practices

Are there ways in which institutional policies and practices exclude certain parent and family configurations? We encourage institutions to examine current policies and practices to ensure that they are not overly restrictive or limiting for first-generation families. How is the term first-generation used by the institution and is it fully explained in institutional documentation? What policies, practices, and departments are in place to help first-generation families feel welcomed? Are these resources limited to one department on campus (i.e., Multicultural Affairs)? Of especially critical importance are policies and practices that create—or alleviate—financial burden: Does the institution charge fees for attending orientation and similar programming, or for participating in parent/family advisory boards? Does it schedule orientation and similar programming that extends over multiple days, requiring families to pay extra for hotel costs, child care, and/or travel— or does it offer affordable housing, childcare, and meal plans for families participating in campus programming?

Implications for Research

The previous section posed important considerations for administrators and practitioners working with first-generation students and families on college campuses. Our study of parents and families in transition also points to important research implications. While there is an abundance of literature on first-generation college students, much less has been written about the role that first-generation families play in the college transition process (see Dennis, Phinney, and Chuateco 2005; Elam, Stratton, and Gibson 2007; Jehangir, 2010; Kiyama and Harper 2018; Stebleton and Soria 2012 for examples of this research over the last ten years). As a result of limited research literature on this topic, institutional actors are often (mis)informed by media and popular culture depictions of first-generation families (Kiyama and Harper 2018), and as a result they miss an opportunity to fully engage these families to support student success. It is with this in mind that we urge researchers to further examine the roles that first-generation, low-income, and families of color may play when supporting the college choice, transition, and success of their students. We understand that family relationships can be complex. Thus, we also suggest that further research explore the challenges or tensions that may exist between first-generation students, their families, and institutions. By further understanding both supporting and limiting roles, research can better inform policy and practice when considering the engagement of diverse families. We discussed at length the programmatic efforts and resources available to first-generation families during traditional orientation and transition sessions. Less is known about continuous efforts to engage first-generation families during students' academic tenure. We also know little about the influence that varying levels of engagement from parents and family members has on students' own development, particularly with regard to their sense of independence and growth as an adult. Likewise, little is known about the perspectives of first-generation families beyond the first year of college transition. Therefore, future studies should examine the role of first-generation families and the role of institutional responsibility for these families beyond the first year of transition.

CONCLUSION

Higher education institutions are welcoming more diverse student bodies than ever before. These students bring with them parents and family members who are equally diverse and who may have different levels of experience with postsecondary education. First-generation families in particular are an important subset of families to whom close attention should be paid, as they may not have the same knowledge or resources to help support their students through the college transition process. Yet, we know that first-generation families do offer emotional and aspirational support for their college-going children. Thus, it is important for institutions to examine the ways in which they communicate with, reach out to, and engage first-generation families in the college-going process. We firmly assert that by creating more inclusive and welcoming campus cultures based on the assets of first-generation families, we can better support their students in navigating college processes and ultimately, in achieving academic success.

REFERENCES

Apprey, Maurice, Patrice Preston-Grimes, Kimberley C. Bassett, Dion W. Lewis, and Ryan M. Rideau. 2014. "From Crisis Management to Academic Achievement: A University Cluster-Mentoring Model for Black Undergraduates." *Peabody Journal of Education* 89, no. 3: 318–35.

Auerbach, Susan. 2004. "Engaging Latino Parents in Supporting College Pathways: Lessons from a College Access Program." *Journal of Hispanic Higher Education* 3, no. 2: 125–45.

Auerbach, Susan. 2006. "'If the Student is Good, Let Him Fly': Moral Support for College among Latino Immigrant Parents." *Journal of Latinos and Education* 5, no. 4: 275–92.

Auerbach, Susan. 2007. "Visioning Parent Engagement in Urban Schools: Role Constructions of Los Angeles Administrators." *Journal of School Leadership* 17, no. 6: 699–735.

Berzin, Stephanie. C. 2010. "Educational Aspirations among Low-Income Youths: Examining Multiple Conceptual Models." *Children & Schools* 32, no. 2: 112–24.

Bradbury, Barbara. L., and Peter C. Mather. 2009. "The Integration of First-Year, First-Generation College Students from Ohio Appalachia." *NASPA Journal* 46, no. 2: 258–81.

Brown, Carrie. L., Keisha M. Love, Kenneth M. Tyler, Patton O. Garriott, Deneia Thomas, and Clarissa Roan-Belle. 2013. "Parental Attachment, Family Communalism, and Racial Identity among African American College Students." *Journal of Multicultural Counseling and Development* 41, no. 2: 108–22.

Budny, Dan. D., and Cheryl A. Paul. A. 2003. "Working with Students and Parents to Improve the Freshman Retention." Unpublished manuscript. Accessed July 29, 2017. http://www.pitt.edu/~budny/transition.pdf.

Carney-Hall, Karla. C. 2008. *Managing Parent Partnerships: Maximizing Influence, Minimizing Interference, and Focusing on Student Success. New Directions for Student Services.* San Francisco: Jossey-Bass.

Castellanos, Jeanett, Alberta Gloria, Nancy Herrera, Marlen Kanagui-Munoz, and Cristina Flores. 2013. "¡Apoyamos La Educación de Nuestros Hija/os!: How Mexican Parents' College Knowledge, Perceptions, and Concerns Influence the Emotional and Behavioral Support of Their Children to Pursue Higher Education." *Journal of Latino/Latin American Studies* 5, no. 2: 85–98.

Chen, Xianglei. 2005. "First Generation Students in Postsecondary Education: A Look at their College Transcripts. (NCES 2005–171)." *US Department of Education, National Center for Education Statistics.* Washington, DC: US Government Printing Office.

Corbett, Mike. 2004. "'It Was Fine, If You Wanted to Leave:' Educational Ambivalence in a Nova Scotian Coastal Community 1963–1998." *Anthropology & Education Quarterly* 35: 451–71. Accessed July 29, 2017. doi:10.1525/aeq.2004.35.4.451.

Council for the Advancement of Standards in Higher Education. 2012. *The Role of Parent and Family Programs.* 8th ed. CAS Professional Standards for Higher Education. Washington, DC: Council for the Advancement of Standards in Higher Education.

Creswell, John W. 2007. *Qualitative Inquiry & Research Design: Choosing Among Five Approaches.* Thousand Oaks, CA: Sage Publications.

Daniel, S. Kate, Kevin Lobdell, Beth Springate, Chelsea Rayome, Rita Bottoni, Daniel Doerr, John R. Saddlemire, and George J. Allen. 2009. "Varying the Frequency of Intentional Communication Between Student Affairs Personnel, First-Year Students, and Their Parents." *Journal of Student Affairs Research and Practice* 46, no. 2: 412–30.

Dennis, Jessica M., Jean S. Phinney, and Lizette I. Chuateco. 2005. "The Role of Motivation, Parental Support, and Peer Support in the Academic Success of Ethnic Minority First-Generation College Students." *Journal of College Student Development* 46, no. 3: 223–36.

Digest of Education Statistics. 2011. "Percentage Distribution of 1990 High School Sophomores, by Highest Level of Education Completed through 2000 and Selected Student Characteristics." National Center for Education Statistics. http://nces.ed.gov/programs/digest/d11/tables/dt11_341.asp. Accessed July 29, 2017.

Elam, Carol, Terry Stratton, and Denise D. Gibson, 2007. "Welcoming a New Generation to College: The Millennial Students." *The Journal of College Admissions* 195: 20–25.

Gassiot, Ken. W. 2012. "Parental Engagement at New Student Orientation and its Influence in Transition of First Year College Students." PhD Diss, Texas Technical University.

Granholm, Katie. 2009. "Parents as Partners: The What, Why, and How of Designing an Effective Parent Orientation Program." Power Point Presentation. University of Minnesota. Retrieved from Innovative Educators Supporting Academic and Professional Growth in Higher Education. http://www.powershow.com/view4/5a8f07-NDQzM/Parents_as_Partners_The_What_Why_and_How_of_Designing_an_Effective_Parent_Orientation_Program_powerpoint_ppt_presentation. Accessed October 12, 2017.

Guiffrida, Douglas A., Judy M. Kiyama, Stephanie J. Waterman, and Samuel D. Museus. 2012. "Moving from Cultures of Individualism to Cultures of Collectivism to Serve College Students of Color." In *Creating Campus Cultures that Foster Success among Racially Diverse Student Populations,* edited by Samuel D. Museus and Uma Jayakumar. New York: Routledge.

Harper, Casandra, Linda Sax, and De'Sha Wolf. 2012. "Parents' Influence on College Students' Personal, Academic, and Social Development." *Journal of Student Affairs Research and Practice* 49: 137–56.

Hernandez, John. C. 2000. "Understanding the Retention of Latino College Students." *Journal of College Student Development* 41: 575–88.

Ishimaru, Ann. M., Kathryn E. Torres, Jessica E. Salvador, Joe Lott, Dawn M. Cameron-Williams, and Christine Tran. 2016. "Reinforcing Deficit, Journeying Toward Equity: Cultural Brokering in Family Engagement Initiatives." *American Educational Research Journal* 53, no. 4: 850–82.

Jehangir, Rashne. 2010. "Stories as Knowledge: Bringing the Lived Experience of First-Generation College Students into the Academy." *Urban Education* 45, no. 4: 533–53.

Jun, Alexander, and Julia Colyar. 2002. "Parental Guidance Suggested: Family Involvement in College Preparation Programs." In *Increasing Access to College: Extending Possibilities for All Students*, edited by William G. Tierney and Linda S. Hagedorn, 195–215. Albany: State University of New York Press.

Kiyama, Judy M. 2010. "College Aspirations and Limitations: The Role of Educational Ideologies and Funds of Knowledge in Mexican American Families." *American Educational Research Journal* 47, no. 2: 330–56.

Kiyama, Judy M., and Casandra Harper. 2018. "Beyond Hovering: A Conceptual Argument for an Inclusive Model of Family Engagement in Higher Education." *The Review of Higher Education.*

LaBrie, Joseph W., and Jessica Cail. 2011. "Parental Interaction with College Students: The Moderating Effect of Parental Contact on the Influence of Perceived Peer Norms on Drinking During the Transition to College." *Journal of College Student Development* 52, no. 5: 610–21.

Lee, Jung-Sook, and Natasha K. Bowen. 2006. "Parent Involvement, Cultural Capital, and the Achievement Gap among Elementary School Children." *American Educational Research Journal* 43, no. 2: 193–218. Doi:10.3102/00028312043002193.

LeMoyne, Terri, and Tom Buchanan. 2011. "Does 'Hovering' Matter? Helicopter Parenting and its Effect on Well-Being." *Sociological Spectrum* 31, no. 4: 399–418.

Lombardi, Allison, R., Christopher Murray, and Hilary Gerdes. 2012. "Academic Performance of First-Generation College Students with Disabilities." *Journal of College Student Development* 53, no. 6: 811–26.

López Turley, Ruth N., Matthew Desmond, and Sarah K. Bruch. 2010. "Unanticipated Educational Consequences of a Positive Parent–Child Relationship." *Journal of Marriage and Family* 72, no. 5: 1377–90.

Martinez, Maria. 2003. "Missing in Action: Reconstructing Hope and Possibility among Latino Students Placed at Risk." *Journal of Latinos and Education* 2, no. 1: 13–21. Doi:10.1207/S1532771XJLE0201_3.

Mayer, Caroline E. 2011. "One Big Happy Family." *Currents* 37, no. 1: 16–21.

Melendez, Mickey C., and Nancy Blanco Melendez. 2010. "The Influence of Parental Attachment on the College Adjustment of White, Black, and Latina/Hispanic Women: A Cross-Cultural Investigation." *Journal of College Student Development* 51, no. 4: 419–35.

Merriam, Sharan B. 1998. *Qualitative Research and Case Study Applications in Education. Revised and Expanded from "Case Study Research in Education."* San Francisco: Jossey-Bass.

Morgan, Elizabeth M., Arvil Thorne, and Eileen L. Zurbriggen. 2010. "A Longitudinal Study of Conversations with Parents about Sex and Dating During College." *Developmental Psychology* 46, no. 1: 139–50.

Perna, Laura. 2000. "Differences in the Decision to Attend College among African Americans, Hispanics and Whites." *Journal of Higher Education* 2, no. 2: 117–41.

Plageman, Paula M., and Chiara Sabina. 2010. "Perceived Family Influence on Undergraduate Adult Female Students." *The Journal of Continuing Higher Education* 58, no. 3: 156–66.

Ramsey, Meagan A., Amy L. Gentzler, Jennifer N. Morey, Ann M. Oberhauser, and David Westerman. 2013. "College Students' Use of Communication Technology with Parents: Comparisons Between Two Cohorts in 2009 and 2011." *Cyberpsychology, Behavior and Social Networking* 16, no. 10: 747–52. Doi:10.1089/cyber.2012.0534.

Sax, Linda J., and Katherine Lynk Wartman. 2010. "Studying the Impact of Parental Involvement on College Student Development: A Review and Agenda for Research." In *Higher Education: Handbook of Theory and Research* vol. 25, edited by John C. Smart, 219–55. New York: Springer.

Sax, Linda. J., and Dayna S. Weintraub. 2014. "Exploring the Parental Role in First-Year Students' Emotional Well-Being: Considerations by Gender." *Journal of Student Affairs Research and Practice* 51, no. 2: 113–27.

Smith, William. L., and Pidi Zhang. 2010. "The Impact of Key Factors on the Transition From High School to College among First- and Second-Generation Students." *Journal of the First-Year Experience & Students in Transition* 22, no. 2: 49–70.

Solorzano, Daniel G., and Tara J. Yosso. 2001. "From Racial Stereotyping and Deficit Discourse Toward a Critical Race Theory in Teacher Education." *Multicultural Education* 9, no. 1: 2–8.

Soris, Krista M., and Michael J. Stebleton. 2012. "First Generation Students' Academic Engagement and Retention." *Teaching in Higher Education* 17, no. 6: 673–85.

Stebleton, Michael J., and Krista M. Soria. 2012. "Breaking Down Barriers: Academic Obstacles of First-Generation Students at Research Universities." *The Learning Assistance Review* 17, no. 2: 7–19.

Taub, Deborah. 2008. "Exploring the Impact of Parental Involvement on Student Development." In *New Directions for Student Services: No. 122. Diversity and Higher Education: Theory and Impact on Educational Outcomes*, edited by Karla C. Carney-Hall, 15–28. San Francisco, Jossey-Bass.

Tekleselassie, Abebayehu, Coretta Mallery, and Jaehwa Choi. 2013. "Unpacking the Gender Gap in Postsecondary Participation among African Americans and Caucasians using Hierarchical Generalized Linear Modeling." *The Journal of Negro Education* 82, no. 2: 139–56.

Terenzini, Patrick T., Laura I. Rendon, M. Lee Upcraft, Susan B. Millar, Kevin W. Allison, Patricia L. Gregg, and Romero Jalomo. 1994. "The Transition to College: Diverse Students, Diverse Stories." *Research in Higher Education*, 35, no. 1: 57–73.

Tierney, William. 2002. "Parents and Families in Precollege Preparation: The Lack of Connection Between Research and Practice." *Educational Policy* 16, no. 4: 588–606.

Tierney, William G., and Susan Auerbach. 2002. "Toward Developing an Untapped Resource: The Role of Families in College Preparation." In *Preparing for College: Nine Elements of Effective Outreach*, edited by William G. Tierney, Zoe B. Corwin, and Julia E. Colyar, 29–48. New York: State University of New York Press.

Wang, Tiffany R. 2014. "'I'm the Only Person from Where I'm From to Go to College': Understanding the Memorable Messages First-Generation College Students Receive from Parents." *Journal of Family Communication* 14, no. 3: 270–90.

Ward-Roof, Jeanine A., Patrick M. Heaton, and Mary B. Coburn. 2008. "Capitalizing on Parent and Family Partnerships through Programming. In *New Directions for Student Services: No. 122. Diversity and Higher Education: Theory and Impact on Educational Outcomes*, edited by Karla C. Carney-Hall, 43–55. San Francisco: Jossey-Bass.

Wartman, Katherine, and Marjorie Savage. 2008. "Parental Involvement in Higher Education: Understanding the Relationship Among Students, Parents, and the Institution" *ASHE Higher Education Report*. San Francisco: Jossey-Bass.

Wood, Mark D., Anne M. Fairlie, Anne C. Fernandez, Brian Borsari, Christy Capone, Robert Laforge, and Rosa Carmona-Barros. 2010. "Brief Motivational and Parent Interventions for College Students: A Randomized Factorial Study." *Journal of Consulting and Clinical Psychology* 78, no. 3: 349–61.

Wolf, De'Sha, Linda J. Sax, and Casandra E. Harper. 2009. "Parental Engagement and Contact in the Academic Lives of College Students." *NASPA Journal* 46, no. 2: 325–58.

Yin, Robert K. 2013. *Case Study Research: Design and Methods*. Thousand Oaks: Sage Publications.

8

Choosing Majors, Choosing Careers

How Gender and Class Shape Students' Selection of Fields

Ann L. Mullen

At some point during their college years, students declare a major field of study and then complete the required courses in that field on the way to earning a bachelor's degree.[1] Majors represent a sort of envisioned future, connecting students to images of the kinds of work they might do and the kinds of people they might become. Choosing a major is also one of the most important decisions students make, influencing not only what they will learn in university but, to an extent, their possible graduate school opportunities, career trajectories, and potential earnings. Not inconsequentially, the choice of a major corresponds to a student's class and gender.

By class, privileged students gravitate toward liberal arts fields of study,[2] while their less privileged peers tend toward applied and preprofessional fields, a pattern identified not just in the United States but in several other countries (Bourdieu and Passeron 1977; Goyette and Mullen 2006; Sanderson 1993; Thomas 1990; Van de Werfhorst 2002). By gender, major choices consistently and sharply diverge. These gender differences in fields of study hold across institutional types as well as across the students' social backgrounds. Highly selective institutions are just as segregated as less selective institutions (Mullen and Baker 2008, 2009). Moreover, high-SES men and women differ as much in their choices of fields of study as low-SES men and women. While high-SES men and women are both more likely to select liberal arts over preprofessional majors, they diverge in terms of which of the liberal arts fields they select. Among high-SES students, men more commonly choose science and math majors, while women choose arts and humanities. Among their lower-SES counterparts, men more commonly choose engineering, while women choose education (Goyette and Mullen 2006). In these ways, the choice of a major becomes a further point of stratification by class and gender. To the extent that a college major is linked to educational and employment outcomes, these patterns contribute to reproducing gender and class inequalities.

Even as little as a year after graduation, salaries vary tremendously according to one's field of study. Generally, graduates in preprofessional fields command higher starting salaries than those in arts and science fields, with graduates in the fields of engineering and computer science enjoying particularly hefty salary advantages. In addition, the fields in which women predominate (e.g., education and the life sciences) correlate with the lowest starting salaries, while male-dominated fields such as engineering and computer science come out at the top (Bradburn et al. 2003).

Yet these trends do not tell the whole story. Students in some fields are more likely than others to continue their education with a graduate or other advanced degree. Indeed, 38 percent of life science majors entered a graduate or professional program within one year of receiving their bachelor's degree. Graduates in the highest-paying majors (engineering and computer science) are among the least likely to continue their education, with only 22 percent and 15 percent, respectively, entering a graduate program (Bradburn et al. 2003). This pattern also follows the liberal arts/preprofessional divide. Forty-one percent of students graduating with a bachelor's degree in the arts and sciences in 1993 had entered a graduate program within four years of graduation, compared with only 24 percent of preprofessional students. The differences are even more pronounced in relation to enrollment in PhD programs; nearly eight times as many liberal arts graduates enroll in PhD programs as do preprofessional graduates (Goyette and Mullen 2006).

These patterns suggest a set of tracks running through the higher educational system. In one track, students attend more prestigious institutions, major in liberal arts fields, and then continue their education with a graduate or professional degree, a package leading to lucrative and high-status jobs. In the other track, students study applied fields at less prestigious institutions and then take their acquired skills directly into the labor market, often earning a relatively decent starting salary. While their earnings in the early years after graduation will be higher than liberal arts majors who choose not to attend graduate school, in the long run there is little doubt that those on the first track do better. The kinds of jobs open to those with graduate and professional degrees generally far surpass the opportunities available to those with bachelor's degrees in preprofessional fields. The probability that a student takes one track or the other varies by social background; children from high-SES families are far more likely to follow the first track, while students from less advantaged backgrounds, if they make it to college, generally take the second track (Mullen, Goyette, and Soares 2003).

In addition to these class-based tracks, there is also a set of gendered tracks. While women now earn a slightly higher share of bachelor's degrees than men, gender differences in the choice of a college major contribute to the earnings disadvantages experienced by women. Graduates in female-dominated majors are more likely to enter female-dominated occupations and earn substantially lower salaries than graduates in male-dominated fields of study. In 2004, for example, the median annual earnings of all full-time working women between the ages of 25 and 34 with bachelor's degrees were $40,300 compared with $50,700 for men, or 79 percent. This percentage has barely changed since 1980, when women earned $34,100 to men's $46,300 (in constant 2004 dollars), or 74 percent (Snyder 2007).

On the surface, it might appear that students simply differ in their proclivities for fields of study. Indeed, the selection of majors is typically portrayed as an individual choice, where students decide based on their particular preferences and career goals (Cebula and Lopes 1982; Davies and Guppy 1997; Hearn and Olzak 1981; Wilson 1978). Certainly, a number of individual characteristics do influence or constrain the choice of a major. This choice will depend in part on one's plans for graduate school. Students planning to attend graduate school have more liberty to postpone their vocational training until after receiving an undergraduate degree. Students intending to complete their education with a bachelor's degree must make sure they have labor-market-ready skills by the time they finish. Because more privileged students have educational aspirations beyond a bachelor's degree (and the means to realize those aspirations), they have more freedom of choice at the undergraduate level. Students may also be limited by their own academic abilities. Those who struggle academically, have difficulty in quantitative-based disciplines, or lack a strong background in science are likely to avoid certain fields. Finally, cultural capital influences choice in at least two ways. First, students with greater levels of cultural capital will have a more extensive knowledge of the various offerings in the higher educational system and the range of possible occupational starting points. Second, because cultural capital facilitates a student's mastery of abstract and theoretical disciplines (Bourdieu and Passeron 1977, 1979; Bourdieu 1984), students with high levels of cultural capital may be more likely to choose fields in these areas.

Beyond these individual characteristics, the features of the institutions students attend also influence their choices. The range of choice is restricted to the majors offered by an institution and further weighted by that institution's focus. The more selective the college or university, the greater the proportion of degrees awarded in liberal arts fields (Brint et al. 2005); indeed, prestigious private liberal arts colleges almost exclusively offer liberal arts degrees. In addition, degrees from more prestigious institutions derive a larger part of their value from the name of the college or university than from the particular kind of degree. If students can count on getting jobs because of the name of the institution on their diplomas, they can afford to be less concerned with acquiring marketable skills during college. Finally, depending on their class backgrounds and the institutions they attend, students likely anticipate entering different segments of the labor market. The segments differ in terms of the types of employment available, the gendered divisions of the labor market, and the varying job requirements. Some labor market segments expect prospective employees to be pretrained with the required job skills, while others are more open and provide training for new hires. In the face of these differences, students may plan their credentials accordingly. Likewise, depending on the market segment, acquiring a job may hinge more on connections than on a particular credential. In these segments, students with a substantial array of social connections may worry less about their marketable skills.

Next to the decision to go to college and the selection of an institution, a student's choice of a major has the greatest bearing on his or her future trajectory. Further, choosing among the 1,056 fields of study currently available depends not only on individual preferences, but also on the particular kinds of constraints and opportunities a student faces. This chapter explores how a largely first-generation and low-income sample of students attending a state college chose their fields of study and how they viewed the knowledge they gained during college. What influenced how these students thought about college majors and went about the process of selecting them? Why did most students gravitate toward applied fields of study? Why did the men and women diverge in their choices? Exploring these questions brings to light not just differences in how students decide on majors, but also the students' perspective on what they were learning in their classes and their opinions about the value of different kinds of knowledge.

DATA AND METHODS

The data for this study come from fifty in-depth, semistructured interviews conducted with a random sample of junior and senior students attending Southern Connecticut State University (Southern), a moderately selective state institution. Just over half of the students (52 percent) would be the first in their families to graduate from college and another 8 percent came from low-income families. First-generation students were more likely than their peers from more highly educated families to report low family incomes (46 percent compared to 17 percent). Still, fourteen of the twenty-six first-generation students did not come from low-income families. Because of the mix of income levels across students and given the small sample sizes, it was not possible to disentangle the separate dynamics related to low-income and first-generation status. The sample was equally divided by gender and comprised 74 percent White students, 12 percent Hispanic students, 10 percent Black students, and 4 percent Asian students. The sample was drawn, using a random numbers table, from a list provided by the university of full-time, non-foreign, junior and senior students under the age of 25. In all, seventy-four students were contacted for a response rate of 68 percent. The interviews (conducted as part of a larger study) took a comprehensive history of students' schooling from high school through college and then asked a series of questions concerning their decisions to attend college and their experiences during college.

A particular focus of the interviews concerned the choice of a major. Students were asked to tell the whole story of how they had come to select their college major, including the fields they had originally considered and later rejected, the range of factors linked to their final choice of a major, their current views on their decision, and what they most liked and disliked about their field. A written survey instrument was employed to collect demographic and family background information. All interviews were taped and transcribed verbatim. In addition to multiple readings of the transcribed interviews, the data were also analyzed using the software program NVivo. Adopting methods outlined by Strauss (1987), the author and two research assistants coded the interview data by section, with new codes allowed to emerge throughout the data analysis. In order to ensure and verify inter-rater reliability, the three coders met regularly to discuss emerging codes, finalize coding schemes, and simultaneously code the same sections and compare the results.

Exactly half of the Southern students did not intend to pursue further education after their bachelor's degree. In addition, of those students intending to go on to graduate school, the majority (fifteen out of twenty-five) planned to enter a master's program. The women in my sample were somewhat more likely than the men to plan to pursue a master's degree.

At Southern, degrees in preprofessional fields constitute around half of all degrees awarded, but if we add in the students earning degrees in liberal arts fields while simultaneously earning their secondary education certificate through the School of Education, the balance shifts to 67 percent applied degrees versus 33 percent liberal arts degrees. These figures are in line with the national average. Over the last several decades, the national trend has shifted in favor of applied fields of study. Currently, about 60 percent of all undergraduate students choose a preprofessional field, up from around 45 percent in the mid-1960s (Brint et al. 2005).

CHOOSING MAJORS AT SOUTHERN

The Southern students regarded majors primarily as career choices, and they prioritized courses and knowledge that would facilitate their career goals. Majors were chosen not for what a student wanted to study, but for the kind of occupation a student planned to enter. While students at liberal arts institutions may first select a major and only then begin thinking about career options, the Southern students worked in reverse, choosing their future occupations and then selecting the most appropriate major. This logic makes sense for those students going into applied fields. After all, why study social work, education, nursing, or business other than to enter those occupations? However, this pattern also held true for those students majoring in the liberal arts, as in the example of a biology student explaining why she chose her field: "I knew that I wanted to work with people or animals, so I was either gonna be bio. or soc[iology], and I wound up choosing to major in biology and minor in soc."

Generally speaking, the students selected fields on the basis of the career options to which they were linked. The process described by the social work student below is typical of most of the Southern students. He initially chose sociology because he wanted to teach, but later switched to social work, not on the basis of what courses he wanted to take or the knowledge he would gain, but in terms of what kind of work he thought he would most enjoy.

> Initially, I wanted to be a sociology major. My senior year in high school, I wanted to be a sociology major and I wanted to teach. But I was confused, and one of my best friend's mom, stepmom, was a social worker, and she goes, "But what do you want to do in sociology?" I said, "I don't know. I want to work with people." She goes, "Sociology's a lot of studying, it's a lot of research." She said, "Why don't you do social work? You'll definitely work with people," and I said, "All right."

For these students, majors represented not bodies of knowledge or academic disciplines, but rather occupational fields. Indeed, these students rarely drew distinctions between an academic field and the occupations associated with it. When comparing different majors, for example, the students did not refer to differences in the academic disciplines as branches of knowledge, but rather to differences in the career lines associated with those majors.

For those Southern students who had difficulty choosing a future line of work, business and psychology remained their preferred choices, because these fields were considered to be more open-ended.

I started out in business because when you don't know what you want, you go into business. I think that Dad helped me along with that one. "When you don't know what you want, Brian, you know, try business. You can always fall back on it." So, it seemed logical to me. So I did that.

I'm not sure what kind of field I want to go into, where business management covers all of them.

In some cases, the students started by considering the available majors and then evaluating them according to their career options. In these instances, liberal arts majors were often the first to be discarded because of their perceived lack of career potential. One student explained why he briefly considered but then rejected the fields of history and sociology.

I really didn't see a future in like sociology, especially. . . . There's no jobs. I don't know, I guess what do you do in sociology? But it's just like, it's hard to get a job, I think. That's what I was told and I've read a little bit. And history . . . what do you do with a history major? Become a teacher with it? And I didn't want to do that.

Two students discarded English and math in part for the same reasons.

I decided to do English because I was always told I was a really good writer, and a very good, you know, grammar, you know, all that kind of stuff. So I tried that and I couldn't stand reading all the books and books of literature. And then I thought about all I could do with it is either write or teach, and that wasn't gonna get me too far.

It was more thinking about the avenue, like, "All right, if I do this major . . . what are the options that this leads to?" If you're a math major, if you think about it, there's not much new research in the field of math. What's there is there, all the problems have been figured out for the most part, so . . . I would see only teaching math . . . and I don't want to be a math teacher.

Students also took into account whether, and how much, graduate education might be required for an occupation. For example, several of the students mentioned an interest in psychology, but once they discovered that they would not be able to practice without a doctorate, they opted for social work instead. An additional factor was the level of difficulty for a given major. Particularly for students already finding their college courses demanding, an easier major often held appeal.

I contemplated biology for some reason. Nah, it's not me. It's a lot of work, and, I don't know, if I was to be a bio major, that's a lot of work, and if I was gonna be a biology teacher say at high school, that would still be a lot of work, because of the amount of knowledge you'd have to take in.

Coming here, taking a couple of psychology classes, I didn't do good, I got Ds in those, and I was, "This is harder than what I thought, you know, I thought it was just sit down and chat with people, know their business," but I found out it takes a lot more.

Finally, in some cases the students arrived at their choice of a major by pragmatically adding up their credits and grades and making a determination as to which major would be the quickest to complete. One student used this method in choosing psychology: "I had the most credits in it. And I had the best grades in it. So I decided on psychology because I thought I would get out faster."

Because the choice of a major was so tightly linked to occupational considerations, the extent of the Southern students' knowledge about possible jobs played a strong role in their decision making. To feel comfortable about their choices, the students wanted to have a clear idea of the exact occupations they would enter. This eliminated a large number of possible but less defined options, such as working in particular industries like publishing or banking.

Moreover, the range of occupations familiar to the Southern students was actually quite limited. Because the students' knowledge and sense of possibility was shaped in part by the occupations of their parents, their parents' friends, and their relatives, these students, particularly those from working-class backgrounds, confined their choices to a relatively small set of occupations. Teaching was a common choice, in part because of its familiarity. Their limited knowledge also meant that students' choices sometimes depended on chance conversations with friends or relatives. They often spoke of choosing a major after learning about a possible occupational field from a friend or relative.

People around me, like my family and friends and stuff, have always said that "you work well with people." And I had no idea, you know. Social work meant nothing to me, you know. I didn't know what it was, but I guess my parents have kind of, had an idea that that would be, you know, psychology, things like that, so, we just looked up in the curriculum and it just said, you know, "social work" and take these kinds of classes, and I was like, "All right, I'll try it, you know," and I just stuck with it.

I was still thinking math, but my grandfather suggested to me if I had thought about computer science. I'd never heard of computer science. I didn't know what he was talking about, but he suggested to try it out and to see if I liked it. So when I became a freshman here I signed up for straight computer science major as a freshman, based on his advice, just to see what it is, and 'cause I figured if I didn't like it I could always change.

My cousin's an architect, and he made a lot of money, so I was like, "Okay, let's try that."

In addition, when discussing various occupational options, the Southern students sometimes revealed a great deal of misinformation about what different careers entailed. For example, one student decided against pursuing law because he didn't want to defend criminals. I asked another student whether she had considered psychology.

No, psychology scares me for some reason. Like I wouldn't want to be a psychologist and like administer drugs and tie people up or something, that whole thing scares me. And I didn't know that psychology, you know, if you were just a psychologist, and not a psychiatrist, it was different. I just assumed it was all different levels of the same thing.

Another student gave a related rationale for choosing social work over psychology.

I enjoy psychology, but even psychology's just like a narrow path, you know? They focus on mental illness, mental health, and that's it. Social work, you can help people find jobs, you know, you can help people find places to live, provide food for people.

Still another student originally declared a major in psychology, only to find out from her adviser that she would need a doctorate to do clinical work. Up until then, she had not considered social work, because she did not know much about it.

I only knew psychology, I didn't know social work. I used to think about social work as welfare. "Oh, welfare people had to take kids out of the homes," that's how I knew social work. I didn't know much about it, so I always used to say, "I'm gonna be a psychologist, I'm gonna sit down and help people with their problems." And also they make good money, that's what I thought about. . . . And I spoke to my advisor and she told me, "Oh, you know, and for psychology, you will need a PhD to really do clinical work. You can't just have a bachelor's and do clinical work. That's not how it works." So I was like, "Oh, then what can I do? I really want to counsel, I really do want to do clinical work." And she said, "Well, you know, you could do social work." And I said, "Oh, what can you do with social work?" And she told me what you could do. . . . So, I said, "Well, I'm gonna give it a try." So I switched from psychology to social work.

In a final example, one student with an initial interest in law turned away from that goal after his teachers explained that he would mostly be doing research.

> One day, my teacher was talking to me and said, "Most of your time's gonna be spent in a library, researching the work." And I thought about that. I never thought about that before, and I was like, "That's not what I want to do. I don't want to be locked up in a room all the time." And so then my mother, at that point, I was confused, I wasn't really sure what exactly I wanted to do. So my mother knew and she one day came with a book full of jobs, different jobs and stuff, job descriptions. And so I was looking through it, and I happened to land on TV reporter, TV anchoring, television news. And I found the qualities, it had a list of qualities, like you can be investigative, you can have your face on TV, all that stuff, so that attracted me to it right away. I said, "This is something I would like to do," you know. I liked writing, I liked creative writing and stuff, I liked to write, and I thought that, you know, I could make a difference in some kind of way, through the stories I do, to help somebody out, and to reveal a lot of the corruption in this world. I mean, that's the best way, TV, that's the biggest medium, and so hopefully that's what I'll be able to do in the future.

While most of the students fit the general pattern described above, there were some exceptions. Of the fifty students I interviewed, thirty-six (72 percent) chose applied fields, while fourteen chose fields in the liberal arts. Students' choices related to their social backgrounds. While just over half of all the students in the sample were first-generation college-goers, only 29 percent of the liberal arts majors were first-generation. However, of the fourteen liberal arts students, eight of them had chosen their major primarily for occupational reasons (such the biology student above). Only six of the students (three men and three women) selected their fields primarily because of their interest in the actual area, with future job considerations playing only a small role. One of these students explained choosing chemistry simply because he really liked it and it was "very interesting," rather than for its career possibilities. He did very well in this major and, at the time of our interview, had been accepted into the PhD program at the University of Arizona. Another student had always loved writing, but initially felt that "it wouldn't be worthwhile to pursue as a major because I wouldn't be able to get a job out of it." She eventually changed her mind after realizing "I was happy doing it and I liked it." Her career interests centered on an ideal, as-yet-undefined job that would allow her to do meaningful work and continue her writing. "I'd like to have a job where I could express, where I could do something that I really cared about, where I could enjoy what I was doing enough, and have enough money and then still have time to write."

GENDER DIVISIONS AT SOUTHERN

Because majors were so tied to future occupations for the Southern students, gendered patterns of choice reflected gender-typed notions of appropriate work for men and women. Women at Southern were more likely to choose majors in education, public health (including nursing), social work, and psychology, while the men more commonly chose computer science and business. These preferences reflected both a gendered occupational structure and the asymmetrical character of gender change (England and Li 2006). Women have made considerable inroads into some previously male-dominated occupations, such as law, medicine, and university professorships. Women made up only 7 percent of all lawyers in 1975, but by 2006 they constituted 26 percent. In medicine, the comparable figures were 13 percent and 32 percent. However, the integration of occupations has mostly been a one-sided process; while women have moved into many previously male-dominated occupations, men have not moved into female-dominated ones. Consequently, the proportion of women in occupations such as nursing, social work, and elementary school teaching has barely changed over the past thirty or so years. Women made up 97 percent of all nurses in 1975; by 2006 this had dropped only slightly, to 92 percent. Women constituted 85 percent of all elementary school teachers in 1975, and 81 percent in 2006. Social work has become even more female-dominated than before: women made up 61 percent of the social workers in 1975, and 83 percent in 2006 (US Bureau of Labor Statistics 2007; Wootton 1997). These patterns reflect the way status in occupations relates to gender. Because our culture devalues women, the kinds of work typically done by women are also devalued. Thus men face a more pronounced stigma for entering nontraditional fields, because they enter the devalued realm of things associated with femininity (England and Li 2006; Williams 1995). However, when women make the nontraditional choice of a typically male occupation, they generally benefit from the higher social value of the occupation (in addition to better pay and elevated status).

Because the Southern students chose majors based on perceptions of their links to occupations, the gender-typing of a particular occupation influenced whether students considered the occupation, and thus the major, to be gender-appropriate. These distinctions were perhaps most strongly reinforced in the major and occupation of education. Because women make up 98 percent of all preschool and kindergarten teachers, and 82 percent of all elementary and middle school teachers (US Bureau of Labor Statistics 2007), the vast majority of the Southern students had gone through their early years of schooling with all-female teachers. It is noteworthy that many of the women in my study discussed forming their aspirations to be teachers at a very young age.

In addition, some came to the realization that they wanted to be teachers by "playing school," a distinctly gendered children's game. Two of the students discussed how the early development of their aspirations to be teachers came partly from this practice of playing school.

> I always wanted to teach. When I was little, I used to play school. I had a nice little chalk board.

> My mother thought that I should be a teacher because she always thought that I would. She'd always observe me with kids, and she always thought that I was good with them and thought that I should be a teacher. And I was always playing school when I was little, so she thought that I would like to be a teacher and she encouraged that.

The influence of the family also comes across in the last quote, with the student's mother encouraging her to take up the teaching profession because she thought her daughter was good with kids. Other students also noted the influence of their families, either through encouragement or by example, such as having female family members in the teaching profession. One student tied her interest in teaching to the fact that she came from a family of teachers, including her mother.

> So I always knew that I wanted to do something around the area of teaching, even if it wasn't 'specially becoming a teacher. So I explored that and then that led me to college because that was my final goal was to. . . .
> *And so you'd always wanted to do something in teaching?*
> Um-hmm. I come from a family of teachers. My mom, I think every single school in the system in the town I live in has a teacher with my last name, and they're all relatives.

Early work experiences, which tended to be gender typed, also influenced the students' choices. Some women linked their decision to go into teaching to their teenage experiences with babysitting.

> *How did you know you wanted to be a teacher?*
> I don't know, I just always, I always loved kids. Every job I've ever had involved kids, so, I don't know, it just sort of happened. Ever since I was, you know, started babysitting I knew that I wanted to be a teacher.

Because babysitting is done almost exclusively by girls, it contributes toward setting more women than men on the track to teaching.

When men do enter education majors, they tend toward higher levels (secondary instead of primary education) and typically male curricular tracks (technology and agriculture). Men also earn the majority of degrees in physical education teaching and coaching (Snyder 2007). For the Southern men, these aspirations, too, were influenced by family and by the students' childhood experiences with gender-typed activities, as shown in the statements by two male students, both studying education in order to be coaches.

> Freshman or sophomore year [of high school], I decided that I probably wanted to go into phys ed and be a gym teacher or coach.
> *How did you make that decision?*
> Well, I played sports all my life since I was five, and it's a major interest is [*sic*] sports, and athletics, and . . . baseball since I was five, hockey since I was nine. So I've been around, my father's coached me since I was five, so he's been involved in sports his whole life, too. So sports is a big background.

> *Tell me the whole story of how you chose your major.*
> I've always played hockey all my life, so I was always involved with the high school teams, and I went back and I'd just skate around with them and stuff even after I graduated . . . I'd skate with them all, through all the practices, and I'd show up at games and stuff. And it happened to be that one of the assistant coaches was quitting, and the guy that I played for said, "Do you want to come aboard and be the assistant coach?" and I said "Yeah, sure." So I started doing that, and I really enjoyed being around the kids and being able to show them "All right, this is the play we want to do and this is how we want to execute it," and then have them go do it in a game, really like gave me, I was satisfied. So I was like, this is something I think I might look into, so that's what I started looking into. . . . I thought about it, and I said, "Yeah, that's something I would like to do."

Because sports activities, and in particular hockey, tended to be a larger part of the boys' childhoods than those of the girls, these earlier experiences laid the groundwork for making coaching a more "natural" choice for men than for women. This also extended to the men who majored in other fields, such as one student who majored in journalism in order to pursue a career in sports information: "'Cause I think the whole sports thing is . . . I mean, I just love being around sports, and it's just, it's something I've grown up with, you know, my dad's very sports oriented, my brother was beyond sports oriented, that was his life, and it still is, and it's something that I can have fun with that." Likewise, another student explained how his interest in business came from watching his father run a store and then helping him.

> *Tell me the whole story of how you chose to major in management.*
> 'Cause, uh, since my father was running a business trade, I was always into business, even in high school . . . And then I said, "Well, since I'm good in business and since I watch my father every day running a store, managing a store," that's what I wanted to do, pursue.

The accounts related above suggest how childhood experiences and observations shaped these Southern students' occupational aspirations. The students' experiences with gender-typed activities and professions influenced their own career inclinations. In addition, gender-essentialist beliefs also contributed to the students' choices. This became most apparent in the comments made by a few of the men who had chosen stereotypically female fields. When asked to describe the kinds of students in their majors, two social work students, both men, immediately focused on the gender composition of their major.

Do you see any similarities among the social work majors?
The only thing I notice is that there's very little males, very small percentage of, I mean, there's some classes where I'm the only male. I think we have like eight in our whole program.
Why do you think that is?
It's a female-dominated field.
Why is that?
Because women are more nurturing by nature, sometimes more sensitive.

Do you see any similarities among the social work majors?
Yeah, they're mostly women. I mean, um, similarities, yeah, I think a lot of them are open, are very open-minded, just have a very caring side to them, and yeah, I think that's . . . but also a lot of women.
Why do you think that's so?
Because, because, ah, maybe it's society the way it is, you know, men are supposed to be, you know, hard core, I don't know, you know, tough, and being a social worker you're kind of, it's kind of the opposite of all that. So maybe that's why, I don't know.

In the first account, the student explained the scarcity of men in social work by attributing what he saw as the necessary characteristics of social workers, nurturing and sensitivity, to women. "By nature," women have more of those characteristics than men. In the second account, the student offered more of a gender-socialization explanation, suggesting that men are supposed to be tough and hard core, rather than open-minded and caring. Both of these descriptions reveal the men's awareness of crossing gender lines when they entered the field of social work. The lines are not so rigid that it becomes impossible for men to enter social work, but strong enough so that only one in ten social work majors is a man (Snyder 2007).

Interestingly, in the interviews none of the women entering traditionally male fields of study made mention of the gender composition of their field. This again suggests that women, while certainly facing other barriers, do not risk the same kinds of stigmatization that men do when entering typically female fields of study.

THE VALUE OF KNOWLEDGE AT SOUTHERN

One of the central ways in which the Southern students evaluated the content of their courses was in the extent to which the materials would be useful in their future lines of work. Most of the time, this meant that they were looking for knowledge that could be directly applied. This point was expressed most clearly in the students' negative evaluations of certain courses.

I had a couple of classes that were a waste of time, I think. Like zoology, it was kind of like memorizing. It was really like, you don't really need it after college.

All we learn is classification, which I'll never use. I'll never say, "All right, what's the Latin name of that animal." No one will ever ask me that.

I had to take physics, and I know that I'll never use physics again.

In each of these cases, students regarded learning they would not later use as a waste of time. On the other hand, the students reserved their praise for knowledge and courses that were directly applicable to their future occupations.

I guess learning what classes I have taken that I have liked and felt that I have learned material that, you know, that does apply, you know, as far as my major goes, I guess. You know, it's not all the classes I've taken I've been fed up with, but, you know, there are quite a few that I have taken that I can really look at the material and say, "Wow, you know, this is like really what goes on in real life," that kind of stuff, where I can really see that it does apply to what I'm gonna need to have to do. . . . Yeah, the teachers, they'll come right out and say, you know, "You're gonna have to know, you need to know this, you have to do this, blah, blah, blah, blah." And I'll say, "Oh, you know, that's great, I'm glad I'm learning that now and not later."

In some fields, this meant that the students critiqued knowledge for being out of date.

Quite a few of the classes I've taken don't seem to, I just feel it's been a complete like waste of time, because they aren't either, I haven't learned anything, or when I get out, it's not gonna do anything for me. . . . I feel it's scary sometimes, 'cause I feel, especially in this field, almost unprepared, like I'm going to be unprepared because there's so much to learn. I mean, I go to, you know, like Walden Books, or, you know, Barnes and Noble, and there's just racks and racks of books in the computer thing and I just look at 'em all, going "I got to know that, I got to know that, I got to know that," and I haven't learned any of it yet. And I just go out and buy the books and just read 'em. You have to, because the things that they teach you, some of it's out of date, or a lot of it's out of date. . . . I just don't feel like I'm learning everything that I need to be.

I'm a computer science major. . . . A couple of [my classes], I was like, "Hmm, I don't see why I have to take this class." Like my assembly language classes. They don't use assembly language anymore in the computer field. It's like "Why do I have to take this?"

Even some of the students who enjoyed liberal arts courses expressed the view that what they learned in their classes should be contemporary or have relevance to their current lives.

Yeah, I don't particularly enjoy writing an eleven-page paper on the *Canterbury Tales*, because, I mean, there's nothing you can really add to it. It's been analyzed for the last 600 years, so I hated doing something like that, because it just seems pointless. And, you know, I mean, I like the *Canterbury Tales*, but I didn't particularly see how the, you know, Wife of Bath or whatever related to anything that was going on today. Not that it has to, but it just seemed a little odd to write about the Black Plague of the thirteenth century.

Because of the emphasis the Southern students placed on courses and learning that would be applicable to their future lines of work, these students showed little patience for general education courses that they did not see as relevant to their careers. While the university itself maintains a system of general education requirements with a stated goal of providing students with a well-rounded education, the students often did not share this goal.

I feel like more of a focus should be on your major, you know. We had to take all these other classes that I don't really feel, and I'm sure a lot of other students feel that way, apply to your major. I mean, I understand having to take a few general courses, but . . . it's like "What am I ever gonna do with this stuff [general requirements]?" you know?

I would never have come to a four-year college if I would have known [about all the requirements]. Like I said, I don't have a problem with the major classes, that's fine, but all these requirements? I didn't think they'd take up at least two years, and then the other two we're doing, that you have to do as far as your major. I'm telling you, if they would have told me, if someone would have told me that I would take all these requirements, I would have never come to a four-year school.

Some of the core requirement stuff, some of 'em I found to be very good, that I'm glad that I was required to take them. Others, they were pointless to my major. I mean, they're something that I might come across but most likely not, and so it was sort of wasted time. Others, like I mean, it just basically took up time away from my other classes, or away from working.

These cases evince the most explicit line of difference between the priorities of many of the Southern students and those of the institution. While the university is invested in providing students with a well-rounded education, this view of education was not always embraced by the students (though to be sure, there were some students who did value the required-curriculum courses).

Along with their appreciation of applied knowledge, these students highly valued hands-on learning (over book learning) and learning that related to real-life experiences.

> Some of the professors are too wrapped up in being professors and reading the book, and then other professors are the complete opposite, are very real, they describe what it's like to be providing therapy, to going out into the field. And those are the professors who make it worthwhile, 'cause they make more sense than the ones that sound like a book.

> I had a radio-broadcast news class . . . which I really enjoyed, because it was a very hands-on class. You got to do all your editing. You were out there in the field getting sound bites and interviewing people.

> I think that more of the education should be hands-on. You should be out in the field, because you learn twice as quick . . . 'cause you have to. Under a controlled environment where you're expected to make mistakes, it's a lot easier than just jumping into it when you graduate.

> The class that I most enjoy is the class that I'm taking now on studio production. And it's hands-on, that's how I know that that is my calling, to do something else where I'm actually physically doing something [other] than taking classes and all that, 'cause I really enjoy it and I'm doing well in the class.

These accounts reflect another way in which the Southern students appreciated a certain efficiency about their education. They wanted to have their education focused as much as possible on their future jobs. For them, what was valuable about learning was what could be readily applied in their future job contexts. Underlying these immediate preferences, the Southern students also expressed a more general appreciation for applied knowledge in and of itself, along with skepticism toward theoretical knowledge.

> I mean, you could read all the theory you wanted about interventions in the book, but until you get to apply it, it doesn't make sense. . . . You use what you have to use and you don't, everything's not a textbook. That's the biggest thing I've learned.

> I was also considering psychology, but I kind of gave up on that because . . . to go back and study Freud and Jung and Erikson, it seemed to be so old that, it seemed so vague, I guess, in a sense. And it seemed like what, bottom line, what

you wind up doing is just talking to people about, you know, trying to, you know
. . . let them vent on you, and kind of guide them. That's all you really can do.

Their comments made clear that theoretical approaches held little interest
for these students, in contrast to their appreciation of the usefulness of knowledge, applicable more for doing than for thinking.

While the above perspectives on the value of knowledge captured the general pattern found at Southern, there were also many students who did take
an interest in their general education requirements and spoke with enthusiasm about their courses in liberal arts fields. Most commonly, the students
described these courses as "interesting," often unexpectedly so. Frequently,
though, these courses, too, were valued for the skills they imparted: "[My
favorite courses] academic-requirement-wise, I would say either any of my
English composition courses, 100, 101, or Major American Authors. I, from
what I understand, I guess I lucked out with the professors I had, and they
were great in helping my writing style, which has been applied in all my
other classes." Like that student, a number of the other Southern students
commented on how their literature courses had been beneficial in improving
their writing skills.

In sum, in both their choices of majors and their views toward knowledge,
the Southern students approached their education from an applied perspective. This corresponds to the rationale employed by most Southern students
of going to college for the explicit purpose of getting a job.

CONCLUSION

While more privileged students often attend university in pursuit of the overall college experience and balance a mix of intellectual and career interests
in their choice of major (Mullen 2010), the Southern students viewed college almost exclusively as career preparation: the project of going to college
involved selecting a career and acquiring the necessary training in that area.
Tying in with this logic of choosing majors, because the Southern students
went to college chiefly to obtain jobs, their priorities rested on acquiring
knowledge that would be useful for those jobs. In contrast with the liberal
arts ideal of learning for learning's sake, they appreciated knowledge largely
for its exchange value in the labor market. This approach to the acquisition
of knowledge may be linked to how graduates from these types of institutions are assessed on the labor market. The Southern students would perhaps
get jobs based on their concrete skills, rather than for demonstrating a broad
intellect.

There is evidence that class-based patterns of choosing majors hold true even within institutions. The first-generation students at Southern were more likely to choose an applied over an arts and sciences field than their peers who came from better-educated families. There are also numerous ways in which the likelihood of adopting a practical versus a liberal arts approach to college can be traced to the privileges or disadvantages of social background.

For starters, the academic preparation of many of the Southern students played a role in the kinds of fields they were willing to consider. Many of the Southern students did not have the appropriate academic preparation to take on some of the more demanding fields of study. Second, the Southern students did not have the luxury of assuming that they could follow up their undergraduate degrees with several more years of graduate training. When the Southern students did consider graduate programs, they mostly imagined two-year master's programs. Third, the institutions themselves played a role. Students attending highly prestigious institutions are no doubt aware that their prospects are assured by the university's name on their diplomas, and that their major carries less importance in obtaining a good job. In contrast, Southern students realized that their future employers would be evaluating their educational credentials less on the name of their university and more on the nature of their studies. In addition, more privileged students often rely on an extensive and powerful family network in their job searches, a resource which helps insulate them from the necessity of acquiring vocational training during their college years. The Southern students operated under a much more limiting set of constraints. Their choices were confined by the extent of their academic preparation, their lower aspirations for graduate education, their restricted knowledge of possible occupations, and the prestige of the institution from which they would graduate. These realities meant that only a particularly courageous or inspired student would pursue a liberal arts path through college.

In Bourdieu's (1984) view, the "distance from necessity" also helps explain class-based patterns in the choice of a major. Those with few economic or cultural resources must direct a large part of their energies toward the practicalities of making a living. The dominant class's freedom from material constraints allows it to develop tastes for the impractical, such as gourmet food and abstract art. This distance from necessity aligns with fields of study, providing privileged groups with the freedom to pursue abstractions having little practical application, such as theoretical knowledge. Put another way, the most privileged have the luxury of choosing liberal arts fields, whereas the least privileged face the necessity of studying something more practical. These varying tastes in knowledge become imbued with cultural distinctions, as such tastes appear to originate from different degrees of natural intellectual aptitude. The choice of a liberal arts field comes to signify the chooser's greater inherent intelligence or broadmindedness, effectively disguising the accumulation of advantages that made this choice possible. A liberal arts degree is certainly no guarantee of an immediate and high-paying job, as satirized by the old joke about what the liberal arts graduate says to the business major ("Do you want fries with that, sir?") Yet research also shows that many firms welcome those with liberal arts degrees and that these individuals are just as likely to advance up the corporate ladder as those with degrees in engineering and business (Useem 1989).

There is also considerable evidence that degrees from elite institutions result in higher long-term earnings and entry into positions of power, as opposed to degrees earned from less selective institutions (Bowen and Bok 1998; Kingston and Smart 1990; Useem and Karabel 1990). Even so, scholars continue to debate the true payoff to earning a degree from an elite institution (Gerber and Cheung, 2008). Students attending elite institutions are generally more talented and more academically qualified than their peers in less selective institutions. Studies can control for academic variables, such as high school grade point averages and SAT scores. However, there are other variables that are more difficult to measure, but that may make a student more likely either to apply to an elite institution or to be accepted at one; such qualities may lead to higher rewards in the labor market, independent of the selectivity of the institution the student attends. In this way, studies may confound the qualities of a graduate with the benefits bestowed by an elite degree. The matter is further complicated because the rates of entry into graduate programs and the types of graduate programs vary, both by the students' characteristics and by the characteristics of the undergraduate institutions they attend. Further, most studies have done a poor job of adequately controlling for major fields of study, often aggregating fields into just a few broad categories. Because less selective institutions will be more likely to offer fields with relatively high, early labor market returns, such as computer science and engineering, it is possible that studies overstate the long-term earnings of graduates from less selective institutions by not including more detailed controls for majors.

Because elite institutions offer majors primarily in the liberal arts, this suggests that some of the effects discussed above may be due to these fields of study. On the other hand, it is possible that the value of a liberal arts degree works best when coupled with a prestigious institution; liberal arts degrees awarded by less selective institutions may not confer the same ennobling status. Answering the question about the precise payoff of a liberal arts degree is quite difficult, because of the problem of disentangling the effect of the institution from that of a particular field of study. Further, liberal arts majors are more likely than students from preprofessional fields to continue their education with one or more graduate degrees (Goyette and Mullen 2006), complicating comparisons between the two groups. It may also be the case that the signaling effect of a liberal arts degree works best for those individuals who already have high levels of inherited cultural capital.

Turning to gender, in some respects the findings presented here confirm earlier studies showing that men gravitate toward fields with higher prestige and better economic payoffs (Berger 1988; Davies and Guppy 1997; Hearn and Olzak 1981). However, my findings also provide a corrective to the simple socialization explanations that predominate in this area of research. Typically, the research on gender and majors either implicitly or explicitly attributes differences in the choice of a field to early childhood socialization. Socialization models conceive of gender primarily as an individual attribute, rather than as an institutionalized system of social practices (Ferree, Lorber, and Hess 1999). These models see men's and women's preferences essentially as the result of socialization without taking structural influences into account. Moving beyond this limited framework in order to demonstrate the powerful effects of institutionalized gender norms on students' preferences for different occupations, Correll (2001, 2004) shows how cultural conceptions of gender work to constrain the early career-relevant choices of men and women. Cultural beliefs about gender and task competence bias individuals' perceptions of their own competence in different areas and consequently influence their preferences for entering fields requiring those skills. Correll's important work points to the inadequacy of early childhood socialization models for explaining gendered preferences; rather, in what is an ongoing process, cultural conceptions of gender bias a person's perceived competence, which then influences that individual's preferences. The results presented here show additional ways in which choice is much more than the result of socialization. Gendered associations with bodies of knowledge, as well as gendered occupational structures, both influence choice. Choice may also be seen as a product of the structure of the curriculum (Charles and Bradley 2009; Gaskell 1992). The organization of the family is important, too, in that it relates to how students anticipate their future roles. Thus, while the socialization that men and woman receive before they arrive at college surely explains some of the differences in their preferences, gender biases in institutions, opportunity structures, cultural beliefs, and social practices also exert a continual and powerful effect on their choices.

Although women have entered higher educational institutions and now attend them in greater numbers than men, this has not resulted in the same kind of success in the labor market. Women and men are still largely segregated into different types of occupations, and women still earn far less than men do. Even more troubling, the narrowing of the gender wage gap has slowed considerably since 1990. These labor market trends are directly linked to the gendered segregation of major fields of study (Bielby 1978; Bradley 2000; Brown and Corcoran 1997; Snyder 2007). In these ways, women's inclusion in higher education has not resulted in commensurate advances in gender equality. In sum, not only does the choice of a major field reflect gender and class divisions among students, it also perpetuates those same divisions, serving as another point of stratification within higher education.

REFERENCES

Berger, Mark C. 1988. "Predicted Future Earnings and Choice of College Major." *Industrial and Labor Relations Review* 41, no. 3: 418–29.

Bielby, Denise Del Vento. 1978. "Career Sex-Atypicality and Career Involvement of College Educated Women: Baseline Evidence from the 1960s." *Sociology of Education* 51, no. 1: 7–28.

Bourdieu, Pierre. 1984. *Distinction: A Social Critique of the Judgement of Taste.* Trans. Richard Nice. Cambridge, MA: Harvard University Press.

Bourdieu, Pierre, and Jean-Claude Passeron. 1977. *Reproduction in Education, Society, and Culture.* Trans. Richard Nice. London: Sage Publications.

Bourdieu, Pierre, and Jean-Claude Passeron. 1979. *The Inheritors: French Students and Their Relation to Culture.* Trans. Richard Nice. Chicago: University of Chicago Press.

Bowen, William G., and Derek Bok. 1998. *The Shape of the River: Long-Term Consequences of Considering Race in College and University Admissions.* Princeton, NJ: Princeton University Press.

Bradburn, Ellen M., Rachael Berger, Xiaojie Li, Katharine Peter, and Kathryn Rooney. 2003. *A Descriptive Summary of 1999–2000 Bachelor's Degree Recipients 1 Year Later, with an Analysis of Time to Degree.* NCES 2003–165. Washington, DC: U.S. Department of Education, National Center for Education Statistics, Institute of Education Sciences.

Bradley, Karen. 2000. "The Incorporation of Women into Higher Education: Paradoxical Outcomes." *Sociology of Education* 73, no. 4: 1–18.

Brint, Steven, Mark Riddle, Lori Turk-Bicakci, and Charles S. Levy. 2005. "From the Liberal to the Practical Arts in American Colleges and Universities: Organizational Analysis and Curricular Change." *Journal of Higher Education* 76, no. 2: 151–180.

Brown, Charles, and Mary Corcoran. 1997. "Sex-Based Differences in School Content and the Male-Female Wage Gap." *Journal of Labor Economics* 15, no. 3: 431–65.

Cebula, Richard J., and Jerry Lopes. 1982. "Determinants of Student Choice of Undergraduate Major Field." *American Educational Research Journal* 19, no. 2: 303–12.

Charles, Maria, and Karen Bradley. 2009. "Indulging Our Gendered Selves? Sex Segregation by Field of Study in 44 Countries." *American Journal of Sociology* 114, no. 4: 924–76.

Correll, Shelley J. 2001. "Gender and the Career Choice Process: The Role of Biased Self-Assessments." *American Journal of Sociology* 106, no. 6: 1691–730.

Correll, Shelley J. 2004. "Constraints into Preferences: Gender, Status, and Emerging Career Aspirations." *American Sociological Review* 69, no. 1: 93–113.

Davies, Scott, and Neil Guppy. 1997. "Fields of Study, College Selectivity, and Student Inequalities in Higher Education." *Social Forces* 75, no. 4: 1415–36.

England, Paula, and Su Li. 2006. "Desegregation Stalled: The Changing Gender Composition of College Majors, 1971–2002." *Gender & Society* 20, no. 5: 657–77.

Ferree, Myra Marx, Judith Lorber, and Beth B. Hess. 1999. *Revisioning Gender.* Thousand Oaks: Sage Publications.

Gaskell, Jane. 1992. *Gender Matters from School to Work.* Milton Keynes, UK: Open University Press.

Gerber, Theodore P., and Sin Yi Cheung. 2008. "Horizontal Stratification in Postsecondary Education: Forms, Explanations, and Implications." *Annual Review of Sociology* 34: 299–318.

Goyette, Kimberly A., and Ann L. Mullen. 2006. "Who Studies the Arts and Sciences? Social Background and the Choice and Consequences of Undergraduate Field of Study." *Journal of Higher Education* 77, no. 3: 497–538.

Hearn, James C., and Susan Olzak. 1981. "The Role of College Major Departments in the Reproduction of Sexual Inequality." *Sociology of Education* 54, no. 3: 195–205.

Kingston, Paul William, and John C. Smart. 1990. "The Economic Pay-Off of Prestigious Colleges." In *The High-Status Track: Studies of Elite Schools and Stratification,* edited by Paul W. Kingston and Lionel S. Lewis, 147–74. Albany: New York University Press.

Mullen, Ann L. 2010. *Degrees of Inequality: Culture, Class and Gender in American Higher Education.* Baltimore: Johns Hopkins University Press.

Mullen, Ann L., and Jayne Baker. 2008. "Gender, Race, and Ethnic Segregation of Science Fields in U.S. Universities." *Journal of Women and Minorities in Science and Engineering* 14, no. 2: 159–76.

Mullen, Ann L., and Jayne Baker. 2009. "Uncovering Multiple Dimensions of Gender Segregation in U.S. Universities." Paper presented at the Gender and Education Assocation Meeting, Institute of Education, March 25–27, London, England.

Mullen, Ann L., Kimberly A. Goyette, and Joseph A. Soares. 2003. "Who Goes to Graduate School? Social and Academic Correlates of Educational Continuation after College." *Sociology of Education* 76, no. 2: 143–69.

Sanderson, Michael. 1993. "Vocational and Liberal Education: A Historian's View." *European Journal of Education* 28, no. 2: 189–96.

Snyder, Thomas D. 2007. *Digest of Education Statistics, 2006.* NCES 2007–017. Washington, DC: US Department of Education, National Center for Education Statistics, Institute of Education Sciences.

Strauss, Anselm L. 1987. *Qualitative Analysis for Social Scientists.* Cambridge: Cambridge University Press.

Thomas, Kim. 1990. *Gender and Subject in Higher Education.* Bristol, PA: Open University Press.

U.S. Bureau of Labor Statistics. 2007. *Women in the Labor Force: A Databook (2007 Edition).* Report 1002. Department of Labor. www.bls.gov/cps/wlf-databook2007.htm.

Useem, Michael. 1989. *Liberal Education and the Corporation: The Hiring and Advancement of College Graduates.* New York: Aldine de Gruyter.

Useem, Michael, and Jerome Karabel. 1990. "Pathways to Top Corporate Management." In *The High-Status Track: Studies of Elite Schools and Stratification*, edited by Paul W. Kingston and Lionel S. Lewis, 175–207. Albany: New York University Press.

Van de Werfhorst, Herman G. 2002. "A Detailed Examination of the Role of Education in Intergenerational Social-Class Mobility." *Social Science Information* 41, no. 3: 407–38.

Williams, Christine L. 1995. *Still a Man's World: Men Who Do "Women's Work."* Men and Masculinity, No. 1. Berkeley: University of California Press.

Wilson, Kenneth L. 1978. "Toward an Improved Explanation of Income Attainment: Recalibrating Education and Occupation." *American Journal of Sociology* 84, no. 3: 684–97.

Wootton, Barbara H. 1997. "Gender Differences in Occupational Employment." *Monthly Labor Review* (April): 15–24.

NOTES

1. This chapter was previously published as Mullen, Ann L. *Degrees of Inequality: Culture, Class, and Gender in American Higher Education.* pp. 156–204. © 2010 The Johns Hopkins University Press. Adapted and reprinted with permission of Johns Hopkins University Press.

2. Liberal arts fields comprise disciplines in the arts, humanities, mathematics, and social and natural sciences. Liberal arts are also sometimes referred to as "liberal arts and sciences."

9

Demystifying Influences on Persistence for Native American First-Generation College Students

Natalie Rose Youngbull and Robin Minthorn

Native American college students are entering and graduating postsecondary education institutions at increasingly higher rates (Brayboy et al. 2012; DeVoe and Darling-Churchill 2008; NCES 2005). With increasing numbers of Native American college students, there is an increasingly urgent need for higher education institutions, including both non-Native colleges and universities (NNCUs) and tribal colleges and universities (TCUs), to understand how to support them—not only in their first year as first-generation students, but also throughout their higher education journey. Numerous factors affect the pathway to college and persistence of Native American first-generation students. Some key areas of consideration are the impact of historical trauma over time from US federal policies as well as the impact of these policies on the socioeconomic status, living standards, and mental, emotional, and physical wellness of these students and their families and communities. It is also important to note that, in spite of the historical trauma Native American students and families face, there is also immense strength and resilience in the culture, language, and values that Native American first-generation college students bring with them in their educational journey. In an effort to understand these lived realities and stories, this chapter begins with a detailed examination of the current literature on Native students and an overview of the student support structures found to promote Native student persistence. Subsequently, we present our study, which specifically examined fifteen American Indian Gates Millennium Scholars who did not persist to graduation; after describing the research design, methods, and reporting our findings, we turn to a discussion of specific recommendations for institutions of higher education to consider implementing to better support first-generation Native American college students. There is increasing representation of Native American college students in higher education. However, there are still many students, particularly first-generation college students, who slip through the cracks despite having full financial assistance, carrying the hopes and prayers of their ancestors and families with them. We hope this chapter helps to strengthen the understanding of the journey

of Native American first-generation college students so that more can persist
and find pathways to graduation.

LITERATURE REVIEW: NATIVE AMERICAN STUDENTS
IN HIGHER EDUCATION

Native students are becoming more visible in higher education and receiving
more bachelor's and graduate degrees than ever before (Brayboy et al. 2012;
DeVoe and Darling-Churchill 2008). Yet increased student services and
incorporation of Native perspectives are also needed for the opposite reason:
because despite the relatively higher numbers of Native students attending
and graduating from college, Native students continue to face obstacles
to college-going and persistence once in college. If the theories of social
networks, social reproduction, and concepts of capital, both cultural and
social, can be applied to certain areas of college access and success for Native
American students, they neglect to address Native American students' low
levels of college persistence through a culturally sensitive and strength-based
lens. The following sections provide a better understanding of the current
literature surrounding Native American students in higher education.

Native Americans are plagued by high attrition rates that begin in high
school and continue throughout college. In 2005, data gathered by the National Center for Education Statistics revealed that less than 50 percent of
Native American high school students graduate. Historically, Native Americans high school students have been plagued with high dropout rates and
low graduation rates (Faircloth and Tippeconnic 2010; Freeman and Fox
2005). As a result, those Native Americans that make it through high school
and continue on to college find that they are few and far between. Although
the latest report from the US Department of Education (2005) shows that
enrollment for Native American college students has more than doubled over
the past twenty-five years, Native Americans remain underrepresented in
higher education. Shotton, Oosahwe, and Cintrón (2007) observed that Native Americans between the ages of 18 and 24 are less likely to be enrolled
in college than their White, Asian/Pacific Islander, and African American
counterparts; only 18 percent of Native Americans in that age group were in
college (Freeman and Fox 2005). Overall, Native Americans comprise about
1 percent of the total population of college students, while students of all minority backgrounds combined comprise nearly 28 percent of college students;
thus, the percentage of Native American college students is very low even in
reference to the overall minority college student population (Snyder, Tan, and
Hoffman 2004; Pavel et al. 1998).

Educational achievement is another staggering problem for American Indians. DeVoe and Darling-Churchill (2008) reported that 9 percent of Native Americans have attained a bachelor's degree, while 19 percent of the general population has attained the same. Even with the increased number of Native Americans attending college, there is a disconnect between students matriculating at college and those students going to graduate. A major issue in the higher education arena is the persistence rates of American Indians. Data reveal that the six-year graduation rate for Native Americans is 36.2 percent, while the general population's rate is 54.4 percent (US Department of Education 2005). The picture that is painted by these statistics is that of the small population of Native Americans that go on to attend college, only a third are persisting to graduation. In sum, Native Americans are matriculating in college at a higher rate than ever before, yet still lagging behind the general population in terms of college completion rates.

Transitional Factors for Native American Students

There are both positive and negative factors affecting Native American students' transition to college. Positive factors include having a strong cultural identity, high self-esteem, and support on campus, while negative factors include poor academic preparation, feelings of isolation on campus, and personal financial difficulties (Benjamin, Chambers, and Reiterman 1993; Gloria and Kurpius 2001; Guillory and Wolverton 2008; Lin, LaCounte, and Eder 1988). Solorzano (1992) found a host of factors that affected the low percentages of American Indians, along with African Americans and Latinos, who meet eligibility requirements for admission; these factors include inadequate preparation, negative teacher expectations, and the disproportionate tracking of students of color into nonacademic and vocational courses. Researchers also assert that cultural discontinuity contributes to the high dropout rates, low academic achievement, and poor self-esteem of Native students (Deyhle and Swisher 1997; Fann 2002; Pavel et al. 1998; Peshkin 1997). Conversely, the opportunity to maintain traditional values and have a positive Native identity has been identified as a factor that helps Native American students to have higher grades, lower dropout rates, and higher self-esteem (Coggins, Williams, and Radin 1997; Dehyle 1992; Fann 2002; Ledlow 1992).

Similarly, Terenzini et al. (1994) found that students from disadvantaged socioeconomic and educational backgrounds experience a considerably different transition to college—academically, socially, and culturally—as compared to their traditional peers. The academic factors that can hinder Native American students who matriculate at college are inadequate academic preparation for college, poor study skills, and insufficient guidance from high school counselors (Brown and Kurpius 1997; Hoover and Jacobs 1992; Swanson and Tokar 1991; Wells 1997). Other factors that researchers have found to play a role in the nonpersistence of Native American students at college can be related to the social and cultural aspects of the transition that Terenzini et al. (1994) describe. Some examples are adjustment to the college environment, feelings of isolation on campus, and feelings that the campus is not accommodating to Native American students' backgrounds (Benjamin, Chambers, and Reiterman 1993; Jackson, Smith, and Hill 2003; Lin, LaCounte, and Eder 1988; Swanson and Tokar 1991; Wells 1997). Jackson, Smith, and Hill (2003) highlight literature that focuses on personal factors influencing the transition to college for Native American students, including students' academic aspirations, confidence in ability to succeed academically, personal financial difficulties, and personal/family problems (Brown and Kurpius 1997; Kerbo 1981; McInerney and Swisher 1995; Swanson and Tokar 1991; Wells 1997).

The majority of research studies addressing Native American students in higher education reflect the deficit approach, with the findings yielding negative statistics and factors that play into students' nonpersistence. In response to the appalling statistics and the many factors that play a role in the nonpersistence of Native American students, researchers have made recommendations as to what could be beneficial in addressing these issues. Some research suggests that students would benefit from finding a mentor and/or a support group on campus (Braithwaite 1997; Brown and Kurpius 1997; Hoover and Jacobs 1992). Other researchers insist that social integration into campus life through active participation in Native American clubs/organizations or building a strong social network could be linked to positive academic performance and persistence of Native American students (Jackson, Smith, and Hill 2003; McClellan 2005; Williams 2012). Some colleges responded to American Indians' inadequate preparation for college and poor adjustment to the college environment by creating peer mentoring programs (Shotton, Oosahwe, and Cintrón 2007), organized tutoring programs, precollege orientation, and academic bridge programs (Wells 1997).

Academic Persistence

Multiple studies have examined factors that contribute to the success and academic persistence of Native American students in higher education. These factors include confidence and self-perception as possible predictors of academic persistence among Native American students (Brown and Kurpius 1997). Jackson, Smith, and Hill (2003) find that confidence and self-efficacy are related to academic persistence. Other studies find that self-efficacy is critical for helping students to overcome obstacles (Coffman and Gilligan 2002; Kalsner 1992). Consequently, as Native students transition from high school to college, nurturing confidence and self-perception is important. Additional factors identified by studies as important for Native student academic persistence include precollege academic preparation, family support, faculty involvement and support, institutional commitment to students and community on campus, financial support, and institutional and individual support for students to stay connected to home communities while at college (Astin 1982; Barnhardt 1994; Brown 1995; Falk and Aitken 1984; Tachine and Francis-Begay 2013). Generally, if Native students who aspire to attend college are supported and prepared for college while in high school, they are more likely to persist academically (Benjamin, Chambers, and Reiterman 1993; Brayboy et al. 2012).

As previously mentioned, both Native and non-Native faculty play a critical role in Native student academic persistence, particularly when faculty seek to understand the concerns and issues that Native students face and demonstrate their support for and connection with Native students (Brown and Kurpius 1997). Studies consistently indicate that positive interactions between faculty members and Native American students are critical for fostering persistence and academic achievement (Jackson, Smith, and Hill 2003). Positive faculty and staff interaction, coupled with demonstration of institutional commitment to supporting Native American students through services and providing an inclusive campus climate, also increase academic persistence (Larimore 1997). Similarly, persistence is promoted by assisting incoming and returning college students with information regarding financial resources, scholarships, and financial management (Aitken 1984; Almeida 1999; Brayboy et al. 2012; Dodd et al. 1995; Reyhner and Dodd 1995). These studies show that American Indian students perceive the campus climate to be inclusive when the institution provides adequate resources in the form of financial assistance, cultural support, and Native faculty representation.

Families and support networks are also critical. Many students draw their strength and motivation to persist from families; this includes the desire to make life better for their families and even the goal to not let their families down (Guillory and Wolverton 2008). The home or tribal community of Native college students helps them persist because they receive emotional, spiritual, and financial support that encourages them to achieve their higher education goals (Bowker 1992; HeavyRunner and DeCelles 2002). As NNCUs acknowledge the important roles that family, community, and support networks play with regard to academic persistence, they increase the likelihood that Native students will maintain cultural ties to their community and benefit from a social support system while away (Guillory and Wolverton 2008).

Current Support Structures and Programs to Support Native American First-Generation College Students

There are various pathways that Native American youth may take during high school, between high school and college, and while in college that can help them navigate the journey to their bachelor's degree as a first-generation student. In the current study, described in more detail below, five American Indian Gates Millennium Scholars (AIGMS) attended college-prep summer programs while in high school to help them prepare for college. The programs they attended, Upward Bound and bridge programs, provided an introduction to college and campus life and fostered smaller, inclusive environments that helped the AIGMS participants feel a sense of belonging once they arrived on campus. In this section, we review these and other programs and opportunities that Native American students might participate in to help them prepare and transition into college. Described in order of progression from secondary education-based support programs to college-based ones, each is important in helping Native American first-generation college students find connections, see themselves belonging on campus, and navigate the completion of their bachelor's degree.

Upward Bound

Part of the TRIO Programs, Upward Bound is a federally funded program that emerged as a result of the War on Poverty during the Johnson administration. Its mission is to help prepare students for college entrance and strengthen their coursework during high school (US Department of Education 2016a). Upward Bound specifically serves students who are low in socioeconomic status or first-generation (i.e., neither parent has a bachelor's degree). The program is housed on university campuses; youth reside on campus for five to six weeks, take classes that strengthen their academics, and become familiar with living away from home and on a university campus. Students also receive follow-ups and check-ins from Upward Bound staff throughout their academic years as long as they are associated with the program. There are a number of Upward Bound programs that help support and prepare Native American college students. One example, at the University of Colorado Boulder, has been in existence for over thirty years and specifically serves students from geographically isolated and reservation-based communities. Others that intentionally and directly serve Native American students are at Ft. Lewis College, Arizona State University, and the University of North Dakota.

GEAR UP

GEAR UP is another federally funded TRIO program that was founded to help low-income middle and high schools that prepare youth for college in order to raise the number of students who attend college and improve their persistence rates (US Department of Education 2016b). GEAR UP facilitates preparation for college through activities such as taking groups of students on college visits and providing specific kinds of college-oriented knowledge and information, including information about the FAFSA and steps in the college choice process. There are a number of GEAR UP programs that serve Native American youth, especially at schools where there are high numbers in addition to high proportions of low-income students.

Early College High School Initiatives

Early College High School Initiatives was created by the Bill and Melinda Gates Foundation in 2002 to increase the number of postsecondary credentials awarded to underrepresented students. To date, there have been 240 Early Colleges started in the United States. In each case, they partner with a university or community college so that upon high school graduation students leave with a high school diploma and an associate's degree or two years of college credits that can be applied toward a bachelor's degree (American Institutes for Research 2016). The Early College High School initiative began with a partnership between the Gates Foundation and Antioch University in the Center for Native Education, where they were able to start fifteen schools, in seven states, that specifically targeted Native students. Of these schools, five achieved graduation rates between 69 and 100 percent and attendance rates between 83 and 94 percent (Akweks et al. 2010). This initiative demonstrates the important role these types of programs can have on Native American students when they are intentional about working with Indigenous peoples (Campbell, Egawa, and Wortman 2003).

Bridge Programs

Bridge programs are a type of program that, as the name suggests, are intended to help students bridge a transition, whether from high school to college or from undergraduate to graduate or professional degree programs. Bridge programs may serve various demographics, including first-generation students, low-income students, and so forth, and there are a number of summer bridge programs that are or have been offered to incoming Native

American freshmen the summer before they formally matriculate to college. They are grouped with a cohort of students living in the dorms for four to eight weeks, during which they earn college-level credit and are encouraged to foster connections to the university campus and with other Native American students on campus. Oftentimes, the purpose of these programs is to help Native American students transition emotionally, physically, and mentally, and to find their social and structural places like home on campus in ways that honor their culture and spiritual ways of being. Colleges and universities with bridge programs include the University of New Mexico, Black Hills State University, the Institute of American Indian Arts, Bacone College, and others.

First-Year Scholars Programs and Living-Learning Communities

Once Native American college students matriculate at their respective institution of higher education, they may be greeted by a first-year scholars program that offers theme-based communities built around common attributes or interests. Particularly if they are attending an institution with relatively high Native American enrollment, or one that has an intentional mission or makes intentional efforts to serve Native students, they may have access to Native-specific living and learning communities (Tachine and Francis-Begay 2013). First-year scholars programs for Native American students often group participating students into a cohort model where they are enrolled in common courses and offered programming specifically intended to help them transition into the university setting. Living and learning communities are also often theme-based and usually involve students living together in a section of student housing, such as one wing of a dorm, which provides students a more community-oriented residential experience that can feel like a home away from home. The structure itself may be helpful for Native American students, and these benefits may be enhanced when the community is focused specifically on Native American students and/or includes intentional efforts to offer programming, meetings, and events to support these Native American students while they are away from family and community.

Peer Mentoring Programs

An important part of supporting persistence among Native American students, first-generation or not, is supporting relationships with their peers. Native American student support services often include a peer mentoring program or component in which first-year or early college students are mentored by upperclassmen college students (Minthorn and Shotton 2014). The intention of the peer mentoring programs is to pair students who have persisted to junior- or senior-year status with newly minted freshmen whom they mentor and guide on issues such as how to navigate the college campus system and how to balance going home and finding home on campus. First-time Native American students are often paired with a fellow Native American student and both are encouraged to attend on-campus programs and events throughout the academic year. These peer mentoring programs seek to provide guidance and support in the areas that will enable Native American college students to persist and graduate (Jackson, Smith, and Hill 2003; Shotton, Oosahwe, and Cintrón 2007).

Native Student Organizations/Building Community on Campus

Native Student Organizations (NSOs) come in a variety of forms. Some are general when other are more specialized. For example, the American Indian Science and Engineering Society is oriented toward academic interests. Other are more social or more service oriented like historically Native American fraternities and sororities. NSOs help Native American students to build shared community on campus through common interests, activities, and events. They fulfil the mission of the organization, promote leadership, and help to develop other skills for Native students (Minthorn 2014; Minthorn and Shotton 2014). NSOs also often work collaboratively with other NSO organizations (and other student organizations as well). For Native college students, the experience of being involved and connected to a NSO offers a deeper sense of community on campus and finding place where it otherwise might not be found.

METHODS

This phenomenological qualitative research study examined the experiences of twenty American Indian Gates Millennium Scholars (AIGMS) who enrolled in but then left institutions of higher education. The Gates Millennium Scholarship Program (GMSP) is a national scholarship program that serves racial minority students from across the nation. Annually, one thousand incoming college freshmen receive awards through the scholarship program. To be eligible, students must fall into at least one of four racial/ethnic categories: African American, American Indian/Alaska Natives, Asian and Pacific Islander American, and Hispanic American. One hundred and fifty Native American incoming freshmen are awarded the scholarship annually. Though GMSP boasts exceptional overall graduation rates among its scholarship recipients, the Native American cohort possesses the lowest persistence to graduation rate of all cohorts (S. Abbott, personal communication, Fall 2009). To date, over 2,000 Native American incoming freshmen have been awarded the Gates Millennium Scholarship since its inception in 1999. For the current study, the sample was drawn from the AIGMS who departed from college. Participants had left college, were labeled as Gates Millennium Scholars alums, and were no longer eligible to receive from GMS. They were identified through informal networks.

Studying this particular group of Native American students contributes to the existing literature by exploring factors beyond financial assistance that impact persistence for Native students navigating higher education institutions. AIGMS are considered among the top academically meritorious incoming Native American college students. The majority of the participants were in the top 5–10 percent of their graduating classes, and some earned top honors such as salutatorian and valedictorian. The fifteen female and five male participants represented over twenty tribes/nations from several regions across the nation, including the Northwest, Northern Plains, Southern Plains, Southwest, and Great Lakes. Half of the participants were the first in their families to attend college, and six participants had one parent who attained an associate's degree. Demographically, ten participants grew up on a reservation and nine came from rural areas or small towns. Over half could understand their Native language and a few could speak it fluently. They were highly involved in their communities and served as examples of hope and possibility to their families and community members. They described themselves as carrying a great deal of responsibility, optimism, and potential with them to college.

AIGMS participants were recruited through purposeful sampling and interviewed one-on-one using a semi-structured interview protocol. All interviews were conducted in 2013 (but participants had left their respective colleges or universities in other years and at varying times in their undergraduate careers). Because the students were living across the nation, fifteen participants were interviewed over the phone and five were interviewed in person. Prior to the interview, participants filled out a participant questionnaire form that collected basic demographic information and asked them about the values that they considered important. One-on-one interviews ranged between forty-five minutes and two hours in length and were audio recorded and transcribed verbatim. Each participant received a transcribed copy of their interview, for the purpose of acknowledging that their stories and experiences belong to them and not the researcher. Having a transcribed copy of their interview also allowed participants to review it and follow up with researchers or clarify any vague information from the interview.

FINDINGS

During AIGMS' transitions to their respective institutions, they encountered issues on both institutional and individual levels. On the institutional level, AIGMS spoke of their institutions and GMSP as not being reflective of Native students. Structures were not in place to serve Native students, and participants acknowledged the significance of relationships—and the absence of relationships on campus and with the American Indian Graduate Center (AIGC), the organization that administered the scholarship, support, and resources to the American Indian cohort of the Gates Millennium Scholarship Program (GMSP). On the personal level, AIGMS felt a lack of support from institutional agents such as their financial aid officers and academic advisors.

Institutions and GMSP Not Reflective of Native Students

The majority of AIGMS interviewed chose to attend mid-to-large four-year NNCUs. These institutions had small Native student populations and multicultural or Native cultural centers, yet some AIGMS felt a lack of connection on campus. Existing structures on these NNCUs were not reflective of Native students' identities and needs, nor were they equipped to serve Native students holistically. Specifically, AIGMS were seeking places to practice their spirituality on campus as well as space within their courses to incorporate that aspect of their backgrounds. AIGMS sought support structures on campus and with the GMSP and the AIGC. In particular, relationships were of central importance for AIGMS to be successful. Though they were disappointed with the lack of connection on campus, they were more frustrated with the absence of relationship-building with the GMSP and AIGC staff.

Structures Not in Place to Serve Native Students

On campus, AIGMS felt there were structures missing on campus that would have made them feel more connected and involved. For Jacob, structures on campus conflicted with his home environment and he struggled to preserve his identity. Jacob explained, "um, at home I was more humble, more settled, more like, grandparents. I was more like that . . . but when I was in college, I was going crazy." There was no place on campus for Jacob to practice the traditional spiritual ways that helped him maintain balance and connection. Dana similarly described a lack of space—and time—on campus for her to represent her spirituality and traditional teachings:

I didn't really feel like there was a place for my spiritual beliefs in the class-room, my cultural beliefs, especially in like all the prereq classes. I mean the prerequisites like English 101, Math. But I took a class, it was a Southwest studies and I felt like me being in that class as a Native person, I contributed in the discussion, you know, my perspective as a Native person. And I felt like it was valued. Especially in the New Mexico history part. I think it was, I felt like my experience and my cultural teachings were valued when it came to, when it came time for, when it was needed, like if it was specifically related or a discussion or if it was celebrating the Indigenous Peoples Day, you know. But other than that, I didn't really feel like there was time . . . time for that to be recognized.

Though Dana did experience her cultural background being acknowledged and appreciated, that recognition occurred in very circumscribed contexts—within the curriculum of one course, or at particular moments and times when "it was needed" or "specifically related," such as Indigenous Peoples' Day. Dana realized this and recognized the limited avenues for incorporating Native perspectives in her overall coursework.

David attended an institution that was located in one of his tribal communi-ties. He had expected to see more Native representation on campus and was disappointed when he did not see or experience any interaction with other Native students. He said, "I had so much ambition and I was so ready, but after I kept going, there was just, there was nothing in the school to keep me there. There was nobody, kind of like saying, there was no support." Beyond the lack of representation on campus, David was disheartened at the lack of connection between his institution and GMSP:

The only thing that I knew from the scholarship was I got money. I kind of remember them saying that someone would keep in touch with me from the scholarship. Um, and so I, I . . . that's all I remember. I used to get the emails, and actually I still do get the emails every now and again. [Laughs.] But I thought there was more of a contact with the actual scholarship people. And I just thought there was a little more to it. And there's no one on campus of course who knew anything about the Gates Millennium Scholarship. The advisor didn't even know, because I had to actually ask them for more money to get all my books because it didn't cover, for some reason they didn't request the right amount. And then I did ask for more money to get a laptop and the advisor said I couldn't do it. And there was just no communication and there was no real knowledge of what I had, what I had received from Gates basically.

David also thought carrying the title "scholar" would be acknowledged by his faculty at the very least. When it went unacknowledged, he concluded that what he brought from home was not valued on campus.

AIGMS spoke of missing structures on campus that represented both their Native and Gates scholar identities. According to TribalCrit, education policies geared toward Native Americans are historically rooted in assimilationist frameworks (Brayboy 2005). Consequently, current mainstream campuses typically are not reflective of Native histories, perspectives, or experiences. Not only did many AIGMS experience feelings of disconnection due to the size and impersonal nature of their institutions, they also experienced feelings of disconnection between their cultural ways of knowing—that is, their teachings and values—and institutional norms. In addition, institutions were not knowledgeable about the resources available to the recipients from the GMSP, such as budget reevaluations and funding specifically for computers. Because of this lack of knowledge, AIGMS were not fully financially supported within the structures on their campuses.

Significance of Relationships for AIGMS

Relationships—or the lack thereof—with their institutions and AIGC/GMSP emerged as a key factor for AIGMS. One AIGMS, Kate, offered an explanation to help institutions and organizations like AIGC/GMSP understand the importance of relationships within the American Indian community:

> The one thing that I really think that AIGC and people who work with Native Americans is they really need to understand that relationships with Native Americans are so essential to be efficient. And I say this because of just anything with my students, I have to build relationships with them before they can trust me to say "ok, you're going to need help with this, let me sit down and help you." It's building those relationships, you know, "what's your favorite color, what's your home like," then I can properly serve them because they're not afraid to ask. They're not afraid to say that "I need help" or "I can't do this" or "Ms. Hamilton, so-and-so's picking on me" or "this is the way I feel about myself." I really can't be effective in what I do if not for relationships and then you look back on the relationships with your parents, building those relationships, they're not going to trust you if they don't respect you or there's no relationship there.

Kate's explanation speaks to the significance of relationships among Native people. In particular, relationships played a central role in the identity of the AIGMS participants. Relationships with family, community, GMSP, AIGC, faculty, and staff were all discussed by AIGMS as being important to their success—and, conversely, the absence or inadequacy of these relationships adversely affected their experiences of college. Many acknowledged the roles within their families and communities that are important to them:

granddaughter/grandson, daughter/son, older sister/brother, auntie/uncle, mother and father. Those roles remained important to them in their transition to college, and they expected to cultivate similar relationships with their peers, faculty, and staff, and especially with AIGC and GMSP. Sahara did not have trouble making friends on campus, but she was unable to make connections with classmates in her courses to study with and share notes. She felt lonely for someone with whom to plan courses to take together in the future. Coming from a small school, Dana struggled with the impersonal, large classes she found in college. She noted, "In my class I graduated from a class of six, and so going to [my university] and being in class of 150, even 500 and not having that personal connection with the professor, that was really hard for me to deal with as well." AIGMS students saw this lack of opportunity to build relationships within classroom environments as a gap in structured institutional supports.

There was also an expectation that the AIGC staff would understand the importance of relationships for Native students. Several AIGMS mentioned attending the National Leadership Conference hosted by GMSP as freshmen. The conference was meant to provide a comprehensive understanding of the scholarship program for all Gates Scholarship recipients while also introducing them to the staff who would be working with the students. AIGMS enjoyed the conference, but they returned to their respective campuses without establishing any meaningful relationships. Rachel elaborated on this topic and discussed the kind of relationship she thought would have been helpful:

> I don't remember them advocating or saying how important it is to make those networking relationships with people. Because then that could be a support system, because you guys are both going through it together. I didn't realize that, again, at the time, how important those networking things are during the whole conference and why they do it. All I knew was that I was going to Los Angeles to this big conference because of the Gates scholarship. And then having someone sit there and say this is important because. . . . I think when you're that young—18, 19, 17—fresh out of high school, that's what you need. You need somebody there not to do everything for you, but to tell you how important it is and to help you along. Someone you could turn to for help that's not like, "oh you should already know this" type of mentality, attitude. Someone's who really there for you as a support system, as a support person, and encouraging in a positive way.

Many expectations that AIGMS had for the Gates Millennium Scholarship Program were unmet. Rachel underscores the lack of AIGC and GMSP staff encouragement to build support networks and relationships at their respective institutions. This particular type of support, building relationships, would have significantly improved Rachel and other AIGMS' experiences on campus.

Lack of Institutional Support

The GMSP is a national scholarship and recipients can attend any accredited institution across the nation. When AIGMS transitioned to their respective campuses, some sought assistance from institutional agents for academic advising, financial aid, and other kinds of support. In seeking guidance and advice from these institutional agents AIGMS put their trust in them. While building trust is important for all college students and particularly those from minoritized communities, it is particularly significant for Native students because even though education is viewed as a valuable commodity in tribal communities, distrust of educational institutions still exists among some students (Fryberg and Markus 2007).

One particular situation in which trust was breached involved the director of the Multicultural Center, a position designed to assist underrepresented students on campus. This individual informed Nadine that she could purchase a computer and that the total cost would be covered by the Gates scholarship, but toward the end of the semester Nadine was told by that same individual that she owed for the computer:

> I really didn't understand the goings-on of the financial part. You know, they told me, "alright, don't worry about it. You're set. Just go ahead and go to class. Pick your classes and those are the classes that you're going to." Yeah, and I didn't really know about anything else, other than classes were paid for. You know, I was just like, "ok, well I'm just going to go to class and do what I have to." And that was about it, until this one year. It was the beginning of the semester, I think, spring semester. Anyways, they said I was supposed to be getting a computer from the Gates Millennium scholarship. And then, like toward the end of the semester, they told me that I needed to pay for the computer because the Gates didn't cover it. And so that really confused me because I was like, "well I thought the Gates covered everything?" And you know, I got the computer from the school. I was like, "um, so what's really going on?" That's toward the end is when I went back and started asking questions because I was like, "oh, ok, now I have to pay for this computer. Where am I going to find the resources right now," because I didn't really take on a job like I wanted to because I had my evenings free. And yeah, so that kind of confused me towards the end, so I was just like, "ok, well, I'll pay for it. Don't worry about it, I'll figure it out."

Nadine also mentioned that she had little correspondence with the AIGC staff and that she was unaware that the GMSP covered costs for expenses such as a computer and travel home. When she asked the director for advice she was told not to "worry about it, just go to class." She went to the financial aid office for help in figuring out the financial situation, and she ended up having to take out a loan to pay off her bursar's account so she did not owe the institution. With little explanation provided by the director of the Multicultural Center, AIGC staff, or the financial aid office, and no effort to help her resolve the situation, Nadine was confused and frustrated from this experience.

Financial Aid Officers

The financial aid office plays a fundamental role in the transition and persistence of AIGMS on campus because they have to work with the students on their financial need analysis and their financial status throughout the time they are students. The majority of AIGMS interviewed understood that Gates provided substantial financial aid toward their cost of attendance, but like Nadine, most did not know that they could ask for additional funding or exactly what expenses the scholarship covered. After speaking with another Gates scholar, Dana learned that they were using funding for purposes other than college expenses and they were able to get the extra funding through working with a financial aid officer. Yet when Dana met with her financial aid officer to gain a better understanding of what the scholarship could cover, she remembers being treated negatively:

> Well, I guess I didn't really know the extent of the scholarship because after my school year had started I heard about other Gates scholars talking about how they got computers and they got this and they got that. And one Gates scholar actually said "yeah, I keep enough money out so I can invest some." And I'm like "how do you do that?" And they're like "well you just have to like convince your financial aid advisor." And I just . . . I just didn't understand that I guess. I didn't know. I just thought it was covering the basics. And I didn't have that good of a financial aid advisor to teach me this, I don't think. And when I asked questions, it was like kind of like "you're just an Indian," you know? I just kind of got that weird vibe, like "oh you're just another kid here and you don't know what you have, so let's give you what's the bare minimum." And I think that person knew what the Gates scholarship was and what it was capable of paying for. And I didn't really know and I just took advantage of it to the extent that I knew was for funding for my books, my room and board, and tuition. And I did get some school supplies and stuff, but that's really about it.

Dana did not feel supported by her financial aid officer; rather she felt the officer treated her as though she was ignorant due to her Native American background. Thus, she felt the officer did not advocate for additional funding for her even though Dana believed the officer knew exactly what the GMSP offered to its recipients.

In general, the scholarship is intended to cover a student's cost of attendance (COA). The financial aid office submits documents declaring this amount and the GMSP sends the funding to the institutions on behalf of the recipients. Some expenses, such as tuition and on-campus room and board, are exact amounts, while others are estimates—books and supplies, food, and utilities, to name a few. Scholarship recipients have the option do a budget reevaluation with a financial aid officer if they are in need of more funding to cover their cost of attendance. This important piece of information was not well understood among AIGMS. Penny did not know she could ask for a budget reevaluation. In her freshman year, Gates covered all her expenses and she received work-study funding. Then, in her sophomore year, the scholarship only covered a small portion of her expenses, so she had to take loans out to pay for the remainder. When asked if she could remember why the funding drastically decreased, she could not pinpoint the reason:

> I couldn't remember if they had said that they had had an increase maybe in applicants that year or awards. And so then therefore the money was disbursed a little bit less. I, honestly, I can't remember. But I remember that because the first year, I remember I got it and I was so excited. And I remember going to the seminar in, not the seminar, but the convention in California. I remember going and I was just so super excited. But then it was like the next year, I went to do my financial aid again and my advisor was like "hey, your scholarship will pay for this much, so for the rest you're going to have to do financial aid." And I was like "ok." And it was funny because at the time I thought, well I wonder if it's just the financial aid advisor wanting me to do student loans.

Because GMSP awards the same number of scholarships each year, Penny's explanation could not have been the reason for her funding decrease. Because she attended a small in-state institution where she was likely the only Gates Millennium Scholar on campus, a more likely explanation is that the financial aid officer may not have been familiar with the GMSP and its funding process. Nevertheless, the cost of attendance should not have radically changed from the prior year, when Penny had received more than enough funding. Additionally, since it was Penny's sophomore year, the financial aid officer should have been familiar with the process. Due to this lack of support from the financial aid officer, Penny's actions seemed to snowball toward leaving the institution. To support herself, she pursued an off-campus job, working the night shift and eventually drifting away from campus. She expressed feeling "burnt out" at that time and decided to take a break from school to focus on work. These examples reveal a troubling disconnect between the GMSP, the institution, and the AIGMS. In this particular case, the financial aid office did not advocate on behalf of the AIGMS to the Gates Millennium Scholarship Program in regard to the scholar's funding. For Penny, ultimately, this lack of support directly impacted her progress and her ability to persist through college.

Academic Advisors

Academic advisors play pivotal roles for students, providing guidance on progress through coursework and degree requirements. Michael attended a large public institution and had difficulty getting in to meet with his advisor. Without academic advising, Michael ended up taking too many electives and not taking the necessary courses toward his degree program:

> I guess I was just taking a lot more electives than I should've been. I should've been taking maybe one or two electives a semester, and then two courses that pertain to the degree that I was taking. However, that wasn't the case. I just kept taking electives. And then from there I had caught up with all the main electives and I think there were just a few that I had left to take. I didn't really concentrate on the courses that I needed for my degree. So that's the reason why I was, I had to, um, the advisor advised that maybe taking a semester off and going to a community college to work on those prerequisites. That way I could come back to the [institution] and start taking the courses.

When he did finally meet with his advisor, Michael's advisor encouraged him to do dual enrollment at the university and a community college, but he did not want to do that because it would mean taking even more credits per semester. Eventually Michael had to take a break from the university because he had exhausted all his elective courses and could not enroll in the required courses for his degree. Though he did not lay blame on his advisor, he might never have had to take a break from the university had he been able to get into the courses required for his major. The advisor could have stressed the importance of building off the prerequisite courses towards upper-division courses.

For another AIGMS, David, his experiences at his institution did not meet his expectations, and the absence of support or communication from his academic advisor was a major influence in his departure. He expressed there not being any support for him at his institution, which took him by surprise because the institution was located in one of his tribal communities and not far from his hometown. He knew the advisor and her family, as she was a tribal member too. Still, that did not make a difference. David felt ignored by his advisor. He recalled, "The advisors they give you had no want for me. And had no emails for forever given to me by my advisor. I never . . . I only spoke to her one time." He shared a defining moment for him on campus where he reached out for counsel and support from his advisor and was never contacted:

I felt like I needed more help, but didn't know how to get it and I was afraid to ask a little. But also, I didn't know who to ask. I didn't, there was not . . . I didn't know if I could ask the advisor. And there was a day that I remember, I was sitting at the school, on the campus and I decided to go ahead and call the advisor. I got on the phone and I called the advisor and it went to voicemail, or message machine, whatever. And I called it and I left her a message. I said "can you call me before the end of the day? I got a decision." I was like "I don't think I want to be here anymore, I don't know what to do." And I never got a call back, and here it is twelve years later . . . I think it's twelve years, and I still ain't got a call back. [Laughs.] And it's just, I just . . . when I never got a call back I was just like, I said "you know what? I guess it's not meant to be." Because obviously, I didn't think the school cared.

It took a lot for David to reach out to his academic advisor because he was a shy young Native college student. In this respect, he viewed himself as typical of many Native American students who matriculate at college. As David put it, "a lot of Indian kids that graduate high school and go to college, they're a shy Indian when they walk onto campus. They don't have that strength to ask a question. They feel embarrassed. And that's how I was." He related this to his traditional upbringing and pointed out that maybe his advisor, and other institutional agents, on campus were unaware of how to support Native American students because they lacked the necessary cultural knowledge and understanding.

Maybe the research hadn't been done. Maybe the knowledge of the advisor wasn't up to code for my race. Maybe they didn't understand, and you know, it took me a lot of years to figure it out because I was pretty upset with [my institution] because I felt like they didn't give me enough as a student to participate.

An academic advisor's role as a guide is critical to a student's progress, and conversely, their absence can be a key factor in students' lack of persistence in college, as was the case for both Michael and David. For Michael, the difficulty of meeting with his advisor led him to take too many electives and not enough required classes, and the resulting bottleneck forced him to take a break from his institution. David's experience demonstrates the importance of touching base with students, especially if they have reached out on their own. David was looking for someone to connect with on campus, and thought that it would have been his academic advisor. Unfortunately, David's experience of disconnection is not unusual and reflects the feelings of many Native American students toward academic advisors and other institutional agents.

Though the GMSP is a national scholarship program that afforded AIGMS the opportunity to attend the institution of their choice, AIGMS experienced an overall lack of support structures within institutions of higher education. Participants expected cultural representation and interpersonal support beyond financial and academic assistance. Potentially, AIGMS anticipated more from GMSP than their own institutions because not only did GMSP provide substantial funding for AIGMS' educations, but the scholarship program also expressly touted the idea that AIGMS would belong to the GMSP family. HeavyRunner and DeCelles (2002) emphasize that sustaining a familial environment positively impacts Native students' academic persistence. AIGMS sought this environment through GMSP and AIGC more than through their respective institutions because they thought GMSP and AIGC understood the importance of relationships and the role of families among Native students. Experiences with certain institutional agents—namely the multicultural director, financial aid officer, and academic advisor—fell short of AIGMS' expectations in regards to receiving guidance and assistance to successfully navigating their institutions. AIGMS' experiences led to feelings of disconnect among institutional agents and within their institutions overall.

RECOMMENDATIONS TO SUPPORT NATIVE AMERICAN FIRST-GENERATION COLLEGE STUDENTS

Below we offer a list of recommended support structures and initiatives to promote success for Native American first-generation college students. The list consists of existing, current programming at certain non-Native colleges and universities as well as recommendations based upon the authors' research and professional experiences on Native student success. These recommendations are in addition to the list of current support structures and programs provided in the prior section. If a combination of the programs and structures listed earlier with those listed below could be implemented, the result would create a strong bridge between secondary and postsecondary education for Native American first-generation college students.

Native American Student Orientations and Blessing Ceremonies

Existing programming to welcome Native American first-generation college students includes hosting a Native American student orientation and/or traditional blessing before or at the beginning of the academic year. For example, the University of Oklahoma's (OU) American Indian Student Association, in collaboration with OU's American Indian Student Services, hosts a Native American new student orientation to introduce incoming students to current Native students, clubs and organizations, faculty, and staff. Another example comes from the University of Arizona (UA), where a Sunrise Ceremony is held at the beginning of the new academic year. A traditional blessing is offered and the tribal liaison offers a welcome and always acknowledges that the land the institution is located on is the traditional land of the Tohono O'odham Nation. These are just two examples of efforts from large NNCUs; there are many more examples of welcoming events at a wide range of schools, from institutions similar to OU and UA to smaller regional institutions as well as tribal colleges and universities. New student orientations and traditional blessings for Native American first-generation students are important because they assist in their transition to college and campus life as well as connect them to existing support structures and involvement opportunities at the very beginning of their college careers.

Relationships and Connections to Home

Relationships are significant for Native students, especially maintaining those relationships from home, with family and home communities. Although many institutions may have an understanding of this connection, relatively few have established specific measures to assist Native students in maintaining their ties to home while also achieving academic success. Guillory and Wolverton (2008) found that maintaining ties to family and communities promoted persistence among Native American students, writing that "The connection for these Indian students to their families, whether nuclear or extended, was so strong that they were willing to overcome many difficult situations, such as an unwelcoming environment, lack of academic preparation, and inadequate financial support" (64). Institutions could emphasize the connection rather than the disconnection between home and college by creating and strengthening opportunities for Native students to return home and give back to their communities through service learning or promoting college knowledge, as well as to foster an inclusive environment for families to feel welcomed on campuses (Minthorn 2014; Minthorn and Shotton 2014).

Culturally Competent Mental Health Services

Mental health issues played into the divergence of AIGMS from institutions of higher education. It was often difficult for them to seek help from the non-Native staff and/or faculty on campus, because these issues were connected back to and entangled with their home communities and families. These

Native students were in need of a trained counselor to help them learn how to cope and take care of their mental health. When they sought counseling services from the campus health centers on their campuses, they often had unpleasant interactions with the available counselors. AIGMS recommended creating a position for a Native counselor within campus health centers—or, at the very least, to require all counselors on campus, particularly non-Native counselors, to have cultural competency training focused specifically on working with Native college students.

Policy Implications

Some of the recommendations emerging from AIGMS's input are related to campus policies that could help foster environments that would be more inclusive of first-generation Native American students. They center on ways to honor and acknowledge the culture of Native American students and the values they bring with them.

Family Involvement on Campus

A first step is to look at ways in which existing policies impact family involvement and inclusion. Are there any policies that prevent family from being involved in the admission, orientation, and enrollment processes? The fact that many Native American students are first-generation means that some families will have limited understanding of college and university climate and structures. In order to garner support from family, they need to feel comfortable and included as part of their student's higher education journey. For Native American college students, moreover, the concept of *family* does not fit within the conventional nuclear definition and often extends to grandmas, grandpas, aunts, uncles, and cousins. Therefore, it is important to reimagine how higher education institutions define family so that it fits all populations of students. As these observations suggest, a comprehensive review and modification of existing policies on family involvement is in order.

Transfer Policies and Memorandums of Understanding (MOUs)

Another area in which college and university policies should be reviewed are current transfer policies. A significant proportion of the Native American college student population begins their college experience at community colleges and especially tribal colleges and universities prior to attend a four-year college or university. Particularly for first-generation Native students for whom college as a whole is an unfamiliar experience, the overall process of transferring schools adds another layer of complexity. These could take the form of intentional efforts to build partnership and transition programs via MOU's between 4-year institutions and local or nearby TCUs and community colleges, simplifying the process and rendering it more transparent and enabling Native American first-generation students to better understand the process of transferring and the university setting.

Enrollment Gap Policies

A final category of policies that may impact first-generation Native American college students is the amount of time allowed for gaps in students' enrollment between terms. It is well established, both in academic studies and in the knowledge base among Native American student affairs professionals, that a significant portion of the Native American college student population ends up "stopping out" so that they can return home to fulfill family responsibilities, take care of family issues or needs, and/or work full time in order to be a financial contributor. Taking this into consideration may encourage administrators and policymakers at the university level to reexamine current policies on allowance of gap years and time for credit hour allowances. Extending the timeline would enable at least some of those students who have stopped out to return back to the institution to finish their degree, whether after a period of one year or five years.

It is important for university administrators and policymakers to take time to better understand the needs of Native American first-generation college students so that their policies reflect the lived realities of this student population. When Native American students see themselves honored in services and policies, they are able to find place on campus, which in turn increases their chances of success and persistence.

CONCLUSION

This chapter examined the experiences of Native American first-generation college students in an effort to provide a better understanding of the realities they face. First, it highlighted literature on the experiences of Native American students in higher education, and it described current support structures and programs for Native American students beginning in high school, continuing through their transitions from high school to college via bridge programs, and ending with the support mechanisms they find when they arrive at college to begin their higher education journey. Then, a description of the AIGMS study analyzed the reasons why these scholars discontinued or stopped out from their higher education journey, despite having a scholarship that at least in principle should have addressed their financial needs while in college. The study highlights the voices of twenty Native American students who experienced isolation, unsupportive staff, and needing to negotiate the unique spaces between family and home life to search for community on campus. Finally, we offered some practical and policy recommendations for staff, administrators, and faculty to consider when exploring ways to support Native American first-generation college students. Native American first-generation college students are umbilically—meaning spiritually and generationally—connected to their families and home communities, yet they desire to find a pathway to complete their higher education degree. It takes everyone to help create the spaces and climate that welcomes, honors, and enables Native American first-generation students to achieve their academic goals.

REFERENCES

Akweks, Kayeri, Nadine Bill, Loretta Seppanen, and Barbara Smith. 2010. *Pathways for Native American Students: A Report on Colleges and Universities in Washington State.* A Report from the Partnership for Native American College Access & Success Project. http://www.evergreen.edu/sites/default/files/nativeprograms/reports/pathways/docs/pathwaysreport.pdf

Almeida, Deirdre A. 1999. *Postsecondary Financial Aid for American Indians and Alaska Natives.* ERIC Digest ED438148. Charleston, WV: Clearinghouse on Rural Education and Small Schools, Appalachia Educational Laboratory.

American Institutes for Research. 2014. "Report Confirms Early College High School Students Much More Likely to Earn a College Degree." News Release, January 15, 2014. http://www.air.org/news/press-release/report-confirms-early-college-high-school-students-much-more-likely-earn-college

Astin, Alexander W. 1982. *Minorities in Higher Education: Recent Trends, Current Prospects, and Recommendations.* San Francisco: Josey-Bass.

Barnhardt, Carol. 1994. "Life on the Other Side: Alaska Native Teacher Education Students and the University of Alaska Fairbanks." PhD diss., University of British Columbia.

Belgarde, Mary Jiron. 1992. "The Performance and Persistence of American Indian Undergraduate Students at Stanford University." PhD diss., Stanford University.

Benjamin, Don-Paul, Stephen Chambers, and Gary Reiterman. 1993. "A Focus on American Indian College Persistence." *Journal of American Indian Education* 32, no. 2: 24–40.

Bowker, Ardy. 1992. "The American Indian Female Dropout." *Journal of American Indian Education* 31, no. 3: 3–20.

Braithwaite, Charles A. 1997. "Helping Students from Tribal Colleges Succeed." *About Campus* 2, no. 5: 19–23.

Brayboy, Bryan McKinley Jones. 2004. "Hiding in the Ivy: American Indian Students and Visibility in Elite Educational Settings." *Harvard Educational Review* 74, no. 2: 125–52.

Brayboy, Bryan McKinley Jones. 2005. "Toward a Tribal Critical Race Theory in Education." *The Urban Review* 37, no. 5: 425–46.

Brayboy, Bryan McKinley Jones, Amy J. Fann, Angelina E. Castagno, and Jessica A. Solyom. 2012. *Postsecondary Education for American Indian and Alaska Natives: Higher Education for Nation Building and Self-Determination.* ASHE Higher Education Report 37, no. 5. New York: John Wiley & Sons.

Brown, Lynn L., and Sharon E. Robinson Kurpius. 1997. "Psychosocial Factors Influencing Academic Persistence of American Indian College Students." *Journal of College Student Development* 38, no. 1: 3–12.

Campbell, Linda, Keith Egawa, and Geneva Wortman. 2003. *Increasing the Achievement of Native American Youth at Early College High Schools.* New Horizons for Learning, The Johns Hopkins University.

Coffman, Donna L., and Tammy D. Gilligan. 2002. "Social Support, Stress, and Self-Efficacy: Effects on Students' Satisfaction." *Journal of College Student Retention: Research, Theory & Practice* 4, no. 1: 53–66.

Coggins, Kip, Edith Williams, and Norma Radin. 1997. "The Traditional Tribal Values of Ojibwa Parents and the School Performance of their Children: An Exploratory Study." *Journal of American Indian Education* 36, no. 3: 1–15.

Dehyle, Donna. 1992. "Constructing Failure and Maintaining Cultural Identity: Navajo and Ute School Leavers." *Journal of American Indian Education* 31, no. 2: 24–47.

Deyhle, Donna, and Karen Swisher. 1997. "Chapter 3: Research in American Indian and Alaska Native Education: From Assimilation to Self-Determination." *Review of Research in Education* 22, no. 1: 113–94.

DeVoe, Jill Fleury, and Kristen E. Darling-Churchill. 2008. *Status and Trends in the Education of American Indians and Alaska Natives: 2008.* NCES 2008–084. National Center for Education Statistics, US Department of Education. https://nces. ed.gov/pubs2008/nativetrends/

Dodd, John M., Florence M. Garcia, Cindy Meccage, and J. Ron Nelson. 1995. "American Indian Student Retention." *NASPA Journal* 33, no. 1: 72–78.

Faircloth, Susan C., and John W. Tippeconnic, III. 2010. *The Dropout/Graduation Rate Crisis Among American Indian and Alaska Native Students: Failure to Respond Places the Future of Native Peoples at Risk.* The Civil Rights Project/Proyecto Derechos Civiles at UCLA and the Pennsylvania State University Center for the Study of Leadership in American Indian Education. https://www. civilrightsproject.ucla.edu/research/k-12-education/school-dropouts/the-dropout-graduation-crisis-among-american-indian-and-alaska-native-students-failure-to-respond-places-the-future-of-native-peoples-at-risk/faircloth-tippeconnic-native-american-dropouts.pdf.

Falk, Dennis R., and Larry P. Aitken. 1984. "Promoting Retention Among American Indian College Students." *Journal of American Indian Education* 23, no. 2: 24–31.

Fann, A. 2002. "Native College Pathways in California: A Look at Higher Education Access for American Indian High School Students." Paper presented at the Association for the Study of Higher Education Annual Meeting, Sacramento, California, November 2002.

Freeman, Catherine, and Mary Ann Fox. 2005. *Status and Trends in The Education of American Indians and Alaska Natives.* NCES 2005–108. National Center for Education Statistics, US Department of Education. https://nces.ed.gov/pubs2005/2005108.pdf.

Fryberg, Stephanie A., and Hazel Rose Markus. 2007. "Cultural Models of Education in American Indian, Asian American and European American Contexts." *Social Psychology of Education* 10, no. 2: 213–46.

Gloria, Alberta M., and Sharon E. Robinson Kurpius. 2001. "Influences of Self-Beliefs, Social Support, and Comfort in the University Environment on the Academic Nonpersistence Decisions of American Indian Undergraduates." *Cultural Diversity and Ethnic Minority Psychology* 7, no. 1: 88–102.

Guillory, Raphael M., and Mimi Wolverton. 2008. "It's About Family: Native American Student Persistence in Higher Education." *The Journal of Higher Education* 79, no. 1: 58–87.

HeavyRunner, Iris, and Richard DeCelles. 2002. "Family Education Model: Meeting the Student Retention Challenge." *Journal of American Indian Education* 41, no. 2: 29–37.

HeavyRunner, Iris, and Joann Sebastian Morris. 1997. Traditional Native Culture and Resilience. Center for Applied Research and Educational Improvement. Retrieved from the University of Minnesota Digital Conservancy, http://hdl.handle.net/11299/145989.

Hoover, John J., and Cecelia C. Jacobs. 1992. "A Survey of American Indian College Students: Perceptions Toward their Study Skills/College Life." *Journal of American Indian Education* 32, no. 1: 21–29.

Hornett, Danielle. 1989. "The Role of Faculty in Cultural Awareness and Retention of American Indian College Students." *Journal of American Indian Education* 29, no. 1: 12–18.

Huffman, Terry. 2001. "Resistance Theory and the Transculturation Hypothesis as Explanations of College Attrition and Persistence among Culturally Traditional American Indian Students." *Journal of American Indian Education* 40, no. 3: 1–23.

Jackson, Aaron P., Steven A. Smith, and Curtis L. Hill. 2003. "Academic Persistence among Native American College Students." *Journal of College Student Development* 44, no. 4: 548–65.

Jackson, A., and Sherri Turner. 2004. "Counseling and Psychotherapy with Native American Clients." In *Practicing Multiculturalism: Affirming Diversity in Counseling and Psychology*, edited by Timothy B. Smith, 215–33. Boston: Allyn and Bacon.

Kalsner, Lydia. 1992. "The Influence of Developmental and Emotional Factors on Success in College." *Higher Education Extension Service Review* 3, no. 2: 3–13.

Kerbo, Harold R. 1981. "College Achievement among Native Americans: A Research Note." *Social Forces* 59, no. 4: 1275–80.

Larimore, Colleen. 1997. *First Person, First Peoples: Native American College Graduates Tell their Life Stories.* Ithaca NY: Cornell University Press.

Ledlow, Susan. 1992. "Is Cultural Discontinuity an Adequate Explanation for Dropping Out?" *Journal of American Indian Education* 31, no. 3: 21–36.

Lin, Ruey-Lin, Deborah LaCounte, and Jeanne Eder. 1988. "A Study of Native American Students in a Predominantly White College." *Journal of American Indian Education* 27, no. 3: 8–15.

Locust, Carol. 1988. "Wounding the Spirit: Discrimination and Traditional American Indian Belief Systems." *Harvard Educational Review* 58, no. 3: 315–31.

Martin, Steven C., and Adrienne L. Thunder. 2013. "Incorporating Native Culture into Student Affairs." In *Beyond the Asterisk: Understanding Native Students in Higher Education*, edited by Heather J. Shotton, Shelly C. Lowe, and Stephanie J. Waterman, 39–51. Sterling, VA: Stylus.

McClellan, George S. 2005. "Native American Student Retention in US Postsecondary Education." *New Directions for Student Services* 109: 17–32.

McInerney, Dennis M., and Karen Gayton Swisher. 1995. "Exploring Navajo Motivation in School Settings." *Journal of American Indian Education* 34, no. 3: 28–51.

Mihesuah, Devon Abbott, and Angela Cavender Wilson, eds. 2004. *Indigenizing the Academy: Transforming Scholarship and Empowering Communities*. Lincoln: University of Nebraska Press.

Minthorn, Robin. 2014. "Perspectives and Values of Leadership for Native American College Students in Non-Native Colleges and Universities." *Journal of Leadership Education* 13, no. 2: 67–95.

Minthorn, Robin, and Heather Shotton. 2014. "Native American Students in Higher Education." In *Today's College Students: A Reader,* edited by Pietro Sasso and Joseph DeVitis, 31–45. New York: Peter Lang.

Pavel, D. Michael, and Raymond V. Padilla. 1993. "American Indian and Alaska Native Postsecondary Departure: An Example of Assessing a Mainstream Model Using National Longitudinal Data." *Journal of American Indian Education* 32, no. 2: 1–23.

Pavel, D. Michael, Rebecca Skinner, Elizabeth Farris, Margaret Cahalan, John Tippeconnic, and Wayne Stein. 1998. *American Indians and Alaska Natives in Postsecondary Education.* NCES 98–291. National Center for Education Statistics, US Department of Education. https://nces.ed.gov/pubs98/98291.pdf.

Peshkin, Alan. 1997. *Places of Memory: Whiteman's Schools and Native American Communities. Sociocultural, Political, and Historical Studies in Education.* Mahwah, NJ: Lawrence Erlbaum Associates, Inc.

Reyhner, Jon, and John Dodd. 1995. "Factors affecting the retention of American Indian and Alaska Native students in higher education." Paper presented at the First Annual Expanding Minority Opportunities National Conference, Tempe, Arizona, January 19–21.

Scott, Wilbur J. 1986. "Attachment to Indian Culture and the 'Difficult Situation': A Study of American Indian College Students." *Youth & Society* 17, no. 4: 381–95.

Shotton, Heather J., E. Star L. Oosahwe, and Rosa Cintrón. 2007. "Stories of Success: Experiences of American Indian students in a Peer-Mentoring Retention Program." *The Review of Higher Education* 31, no. 1: 81–107.

Snyder, Thomas D., Alexandra G. Tan, and Charlene M. Hoffman. 2004. *Digest of Education Statistics 2003.* NCES 2005–025. National Center for Education Statistics, US Department of Education. https://nces.ed.gov/pubs2005/2005025.pdf.

Solorzano, Daniel G. 1992. "An Exploratory Analysis of the Effects of Race, Class, and Gender on Student and Parent Mobility Aspirations." *The Journal of Negro Education* 61, no. 1: 30–44.

Swanson, Jane L., and David M. Tokar. 1991. "College Students' Perceptions of Barriers to Career Development." *Journal of Vocational Behavior* 38, no. 1: 92–106.

Swisher, Karen, and Donna Deyhle. 1989. "The Styles of Learning Are Different, but the Teaching Is Just the Same: Suggestions for Teachers of American Indian Youth." Special Issue, *Journal of American Indian Education*, 1–14.

Tachine, Amanda, and Karen Begay-Francis. 2013. "First-Year Experience for Native American Freshmen." In *Beyond the Asterisk: Understanding Native Students in Higher Education*, edited by Heather J. Shotton, Shelly C. Lowe, and Stephanie J. Waterman, 25–38. Sterling, VA: Stylus Publishing.

Terenzini, Patrick T., Laura I. Rendon, M. Lee Upcraft, Susan B. Millar, Kevin W. Allison, Patricia L. Gregg, and Romero Jalomo. 1994. "The Transition to College: Diverse Students, Diverse Stories." *Research in Higher Education* 35, no. 1: 57–73.

Tippeconnic, John W., and Smokey McKinney. 2003. "Native Faculty: Scholarship and Development." In *The Renaissance of American Indian Higher Education: Capturing the Dream*, edited by Maenette Benham and Wayne Stein, 241–255. New York: Routledge.

US Department of Education. 2005. *Status and Trends in the Education of American Indians and Alaska Natives.* Washington, DC: U.S. Government Printing Office.

US Department of Education. 2016a. "Programs: Upward Bound Program." Website. Last modified October 24, 2016. http://www2.ed.gov/programs/trioupbound/index.html.

US Department of Education. 2016b. "Programs: Gaining Early Awareness and Readiness for Undergraduate Programs (GEAR UP)." Website. Last modified March 22, 2017. http://www2.ed.gov/programs/gearup/index.html.

US Department of Education, National Center for Education Statistics. 2005. *The Condition of Education 2005* (NCES 2005–094). Washington, DC: US Government Printing Office.

Wells, Robert N. 1997. *The Native American Experience in Higher Education: Turning around the Cycle of Failure II.* Report. ERIC Document Reproduction Service No. 414108. Retrieved from http://files.eric.ed.gov/fulltext/ED414108.pdf.

Williams, Robin Starr. 2012. "Indigenizing Leadership Concepts through Perspectives of Native American College Students." PhD diss., Oklahoma State University.

Science Posse

The Importance of the Cohort in Normalizing Academic Challenge

Kim Godsoe

The most highly selective colleges and universities in the United States have been found to graduate Blacks and Latinos/as at a higher rate than less selective colleges and universities, yet these same institutions are less likely to graduate underrepresented students in the sciences (Alon and Tienda 2005; Bowen and Bok 1998; Huang, Taddese, and Walter 2000; NSF 2004). Underrepresented students of color in the sciences enter college with an interest in science that is equal to their White and Asian American peers (HERI 2010). However, in spite of having similar levels of interest in STEM at college entry, there are notable differences based on race in the rates with which students graduate with STEM majors. Within selective institutions, 55 percent of White students and 63 percent of Asian American students graduate with majors in STEM fields, compared to only 38 percent of Blacks and Latinos graduating with majors in STEM fields (Smyth and McArdle 2004). One of the major areas of debate in higher education is how to best retain underrepresented students of color in the sciences, including first-generation college students in Science, Technology, Engineering, and Math (STEM).[1]

This paper draws from data collected through student interviews conducted during a consecutive two-year period from 2012 to 2015 to examine how the cohort model of the Science Posse Scholars program at Brandeis University helped students navigate the academic and social challenges of studying science at a predominantly White research institution. Because the Posse Scholars Program is so small, the precise two-year period for interviews is not identified in order to protect the confidentiality of the participants. While leadership skills is the only criteria for being selected as a Posse Scholar, participants in the Science Posse Scholars program at Brandeis are primarily first-generation college students, low-income students, and students of color underrepresented in the sciences, defined as Blacks, Latinos, Native Americans, and Pacific Islanders.

Some studies have found that parental education and occupation impact the degree to which a student continues to study STEM fields. Shaw and Barbuti (2010) analyzed a national data set of students at four-year colleges who had indicated while taking the SAT that they had an interest in majoring in science. They found that by the third year of college, 62 percent of first-generation college students were not continuing in STEM majors, compared to 56 percent of students with a college-educated parent. The American Council on Education (2006) studied students who entered college with an interest in majoring in STEM and those who did not continue in STEM disciplines. In this study, 64.4 percent of students who completed a STEM major were from families in which at least one parent had a bachelor's degree. For students who did not complete the STEM major, only 38 percent were from families in which at least one parent had a bachelor's degree. Astin and Astin (1993) found that when parents were employed in science or engineering fields, it contributed to students graduating with a major in a STEM field.

The Science Posse Scholars Program, founded at Brandeis University and now expanded to ten other schools, is a leadership-based scholarship program that uses a cohort model to support students who are interested in majoring in STEM disciplines at highly selective colleges and universities. At Brandeis University, the data about perseverance in STEM disciplines show the same general trends as previous research. Excluding Science Posse Scholars, 49.4 percent of White students who entered with an interest in STEM declared a major in the field. For Asian American students, 59.6 percent declared a major in a STEM field. Underrepresented students of color in the sciences (Blacks, Latinos, Native Americans, and Pacific Islanders) who had an interest in STEM disciplines declared a major in a STEM discipline at a rate of 40.0 percent. Students who were race/ethnicity unknown declared a major in STEM fields at a rate of 61.6 percent. As with race, first-generation college student status had a negative effect on the likelihood of declaring a major in STEM, with 20.0 percent of first-generation college students declaring a STEM major compared to 22.9 percent of non-first-generation college students. However, the intersectionality of students' race and first-generation college status has profound implications for their success of studying college level science. Table 10.1 shows STEM declaration rates by race and first-generation status.

Table 10.1 STEM declaration rates at Brandeis University by race and first-generation college status—U.S. citizens and permanent residents who entered Brandeis in Fall 2008, 2009, and 2010, and who would have been required by the institution to declare a major by Summer 2012.

All Undergraduate Students						
		STEM Major	Other Major		STEM Major	Other Major
First-Generation	N	116	464	Not First-Generation	980	3,302
	%	20.0%	80.0%		22.9%	77.1%
White and Asian-American Students						
First-Generation	N	82	245	Not First-Generation	752	2,350
	%	25.1%	74.9%		24.2%	75.8%
Underrepresented Minority Students						
First-Generation	N	15	175	Not First-Generation	49	231
	%	7.9%	92.1%		17.5%	82.5%
Race Ethnicity Unknown Students						
First-Generation	N	19	44	Not First-Generation	179	721
	%	30.2%	69.8%		19.9%	80.1%

Source: Brandeis University, Office of the University Registrar

The data in table 10.1 shows that only 7.9 percent of underrepresented students of color in the sciences who were first-generation college students declared a major in a STEM discipline. These statistics demonstrate how multiple facets of a student's identity (race/ethnicity, first-generation college student status, etc.) may constitute specific needs for support programs in the sciences. The purpose of this study is to understand why the Posse Scholars Program—which includes a large number of students of color who are first-generation and low-income—is so successful.

THE BRANDEIS UNIVERSITY SCIENCE POSSE SCHOLARS PROGRAM

The Brandeis University Science Posse Scholars Program provides a useful example of how institutions, particularly highly selective colleges and universities, can support the success of students interested in majoring in STEM disciplines. The Posse Foundation is a nonprofit organization founded in 1989 with a threefold mission. These goals are "To expand the pool from which top colleges and universities can recruit outstanding young leaders from diverse backgrounds, to help these institutions build more interactive campus environments so that they can be more welcoming for people from all backgrounds, and to ensure that Posse Scholars persist in their academic studies and graduate so they can take on leadership positions in the workforce" (http://www.possefoundation.org/about-posse/our-history-mission). Posse is based in New York City and has additional sites in Atlanta, Boston, Chicago, Houston, Los Angeles, Miami, New Orleans, Washington, DC, and San Francisco. Each Posse site partners with different highly selective colleges and universities, and each college or university agrees to take a cohort of ten students—a Posse—each academic year.[2] When Posse Scholars are selected, all ten of the Scholars from the same city will attend the partner college or university. This city-based model allows the ten Scholars to meet regularly as a group prior to their enrollment in college, a key component of the program as it begins the work of the Scholars identifying as a supportive cohort for each other before they even enter college. Posse has been an extremely successful program, with 90 percent of Posse Scholars graduating from the college or university in which they first enrolled (http://www.possefoundation.org/about-posse).

In 2008, Brandeis launched the first Science Posse Scholars Program, which has now been replicated in ten other colleges and universities.[3] Rather than placing an emphasis on the traditional admission metrics of SAT scores and grades, the Posse selection process emphasized leadership traits, as well as communication and problem-solving skills and a strong interest in science.[4] At Brandeis University, Science Posse Scholars were overwhelmingly under-represented students of color in the sciences, particularly Black students, Latino/a students, first-generation college students, low-income students, or some combination of these characteristics, all of which are factors that have been found to negatively impact a student's likelihood of declaring a major in a STEM discipline (American Council on Education 2006; Brandeis Office of the University Registrar 2013; Center for Institutional Data Exchange 2000; Shaw and Barbuti 2010).[5] Table 10.2 shows key demographic factors among Brandeis Science Posse Scholars and all other Brandeis students who are US citizens and permanent residents who entered the institution in Fall 2008, 2009, 2010, and 2011.

Table 10.2 Comparison of Brandeis Science Posse Scholars and all other students.

	Science Posse Scholars	All Other Students
Number	40	2,753
Percent Majoring in Science	70.0%	17.8%
Average Math SAT	609	669
Average Verbal SAT	558	662
Female	47.5%	56.6%
First-Generation	77.5%	14.4%
Pell Grant Recipient	70.0%	19.3%
First Gen and Pell Grant	60.0%	7.8%
White and Asian-American	25.0%	70.3%
Blacks, Latinos, Native Americans, and Pacific Islanders	72.5%	12.5%
Race/Ethnicity Unknown	2.5%	16.9%

Source: Brandeis University, Office of the University Registrar

Unlike many STEM retention programs, the Brandeis Science Posse Scholars Program was not designed as an academic bridge program. There is virtually no remediation provided to students. Instead, the Science Posse Scholars program focuses on team-building, mentoring, and preparing students for the culture of science at a highly selective university. The program does not assume that students were in deficit because of their race, levels of parental education, family income, or even their academic preparation. Rather, the emphasis of the program is preparing the Scholars for the challenges they will face in a highly competitive science classroom. The assumption is that all students who are studying science at the college level will be challenged, and an important intervention is to prepare students for those challenges. Each of these program activities emphasizes not only the progress of the individual but also the success of the group as a whole. Table 10.3 outlines the activities that are mandatory and voluntary as part of the Science Posse Scholars Program.

Table 10.3 Structure of the Science Posse Scholars Program.

Event	Time of Year	Time Commitment	Mandatory or Optional
Weekly Pre-Collegiate Training (PCT) with Posse staff emphasizing leadership and communication skills	January through August of the Scholars' senior year of high school	2 hours per week	Mandatory
Three STEM workshops within PCT are devoted to science, 1 chemistry, 1 biology and 1 math	1 workshop per month in February, March or April	2 hours for each workshop	Mandatory
Summer Science Immersion Program	July	10 days	Mandatory
Weekly group meetings of the Scholars emphasizing leadership skills, the transition to college, and the success of the group	September through May for the first two years of college	2 hours per week	Mandatory
Individual meetings with the Science Posse Mentor in which both individual progress and the progress of the group is emphasized	September through May for the first two years of college	1 hour every other week	Mandatory
Research Lab Experience	September through May	Varies	Optional

Source: http://www.brandeis.edu/science-posse/about/index.html

At the time of this study, 70 percent of the Science Posse Scholars had declared a major in STEM fields, which included biochemistry, biology, biophysics, chemistry, computer science, mathematics, neuroscience, or physics. Since the time of this study, the number of Posse Scholars who have declared a major in science has increased to 85 percent.

LITERATURE REVIEW

Several factors have been found to contribute to students being retained in STEM disciplines including race, college preparation, college selectivity, grades in entry-level college courses, and having the skills to navigate a challenging academic culture. The ability to attend a well-resourced high school has been identified as a critical factor in graduating with a major in a STEM field (Kerr 2001; National Science Board 2010; Report of the

Congressional Commission on the Advancement of Women and Minorities in Science, Engineering and Technology Development 2001). High schools with high minority populations tended to have fewer science and math classes, fewer Advanced Placement (AP) classes, a less demanding curriculum, and less qualified teachers, resulting in students who are less prepared for the demands of college (Report to the Congressional Commission on the Advancement of Women and Minorities in Science, Engineering and Technology Development 2001). When students perceive that there is a hostile racial climate on campus, they experience a lack of belonging that negatively impacts their academic adjustment (Hurtado et al. 2007).

Astin and Astin (1993) found that attending a liberal arts college had a positive effect on graduating with a major in STEM, while attending a large research university had a negative effect. However, students who attended selective institutions that had higher undergraduate to graduate-student ratios, or that focused on teaching and research opportunities for undergraduates, were more likely to graduate with a major in STEM fields than students who attended selective institutions focused on graduate education (Astin and Astin 1993). Chang (2008) conducted a survey of 26,000 first-year students in 203 four-year institutions who expressed an interest in majoring in STEM. He found that all students, regardless of race, were more likely to leave the sciences if they attended a highly selective college or university where the undergraduate population was predominantly White. Arcidiacono (2004) examined how students selected science majors and how this related to college selectivity. He found that when students received grades in their initial science and math courses, they adjusted their choice of majors. Strong skills in mathematics and "positive ability shocks" or the ability to feel a sense of academic achievement due to high grades in entry level classes made students more likely to continue with their study of STEM fields (29). Weaker skills in mathematics resulted in lower grades and an increased likelihood of not continuing in STEM fields. Mau (2016) found that having a higher cumulative grade point average in college contributed to majoring in a STEM field.

Another key factor in retention in STEM fields is a student's ability to navigate a challenging academic environment. Seymour and Hewitt (1997) found that competition had a negative effect on retention in the sciences for all students, regardless of race. They found that even students who could have succeeded in the sciences decided to leave the field unless they developed coping skills to navigate the competitive culture of the sciences. Bonous-Hammath (2006) cites the competitive atmosphere of highly selective schools and their lack of diversity as the primary reasons for the negative correlation between continuing to study a STEM discipline and attending a selective institution. Yee (2016) found that first-generation college students are more likely than their middle-class peers to study in isolation rather than accessing resources such as faculty, tutors, and other peers.

Resilience is therefore instrumental to students being able to navigate times of academic challenge. Many definitions of resilience emphasize the importance of the community in navigating challenging events. Luthar, Cicchetti, and Becker (2000) found that resilience is not a fixed trait but a relationship between oneself and others. McGee (2009) defined resilience as "self-confidence, realistic self-assessment, awareness of racism and seeking out like-minded friendships" (12). Stanton-Salazar and Spina (2000) identified resilience as a navigational tool that allows students to not only survive stressful events but use those events to positively shape future events. These definitions highlight the importance of having a supportive peer group in developing resilience.

Research on retention in STEM also emphasizes the importance of peers. Astin and Astin (1993) found that when a student has a greater number of peers majoring in STEM fields, the student was also likely to major in STEM. Similarly, McGee (2009) found that underrepresented minority students were more likely to major in STEM fields when the students had "like-minded friendships" (12). Peer support, or creating intentional cohorts of students interested in studying science, has been at the center of other science support programs, including the Meyerhoff Scholars at University of Maryland at Baltimore County, the Biology Undergraduate Scholars Program at University of California at Davis, and the University of Central Florida EXCEL Program (Stolel-McAllister 2011; Ovink and Veazey 2011; Young 2016). Similarly, research experience which allowed students to experience "the collaborative and empowering culture of science" rather than the competitive nature of the classroom was found to be critical to retaining students in STEM disciplines (Hurtado et al. 2009, 211). The research on the challenges of studying science and the importance of peer support in navigating these challenges is directly applicable to the cohort model used by the Science Posse Scholars program.

METHODOLOGY

The research for this study included both quantitative and qualitative data. The research design chosen for this study is unique in that it uses three comparison groups: Science Posse Scholars, students with backgrounds similar to Posse Scholars, and well-resourced students. Too often, research has focused on only students who have had limited access to resources. The purpose of this study was to understand how resources—whether provided by the home culture, local community, or by a program such as Science

Posse—contributed to students' success in the sciences. The three questions guiding the research were: (RQ1) What source of social and cultural capital do the three groups of students (Science Posse Scholars, students from backgrounds similar to Science Posse, and well-resourced students) draw on to be successful? (RQ2) Are there traits of individual resilience in the three groups of students that also contribute to their success in the sciences? and (RQ3) How are the social and cultural capital of the three groups of students similar and how are they different? This chapter focuses on findings from the qualitative data using the theoretical framework of resilience.

It is also important to discuss how the comparison groups were defined. The Posse Scholars Program is a leadership scholarship, and race, parental education, or income levels are not criteria used in deciding which students receive the scholarship. At the time of the research, forty Posse Scholars were on campus, and thirty were Black and/or Latino/a, while ten were White and/or Asian American students. Thirty-six of the forty Science Posse Scholars on campus were first-generation and/or low-income. The mean family income for all Science Posse Scholars was $42,734. Because Science Posse Scholars were not all Black and Latino students, but rather represented a more racially and ethnically diverse group of students, race was not used in the creation of the comparison groups. Instead, the comparison groups focused on parental education and family income level. Table 10.4 provides an overview of the comparison groups.

Table 10.4 Overview of the comparison groups for qualitative research.

Comparison Group 1: *38 Brandeis Science Posse Scholars*	• Students who were Science Posse Scholars • 90% were first-generation college students and/or low-income • 9 White or Asian American students, 29 Black and/or Latino students the sciences • First-years, sophomores, juniors, and seniors • Students entered college with the intention to major in biology, biochemistry, chemistry, neuroscience or HSSP and who attempted at least one semester of sciences intended for these majors (Science Posse students who leave the sciences are still part of the program and participate in all program activities)
Comparison Group 2: *24 Brandeis Students from Backgrounds Similar to Science Posse Scholars (Underrepresented Students)*	• Students not in Posse (Science or Liberal Arts) • 100% were either first-generation college students and/or Pell grant recipients • 10 White or Asian American students, 14 Black and/or Latino students in the sciences • First-years, sophomores, juniors, and seniors • Students entered college with the intention to major in biology, biochemistry, chemistry, neuroscience, or HSSP and who attempted at least one semester of sciences intended for these majors
Comparison Group 3: *25 Brandeis Students from Well-Resourced Families*	• Students not in Posse (Science or Liberal Arts) • Students from families with adjusted gross incomes of $80,000 or more (one-third of these students were not receiving need-based financial aid) • Students had at least one parent with a bachelor's degree (most students had one parent with a graduate degree, approximately half came from families in which both parents had graduate degrees) • 21 White or Asian American students, 4 Black and/or Latino students in the sciences • First-years, sophomores, juniors, and seniors • Students entered college with the intention to major in biology, biochemistry, chemistry, neuroscience or HSSP and who attempted at least one semester of sciences intended for these majors

Source: Brandeis University, Office of the University Registrar

All forty Science Posse Scholars volunteered to participate in the study, and thirty-eight completed interviews in April and May of 2012. The remaining two Scholars said they wanted to participate, but they did not schedule an interview time. Twenty-six well-resourced Brandeis students and twenty-five underrepresented Brandeis students were interviewed in April and May of 2013.The goal was to interview a wide range of students in all class years, males and females, and students from different racial and ethnic backgrounds. Well-resourced and underrepresented students were recruited through multiple means. Faculty in introductory chemistry, biology, and neuroscience classes were told about the study, and they were asked for names of students who might be willing to participate. Faculty and administrators who have an interest in supporting underrepresented students in STEM disciplines were also contacted to see if they would recommend possible students. The students were then screened to see if they met the eligibility criteria for the study. Eligible students were sent a personal email inviting them to participate. Twenty of the twenty-six (77 percent) well-resourced students and all twenty-five (100 percent) underrepresented students were recruited using this method.

In addition to faculty and staff referrals, students were told about the study via email by the undergraduate departmental representatives for biology, biochemistry, chemistry, and neuroscience. Undergraduate departmental representatives are sophomores, juniors, and seniors who are peer advisors within a major and who organize departmental events for undergraduates. Six of the twenty-six (23 percent) well-resourced students were recruited using this method. No underrepresented students responded to this recruitment method.

Students received a $10 gift card to the bookstore or a local ice cream store for their participation. Participants were also able to select their pseudonym to be used in the research, and several students delighted in selecting whimsical names that reflected personal characteristics, literary or film characters, or role models.

In general, students were very willing to candidly speak about their experiences in the sciences. Science Posse Scholars knew the researcher very well, and at the time of the interviews, most had already had at least one or more conversations with her about their experiences in sciences. The interviews often were perceived as an extension of previous conversations. Students in the underrepresented student comparison group may have heard of the interviewer from friends, but few had spoken to her about their experiences in the sciences. Underrepresented students were often trying to understand their own experiences in the sciences, and they saw the interview as a way to potentially help others. The majority of students in the well-resourced comparison group had not spoken to the interviewer about their experiences in the sciences. For the well-resourced students, they largely viewed their progress in the sciences as successful, so there were few reasons to be wary of the interview process.

Interviews were conducted on campus, recorded, transcribed by a professional company, and analyzed using ATLAS.ti. For the qualitative data analysis, inductive reasoning was used. As described by Creswell (2007), data was analyzed using the "patterns, categories, and themes from the 'bottom-up' by organizing the data into increasingly more abstract units of information" (38). Interviews from the Posse Scholars were coded first, followed by interviews from the underrepresented students and then the well-resourced students. The themes that emerged from the data analysis were then assigned to the theoretical framework of social capital, cultural capital, and resilience. The themes for resilience that were explored included competition in the sciences, time and effort in studying, the impact of gender and race on a student's experience, perceptions of whether science is a level playing field, whether the student feels successful in the sciences, and personal traits that kept the students in the sciences.

FINDINGS

One of the benefits of this research was that it included interviews not only with Posse Scholars but with students from well-resourced backgrounds and from backgrounds similar to the Science Posse Scholars.[6] This allowed for a better understanding of the dominant campus culture in the sciences and the challenges that nonmajority students (Science Posse Scholars and other underrepresented students) faced in navigating that culture.

It is also important to explicitly state that while race was not used as a factor in selecting in the comparison groups, students who were underrepresented students of color in the sciences regularly felt ostracized regardless of family or economic background. Diane, a Black student in the well-resourced comparison group, said she was acutely aware of race and said, "you feel like you're alone most of the time." Diane recounted how difficult it was to be a Black woman in the sciences.

> I think that is especially hard because there are so few. In the faculty, in my classes, or in my like Organic Chemistry class there are like three to five people on average on any given day who are like Black or Hispanic. I'd say that, more so than being a woman. And even like combined being like a Black woman in the sciences and coming from an immigrant family and going to the sciences I would say it's hard because there's really not—you know you feel like you're alone most of the time, you feel like, "well I don't really have an incentive to

stay here, I should probably just end up doing something else." So yeah, I think it's difficult being a minority in the sciences.

For Diane, being in the sciences was not only isolating, it also regularly made her question whether she should continue. These same feelings were expressed by Danielle, a first-generation Black student in the underrepresented student comparison group. She said, "You just think of your race way more, especially being in a room full of people who don't look like you." Marie, a first-generation Black student in the underrepresented student comparison group, described how being a student of color made her feel not only isolated but wondering if she should continue to major in science. She said, "I think it's a little intimidating because there's only a few in the sciences, and most students that are minorities say, 'Oh, I can't do the sciences, sciences are not for minorities.'" Marie's comments demonstrated her making an active evaluation of where she does and does not see other students of color and internalizing those observations into questioning where she belonged.

These feelings of inclusion and exclusion are even more apparent as students reflect on how race, parental education, and family income intersect. Zara, a first-generation Latina Science Posse Scholar who is majoring in science, explained:

Not to be narrow-minded, but in seeing all the people that are in chemistry, or in the sciences, it's mainly Asians and Caucasians and Indians. And there's not that many Latinas there. There's not many Hispanics there. There's not many people from urban cities that are there. So, it's definitely hard, especially when you're talking to your friends, and they're like, "Yeah, my mom used to make me study all night long." And I'm like, "Well, my mom used to make me clean the house all the time. That's what my mom cared about most, you know?" My mom used to make me do chores, and like it's—it's hard.

Zara's description demonstrated how keenly the underrepresented students and Science Posse Scholars experienced their difference from the majority of their peers who were studying the sciences. Feeling isolated because of any single element of one's background could be discouraging. However, to immediately feel multiple sources of isolation in their first days of studying science at college made students question if they belonged in the sciences.

The themes of race and first-generation college status are intrinsically linked in this research. While the comparison groups were defined by parental education and family income, race was intertwined throughout most of the discussions and served to inform the three key findings about why the Science Posse Scholars program is so successful. The first finding is the importance of the cohort model. The cohort model provided not only academic support to Scholars; it also provided students with a group of peers who felt safe and supportive. This positive peer group was especially important, as the majority peer culture was often perceived as judgmental and unwilling to offer help. The second finding is the importance of the program in normalizing challenge when studying STEM disciplines. Whereas many students internalize their struggles in science as a reflection of their academic abilities, the Science Posse Scholars Program helped students understand that everyone struggles in the sciences, thus externalizing the academic challenge. Finally, the findings showed that Science Posse Scholars demonstrated resilience. They not only declared majors in science but they were also able to view their success as an upward trajectory implying hope about the future. This ability to measure their academic self-worth not simply as their grades or class standing reflects Stanton-Salazar and Spina's definition of resilience as a way to use difficult past events to positively shape future events (2000).

Finding 1: The Importance of the Cohort

This study found that how students perceive competition in the sciences is very different based on their family background. When well-resourced students were asked about competition in the sciences, their responses addressed competing against one's self, competing against the test, or helping others with science. In contrast, when Science Posse Scholars or underrepresented students, including first-generation college students, were asked about competition in the sciences, they overwhelmingly described it as unhealthy and even unsafe. This distinction is important, as the well-resourced students are in the majority at Brandeis, and therefore they determine the dominant peer culture. It is important to remember that if the Science Posse Scholars did not have the strong cohort of their peers and the support of the program, their experiences would likely be very similar to those of the underrepresented students in the sciences. By examining the experiences of both well-resourced students and underrepresented students including first-generation college students, we begin to understand both the majority culture in the sciences and the struggles of not belonging to that culture.

Allie, a well-resourced White student with college-educated parents who was still deciding which field of science she wanted to pursue, described competition in the sciences as about wanting to be personally successful. She explained, "I don't think it's competition between each other but just I feel like it's more for yourself to do well, and if you don't do well, then you wouldn't want to stay on the track." Faith, another well-resourced White student with college-educated parents, who was interested in health, described competition as being centered in the self and said that students actively decided whether or not they wanted to participate in the competitive environment associated with science. She explained:

> I guess it really depends how you are. I'm competitive with myself, but I really don't compete with anyone else. I don't want to know, and I don't talk about grades to anyone. I don't want to know people's grades. It's really for me, but other people can make it a competition. It's really what you want it to be, and personally, I don't like competing with other people. . . . So it doesn't have to be a competitive environment if you don't want it to be.

Both Allie and Faith felt like students have a choice about whether or not to engage in the competition.

For underrepresented students, the competition was an experience that impacted peer groups, where to study, and even whether or not to ask for help. Jane, a first-generation White student in the underrepresented student group, expressed relief that Brandeis was less competitive than other institutions but still noted, "It's been hard to form [friendship] groups in the sciences because I feel like it gets competitive and cutthroat. There was an uncomfortable tension between a lot of the students, so it was hard to get close to other science peers." Similarly, Sarah, a Black student in the underrepresented comparison group who was interested in health, recalled such strong feelings of competition that she wouldn't feel comfortable going to the library. Sarah remembered:

> There's a competition in the class which you feel right away. I had come from getting As in all my [high school] classes because I was really pumped about it . . . and I would talk about it with my friends and everything, to coming here [to college]. . . . For some reason, I was afraid to go to the library because I didn't want to be alone in that big space. So I would always try and study in my room. And no matter how much I seemed to try and figure out how to do everything, once the exam came, I just felt confused and like my studying amounted to nothing.

Later in the interview, Sarah recounted once approaching her well-resourced peers in the library and asking for help and to join their study groups. Sarah remembered, "It seemed like people would try and squirm around it, which was really off-putting to me." She described the feelings of "loneliness" as making her explore majors outside of the sciences.

Science Posse Scholars also described feelings of competition, which like underrepresented students made them highly uncomfortable. Julian, a first-generation Latino Science Posse Scholar majoring in the sciences, spoke about the competition he felt in his major. He was one of the Science Posse Scholars who had attended an academically rigorous high school, and he described himself as very academically confident in his first year at Brandeis. As with underrepresented students, Julian spoke about how he did not develop friendships with peers in his major. He did have friends who were Science Posse Scholars, but as a first-generation college student, he felt too much competition from his well-resourced peers. He recounted:

> It's not that I don't like them [other students in his major], though. It's just that . . . [Department Name] majors here are pretty competitive. And I don't know how it is in other sciences, but even in [another STEM discipline] . . . people get pretty competitive, and it gets a little gross. And, at that point, I don't like to affiliate with [them] outside of an academic setting, like a social setting. . . . They're just like—a lot of them are very cocky, and I [can] kind of tell they've been put through private school their whole life. And they're just . . . too different. . . . I just don't see myself interacting with them, at least comfortably, in a social setting.

Julian, like other Posse Scholars, described how much he noticed the difference in his background compared to his peers.

These differences could have been isolating, but because the Science Posse Scholars had a cohort of students that they had known since their senior year of high school, they felt that they had an important support system. Each Posse Scholar participated along with their cohort in Pre-Collegiate Training (PCT) from January through August of their senior year of high school. PCT includes only three sessions on science instruction. The remaining sessions are dedicated to leadership training. Science Posse Scholars regularly spoke about how PCT prepared them for the challenges that they would face on campus, including academic expectations, social norms, and conflict resolution. Kay, a first-generation Black Science Posse Scholar who planned on majoring in science, explained that the workshops in PCT taught her that if "something [made] you . . . uncomfortable, you could handle it" and that PCT "brings you [the Posse] together." Jochaim, a first-generation Asian American Posse Scholar planning on majoring in science, said how important PCT was in "prepar[ing] us for . . . some issues [with racism] that may have arisen at Brandeis." He explained that when an event occurs on campus, the PCT training made him "not shocked about it." He went on to describe PCT as "social preparedness, not just academic preparedness." The PCT thus gives Science Posse Scholars, particularly first-generation Scholars, important information about what to expect from college, so they can be successful.

The experiences of PCT also were critical in helping to combat feelings of isolation in the sciences. Harrison, a Black Science Posse Scholar, described his experiences in the sciences as "So competitive, and it can be dangerously competitive at the same time. You need people who are supportive and help

you to not get down on yourself because it's very easy . . . for that to happen."
For Harrison, having a supportive peer group was one of the key features of
the Science Posse Scholars Program. Steve, a first-generation Latino Science
Posse Scholar majoring in science, said that "I'm begging [another Scholar]
to take [an advanced science] class with me next semester. But without anyone in my Posse in my class, it's a little daunting." Steve went on to explain
that he would be "afraid" to ask questions of his peers because he did not
want to be perceived as less intelligent than them. However, with his fellow
Science Posse Scholar, he could express academic vulnerability. He said
when he was able to take classes with another Science Posse Scholar, he felt
comfortable approaching him to say, "I'm like, dude, I have no idea what I'm
doing. Do you understand this?" The cohort provided a safe place to disclose
a lack of understanding and ask questions.

Similarly, the cohort provided encouragement when Scholars were struggling. Macbeth, a first-generation Latina Science Posse Scholar who was
interested in science, described this support in greater detail. She said that
within her Posse, the attitude was not "Ha, we're doing better." Instead, she
said if someone was struggling, "we're going to sit down, and we're going to
try to explain this, and if you don't understand it, then we'll try to figure out
something else." In addition, when a fellow Scholar excelled, it often made an
achievement seem doable for the other members of the Posse. Celina, a first-
generation Latina Science Posse Scholar from that same Posse cohort, said
that seeing one of her fellow Scholars, also a first-generation college student,
do well made her think "Someone else [is] doing better, it's like, wait, I've
got to do that." Alisha, a first-generation Black Science Posse Scholar majoring in science, said that in her Posse, the Scholars actively don't compete with
each other. She recounted that as a Posse, they "don't worry about getting a
higher grade than someone else in the Posse." Instead, she explained, "We
just care that everyone moves along with us. Like, no one's left behind."
Andrea, a Black Science Posse Scholar interested in health, gave a more nuanced description of the competition within Science Posse. She said: "The
reality is that we are in competition with each other. But we are in support
of each other, even though we are in competition with each other." Andrea
explained that when one of her fellow Posse members was selected to present at a conference in California, the attitude in the Posse was celebrating her
success and achievement. A success for one Scholar was often perceived as a
success for the group, even if the achievement was only awarded to the individual. The support that Scholars felt for each other was a strong counterpoint
to the negative feelings of competition they felt from their well-resourced
peers. The Scholars perceived the Posse as a place of support and motivation
for the study of science, while the larger culture of science was perceived as

uncomfortable and unwelcoming. The importance of peer support in developing resilience has likewise been found in other research on success in STEM disciplines (Cavazos et al. 2010; Lee et al. 2013; McGee 2009).

Finding 2: Normalizing Challenge

All students who were interviewed, regardless of background, described studying the sciences as challenging. This research found that choice of major also reflected family background. Well-resourced students were more likely to describe other academic interests as a reason why they wouldn't pursue science, while underrepresented students and Science Posse Scholars were more likely to question their academic abilities. Normalizing challenge and developing resilience emerged as key factors in counteracting this tendency and therefore contributed to these students' being retained in the sciences.

Well-resourced students described the study of science as difficult but manageable with hard work. For these students, success in the sciences was the result of a meritocracy, and the students who were the most motivated earned the highest grades. They used a framework of hard work to explain their individual success. In contrast, underrepresented students were keenly aware of the differences in academic background and the ways that these differences played out amongst different student groups. Underrepresented students felt judged by their peers, and they tended to internalize feelings of academic struggle as personal failures. Science Posse Scholars also experienced feelings of academic challenge. However, when they saw other members of their Posse struggling with the sciences, they were able to externalize the challenge as being inherent to studying science rather than internalizing feelings of personal failure.

The first academic challenges that students faced were introductory science courses. Usually large-lecture courses graded on a curve, these courses provide students their initial glimpse into how well they do in comparison to their peers. Well-resourced students regularly described the introductory classes as important not because of the content of the course but because they helped to ensure that only students who were dedicated to their studies continued in the sciences. Reuben, a well-resourced student majoring in the sciences, with college-educated parents, said "Those who put in work, those who put in the hours; they have a shot." Mollie, a well-resourced White student with highly educated family members, believed that General Chemistry was an important screening mechanism for determining who was serious about studying science. She explained:

> Chemistry was hard because it's a weed-out [class], and it really should be though. If you're thinking about it because you can't have—it's just not possible

to have a lot of people just coasting through the sciences because you really need to dedicate a lot of time to it, so it was definitely a weed-out. But I think that figuring out how to work hard and figuring out what study habits work best for me is something that really got me through it.

Django, a well-resourced White student majoring in science whose parents had attended graduate school, described his experiences in Honors Chemistry by saying "it wasn't that rough." In spite of the personal ease of his transition to college-level chemistry, he also described success in the sciences as being linked to how hard a person was willing to work. He recalled, "I mean I wish they [other students] could [be successful in the sciences]. . . . I mean there's a lot of people that weren't as successful freshman year 'cause they weren't as prepared, but they get their shit together. And now they're doing perfectly well." While Django's choice of words was crass, it reflected the feelings of his peers. Well-resourced students repeatedly emphasized this theme of hard work and meritocracy as the key component of success in the sciences.

In contrast, underrepresented students regularly described working harder than their peers. Jane, a first-generation White student in the underrepresented student group, who was majoring in science, expressed the disconnect that she felt between her grades and the amount of work she was completing. She remembered feeling "inadequate" and that "other people were studying just as hard, less hard sometimes . . . and doing better." Daisy, a Black student in the underrepresented comparison group, who had wanted to major in the sciences, described herself as "heartbroken" about dropping biology. She first explained her experiences in high school and then her experience at Brandeis University:

People [in high school] don't know what school I go to. They just call it the smart people school because I was one of the smart kids. Most people go to state schools. The majority go to community college. So not many people go out of state and not many people go to private colleges. . . . [At Brandeis] I was putting in so much effort . . . that I was not doing as well in my other classes because I was trying to put so much into bio because it was so much to handle.

Underrepresented students did not see a lack of success in the sciences as a lack of hard work, but they still had the tendency to internalize the failure. John, an underrepresented Black student who was not first-generation, described working hard and dropping Introduction to Chemistry, said that he "ended up crying" and that "I felt like I failed, like I just didn't deserve to [be in college]." In John's case, he not only questioned his abilities in the sciences, he questioned whether he was intelligent enough to be in college. These same themes of questioning one's own intelligence and sense of belonging were found in interviews with first-generation college students.

Like underrepresented students, Posse Scholars struggled with the academic intensity of science classes. Alisha, a first-generation Black Science Posse Scholar majoring in science, remembered how important the Science Posse cohort was in normalizing the academic challenge of science at a time when she doubted herself. She explained: "[I thought] I can't do the science anymore. I was like, 'I can't.' And then I realized everyone was, like, 'Ahh, science is horrible.' And then we still had to, you know, get through it. So, I was like, 'I can stick through it. If my Posse can stick through it, of course I can stick through it and just go along with them and hopefully we all survive.'" Alisha was able to understand her moments of individual struggle in the context of her Posse. She saw that her fellow Scholars were struggling in the sciences, too, and this helped to normalize her individual struggle. Alisha valued the idea that the group would make it through the challenging experience of studying science together. Zara, a first-generation Latina Science Posse Scholar majoring in science, also described how important it was to see other Scholars struggling and how this inspired her to continue in the sciences. She recalled when she had moments of doubt about the sciences:

> Everyone else was like, "No, you can do this, you can do this, you can do this." If it wasn't for people telling me things, and me being determined to find something in the sciences I wanted to do, I wouldn't have kept on in science . . . If I saw, like, [another Posse Scholar] freaking out, but still cracking down, it was like, "Okay, she can do it; I can do it. We're in the same Posse. She'll teach me how to do it if I don't know how to do it." Or even seeing [two other Posse Scholars from well-resourced high schools] . . . just continue on and see other people struggling and still doing it, it's a motivation. And it's like—you can keep going, because people show you how to keep going, and you can learn how to keep going.

Zara's comments showed that the struggles of other Scholars made her feel more comfortable about her own struggles, and that resilience is not simply an internal trait but can be learned from other students. This learned resilience can also occur in a positive form as described by Navitas, a first-generation Latino Posse Scholar planning on majoring in science. Navitas described members of his own Posse as role models in science, saying, "Every time they succeed and do well, I want to be just like them." Nasir, a first-generation Black Science Posse Scholar majoring in science, remembered that in his first year, he "really had to really work hard" to understand the material. However, in Nasir's case, he had attended an under-resourced high school, and unlike well-resourced students, he did not describe success as only being a result of hard work. Nasir also emphasized the importance of the Posse in helping him navigate academics:

Let's begin with the fact that science is hard. Science is just extremely hard. . . . Everybody in the [Science Posse] understand[s] that, "Hey, you know, we're all in this together, and it's all hard." . . . Just having an automatic person to fall on, that you already knew, that you could study with and ask questions, and, like, you know, joke around with in a sense. Because, you know, it would suck if I was just a regular admitted student that came into science and didn't know anybody . . . I know that I got my Science Posse to talk to. And also, previous Science Posses that [have] been through the same thing as me, and [I] can ask them for advice.

Scholars regularly described Posse as a family, with the older Posse Scholars supporting the younger Posse Scholars, particularly in the first two years of coursework.

In addition to the personal support of having a Posse, Science Posse Scholars regularly credited the ten-day Summer Science Immersion program as preparing them for the academic intensity they would face in the sciences in college. The immersion program tried to provide entering Science Posse Scholars with an accurate understanding of what the culture of the sciences would be like prior to their arrival on campus. The program was designed to familiarize students with the intensity of studying college-level science, the grading curve, the competitive culture of the sciences, and the freedom of being on a college campus. Unlike many other summer bridge programs, the Summer Science Immersion program, fondly referred to as "boot camp," was not remedial and did not focus on science content mastery.[7]

The Summer Science Immersion program also emphasized the cohort model of Posse and the importance of supporting each other, rather than competing with each other. This was important because in the Summer Science Immersion program, Science Posse Scholars realized that there were significant differences in how their respective high schools prepared students for college. For a few Science Posse Scholars from stronger academic backgrounds, the program was not challenging. These students said that the program gave them a false sense of security or caused them to be overconfident in their abilities. However, for most Science Posse Scholars, including first-generation Posse Scholars, the Summer Science Immersion program was essential for their transition to college-level science. Michelle, a first-generation Latina Science Posse Scholar who had not yet decided her major, said of the program, "Our grades were horrible. We stayed up until really late working on things, and it was like a taste of what college was going to be like." Cornelius, a first-generation Latino Science Posse Scholar who planned to declare a major in science, recounted that this was the first time he had doubted his ability in science. He remembered that "Science boot camp was rough. I just broke down and wanted to go back home just because I felt like

I wasn't doing good on anything." Alisha, a first-generation Black Science Posse Scholar who was majoring in science, described the program as a "real eye-opener to science."

In spite of all of the challenges of boot camp, students overwhelmingly described it as a positive experience. Jess, a first-generation Latina Science Posse Scholar interested in science, explained:

> It was hard. I did not expect so much work, but it was—I feel that it was really helpful. Like, just knowing how, like, labs are so much different than the lab that I was accustomed to back in high school and, like, seeing all this technology was also amazing. But, I mean, all the work that we got that whole—those two weeks, it was just—it was hell. It was just that—it was so different from high school, especially being out of, like, senior year of high school where you, like, you know, well, for me it was, like, a short schedule, barely did anything, and then coming here and it was just, like, all right now you have a lot of work to do, here it is. And it was just hard. But I managed, so that was, like okay now I think I know what college is going to be like if this is boot camp.

For the Science Posse Scholars who did not attend academically rigorous high schools, the Summer Science Immersion program provided them with an opportunity to understand the academic norms that they would soon face as full-time Brandeis students. Kay, a first-generation Black Science Posse Scholar who planned to major in science, explained how the Summer Science Immersion program prepared her not only for the rigor of science but the culture of science.

> I remember we took one of Dr. KC's tests and took a chemistry test, and I remember I did so bad. . . . I was like oh my God. I think that was the first test I had failed. I was like flipping out, and I was like "Oh, my gosh. If this is [what it's] like before I even get here, what is it going to be like when I actually get to Brandeis?" I don't know, I feel like boot camp really prepared us for being able to cope with that and then like the whole curve thing too. So even if you get a low [numerical] grade that you know, in the scope of things, it's [a different letter] grade. I remember the first chemistry grade I got back [at Brandeis, and] if I hadn't gone to boot camp, I'd probably be crying right now. I would be breaking down in tears so sad, but boot camp definitely helped with that. . . . And so that the shock that you have during boot camp, you don't have it here [in the fall] and you don't break down.

By providing Science Posse Scholars with a realistic understanding of the challenges that they would face in the sciences at Brandeis, boot camp helped to ease the transition to college-level science. Scholars of all backgrounds, including first-generation students, still had negative experiences in the sciences and doubted their abilities in the sciences, particularly when they compared themselves to their more well-resourced peers. However, Scholars felt that if they could make it through boot camp together, they could make it through science at Brandeis together.

The Summer Science Immersion program was also central to helping to solidify the idea of being a cohort. Joseph, a first-generation Black Science Posse Scholar majoring in science, described the program as "a lot of work" but emphasized that it was also "the highlight of Posse bonding." Dennis, a first-generation Black Science Posse Scholar majoring in science, also emphasized the importance of the program in fostering loyalty among the Scholars. He said the program made him realize that the members of his Posse were "all in this together." Monica, an Asian American Science Posse Scholar interested in health, described the transformative nature of boot camp on her Posse. She recalled:

> I think after boot camp is when it really hit me that "Okay, we're in this together, no matter—whether we like it or not, we're the only ten that know what it feels like to be," at that point, "a Science Posse." . . . I didn't understand the full concept of what Posse meant until we got to boot camp, and we had to take those classes, and how we could help each other, and how sometimes it could get a little, you know, frustrating to be in a group of ten very individual people. I think that's the perfect way to put it.

In addition to strengthening the cohort and providing an accurate understanding of the academic rigors of the sciences at Brandeis, the Science Posse Scholars also described the summer program as essential in three other areas: it helped them develop connections with faculty and staff, allowed them to become familiar with the physical layout of the campus, and made them recognize that they would have to ask for help to succeed in college-level science. While these skills are essential for any student, they are even more critical for first-generation college students as they do not have the social, cultural, and informational capital of their more well-resourced peers.

Finding 3: Defining Success

Whether or not students perceive themselves as successful in science is also an indicator of resilience. If a student feels successful in the science classroom, they are more likely to enroll in additional STEM classes. Previous research has demonstrated that the greatest predictor of continued enrollment in STEM classes at highly selective colleges and universities was first-year and second-year science grades (Strenta et al. 1994). This research study found that most well-resourced students described themselves as successful in science based on their academic performance. Some well-resourced students did not value their grades but contextualized their success in terms of accomplishments in research or professional goals. Underrepresented students, including first-generation college students, also described themselves as successful, but typically used a different context for understanding their success. The majority of underrepresented students defined success in the sciences as the progress they had made in learning to study science and/or the fact that they did not leave the sciences for another academic discipline.

Allie, a well-resourced White student with college-educated parents who was interested in science, said, "I think I'm successful. I definitely have to work hard to succeed, but I am doing well." For Malcom, science major and a well-resourced White student with well-educated family members, his success was very much a reflection of his grades:

> I haven't calculated my science GPA, because I haven't needed to. But I have a good GPA. I'm planning on hopefully graduating with whatever that first honors is. And yeah, I do fine, as I said. I think one time I got a B– in a science class. One time. Or maybe it was a B. No, it was a B. And that I was like, "Okay. That stinks, but I'll do better." And then, usually I get B+s, A–s, which I'm perfectly—I'm very happy with that.

Django, a well-resourced White student majoring in science, had been working in a research lab since his first year of college. When asked about success, he said, "I am not proud of my grades anymore because I've been getting good grades for so long. The next level of success is research, which I haven't been successful in." For Django, being a coauthor of an article published in a peer-reviewed journal was his definition of success in science.

In sharp contrast, underrepresented students, including first-generation students, described success as staying in the sciences in spite of all the difficulties they faced. Rose Ann, a first-generation White student in the underrepresented group who was majoring in science, described how she felt there were different types of success. She said: "I am happy with how I have done. I feel like I struggled, I mean it will always be there, my GPA . . . that freshman year. But in terms of where I've gotten to . . . I feel like I have been able to succeed. . . . I wish that I could have entered with what I know now, but that's part of growing. I have to keep reminding myself that." Chipmunk, a first-generation Black student in the underrepresented group who was majoring in science, explained how emotionally difficult it was for her to stay with the sciences, yet she persevered. She said "So it wasn't a clean shot. Of course not, and I wish it was. But, I don't regret that it wasn't. . . . You know, [I] really cried a lot. You know, this is very instrumental in making me in every way. Wherever I go from now, I will remember those moments."

Mark, a first-generation Asian American student in the underrepresented comparison group who was interested in science, described how he thought of his academic success both in the context of grades and in the context of his family background:

> I feel like I am [successful] because I always tell myself it's always—it's about this journey. And if I look at it in terms of grades, I would just—I would just transfer or something. I would just be depressed all the time. But I know I can't do that to myself. So, I measure success in terms of where I started from . . . all I have learned, and all I have gained, all I've been through. So, I feel like in that aspect, you know, no, I don't have a 3.7; I'm barely staying above 3.0. . . . If I look at just everything I've learned, I feel like it's been a very successful journey, and I'm glad I'm at Brandeis. You know, because even—I told myself I would be getting As, or whatever, at U Mass, I feel like that type of journey would not be as rewarding because it was just easier. But I know being gay, having a father with a mental disability, being first-gen, I feel like, yes, I face obstacles in my life, but those obstacles helped shape who I am. And I feel like the sciences here also shaped who I am. So, I look at it with absolute success, because I'm still here; I'm still doing it. I'm still—I still want to learn science. I'm not—it hasn't pushed me away.

Rose Ann, Chipmunk, and Mark, all first-generation college students, made an active decision not to define their success by their grades. While still being keenly aware of their grades being lower than what they would have liked, they were able to create a narrative of success that acknowledged that they had overcome academic challenges.

Science Posse Scholars also had mixed responses to whether or not they considered themselves as successful in science. A few Scholars said they felt successful, which was a reflection of their academic achievement. Jeff, a first-generation Latino Science Posse Scholar interested in science, said, "I guess [I'm successful]. I mean like I do pretty well in the classes." Zara, a first-generation Latina Science Posse Scholar planning on declaring a major in science, had similar feelings of accomplishment. She said, "Not to toot my own horn, but yeah . . . I feel like I can teach people about the sciences and be happy when I'm teaching them." For these Scholars, the definition of success was similar to the well-resourced students' definition of academic achievement.

However, the majority of Science Posse Scholars did not feel successful in the sciences or felt they were in the process of becoming successful in the sciences. Harrison, a Black Science Posse Scholar interested in science, defined his success using both the framework of grades and the ability to learn from his mistakes and work toward achievement. He said that he was "not as successful as I want to be" but he had been "successful in learning . . .

learning from what I've done, and trying to do things right the next time." This theme of an upward trajectory was also expressed by Phoebe, an Asian American Science Posse Scholar science major. She said, "I guess that I am becoming successful in the sciences." She thought of her success as how she "learned to study a little bit more, a little bit better for the sciences." Kay, a first-generation Black Science Posse Scholar interested in science, described herself as both unsuccessful and successful in the sciences: "Oh, Jesus. Oh, man. If I go off my grades solely I'd say no, but if I think about what I've learned and what I've taken away from science and like what it has taught me about myself and about myself as a student, myself as a person, then I'd definitely say yeah that I'm successful in science. . . . But as far as success like grade-wise, not so much. Not so much." This idea of science as a journey was similar to how underrepresented students, including first-generation students, described their success; they valued the progression they had made over time. Students recognized their current level of accomplishment as defined by their grades, and they also valued the improvements they had made in their approach to studying.

One of the key program elements in helping students understand their academic journey was the Posse mentor. Once Brandeis Science Posse Scholars were enrolled as full-time students at Brandeis, the Scholars continued to meet as a cohort under the guidance of a mentor for their first two years of college. The mentor was a graduate student or postdoctoral research fellow in the sciences who met weekly for two hours with the cohort as well as individually for an hour with each Scholar every other week.[8] The mentor was a paid position, selected by faculty and administrators who worked closely with the Science Posse Scholars. At the time of this research, the Science Posse mentors were from biology, neuroscience, and chemistry. The mentor was expected to help the group function as a cohesive unit, address academic and social challenges that the Science Posse Scholars faced in college, and encourage the Scholars to study science, particularly in times of difficulty. The mentor was not hired to provide tutoring or academic support to the students.

Scholars regularly described the mentor as an important resource to them and as being equivalent to a family member. Scholars said that they could turn to their mentor for advice, particularly when their families could not provide guidance about how to navigate the sciences at Brandeis. Because so many of the Posse Scholars were first-generation college students, the mentor played an important role in being a motivating influence, offering positive encouragement when students received a poor test grade, offering realistic feedback about the student's academic progress, and helping Scholars to perceive themselves as successful. RJ, a Black Science Posse Scholar interested in health, described her mentor:

[My mentor] is kind of like my mom away from home. She's that person. I always look forward to our one-on-ones. The fact that she was going for her PhD was a huge inspiration. She's just always—she offered tough love so to speak. Like, I know that I could talk to her about anything. But she'd always be open and honest with me in terms of what she thought about whatever it is that I was going through. . . . I love her to pieces.

This idea of "tough love" was expressed by multiple Scholars. The mentor would hold Scholars accountable for their grades and discuss ways to academically improve, but also they would offer encouragement in times of doubt. Many mentors self-disclosed their own academic struggles as undergraduates, which was very valuable to Scholars, as it demonstrated that an individual who was perceived as having power and success may also have had times of difficulties.

Mentors also offered important guidance about how to navigate the culture of the sciences at Brandeis, information that was particularly useful for first-generation Scholars. Because the mentors were graduate students in the sciences, they were very familiar with the reputations of faculty members and how to best communicate with the faculty. Navitas, a first-generation Latino Posse Scholar interested in science, had a different mentor than RJ, and one can understand how important his mentor was to him and his experiences in science. He remembered:

[I] talked with my Posse mentor about how to approach professors. . . . Probably my second test in organic chemistry, first semester. I got a low grade and [my mentor] was telling me, "You know, just go to the professor and ask him how you can improve," and I was just really nervous, one, because I couldn't stand that I got a dissatisfactory grade, and two, because I was just really nervous about approaching a professor who I knew was—might have been doing research on his own time and had a lot of students that he had to care about, and I didn't know that he would be really interested in talking with me. . . . [My Mentor's] push helped me to ask for help from the professor. The professor's words helped me in my studying and also realizing that professors, as many students as they may have, that they are attentive to individuals.

The mentor was able to provide guidance on how to talk to a faculty member, and in this case, the faculty member was one who had a reputation of being very direct and at times dismissive of student questions. As demonstrated by this example, the mentor was in many ways a translator between the dominant culture within the sciences at Brandeis and the lived experiences of the Scholars. This also contributed to the Scholars being able to understand their success in the sciences as a journey. Prior research has found that positive student interactions with faculty has a significant impact on students' academic success, social integration into the campus, and satisfaction with the undergraduate experience (Astin 1993; Cole 2007; Kuh 1995; Pascarella et al. 2004). Other research has found that the effects of mentoring can be even more significant for African American and Latina/o students than for White students (Cole and Espinoza 2008). This research implies that graduate students, particularly doctoral students in the sciences, can also be effective mentors and role models and contribute to undergraduates' success in the sciences.

DISCUSSION

All students, regardless of background, face challenges in studying STEM disciplines. However, students who are underrepresented racial minorities and/or first-generation and/or low-income students at a highly selective college or university are regularly required to navigate feelings of legitimacy and inclusion for simply being at an elite institution in which they are in the minority. These students can feel estranged from the dominant culture of highly selective colleges and universities, which becomes even more noticeable in STEM disciplines in which so few underrepresented students are retained.

The Science Posse Scholars Program was instrumental in developing feelings of cohesion among the Scholars. This supportive peer group provided both academic and emotional support in times of academic challenge. The Summer Science Immersion program provided multiple experiences that allowed Scholars to understand the academic challenges they would face in pursuing a STEM discipline. As a result, Science Posse Scholars were able to externalize rather than internalize feelings of struggle. Posse Scholars understood the sciences as a challenging discipline, rather than viewing themselves as lacking the skills to succeed. Because of this understanding of the sciences as a challenging discipline, Science Posse Scholars viewed their academic success as not only a reflection of their grades, but also of their academic journey, which often included an upward trajectory in their grades. Each of these factors—along with program services such as Pre-Collegiate Training, the Summer Science Immersion Program, and the Posse mentor—were found to positively contribute to Science Posse Scholars being retained in STEM disciplines. For first-generation college students, this type of programming is essential as it helps to reduce their gap in social, cultural, and informational capital relative to those of more well-resourced students with college-educated parents.

LIMITATIONS TO THE RESEARCH

These findings had three major limitations and, as a result, suggest areas for future research. The first limitation was that Science Posse was still very new at Brandeis. With only three cohorts having declared majors, future research should examine the rates at which Science Posse Scholars graduated with STEM majors as well as whether or not they pursued STEM careers. Second, this study only examined students' records data, attitudes about studying science based on the science survey, social capital, cultural capital, and resilience; it did not ask the question of whether or not Science Posse Scholars were fundamentally different from other students, particularly students with similar family and educational backgrounds. Given the highly competitive nature of the Science Posse Scholars Program and the method of selecting Scholars based on qualitative factors such as leadership and communication skills, it could be that Science Posse Scholars who participated in this study had personal qualities that were significantly different from their Brandeis peers. A third limitation of the study was that it was limited to the Brandeis campus. As Science Posse programs are established at nine other institutions across the country, it will be important to conduct further research. By researching the impact of Science Posse on other college campuses, important information could be learned, including whether the success of the Science Posse Scholars Program is limited to Brandeis or can be replicated at other highly selective colleges and universities.

In addition, since the time of this research study, the national conversation has begun to shift from how to best serve students who face challenges in pursuing STEM majors to how to create more inclusive learning environments. In this study, the voices of the well-resourced students show the degree to which they understand their own academic success as the result of a functioning meritocracy rather than as a reflection of academic preparation. Additional research is needed to better understand dominant academic cultures and how they contribute to or work to undermine inclusive learning environments.

CONCLUSION

Universities and funding agencies should determine if they could successfully adopt policies, programs, and practices that replicate the aspects of the Science Posse Scholars program that were critical to resilience and success among underrepresented students in the sciences, including first-generation college students. The Science Posse Scholars Program provided important sources of science support, including the development of a supportive cohort through the Pre-Collegiate Training, the norming of academic challenges in the sciences (rather than a focus on remediation) through the Summer Science Immersion program, and the creation of an identity of success in the sciences as facilitated by the Posse mentor. These components appeared to be central to Scholars' success and changed the paradigm of remediation that is so common in STEM support programs to a paradigm of acculturation. The Science Posse Scholars provided positive reinforcement to individual students and emphasized the group achieving a common goal of being retained in the sciences.

REFERENCES

Alon, Sigal, and Marta Tienda. 2005. "Assessing the 'Mismatch' Hypothesis: Differences in College Graduation Rates by Institutional Selectivity." *Sociology of Education* 78, no. 4: 294–315.

American Council on Education. 2006. *Increasing the Success of Minority Student in Science and Technology.* Washington, DC: American Council on Education.

Arcidiacono, Peter. 2004. "Ability Sorting and the Returns to College Major." *Journal of Econometrics* 121, no. 1–2, 343–75.

Astin, Alexander. 1993. *What Matters in College? Four Critical Years Revisited.* San Francisco, CA: Jossey-Bass.

Astin, Alexander, and Helen Astin. 1993. *Undergraduate Science Education: The Impact of Different College Environments on the Educational Pipeline in the Sciences.* Los Angeles: UCLA Higher Education Research Institute.

Bial, Deborah, and Alba Rodriguez. 2007. "Identifying a Diverse Student Body: Selective College Admissions and Alternative Approaches." *New Directions for Student Services* 118: 17–30.

Bonous-Hammarth, Marguerite. 2006. "Promoting Student Participation in Science, Technology, Engineering and Mathematics Careers." In *Higher Education in a Global Society: Achieving Diversity, Equity and Excellence*, edited by Walter Allen, Marguerite Bonous-Hammarth, Robert Teranishi, and Ophella Dano, 269–82. West Yorkshire: Emerald Group Publishing.

Bowen, William, and Derek Bok. 1998. *The Shape of the River.* Princeton, NJ: Princeton University Press.

Cavazos, Javier, Michael Johnson, Cheryl Fielding, Alyssa Castro, and Luti Vela. 2010. "A Qualitative Study of Resilient Latina/o College Students." *Journal of Latinos & Education* 9, no 3: 172–88.

Center for Institutional Data Exchange Analysis. 2000. *1999–2000 SMET Retention Report.* Norman, OK: University of Oklahoma.

Chang, Mitchell. 2008. "The Contradictory Roles of Institutional Status in Retaining Underrepresented Minorities in Biomedical and Behavioral Science Majors." *Review of Higher Education* 31, no 4: 433–64.

Cole, Darnell. 2007. "Do Interracial Interactions Matter? An Examination of Student-Faculty Contact and Intellectual Self-Concept." *Journal of Higher Education* 78, no. 3: 249–81.

Cole, Darnell, and Araceli Espinoza. 2008. "Examining the Academic Success of Latino Students in Science, Technology, Engineering, and Mathematics (STEM) Majors." *Journal of College Student Development* 49, no. 4: 285–300.

Commission on the Advancement of Women and Minorities in Science, Engineering and Technology Development. 2001. "Land of Plenty: Diversity as America's Competitive Edge in Science Engineering and Technology." Leadership and Management in Engineering 1, no. 4. https://doi.org/10.1061/(ASCE)1532-6748(2001)1:4(27).

Creswell, John. 2007. *Qualitative Inquiry and Research Design: Choosing Among Five Approaches.* Thousand Oaks, California: Sage Publications.

Huang, Gary, Nebiyu Taddese, and Elizabeth Walter. 2000. "Entry and Persistence of Women and Minorities in College Science and Engineering Education." *Education Statistics Quarterly* 2, no. 3: 59–60.

Hurtado, Sylvia, June Chang, Victor Saenz, Lorelle Espinosa, Nolan Cabrera, and Oscar Cerna. 2007. "Predicting Transition and Adjustment to College: Minority Biomedical and Behavioral Science Students' First Year of College." *Research in Higher Education* 48, no. 7: 841–87.

Hurtado, Sylvia, Nolan Cabera, Monica Lin, Lucy Arellano, and Lorelle Espinosa. 2009. "Diversifying Science: Underrepresented Student Experiences in Structured Programs." *Research in Higher Education* 50, no. 2: 189–214.

Kerr, Clark. 2001. *The Uses of the University*. Cambridge, Massachusetts: Harvard University Press.

Kuh, George. 2008. "Why Integration and Engagement are Essential to Effective Educational Practice in the Twenty-First Century." *Peer Review* 10, no. 4: 27–28.

Lee, Ji Hee, Suk Kyung Nam, A-Reum Kim, Boram Kim, Min Young Lee, and Sang Min Lee. 2013. "Resilience: A Meta-Analytic Approach." *Journal of Counseling and Development* 91, no. 3: 269–79.

Luthar, Suniya, Dante Cicchetti, and Bronwyn Becker. 2000. "The Construct of Resilience: A Critical Evaluation and Guidelines for Future Work." *Child Development* 71, no. 3: 543–62.

Mau, Wei-Cheng, 2016. "Characteristics of US Students That Pursued a STEM Major and Factors that Predicted their Persistence in Degree Completion." *Universal Journal of Educational Research* 4, no. 6: 1495–1500.

McGee, Ebony. 2004. "Race, Identity, and Resilience: Black College Students Negotiating Success in Mathematics and Engineering" (PhD diss., University of Illinois at Chicago).

National Science Board. 2010. *Preparing the Next Generation of STEM Innovators: Identifying and Developing our Nation's Human Capital*. NSB-10–33. Arlington, VA: National Science Foundation.

National Science Foundation. 2004. *Women, Minorities, and Persons with Disabilities in Science and Engineering*. NSF 04–317. Arlington, VA: NSF, Division of Science Resources Statistics.

Ovink, Sarah, and Brian Veazey. 2011. "More Than 'Getting Us Through': A Case Study in Cultural Capital Enrichment of Underrepresented Minority Undergraduates." *Research in Higher Education* 52, no. 4: 370–94.

Pascarella, Ernest, Christopher Pierson, Gregory Wolniak, and Patrick Terenzini. 2004. "First-Generation College Students: Additional Evidence on College Experiences and Outcomes." *Journal of Higher Education,* 75, no. 3: 249–84.

The Posse Foundation. About Posse, retrieved from http://www.possefoundation.org/about-posse on December 22, 2017.

Seymour, Elaine, and Nancy Hewit. 1997. *Talking About Leaving: Why Undergraduates Leave the Sciences.* Boulder, CO: Westview Press.

Shaw, Emily, and Sandra Barbuti. 2010. "Patterns of Persistence in Intended College Major with a Focus on STEM Majors." *NACADA Journal* 30, no. 2: 19–34.

Smyth, Frederick, and John McArdle. 2004. "Ethnic and Gender Differences in Science Graduation at Selective Colleges with Implications for Admission Policy and College Choice." *Research in Higher Education* 45, no. 4: 353–81.

Stanton-Salazar, Ricardo, and Stephanie Spina. 2000. "The Network Orientations of Highly Resilient Urban Minority Youth: A Network-Analytic Account of Minority Socialization and its Educational Implications." *The Urban Review* 32, no. 3: 227–61.

Stolel-McAllister, Kathleen. 2011. "The Case for Summer Bridge: Building Social and Cultural STEM Students." *Science Educatator* 20, no. 2: 12–22.

Strenta, Christopher, Rogers Elliott, Russell Adair, Michelle Matier, and Jannah Scott. 1994. "Choosing and Leaving Science in Highly Selective Institutions." *Research in Higher Education* 35, no. 5: 513–47.

Yee, April. 2016. "The Unwritten Rules of Engagement: Social Class Differences in Undergraduates' Academic Strategies." *The Journal of Higher Education* 87, no. 6: 831–58.

Young, Cynthia. 2016. "Increasing Retention and Graduation Rates through a STEM Learning Community." *Journal of College Student Retention: Research, Theory and Practice* 18, no. 2: 167–82.

NOTES

1. *Underrepresented students of color* in the sciences is defined as students who are Native American, African American, Latina/o, or Pacific Islander. The term *underrepresented racial minority* is a more accurate description of this population. However, the term *underrepresented students* is used later in this research to indicate students who are first-generation and/or low-income. Therefore, for ease of reading and to better differentiate the two populations, the term underrepresented students of color in the sciences is used rather than the term underrepresented students of color in the sciences.

2. Posse Scholars receive a four-year, full-tuition scholarship which is funded by the college or university that they attend. Once selected for the scholarship, Science

Posse Scholars will continue to receive the funding even if they decide not to major in a STEM discipline.

3. Brandeis chemistry professor Irv Epstein and Posse president Deborah Bial developed the idea of a Science Posse with initial funding from the Howard Hughes Medical Institute and the Carnegie Corporation. Epstein's premise was that students who were recruited together to major in science and who continued as a cohort in their initial years at Brandeis would be more likely to graduate with a major in the sciences.

4. Students were nominated for the Science Posse Scholarship by schools and nonprofit organizations in New York City because of their academic success, leadership skills, and demonstrated interest in the sciences. Students were then selected for the scholarship through a three-step process. The Dynamic Assessment Process was a group interview with guided activities that allowed trained observers to identify students with outstanding communication and problem-solving skills (Bial and Rodriguez, 2007). The top 50 percent of students who participated in the Dynamic Assessment Process were invited to the second step in the admissions process, which was an individual interview with members of the Posse staff. At these interviews, students selected their top three choices of partner colleges or universities. This was also when students expressed an interest in being in a Science Posse, rather than a Posse in which there were no expectations about the field of study in which a student would major. To be in the Science Posse Scholars Program, a student must have expressed an interest in majoring in a STEM discipline. From these interviews, a finalist group of twenty students was selected for the Brandeis campus. Representatives from Brandeis University and from the Posse Foundation then completed another group interview with the twenty finalists, and the cohort of ten Posse Science Posse Scholars was selected in the middle of December of the students' senior year of high school. At no point in the selection process were the students nominated for the Science Posse Scholars program given a diagnostic exam for abilities in math or science.

5. The Posse Foundation does not use race, ethnicity, parental education level, or family income in selecting the finalist pools of Scholars. However, given Brandeis's history as an institution founded when quotas and restrictions in admissions were common to higher education, the university cites social justice as one of its core tenets. Because of this, the selection teams from Brandeis tend to pay careful attention to students in the finalist pool who are first-generation college students or who come from backgrounds with limited financial resources. In general, Brandeis tends to have a greater number of Posse Scholars who are first-generation and/or low-income compared to other Posse partner schools. Therefore, the demographics of Brandeis Posse Scholars should not be generalized to all Posse Scholars.

6. It is important to note that Science Posse Scholars go through an extensive and highly competitive screening process in order to receive the scholarship. The comparison group of students who are similar to Posse Scholars—using criteria such as race, parental education, and whether or not a student was a Pell Grant recipient—were admitted to Brandeis using the traditional admissions process. Therefore, they were not screened for their skills in leadership, communication, or problem-solving. In spite of these differences, they offer a useful comparison group to the Science Posse Scholars.

7. The Summer Science Immersion program was developed by Dr. Melissa Kosin-ski-Collins, a professor at Brandeis University. She structured the program to include a scientific book report, a poster presentation using primary scientific sources, as well as lectures and/or labs in chemistry, biology, and physics.

8. Previous research on factors that positively impact students declaring majors in STEM disciplines has overwhelmingly focused on the importance of faculty mentoring rather than on mentoring by graduate students or postdoctoral research fellows. One of the few studies of the differences in mentoring was conducted by Cox and Androit (2009), who studied differences in perceptions of undergraduates' lab skills in college among faculty mentors and graduate student mentors. However, this research did not compare how mentoring by graduate students differed from mentoring by faculty.

11

Toward a Local Student Success Model

Latino First-Generation College Student Persistence

Trista Beard

First-generation college students (FGS) are a diverse population, and yet an invisible minority at most four-year colleges, with no outward identity markers. Researchers have established that there is a definite completion gap between FGS and their non-first-generation student (NFGS) peers (Chen and Carroll 2005). FGS are less likely to take advantage of study groups, professors' office hours, tutoring, writing coaches, and other support services that could help them achieve better marks in the first year of college (Chen and Carroll 2005). FGS also enroll in fewer credit hours in the early years of college, contributing to slower progress and higher attrition rates, especially after the first year, when FGS are half as likely to return to school as NFGS (Choy 2001; Pascarella et al. 2004; Soria and Stebleton 2012).

Latino students are also a rapidly rising population entering four-year universities, and half of them are the first in their families to attend college (Santiago 2011). In looking at how Latino students succeed in college and why they depart, researchers have used variable such as campus climate (Castillo et al. 2006; Hurtado and Carter 1997), minority stress (Wei, Ku, and Liao 2011), campus involvement (Museus, Nichols, and Lambert 2008; Próspero and Vohra-Gupta 2007) and students' support networks (Bordes-Edgar et al. 2011; Hurtado, Carter, and Spuler 1996). Much of the educational research on persistence has focused on barriers to persistence in college for Latino students *or* for first-generation college students, but little has honed in on the intersection of these populations.

In thinking about the theme of this book, it is important to consider how institutions, educators, families, and policymakers can clear the path *to* college, but also clear the path *through* college. "Access without support is not opportunity" (Engstrom and Tinto 2008, 46). This chapter focuses not on student access, but on student *success*. While there is an abundance of quantitative studies examining factors that influence college departure, there is a need for more qualitative studies that seek to examine how first-generation students of color overcome obstacles and complete four-year degrees. Qualitative studies allow researchers to explore a participant's world, culture, and experience in its entirety, allowing those voices to speak to the complexity of intersectional identity. Instead of trying to control for demographic characteristics or to disentangle identity markers, it was the aim of this study to learn directly from Latino first-generation college students (LFGCS) about their unique experiences at a large, research-intensive, predominately white institution (PWI). A single research question drove this study: *How do Latino first-generation college students at this elite PWI navigate and negotiate barriers to persistence?*

LITERATURE REVIEW

In considering what promotes student persistence in college from year to year, many researchers have looked to Astin's (1984) theory of student involvement. Astin asserts that the more a student is involved in academic activities, extracurricular activities, faculty and staff interactions, and residential programs that engage the student's time, the greater the amount of learning. Kuh (2001) defines engagement as cocurricular activities such as campus clubs and societies, relationships and interactions with peers and faculty, mentoring programs, and educational activities like group projects, study groups, and course-related field trips. The concept of *high-impact practices* has also been associated with engagement activities that make the most impact on student commitment and persistence—i.e. capstones, internships, service learning, global learning, and undergraduate research, all of which require application of classroom skills in new contexts (Kuh 2008). First-gen students often find it more difficult to decode the behaviors necessary to succeed in college, such as "attending class, asking questions, visiting professors, and being involved on campus in organizations and with peers" (Mehta and Newbold 2011, 30). Mehta and Newbold found that FGS were less likely to be engaged in campus activities, both academic and social, and that GPA and completion rates were affected by this.

Museus, Nichols, and Lambert (2008) suggest that the relationship between campus racial climate, academic and social involvement, and institutional commitment all relate to degree completion in unique ways for students of color. For Latino students, the most significant positive effect on degree completion was a lower amount of social involvement, assuming that social time detracted from academic engagement (Museus, Nichols, and Lambert 2008). Próspero and Vohra-Gupta (2007) also found a strong correlation for FGS between engagement and academic achievement. Hernandez (2002) validated this experience through interviews with Latino students at a four-year PWI who reported that because they felt underprepared, they specifically chose not to get involved in student organizations the first year so that they could focus on meeting academic expectations. The benefit of academic activities is higher for FGS "because these experiences act in a compensatory manner and thus contribute comparatively greater incremental increases in first-generation students' stock of cultural capital" (Pascarella et al. 2004, 280).

How LFGCS negotiate the campus climate impacts their commitment and persistence at an institution (Hurtado and Carter 1997). First-gen students of color have unique intersectional identities. In a qualitative study, Orbe (2004) found that the first-generation student identity was most salient for those who also identified as an underrepresented minority on their campus. It was the intersectional identities of race and class that exacerbated students' feelings of difference and minority status, especially at the most selective colleges. When the students felt that they were the minority within the minority, they kept their first-gen status hidden until they found individuals like them, with whom they could share their status.

Social support from peers then becomes a lifeline for students marginalized by the dominant institutional culture. Specifically, mentoring (formal and informal) by either peers, faculty, or staff increases the likelihood of persistence for Latino students (Bordes-Edgar et al. 2011). Mentors can guide students in turning desire to complete college into behaviors that will aid persistence. The literature also suggests that FGS who perceive they have the support they need feel less stress, have more confidence, and adjust and perform better. Those who feel they lack support struggle to adjust and persist (Dennis, Phinney, and Chuateco 2005). Students who perceived they had less social support also had low self-efficacy scores (Phinney and Haas 2003). Disentangling self-efficacy and social support as influential variables in how first-gen students of color cope with stressful situations in college is incredibly difficult. Using a narrative approach allows for this complexity. Just as intersectional identities cannot be unraveled, neither can the intrinsic mechanisms students use to succeed in college. Instead of controlling for variables looking for causation, starting this study with an awareness of students' multiple identities and compound strategies for problem-solving gives credit to students' funds of knowledge and community wealth.

Yosso (2005) explains that traditional notions of cultural capital ignore the unique knowledge that students of color bring with them to college, and that their home communities have infused them with cultural wealth that they can use to succeed in dominant spaces. An example of how students use community cultural wealth is found in Muñoz and Maldonado's (2012) case study of four undocumented Mexican women, all first in their families to attend college. The students reported that they were able to persist because of family support, and that they created their own peer support and cultural circle. The students, through their stories, also expressed a strong desire to complete college, and were able to navigate home life, work life, and school life in different ways, and still maintain their aspirations (Muñoz and Maldonado 2012). Padilla's (1996) qualitative study of students of color at a single college campus allowed students, in focus groups, to respond to a list of established barriers to persisting in college and to report how they faced those barriers, what they had to know to overcome them (heuristic knowledge), and actions taken by the students to succeed and persist. Padilla's (1996) results demonstrated that students of color were successful because they learned how to get the support they needed in their campus environment. His argument necessitated my own study: if we know, based on tested theoretical models, that integration and involvement increase persistence (Astin 1984; Tinto 1993), and yet graduation rates have changed very little in fifty years (see Iffert 1957; NCES 2016), then we must look more deeply at student experiences to see what actions work for students and what institutions might do to eliminate barriers and better serve students. A singular focus on models of student success allowed me to learn from students' expertise. This focus situates the study on a longer line of action research that acknowledges LFGCS' funds of knowledge.

METHODS

The expertise model put forth by Padilla (1994) allowed me to explore the process by which LFGCS at an elite PWI gained heuristic knowledge that impacted their persistence. A focus on success rather than deficits allows for the development of new models of student completion from which asset-minded strategies and interventions can be drawn. This study aimed to explore the ways successful LFGCS persisted and navigated the college and to examine the role that students play as agents of their own academic success, as measured by persistence to degree completion. One research question drove this study: *How do Latino first-generation college students at this elite PWI navigate and negotiate barriers to persistence?*

Padilla's (1994) expertise model fit this study because it validates students' sense of agency and funds of knowledge, acknowledging that successful LFGCS are experts on how to persist at an elite PWI. Yosso's (2005) community cultural wealth framework also informed the study, keeping the focus on what assets LFGCS brought to campus with them. Yosso's theory allows for a wider conceptualization of cultural capital that values aspiration, bilingualism, interdependence, familial strength, and resistance, among other values. The community cultural wealth model combined with Padilla's expertise model helped center the study on the participants as I sought to highlight their lived experiences and their unique ways of getting through the new terrain of college as Latino students *and* first-gen college students.

To build a local model around LFGCS and their pathways to persistence was the goal of this study. The primary form of data collection for this study was interviews, which allowed me to gain insight into the experience and perceptions of others (Patton 2002). I conducted in-depth interviews (on average, ninety minutes) with ten participants (five men and five women), using a semistructured interview guide, based on Padilla's (1994) unfolding matrix model. Padilla's unfolding matrix technique helped to draw out expert tacit knowledge that students may not be explicitly aware that they even possess. Where Padilla used this technique with focus groups, I conducted one-on-one interviews in order to explore with each participant the barriers to their integration and engagement in college and the ways in which they faced and overcame those barriers.

Site and Sample Selection

The site was a single predominately white research university in the West: highly selective, with nearly 18,000 undergraduates, 23 percent low-income (Pell-eligible), about 20 percent first-generation and 14 percent Latino. As with the national average (Santiago 2011), half of the Latino undergrads are first-gen. All interview participants were rising seniors and first-generation college students who self-identified as Latino. This study used the federal TRIO programs' definition of first-generation: students whose parents have not earned a bachelor's degree. The university has three single-ethnicity cultural centers and an LGBT resource center, but no transfer center or first-gen office. The culture is one where, like many colleges, ethnicity is part of the diversity discussion but class is not yet. Some students' identities are validated by the university, as cultural centers are a visible way the university says "you belong," but for many others, when there is no space, there is no place, and it is more difficult to find community and sense of belonging.

All ten participants were the children of immigrants, and high financial-need students (also described as low-income). All interviews took place in the fall term of the students' senior year. Participants were purposefully invited to interview because they were LFGCS and were seniors making successful progress toward graduation. Invitations to interview were sent out via academic advisors across the campus, student organizations, including Latino student government, and through scholarship program offices that support first-generation and low-income students.

Data Analysis

All interviews were transcribed and then analyzed for common themes and categories following Padilla's unfolding matrix method, detailed in *Student Success Modeling* (2009). Transcripts were coded first for open codes and then grouped into cover terms developed through interpretive analysis. All categories related to barriers and obstacles were listed under one domain, and the strategies used to overcome reported barriers and obstacles were listed under the second domain. The purpose of the domain analysis was to establish a model of how first-generation students perceived and overcame challenges as they arose, within the boundaries of the college years and the college environment. All interviews were viewed as a single case study, representing a collective experience at one particular site. Themes that were reported by only a single participant were considered outliers as they were not corroborated by additional participants, and as such, were not included in either domain. Interview texts were analyzed to the point of saturation.

FINDINGS

In participant interviews, students described the obstacles to successful completion of college as well as the ways in which they were able to take action to overcome such difficulties as they arose. The following tables present the barriers by category (table 11.1) and the strategies for navigating such impediments (table 11.2). While the sample is small, and not generalizable to all LFGCS at large research universities, there is value in learning how a particular group of students interpreted the institution, reported the obstacles that could derail student success, and suggested their own tested strategies.

Table 11.1 Barriers to Latino first-generation college student persistence at a large PWI.

Type of Barrier	Barriers and Obstacles to Persistence
Academic	1. academic struggle
	2. felt academically underprepared
	3. afraid to speak up in class
	4. lack of academic support
	5. lack of study skills
	6. did not seek out advice from instructors

Behavioral	7. did not want to try new things 8. lack of help-seeking behaviors 9. lack of willingness to share emotions and struggles
Cultural	10. cultural stigma to counseling 11. negative perception of help-seeking 12. culture shock 13. feeling separated from home 14. feeling stereotyped 15. feeling "minoritized"[1] 16. to not assimilate takes energy
Emotional	17. afraid of being seen as an imposter/not good enough 18. afraid to ask for help (fear of rejection) 19. anxiety 20. difficulty managing emotions 21. fear of not belonging 22. fear of talking to instructors/faculty 23. feeling isolated 24. lack of sharing emotions/struggles 25. overwhelming stress (distraction)
Familial	26. family issues at home (takes energy) 27. difficult to explain academic challenges 28. difficult to explain social challenges 29. lack of parental involvement/advocacy at college
Financial	30. worry over finances 31. lack of clear understanding of financial aid 32. works more than twenty hours per week 33. work conflicts with office hours on campus 34. works off-campus 35. works to send money home 36. work conflicts with clubs/co-curricular activities 37. work conflicts with tutoring/academic support

(continued)

Institutional	38. competitive peers in class
	39. poor advising
	40. distrust of academic advisor
	41. professors are not approachable
	42. support resources are hidden
Integrational	43. commutes from home
	44. work conflicts with clubs/co-curricular activities
	45. does not join social or academic communities
	46. feels lost
	47. does not feel a sense of belonging
Knowledge	48. does not know how to navigate campus resources
	49. does not know how to network
	50. difficulty with time management
	51. difficulty balancing work and academics
	52. difficulty balancing academic and social engagement
	53. lack of study skills
	54. lack of heuristic knowledge (how to learn)
Motivational	55. lack of commitment
	56. lack of goals/sense of purpose
Self-efficacy	57. lack of confidence
	58. self-doubt
	59. lack of effort to access support resources
	60. lack of models
Social	61. does not join social communities
	62. difficulty finding "people like me"
	63. lack of models

1. I use "minoritized" in this study as used by Shaun Harper in his work *Race Without Racism* (2012). Harper explained that many students of color do not feel like a minority until they enter the predominately white space. Minority status is a social construction put upon them, not a natural state of being.

The research question that drove this study was *How do Latino first-generation college students at this elite PWI navigate and negotiate barriers to persistence?* The detailed items in table 11.1 provide a clear picture of the difficulties students encountered at this particular college. As I sat through interviews and listened to students talk about their frustrations and successes, their ups and downs in college, I asked them to tell me more about *how* they got past obstacles such as fear of speaking to professors, or lack of study skills, or feeling that they didn't have a purpose. Table 11.2 comprises the aggregate responses from this line of inquiry.

Table 11.2 Strategies identified by Latino first-generation college students as ways to overcome obstacles to persistence in college.

Type of Barrier	Strategies and Actions for Persistence
Academic	1. ask for advice 2. ask professors for study advice particular to field of study 3. ask TAs for study tips 4. connect with a professor over shared interests 5. sign up for enrichment programs 6. find mentors 7. find models 8. find study groups 9. follow others 10. participate in high-impact practices 11. take peer advice and share resources 12. identify peer models/mentors 13. view professors as models 14. study with trusted peers 15. talk to advisors 16. talk to professors about coursework and college life 17. talk to professors about career ideas/paths 18. use academic support resources (tutoring/SI) 19. use learning center (academic coaching) 20. find a job that allows for study/time space 21. join learning communities around field of study
Behavioral	22. explore your interests 23. show your interests 24. speak up in class 25. talk about career ideas/pathways 26. talk about your goals 27. be willing to try new things 28. practice help-seeking behaviors
Cultural	29. find a way to connect with ethnic community/-ies 30. connect with others around all identity markers

Table 11.1 (*continued*)

Type of Barrier	Strategies and Actions for Persistence
Emotional	31. de-stress with peers 32. gain emotional support and encouragement from peers 33. find a confidante
Financial	34. financial aid is an incentive to stay 35. campus job provides funds and connections 36. find a job which allows study time/space
Institutional	37. advisors are bridges to resources 38. professors offer advice and mentorship 39. learning center offers coaches
Integrational	40. assimilate or code-switch 41. claim space 42. be active in cultural centers 43. live in dorms 44. cultivate fictive kin/trusted peer network 45. find a sense of home 46. join communities 47. join a team 48. be active in dorm events 49. stay involved in campus activities/groups 50. join learning communities around field of study and professional interests
Knowledge	51. ask advisors questions to get referrals 52. find study spaces that work for you 53. learn to study 54. use resident advisors as near peer coaches 55. take advantage of academic and pre-professional opportunities
Motivational	56. find purpose 57. find role models 58. set goals beyond college 59. help others 60. join organizations with a purpose/ideology 61. remember your success is part of a collective success 62. be part of a peer group that motivates you 63. put in effort 64. feeling a sense of duty 65. set higher, long-term life goals

Self-efficacy	66. ask for advice from models
	67. accept short-term failure as part of skill-building
	68. be willing to make changes
	69. focus on a few goals
	70. go to offices for help
	71. practice self-care
	72. self-exploration (goals, interests)
	73. self-talk
	74. gain confidence through navigating challenges
Social	75. awareness of need to build new ties
	76. connect over shared identity
	77. connect with peers
	78. develop a support network
	79. find peers who share values
	80. find trusted peers for emotional support
	81. join social events
	82. meet a wide range of people
	83. join learning communities around field of study and professional interests

First, the matrix of reported barriers revealed little in the way of new insights. The categories of barriers and examples (table 11.1) described by the participants in this study are in line with previous literature (Chen and Carroll 2005; Choy 2001; Pascarella et al. 2004; Tinto 1993). One category of barriers that is not present in the first-gen persistence literature was the institutional barriers that students described here (table 11.1, items 37–41). These items are particularly important to consider since they convey how LFGCS interpret and understand the institution. Students do not depart college simply because they are not motivated, committed, or connected to the university; they also may be repelled and pushed out by hostile campus climate or unnavigable bureaucratic systems.

The first item in this category was "competitive peers in class." Multiple participants reported that they could not connect with peers in classes, particularly in biosciences, because the courses were large and graded on a curve. No one wanted to study together or support others. They explained that there were only so many high scores to be doled out and students were afraid they would be sabotaged by their peers.

It's weird, because it feels like at any moment you can't really trust other students, because it's a huge curve, and everyone's like "oh, it's a 50 percent acceptance rate to get into medical school." You want to be above the curve, so if you're helping anyone, that might put you down a little bit.

Students interpreted grading on a curve as being measured against—and therefore in competition with—their classmates. Faculty could mediate this problem by explaining that students working together to review and study material before each exam generally do better. The benefits of study groups are academic, but they also provide opportunities for social engagement, which students reported as a helpful strategy for persistence in college.

Also in the institutional barriers category, participants reported that they received poor advising from professional academic support staff, and that they were mistrustful of advising staff. Positive interactions with faculty and staff can increase student persistence (Schreiner, Noel, and Cantwell 2011). A negative experience or repeated negative interactions caused distress for the students in this study and increased the difficulty they were already having in navigating the college environment.

When I was here at orientation, my first day, like officially as a student here, the advisor was . . . just pressuring me into other [classes], so I really had to figure it out on my own, I feel like, in terms of navigating [this school], especially because they're not—at least the advisors that I've encountered, not many of them are first-gen and not many of them are people of color, so they don't—and they're also not—at least from what they've expressed to me, they don't come from low socioeconomic backgrounds, so they don't understand the specific perspective that I have and that my friends have.

The students who felt they were not listened to, or not understood as first-gen, working-class students of color, were dissuaded from further help-seeking because they lost trust in the institution and its agents. This exemplifies institutional failure to serve students who are both first-gen and Latino. *Every* interaction with students is key to building their connection to the institution and their academic journey.

The last two items in the institutional barriers category (table 11.1) were "professors are not approachable" and "support services are hidden." Much like the negative impact of advisors, students perceived their instructors as unapproachable. Students spoke of professors as "not even human." None of the students felt empowered early in their college years to speak with their professors. Some participants explained that they were able to speak to professors once they gained confidence and heard from other people (e.g., peers, peer mentors/models, advising staff) that they were *supposed* to go to office hours, ask professors questions, and talk about their own interests and goals as a way to get feedback. Endorsements and advice from trusted sources, especially peers—that is, fellow LFGCS—is one of the most noteworthy findings from the analysis of the strategies used to overcome barriers (table 11.2).

Peer networks were a valuable way to adjust to the new terrain, learn about and gain entry to other communities, and acquire academic advice. The use of social support came up as a strategy under the academic, cultural, emotional, integrational, motivational and self-efficacy cover terms. This excerpt demonstrates how LFGCS's network-building impacts integration, engagement (both academic and social), and even aspirational capital:

> So when I got there, I got connected with some friends who liked the same things I like. They were pre-med or they were studying bio too. And we got involved with different community outreach organizations, so for example, Chicanos for Health Education. We'd go to the weekly meetings, and I think it helped that we would all go together kind of. And I also got interested in a Latina sorority my first year and I would just go and hang out with them and see what it was all about, kind of just trying to meet new people and things like that. . . . One of the first girls I met, we got in contact because she was my same major and she was already a senior but I was a freshman. I was like "oh, what about this class?" or you know, "what about this professor?"

These students had a natural impulse to tap into the local community cultural wealth (Yosso 2005) within the college. Participants explained that when they saw people "like me," they felt a sense of trust. For one student, that person was her resident advisor (RA) in the dorm, a Latino student just a few years older than her, who provided emotional support, but also served as a credible model of success. "He was just the first person that I considered someone like me, but older, that has gone through what I was going through." She stated that the support of peers and her RA helped her through the "culture shock. 100 percent culture shock. . . . I felt lost and confused." Others found empowering, credible models through joining a cultural organization that offered a community of peers who shared class, gender, and ethnic identity, as well as navigational capital.

> When I found these girls they all knew the same music I was talking about, who I was talking about or what shows I was talking about . . . and all of us were kind of in the same income level, so it was really easy to fit in with them. It is easy to fit in with the girls there [in Las Hermanas]. . . . They really were helpful in the sense that they could guide me. There was one girl who was a psychology major and I would ask her what professors or what classes she would recommend. They would share their own stories of what they were feeling at the moment so it prepared me of what I had to look [forward] to. It wasn't like guiding in the

sense of advising, but guiding in the sense of what they were feeling or what they went through and it prepared me for what I would face.

Beyond the power of peers to support many of the strategies used by these LFGCS and the drawing upon of community cultural wealth, it is important to note that there is no consistent correlation between a struggle and its resolution. The barriers and strategies are categorized and can be coupled by matching theme. For instance, a student who felt they were academically underprepared (table 11.1, item 2) might have tried strategies from the academic section (see table 11.2) as well as strategies from the institutional section. For each barrier there are multiple strategies that will help to mitigate the problem. For cultural barriers (table 11.1, items 10–16), there are few specific "cultural" strategies that align with these obstacles. Students in this sample, Latino first-gen college students, used a multipronged approach to resolving those kinds of difficulties.

Like my mom worked all day and she didn't really speak English so I was the one handling stuff at high school and [college], but here it's like, parents fight for their kids with their counselors, it's like—that's cool, but when are you going to learn to do that for yourself, you know? So all that was very confusing to me. Um, yeah, I think I was blessed too, because I was American Studies, I took a lot of classes that were already empowering with professors of color, or professors from different backgrounds, so I think I'm very lucky in that sense.

This student felt separated from home, felt a lack of familial support in the college environment, but was empowered to persist because of models she found in faculty of color, coursework that validated her experiences, and the independence and self-efficacy she brought with her to college. A cultural barrier ("feeling separated from home") and a familial barrier ("lack of parental involvement/advocacy") were alleviated by academic ("view professors as models") and motivational solutions ("put in effort" and "find role models"). Another way to look at this is that a high-impact solution, like finding models, helps to diminish multiple obstacles, hurdles, and/or stressors. Since barriers and obstacles are often compounded for working-class minority youth, then so must their strategies for persistence be compounded, complex, and multipronged. Because there is not a clear alignment of strategies to barriers, I found it essential to look more closely at the most "high-impact" actions that yielded multiple benefits, and from there begin to create models of the most advantageous actions.

DISCUSSION

The results indicate that barriers to persistence for LFGCS are in line with prior research on Latino students and first-gen college students, although little research has been done on this intersectional population. Barriers such as familial demands, conflicts between needing to work and needing time for engagement activities, feeling minoritized, and difficulty finding community are not surprising. The LFGCS's discussion of specific institutional barriers was unique to this study: competitive peers, negative advising experiences, and the perception that support services are hidden. Whether these barriers are particular to the population, the type of university, or this site specifically is not clear without investigating the perception of these barriers at other sites.

As students explained that they felt isolated, overwhelmed, underprepared, and cut off from familial communities, I thought of the unique situation they are in, where they have to navigate a maze from *within* the maze. Latino students have been found to scale down the geography of the university in order to be able to find a way through the unfamiliar terrain (Attinasi 1989). I found this to be true for these LFGCS as well. What becomes important here is to illustrate *how* they were able to accomplish this. All the students demonstrated through their strategies that a sense of agency and social learning were integral to their persistence.

First, a sense of agency was exemplified through the students' action-oriented strategies, such as asking for advice, exhibiting help-seeking behaviors, joining communities, and participating in "high-impact practices" (Kuh 2008). While all the students explained that their first-year adjustment was particularly difficult and they "felt lost," they were still willing to ask questions, to talk to peers about their struggles, and build some initial support networks that could be scaffolded and built upon as their confidence grew. Many students were aware of their poor help-seeking behaviors and talked about their lack of confidence or cultural barriers that kept them from asking for help and advice. However, participants expressed that after some critical incident of failure or faltering, they realized that if they want to be successful and complete college (i.e., if they were motivated to persist), they would have to be active in help-seeking and community-building. Many of the students also elected to participate in cocurricular *high-impact practices* (Kuh 2008). These activities were not part of the required course of study, but the fact that 90 percent of these successful students voluntarily took part in undergraduate research, service learning, overseas studies, internships, or capstones validates the students' sense of agency and supports the powerful effect of such activities on persistence in college.

Secondly, *social learning* (Bandura 1963) was demonstrated through the intricate system of mentors, models, and brokers that students reported were integral to their persistence. One student described her varied networks as "ropes of people" while another said, "I have a lot of role models. I look up to a lot of people because I want to be a lot of things, you know?" Each described peer models and coaches who gave them emotional support; advice about campus resources; academic advice on study skills, courses, and professors; as well as connected them to other communities on campus. Learning how to navigate college and how to be a successful student was learned in a social context. Students spoke to peers and near-peer models about their goals. This allowed for articulation of goals and immediate feedback or advice on local resources that could be utilized. Many of the success strategies that participants identified are dependent on activating social networks and social learning. The community cultural wealth model helps to explain how the Latino first-gen students in this sample motivated and inspired each other and bonded over aspects of shared culture. They exchanged navigational, social, and aspirational capital among their trusted peers, and they invested in others without any expectation of favors being reciprocated. The peer network became a fictive kin network, and trusted peers took the place of familial networks within the college environment.

A final point for discussion is the finding that some strategies for persistence identified by participants addressed multiple barrier types. For instance, two male students described their time volunteering at a local hospital and being allowed to shadow healthcare professionals as significantly contributing to different categories of barriers to persistence (figure 11.1). "Helping others" diminished motivational, emotional, social, and academic difficulties. The many benefits that this volunteer experience provided to the students validate that this is a type of high-impact action, even though volunteering is not one of the cocurricular activities described among the high-impact practices that increase retention (Kuh 2008).

For three of the female participants, their first year in the dorms living in an ethnic enclave (an all-Latino dorm floor) made a positive impact on their initial adjustment to college life at the large urban PWI, providing them with access to various networks that again helped them face multiple types of barriers (figure 11.2). These are just a few examples of how actions taken by successful Latino first-generation college students were a type of significant investment that paid dividends in breaking down other barriers they encountered as they worked to persist to graduation. Models like these can help students see the value of their actions and may increase motivation to persist. A future project will be to continue mapping key actions that yielded such a powerful effect in mitigating obstacles.

LIMITATIONS

The generalizability of this study is limited because of the single site and small sample. It was not my intention that the findings be scaled up to a larger population or be interpreted as applicable at other institutional types. The findings present a starting point for action research and analysis of student success strategies at other sites. The second limitation is the complex entanglement of barriers and strategies for success, and in particular, the compounded struggles with which Latino first-generation students at an elite PWI have to contend. Culture shock as a barrier to student persistence was reported by nearly all the students and explained in so many ways that it was difficult to unpack. The jumble or piles of frustrations and roadblocks that come along with encountering so much new "culture" (for example, socio-economic class difference, racial and ethnic difference, linguistic difference, differences in parental educational history and parental occupations, new unspoken social norms and rules, privilege, minoritization, and other "shocks") are very difficult to tease out. I would suggest a project that focuses solely on culture shock as a barrier to student adjustment and integration, and that a dynamic model should be created to demonstrate what aspects of "culture" push levers on LFGCS's sense of belonging and how they negotiate or as-similate to each facet of "culture."

The third limitation of this study is that it cannot separate, and therefore control for, ethnicity, socioeconomic status, immigrant status, or parents' educational level in sorting out which factors might contribute more heavily to barriers and which strategies mitigate those. The delimitation of this is that I remained focused on the homogenous nature of the sample. All participants met the same criteria, and so from them I could learn something about the experience of this population at this institution. Unable to tease the identity markers apart, I accepted my participants as complex subjects, and acknowl-edged that all the barriers, and strategies for diminishing them, were unique to the reporting population, a sample of students with intersectional identities. The results presented here inform the discussion on models for student suc-cess, but cannot be presumed to represent a solution for all students.

IMPLICATIONS FOR PRACTICE AND FURTHER INQUIRY

In terms of using these findings to create an action plan or interventions to improve graduation outcomes for Latino first-generation college students at four-year universities, I recommend first creating intentional programming around the strategies identified by the study participants. The high-impact ac-tion models (figures 11.1 and 11.2) presented here demonstrate the numerous benefits that productive activities provide. Many of the strategies that stu-dents identified for overcoming obstacles can be grouped together and can be modeled and taught to first-year students. Having resident advisors and peer mentors explain how certain high-impact actions yield multiple results may increase sense of agency and encourage help-seeking behaviors early in col-lege. Since LFGCS do not have their parents' college knowledge to fall back on, they must get all their information *about* college from *within* college, and so faculty, staff, and students become the teachers and disseminators of that knowledge. Every interaction matters, and I would add, *especially* those interactions with people employed by the university to teach and administer programs and services. How might faculty training on heuristic knowledge and the geography of the college impact students' help-seeking behaviors and sense of belonging?

Faculty should receive overt training on minimizing the power distance between themselves and first-gen students of color, particularly those who may feel marginalized or feel that their voice does not matter. There may be implicit bias at work in the way instructors communicate (too subtly) that they are available to students. If instructors are explicit about wanting to see students at office hours and conferences, and explain *why* students should be speaking with professors about coursework, study practices, and academic opportunities across and beyond the college, could this improve cultural capital building for first-gen students? These actions are not obvious to first-gen students, as many were not socialized to engage in help-seeking or network-building behaviors, and therefore would need extra encouragement to build that bridge with staff and faculty.

As for students' perception that "support services are hidden" or difficult to find, how might the institution remedy that? Administrators say that support services are available, but they cannot make students use them. From student reports, we learn that first-gens were often not aware of free campus resources, such as tutoring, supplemental instruction, writing centers, academic coaches, support groups, career coaching, and other spaces where students get advice and assistance with academic, social, and other types of difficulties. It is necessary to realize that students with little knowledge of the college terrain will not be expecting these types of services or know that they are free and accessible to them. LFGCS need a clear map and an overt welcome mat in the form of institutional agents who meet them where they are. Could faculty, especially those teaching first-year students, involve support services staff in the classroom experience, integrating heuristic and content knowledge, as well as endorsing campus support services and normalizing help-seeking behaviors? Another opportunity might be to assign first-year students to visit support service offices as part of assignments, aligning the course content with exploration of campus resources.

Lastly, I would advocate for a visible First-Generation Students' Services office. First, this would add depth and counterpoint to race-based diversity efforts in bringing socioeconomic class and privilege to the forefront. Second, through its very existence such an office would raise the profile of and celebrate students who are doing something extraordinarily challenging by being the first in their families to attend college. Third, a campus center would allow for this population with no visible markers to share an identity and to connect and share resources. If trusted peers that are "people like me" are so important for community-building and social support, but there is no space to connect on campus, how does one find their first-gen and low-income peers? The institution can ease this burden, especially at a campus with 20 percent first-generation college students. The larger question is whether it is the institution's responsibility to provide spaces for students to connect around socioeconomic class. Class is left out of the diversity initiatives at most universities. Could a more intentional and open acknowledgment of class as an identity marker strengthen community on campus and mitigate marginalization? First-gen status often becomes a proxy for low-income (although this is not always the case). A center that celebrates student achievement, offers space for community-building, and increases awareness of underrepresented populations would allow for class-based diversity work to come out of the shadows, further supporting students with intersectional identities across the campus.

CONCLUSION

When we explore the lived experience of students, we validate their funds of knowledge and we demonstrate that students are what make a college a place of learning and growth. Even the most prestigious research university is only a think tank (at best) without students. This study aimed to explore the college life experiences of Latino first-generation college students at an elite PWI, particularly inquiring as to how these students navigate and negotiate barriers to persistence. This rich data, even from a small sample, yielded a comprehensive list of barriers and obstacles that Latino first-gen students faced, as well as an extensive list of strategies for overcoming such obstacles. These successful seniors created their own support networks and shared heuristic knowledge and their understanding of the geography of the campus with each other. They also identified peers and mentors who were credible models from whom to learn, building their self-efficacy and sense of belonging in the process. Studying successful students allows us to build up the literature focused on assets and to develop models of student potential and achievement. As educators, we must continue to learn from our students and be mindful and accepting of the lessons they can teach us.

REFERENCES

Astin, Alexander W. 1984. "Student Involvement: A Developmental Theory for Higher Education." *Journal of College Student Personnel* 25, no. 4: 297–308.

Attinasi, Louis C., Jr. 1989. "Getting In: Mexican Americans' Perceptions of University Attendance and the Implications for Freshman Year Persistence." *The Journal of Higher Education* 60, no. 3 (May-June): 247–77.

Bandura, Albert. 1963. *Social Learning and Personality Development.* New York: Holt, Rinehart, and Winston.

Bordes-Edgar, Veronica, Patricia Arredondo, Sharon Robinson Kurpius, and James Rund. 2011. "A Longitudinal Analysis of Latina/o Students' Academic Persistence." *Journal of Hispanic Higher Education* 10, no. 4: 358–68. doi: 10.1177/1538192711423318.

Castillo, Linda G., Collie W. Conoley, Catherine Choi-Pearson, Debra J. Archuleta, Marion J. Phoummarath, and Alisa Van Landingham. 2006. "University Environment as a Mediator of Latino Ethnic Identity and Persistence Attitudes." *Journal of Counseling Psychology* 53, no. 2: 267–71.

Chen, Xianglei, and C. Dennis Carroll. 2005. "First-Generation Students in Postsecondary Education: A Look at Their College Transcripts. Postsecondary Education Descriptive Analysis Report. NCES 2005–171." *National Center for Education Statistics.* http://nces.ed.gov/pubsearch/pubsinfo.asp?pubid=2005171.

Choy, Susan. 2001. "Students Whose Parents Did Not Go to College: Postsecondary Access, Persistence, and Attainment. Findings from the Condition of Education, 2001." http://nces.ed.gov/pubsearch/pubsinfo.asp?pubid=2001126.

Dennis, Jessica M., Jean S. Phinney, and Lizette Ivy Chuateco. 2005. "The Role of Motivation, Parental Support, and Peer Support in the Academic Success of Ethnic Minority First-Generation College Students." *Journal of College Student Development* 46, no. 3: 223–36.

Engstrom, Cathy, and Vincent Tinto. 2008. "Access without Support Is Not Opportunity." *Change: The Magazine of Higher Learning* 40, no. 1: 46–50.

Harper, Shaun. R. 2012. "Race without Racism: How Higher Education Researchers Minimize Racist Institutional Norms." *The Review of Higher Education* 36, no. 1: 9–29.

Hernandez, John C. 2002. "A Qualitative Exploration of the First-Year Experience of Latino College Students." *NASPA Journal* 40, no. 1: 69–84.

Hurtado, Sylvia, and Deborah Faye Carter. 1997. "Effects of College Transition and Perceptions of the Campus Racial Climate on Latino College Students' Sense of Belonging." *Sociology of Education* 70, no. 4: 324–45.

Hurtado, Sylvia, Deborah Faye Carter, and Albert Spuler. 1996. "Latino Student Transition to College: Assessing Difficulties and Factors in Successful College Adjustment." *Research in Higher Education* 37, no. 2: 135–57.

Iffert, Robert E. 1957. *Retention and Withdrawal of College Students.* U.S. Department of Health, Education, and Welfare, Office of Education, Bulletin 1958, no. 1. Washington, DC: US Government Printing Office. http://files.eric.ed.gov/fulltext/ED543830.pdf.

Kuh, George D. 2001. "Assessing What Really Matters to Student Learning Inside the National Survey of Student Engagement." *Change: The Magazine of Higher Learning* 33, no. 3: 10–17.

Kuh, George D. 2008. "High-Impact Educational Practices: A Brief Overview." (Excerpt from *High-Impact Educational Practices: What They Are, Who Has Access to Them, and Why They Matter.* Washington, DC: Association of American Colleges and Universities.) https://www.aacu.org/leap/hips.

Mehta, Sanjay S., and John J. Newbold. 2011. "Why Do First-Generation Students Fail?" *College Student Journal* 45, no. 1: 20.

Muñoz, Susana María, and Marta María Maldonado. 2012. "Counterstories of College Persistence by Undocumented Mexicana Students: Navigating Race, Class, Gender, and Legal Status." *International Journal of Qualitative Studies in Education* 25, no. 3: 293–315.

Museus, Samuel D., Andrew H. Nichols, and Amber D. Lambert. 2008. "Racial Differences in the Effects of Campus Racial Climate on Degree Completion: A Structural Equation Model." *The Review of Higher Education* 32, no. 1: 107–34.

National Center for Education Statistics. 2016. "The Condition of Education 2016. NCES 2016–144." Retrieved from http://nces.ed.gov/pubs2016/2016144.pdf.

Orbe, Mark P. 2004. "Negotiating Multiple Identities within Multiple Frames: An Analysis of First–Generation College Students." *Communication Education* 53, no. 2: 131–49.

Padilla, Raymond V. 1994. "The Unfolding Matrix: A Technique for Qualitative Data Acquisition and Analysis." In *Studies in Qualitative Methodology* vol. 4, edited by R. G. Burgess, 273–85. Greenwich, CT: JAI Press.

Padilla, Raymond V. 1996. "The Unfolding Matrix: A Dialogical Technique for Qualitative Data Acquisition and Analysis." Paper presented at the Annual Meeting of the American Educational Research Association, New York, NY.

Padilla, Raymond V. 2009. *Student Success Modeling: Elementary School to College.* Herndon, VA: Stylus Publishing, LLC.

Pascarella, Ernest T., Christopher T. Pierson, Gregory C. Wolniak, and Patrick T. Terenzini. 2004. "First-Generation College Students: Additional Evidence on College Experiences and Outcomes." *Journal of Higher Education* 75, no. 3, 249–84.

Patton, Michael Q. 2002. *Qualitative Research & Evaluation Methods.* Third edition. Thousand Oaks: Sage Publications.

Phinney, Jean S., and Kumiko Haas. 2003. "The Process of Coping Among Ethnic Minority First-Generation College Freshmen: A Narrative Approach." *The Journal of Social Psychology* 143, no. 6: 707–26.

Próspero, Moisés, and Shetal Vohra-Gupta. 2007. "First Generation College Students: Motivation, Integration, and Academic Achievement." *Community College Journal of Research and Practice* 31, no. 12: 963–75.

Santiago, Deborah A. 2011. *Roadmap for Ensuring America's Future by Increasing Latino College Completion.* Washington, DC: Excelencia in Education.

Schreiner, Laurie A., Patrice Noel, and Linda Cantwell. 2011. "The Impact of Faculty and Staff on High-Risk College Student Persistence." *Journal of College Student Development* 52, no. 3: 321–38.

Soria, Krista M., and Michael J. Stebleton. 2012. "First-Generation Students' Academic Engagement and Retention." *Teaching in Higher Education* 17, no. 6: 673–85. doi:10.1080/13562517.2012.666735.

Tinto, Vincent. 1993. *Leaving College: Rethinking the Causes and Cures of Student Attrition.* Second edition. Chicago: University of Chicago Press.

Wei, Meifen, Tsun-Yao Ku, and Kelly Yu-Hsin Liao. 2011. "Minority Stress and College Persistence Attitudes Among African American, Asian American, and Latino students: Perception of University Environment as a Mediator." *Cultural Diversity and Ethnic Minority Psychology* 17, no. 2: 195–203.

Yosso, Tara J. 2005. "Whose Culture Has Capital? A Critical Race Theory Discussion of Community Cultural Wealth." *Race, Ethnicity and Education* 8, no. 1: 69–91.

Afterword

Jenny Stuber

In 1989, I enrolled at Northwestern University as a working-class, first-generation college student. Like many of the students profiled in this volume and elsewhere in the literature, I was a smart, motivated high school student who envisioned similar success at the college level. And yet my undergraduate experience, while resulting in timely graduation, was marked by psychological, academic, and professional challenges and roadblocks. Indeed, it was these roadblocks that led me to majoring in sociology and, ultimately, building a rewarding and successful career as a sociologist. But this path was not foreordained.

I entered college as an aspiring lawyer or investment banker. These aspirations gradually fell from view, as my sociological imagination was piqued. As a first-year student, I became curious and concerned over the gender relations I saw around me and even participated in: in this seemingly evolved academic environment, why was it that young fraternity men hosted young women at alcohol-fueled parties, while sorority women and their spaces were off-limits to men and alcohol and were generally regulated in a highly paternalistic fashion? I was also curious about the racial segregation I saw around me on campus, as well as the sense that many of the Black students at Northwestern University came from families of privilege—despite the broader media images depicting Blacks as poorly educated and lower-income. Class privilege was also cast into a new light: while I had attended a high school with a strong upper-middle-class presence, the intergenerational wealth and privilege I saw around me seemed to exist on a more profound and more systematic level. But more than anything else, I wondered how, as a lower-income student, I had gotten to the elite Northwestern University in the first place, and why my experiences were characterized by a strange combination of joy, intellectual inspiration, and pain and sadness.

It was this question that I sought to answer in my senior thesis as a sociology major. In the vaunted tradition of "me-search" (research inspired by a desire to understand one's self), I wanted to understand how White, lower-income, first-generation students arrived at an elite college education, and what they experienced once there. Alas, in 1993, the literature on this topic sent out a deafening radio silence. My exploration into the research on first-generation students did not speak to *me*: within the literature, this term seemed to be synonymous with—or at least inextricably intertwined with—students of color, nontraditional-aged students, students attending community college, and other social locations and identities that were not *me*. Despite being fa-

343

miliar with and inspired by Pierre Bourdieu's theory of social reproduction, I seemed unable to apply his notions of social, cultural, and economic capital to situations like mine: students who lacked economic capital, but were able to use their social and cultural capital to navigate educational institutions. In the absence of a literature on first-generation college students that resonated with me, I wrote my senior thesis on how Black students used their stocks of social and cultural capital to navigate the path that led them toward an elite college education.

My, how things have changed. The current state of knowledge concerning first-generation college students is now remarkably richer, more diverse, and more powerful due to the intellectual persistence of individuals like myself and the scholars assembled in this volume. Methodologically, research on first-generation students reflects both continuity and change. From its inception, those researching first-gen students have used both quantitative and qualitative methods. Early on, scholars used large-scale datasets to document correlates of college outcomes, namely college completion, among a wide array of students. This research established the now well-known insight that first-generation college students persist through college at much lower rates than their non-first-generation peers. Over time, scholars like Vincent Tinto, Alexander Astin, Ernest Pascarella, Patrick Terenzini, and George Kuh have elaborated their models of integration and engagement to shed greater light onto the experiences of first-generation students, while others—like Trista Beard in this volume—have used their research as inspiration to develop new models and understandings. Yet it may be safe to say that the early quantitative approach to understanding first-generation students has, in some ways, not kept pace with the formative questions that have emerged from the qualitative literature, nor has it reached its potential, given increasingly sophisticated analytic techniques and datasets.

There are, of course, noteworthy exceptions. For example, Sara Goldrick-Rab's research is essential for understanding how social class shapes students' college pathways (e.g., their choice to enroll, where to enroll, etc.); her research also provides insight into the perils and possibilities of community colleges, especially as a starting point for lower-income, first-generation students. Yet as excellent as her work is, namely in terms of understanding financial barriers to access, she has not taken first-generation students as the focal point of her inquiry (they are, instead, an important constituent group within a broader set of processes). Similarly noteworthy is the recent work on college choice by Caroline Hoxby and her coauthors. Focusing on the college-choice process, Hoxby uses quantitative analyses to show that knowledge and beliefs about higher education, and especially its costs, often inhibit high-ability, lower-income students, most of whom are presumably first-generation students, from applying to more selective schools for which they are qualified—and where they would face a higher likelihood of eventual graduation.

Persistent gaps in the quantitative literature leave plenty of room for other scholars to pick up the mantle and do meaningful research that disentangles the effects of age, ethnicity, immigration status, income, and parental education on college experiences and outcomes. Largely unknown is the process by which some first-generation and/or lower-income students "break away" and achieve social mobility. While qualitative work included in this volume contains hints of this process—for example Anthony Jack and Véronique Irwin's work on high school pathways and early exposure to elite cultural capital, and Ashley Rondini's work on parental encouragement and influences—quantitative researchers should explore the patterns by which some students "beat the odds," whether they reflect seemingly idiosyncratic exposure to social and cultural capital in one's network, or more systematic dynamics of neighborhood and educational segregation, and the ways in which these patterns and processes facilitate the educational experiences of some seemingly less advantaged students.

Extending this thought, we know little about how parental education intersects with social class in the lives of college students. Quantitative scholars might build on work like Thomas Piñeros Shields's in this volume and ask: How do the college experiences of lower-income students vary depending on whether their parents have a college education? Does the cultural capital associated with higher levels of parental education moderate the effects of low-income status on the college-choice behavior and college experiences of less advantaged college students? Quantitative analyses should be able to answer such questions, further illuminating the relationships between social, cultural, and financial capital, and educational attainment and social mobility.

Continuity and change is also seen in the qualitative literature. In 1989, the year I myself became a first-generation student, Howard London published the first of his qualitative accounts of first-generation college students. His work lent poignancy, empathy, and nuance to the experiences of this unique group. Taking a psychological perspective, one focused on identity and social relationships, he showed that some of those who were gaining educational credentials simultaneously experienced a sense of loss (London 1989, 1992). Gaining educational credentials is not merely or exclusively an educational process, nor is it an unmitigated gain; it is also a cultural process, one governed by middle-class norms operating within middle-class institutions. Those who are among the first in their families to navigate such institutions may endure the hidden injuries of class as they acquire new forms of social and cultural capital and confront the possibility that higher levels of education mean dislocation from friends and family from home. This research laid the foundation for much of the qualitative inquiry that exists today, especially that which focuses on the lived experiences, worldviews, and narrative accounts of first-generation students.

Change, within the qualitative tradition, has moved the research into richer territories, especially by providing insight into institutional contexts and variations. While students' identities and demographic traits are important predictors of their college experiences, none of these experiences play out in a vacuum. Instead, moving from the work of Howard London and others who focused on community college settings, we now know that first-generation students have different experiences and different outcomes depending on the type of institution they attend. Taking a comparative approach, I showed in my research that first-generation students were more likely to get pulled into social networks and extracurricular activities at a small, private liberal arts college than they were at a large public university. Normative institutional arrangements, including housing policies and financial aid/work study opportunities, played an important role in these processes. Also working from a comparative frame, within this volume Minthorn and Youngbull show very powerfully that institutions that devote greater resources to programming for Native American students can significantly increase retention among this at-risk population by providing culturally relevant programming and creating a sense of belonging. Similarly, Kiyama, Harper, and Ramos show that institutions differ in the ways that they welcome first-generation students and their families, which likely has consequences for their attachment and engagement to higher education.

Other researchers have focused exclusively on the experiences of first-gen students at elite colleges and universities. In this volume, Anthony Abraham Jack and Véronique Irwin show that among first-generation students at an elite institution of higher education, some are more inclined than others to engage in help-seeking behavior; differences in help-seeking among first-gen students emerged from earlier educational socialization and exposure to college-related cultural capital among what the authors call the *privileged poor*. Published in 2016, Elizabeth Lee's book *Class and Campus Life* makes perhaps the most detailed contribution to our understanding of how working-class, (mostly) first-generation students navigate an elite educational environment. She shows that beliefs about social class, morality (hard work), and group membership tend to collide within the elite Linden College, creating a sense of outsider-ness among less advantaged students—even as they persist through graduation.

As a *sociologist* of higher education, perhaps the most encouraging evolution in the literature on first-generation students has been the increased attention to identity and processes. Like much research in higher education, there has been an historical focus on social disparities in educational outcomes, in this case focusing on differences between first-generation and non-first-generation students in enrollment, retention, and completion. While it is critically important to understand these disparities, focusing only on such outcomes obscures the fact that educational institutions are major sites of socialization and identity development, and that many socially significant processes occur on campus that are not directly related to achievement or attainment. In their seminal review article, Mitchell L. Stevens, Elizabeth A. Armstrong, and Richard Arum (2008) drew attention to the ways in which institutions of higher education function as *incubators*—spaces where students become socially competent actors as they form their identities and acquire social and cultural capital that can be used to navigate the college setting and beyond. This shift in attention has animated the research on first-generation students.

Looking at educational attainment as a process—one that is as much about acquiring a credential as it is about acquiring an identity, along with social and cultural capital—researchers including myself (Stuber 2008) have examined how students draw on their cultural repertoires to navigate higher education. Within this volume, chapters by Ann Mullen, Anthony Abraham Jack and Véronique Irwin, and Trista Beard look at how students draw on their cultural beliefs about higher education as they decide what school to attend, what to major in, and whether and how to engage professors and peers. Much of this research comes to a common conclusion: first-generation students do, indeed, hold different cultural understandings of higher education compared to their non-first-generation peers. These differences—which often come down to an instrumental or career-focused approach to higher education—tend to limit their engagement with peers and faculty as well as their extracurricular engagement. Jack and Irwin show, however, that the high school experiences of lower-income/first-generation students can equip some such students with cultural repertoires that prove useful when navigating an elite academic environment. Their work shows that terms like *lower income* and *first generation* may be overly blunt, especially given the considerable heterogeneity that exists within the high school landscapes, where the privileged poor attend high-resourced magnet and college-preparatory schools and the doubly disadvantaged come to college having attended lower-resourced public schools. Differences in high school experiences and exposure to cultural capital, then, differentially equip first-gen students for college life.

Researchers have also given greater attention to the family in trying to understand the process of college-going and college completion. For several authors in this volume, having non-college-educated parents is not an impediment to educational attainment—as it is often framed in the literature—but a key facilitator. Ashley Rondini, in particular, shows how first-generation parents may draw on their own life experiences and offer their children "cautionary tales" about educational and occupational decisions not to make. Similarly, such parents may see their children as a means of redemption: by encouraging their children to attend college and achieve occupational autonomy and a middle-class lifestyle, they are able to redeem themselves and show that they are good parents of successful children (Rondini 2016). Fanny Yeung similarly explores the family as a unit of analysis, showing that the sense of familism among Asian American immigrants locks children and their parents into interdependent relations, characterized by giving and receiving social support. Yeung shows that as college students, first-generation immigrant students may feel a sense of accountability and gratitude towards their parents for making their educational aspirations possible.

Despite these positive narratives of family influence and interaction, an enduring theme in the literature on first-generation college students is that the process of becoming an educated person can be quite difficult. A college degree is much more than an educational or occupational credential; it is a credential that is earned via a cultural process. This cultural process plays out over several years, within a cultural space inhabited by people—students, staff, and faculty—with class-based identities, interacting in a setting that operates according to class-based assumptions. As Elizabeth Lee and Rory Kramer show, first-generation college students may acquire a cleft habitus, a way of acting and being that combines the working-class habitus of their youth and the middle-class habitus generated on campus. The tension presented by this cleft habitus guides how students enter into conversations with friends and family from home, and it shapes how they think about their emerging class identities. Allison Hurst echoes these themes in her analysis of how first-generation students balance their cleft social class identities and grounding in distinct class cultures. While some of her respondents were Loyalists, remaining identified with and in solidarity with their working-class origins, others reinforce the finding that social mobility can be hard. It can involve a sense of betrayal, and for some the need to become a Renegade who seeks to escape their working-class origins. Double Agents, by contrast, move between cultural identities and groups, somehow managing to find a balance. Together, what Lee and Kramer and Hurst show is that despite the more redemptive narratives of first-generation students from immigrant families, there still exists a sense of loss among some socially mobile first-generation students, who describe a weakening rather than strengthening of family ties.

Finally, one of the emerging themes within the literature on first-generation students—evident in this volume and elsewhere—is a shift away from looking at first-generation and working-class status from a deficit perspective. To characterize first-generation status as a deficit is to suggest that academically, financially, and culturally, this segment of students arrives on campus at risk—with lower likelihoods of engaging and integrating, of expanding their social and cultural capital, and of persisting through graduation. Yet many of these students *do* graduate. And many also return to be important members of their families and their communities. Accordingly, scholars now recognize the importance of looking at the strengths that these students possess. Several chapters in this volume do justice to this notion, showing that the family of origin is not a hindrance, but rather can play a critical role in encouraging first-generation students' college aspirations and enhancing their sense of resiliency. Further challenging the deficits perspective, another set of chapters in this volume shows that peer connections and group identity are assets that first-generation students can draw on to facilitate their success. As shown by Kim Godsoe, the peer relations built by less advantaged groups in the Posse STEM program can be harnessed to draw out the skills, aptitudes, and resilience of these students. Similarly, Minthorn and Youngbull show that Native American students enter college with important cultural assets and identities, but that the institution must put programming in place to draw out these strengths. Unfortunately, they too rarely do so, contributing to the higher rates of attrition among Native students.

Ever since the publication of Pierre Bourdieu's groundbreaking work in the early 1970s, sociologists and other educational researchers have been attentive to the ways in which institutions of education do not operate in a class-neutral way, but instead according to class-based assumptions. This institutional critique is essential for challenging the deficit perspective. Although not published within this volume, psychologist Nicole Stephens's work provides a powerful critique of the class-based assumptions of higher education, and how these assumptions disadvantage first-generation and lower-income students. Her work shows that at an institutional level, colleges and universities send messages—during recruitment, orientation, and beyond—that frame the acquisition of a college degree as an individual project, motivated by individual aspirations and individual goals. Stephens and her colleagues have shown that lower-income and first-generation students do better—are more likely to apply, persist, and have higher GPAs—when colleges and their representatives send students messages that emphasize collective efforts, the role of family and community in facilitating success, and the positive impacts for family and community of acquiring a college degree (Stephens et al. 2012; Stephens, Hamedani, and Destin 2014). This research, in particular, shifts the emphasis away from a deficit approach and shows that first-generation students are disadvantaged by an educational environment that is at odds with many of their cultural orientations and assumptions.

Despite the massive, high-quality growth in the literature on first-generation students, some challenges remain. As noted above, when this scholarship first began making its mark in the late 1980s, researchers often failed to disentangle the ways in which various social identities exacerbate or mediate the experiences of first-generation students. First-generation status was often analytically bundled up with a host of other identities, including age, race/ethnicity, social class, and family status. Over time, greater care has been taken, often through research design, to analytically separate the ways in which these identities come into play. Yet to some extent, these challenges remain. While taking an intersectional approach is absolutely essential in research on education, inequality, and marginality, researchers still need to develop careful research designs in which immigration status, social class, race, and other such identities are understood as both *distinct from* and *complexly interacting* with parental education. Reinforcing another point made earlier, researchers must also continue to examine how these complex identities are molded within particular institutional settings, and how these processes impact educational outcomes. Educational institutions vary considerably, and researchers should understand how these variations may enhance or impede the educational experiences of first-generation students.

Finally, it is not simply that first-generation students are molded by the institutions they attend; they also mold those institutions in return. One of the most powerful and exciting results of the growing attention to first-generation students is the activism that first-generation students themselves have undertaken. 1vyG, for example, is an "organization that strengthens and empowers the first-generation college student network by convening communities of students and administrators, sharping and building best practices of support, and advocating for change," as the About section of their Facebook page puts it (www.facebook.com/pg/team1vyG/about/?ref=page_internal). Founded by students at Brown University in 2015, 1vyG is a cross-campus network of students at Ivy League schools and other highly selective colleges and universities that seeks to understand their own experiences as first-generation students and to harness the power of research and peer support to make change on their campuses and beyond. Each year, this organization's work culminates in a student-run conference on one of their campuses, with a schedule full of scholarly presentations, student workshops, and late-night bonding over an often invisible sense of difference.

At other colleges and universities, students have similarly banded together in organizations aimed at raising an awareness of social class issues and, especially, at providing a forum for lower-income students to understand their own experiences as potentially socially mobile young adults. As Elizabeth Lee shows in her nuanced book *Class and Campus Life*, this is a challenging process within the context of a society that celebrates social mobility and where middle-class status is treated either as the default or an unmitigated good. The fact that students are now banding together around parental education and social class is an incredibly powerful commentary on the complicated intersection around education and class identity. While the scholars in this volume have documented these compelling dynamics, students have admirably taken up the charge of transforming their institutions. Schools and institutions seem to be recognizing this work, offering more orientation programming, resources, and scholarships for those who are the first in their families to pursue a college degree.

Which brings me to a final question: What have I learned as a researcher and as a human, given the changes in scholarship and campus activism over the last several decades? For one, I have learned that being a first-generation student is an experience that typically presents multiple barriers within higher education. Some of these derive from the lower-income status that often accompanies first-generation status, but other barriers reflect a mismatch between the student's cultural resources and repertoires and those privileged by educational institutions. Additionally, as a scholar and as a human, I have learned that first-generation status is a complex status and, as this volume admirably shows, one that is deeply intertwined with other identities and social statuses. Although I may share some commonalities with a first-generation student from an immigrant background, there are also substantial differences between their lives and mine (as a White woman from a lower-income background). For many immigrant students, family support acts as a resource. For many White students, race privilege may act as both asset and liability, providing the opportunity to pass and blend in, but also limiting a sense of community and identity. Finally, and on a most personal level, I have learned that the academic hunches and deeply complex emotions that I experienced as an undergraduate many years ago are worthy of scholarly consideration. The work of the scholars in this volume makes an important contribution by providing theoretical and practical insight into the lives of first-generation students—those like me and those quite unlike me. This research powerfully documents the enduring challenges faced by first-generation students, the ways in which colleges and universities can and should change to better meet the needs of these students, and the resilience and often unrecognized strengths of these educational pioneers. I look forward to the opportunity, in another twenty years, to reflect on what has changed and what has not in the lives of first-generation students and the associated scholarship.

REFERENCES

1vyG, *1vyG: The inter-Ivy, First Generation Students' Conference,* retrieved from www.facebook.com/pg/team1vyG/about/?ref=page_internal on December 22, 2017.

Goldrick-Rab, Sara. 2006. "Following Their Every Move: An Investigation of Social-Class Differences in College Pathways." *Sociology of Education* 79, no. 1: 67–79.

Goldrick-Rab, Sara, Douglas N. Harris, and Philip A. Trostel. 2009. "Why Financial Aid Matters (or does not) for College Success: Toward a New Interdisciplinary Perspective." In *Higher Education: Handbook of Theory and Research,* vol. 24, edited by John C. Smart, 1–45. London: Springer.

Lee, Elizabeth M. 2016. *Class and Campus Life: Managing and Experiencing Inequality at an Elite College.* New York: Cornell University Press.

London, Howard B. 1989. "Breaking away: A Study of First-Generation College Students and Their Families." *American Journal of Education* 97, no. 1: 144–70.

London, Howard B. 1992. "Transformations: Cultural Challenges Faced by First-Generation Students." *New Directions for Community Colleges* 1992, no. 80: 5–11.

Rondini, Ashley C. 2016. "Healing the Hidden Injuries of Class?: Redemption Narratives, Aspirational Proxies, and Parents of Low-Income First Generation College Students." *Sociological Forum* 31, no. 1: 96–116.

Stephens, Nicole M., Stephanie A. Fryberg, Hazel Rose Markus, Camille S. Johnson, and Rebecca Covarrubias. 2012. "Unseen Disadvantage: How American Universities' Focus on Independence Undermines the Academic Performance of First-Generation College Students." *Journal of Personality and Social Psychology* 102, no. 6: 1178–97.

Stephens, Nicole M., MarYam G. Hamedani, and Mesmin Destin. 2014. "Closing the Social-Class Achievement Gap: A Difference-Education Intervention Improves First-Generation Students' Academic Performance and All Students' College Transition." *Psychological Science* 25, no. 4: 943–53.

Stevens, Mitchell L., Elizabeth A. Armstrong, and Richard Arum. 2008. "Sieve, Incubator, Temple, Hub: Empirical and Theoretical Advances in the Sociology of Higher Education." *Annual Reviews in Sociology* 34: 127–51.

Stuber, Jenny M. 2009. "Class, Culture, and Participation in the Collegiate Extra-Curriculum." *Sociological Forum* 24, no. 4: 877–900.

Stuber, Jenny M. 2011. *Inside the College Gates: How Class and Culture Matter in Higher Education.* Maryland: Lexington Books.

Index

About the Contributors

TRISTA BEARD

Trista Beard is an adjunct instructor at University of Southern California's Rossier School of Education. She earned her EdD at USC and currently administers the Topping Scholars Program which supports high financial need, first-generation college students. Her research interests include first-generation student success, social capital building and exchange, the impact of mentorship, and critical incidents in the journey to college completion. She comes from a White working-class rural community where most people go to work at a factory or farm after high school. She was the first in her family to attend college and felt a great sense of isolation being a low-income student at an elite private university (because of her lack of cultural capital). Her first-gen experience drives much of her research and advocacy work. She is interested in learning from different populations of students, how they use agency to persist in college. She is also committed to discourse on class as she works to design and improve support services for underrepresented college students.

KIM GODSOE

Kim Godsoe currently serves as the Associate Provost for Academic Affairs at Brandeis University. Much of her career in higher education has been developing programs for students who are the first in their families to go to college and/or who come from low-income backgrounds. She is particularly interested in how to support these students in highly selective colleges and universities, places that traditionally have served well-resourced students. Godsoe holds a PhD in social policy from the Heller School for Social Policy and Management, where her research focused on retention of undergraduates in STEM disciplines. At the time of this research, Godsoe served as the Dean of Academic Services, a role which allowed her to provide academic advising to students, serve as the Posse Liaison for Brandeis University, and to sit on the University's Pre-Health Board. Her familiarity with the institution, students, staff, and faculty gave her a unique understanding of the campus and the challenges that students faced as they studied science. Godsoe received a Bachelor of Arts from Bryn Mawr College and a Master of Fine Arts in writing from Columbia University. In 2000, Kim became the Posse Liaison for Brandeis University, a role in which she helped to establish the first Science Posse Scholars program in the country. The Science Posse Scholars Program has been recognized by the Howard Hughes Medical Institute as an innovative model for science education. Currently, ten colleges are now sponsoring Science Posses as a way to support students in STEM disciplines.

CASANDRA E. HARPER

Casandra E. Harper is an Associate Professor of Higher Education in the Educational Leadership and Policy Analysis Department at the University of Missouri. Her research is focused on the diversity of the individual student experience, including: multiracial identity and racial identification, parent and family engagement in higher education, perceptions of campus climate, openness to diversity, and financial aid outcomes. As the daughter of a Dominican mother who worked three jobs to get through high school and was a first-generation college student, Dr. Harper is interested in understanding the resilience and unique experiences of first-generation, and low-income, and families of color. She was awarded a National Academy of Education/ Spencer postdoctoral fellowship in 2012, ACPA emerging scholar in 2013, and the Richard Caple award from MoCPA in 2014. Her work has been published in *Research in Higher Education*; *The Review of Higher Education*; *Race, Ethnicity, and Education*; the *Journal of College Student Development*; the *Journal of Student Affairs Research and Practice*; *New Directions for Institutional Research*; and the *Journal of College Orientation & Transition*. Casandra received her BS in Psychology and her MA in Higher Education from the University of Arizona and her MA and PhD in Higher Education and Organizational Change at UCLA.

ALLISON L. HURST

Allison L. Hurst is an Associate Professor of Sociology at Oregon State University, where she teaches courses on the sociology of education and theory. She has written two books on the experiences and identity reformations of working-class college students, *The Burden of Academic Success: Loyalists, Renegades, and Double Agents* (2010) and *College and the Working Class* (2012). Her current research focuses on the outcomes of college graduates, specifically the role of class and the impact of student debt. She was one of the founders of the Association of Working-Class Academics, an organization composed of college faculty and staff who were the first in their families to graduate from college, for which she also served as president from 2008 to

2014. She is currently serving as Chairperson of the Working-Class Academics Section of the Working Class Studies Association.

VÉRONIQUE IRWIN

Véronique Irwin is a graduate student in Sociology at University of California, Berkeley, where she is a National Science Foundation Graduate Research Fellow. Her research interests include selective enrollment, public schools, teacher effects, and educational stratification.

ANTHONY ABRAHAM JACK

Anthony Abraham Jack is a Junior Fellow at the Harvard Society of Fellows and Assistant Professor of Education at the Harvard Graduate School of Education. He also holds the Shutzer Assistant Professorship at the Radcliffe Institute for Advanced Study. His research documents the overlooked diversity among lower-income undergraduates: the *Doubly Disadvantaged*—those who enter college from local, typically distressed public high schools—and *Privileged Poor*—those who do so from boarding, day, and preparatory high schools. His scholarship earned awards from the American Sociological Association, Eastern Sociological Society, and the Society for the Study of Social Problems. Tony holds fellowships from the Ford Foundation and the National Science Foundation and is a 2015 National Academy of Education/ Spencer Foundation Dissertation Fellow. The National Center for Institutional Diversity at the University of Michigan named him a 2016 Emerging Diversity Scholar. The *New York Times, Boston Globe, The Huffington Post, The National Review, American RadioWorks*, and *MPR* have featured his research as well as biographical profiles of his experiences as a first-generation college student.

JUDY MARQUEZ KIYAMA

Judy Marquez Kiyama is an Associate Professor in the Higher Education department at the University of Denver's Morgridge College of Education. Dr. Kiyama's research examines the structures that shape educational opportunities for underserved groups through an asset-based lens to better understand the collective knowledge and resources drawn upon to confront, negotiate, and (re)shape such structures. Her research is organized in three interconnected areas: the role of parents and families; equity and power in educational research; and underserved groups as collective networks of change. Dr. Kiyama's current projects focus on the high school to college transition experiences of first-generation, and low-income, and families of color and their role in serving as sources of cultural support for their college-aged students. As a first-generation, Mexican-American college student, Dr. Kiyama draws on her own experiences with her family to connect with the sources of support that first-generation families offer their students in the transition to college. The recipient of the Association for the Study of Higher Education—Council on Ethnic Participation 2014 Mildred García Junior Exemplary Scholarship Award and named a 2011 Emerging Scholar by the American College Personnel Association, Kiyama's research has been published in the *American Educational Research Journal*, the *Journal of Higher Education*, and the *Review of Higher Education*.

RORY KRAMER

Rory Kramer is an Assistant Professor of Sociology at Villanova whose research focuses on race, space, inequality, and education. His research appears in journals such as *American Journal of Sociology*, *Du Bois Review*, *Sociology of Race and Ethnicity*, and *Sociology of Education*. He is currently completing a book project on Black diversity in selective higher education as part of an Andrew W. Mellon grant.

ELIZABETH M. LEE

Elizabeth M. Lee is an Assistant Professor of Sociology at Ohio University. Her research focuses primarily on class inequality in higher education and has been published in Sociology of Education, Poetics, and Sociology Compass. Her book, *Class and Campus Life: Managing and Experiencing Inequality at an Elite College,* was published by Cornell University Press in 2016, and her edited volume (with Chaise LaDousa), *College Students' Experiences of Power and Marginality: Sharing Spaces and Negotiating Differences*, is available from Routledge.

ROBIN MINTHORN

Robin Minthorn is an enrolled member of the Kiowa tribe of Oklahoma. She is an Assistant Professor at the University of New Mexico in Educational Leadership and Native American Studies and teaches courses surrounding Indigenous leadership, leadership and organizations in educational settings, and conflict resolution. Prior to becoming a faculty member at the University of New Mexico she served as coordinator of Native American affairs at Oklahoma State University, an adjunct faculty at Pawnee Nation College; preceding that, academic advisor at Comanche Nation College, Oklahoma's first tribal college. She is also a cofounder of Gamma Delta Pi, American Indian Sisterhood, RAIN (Retaining American Indians Now) as an undergraduate, and as a professional she cofounded ONASHE (Oklahoma Native American Students in Higher Education). Her professional experiences and student leadership experiences as a Native American directly influence her research and more specifically this book chapter. Her research interests include areas around Indigenous leadership in higher education, inter-generational leadership perspectives in tribal communities, supporting Native American college students, campus climate for Native American college students, and Native student participation in study abroad. Robin recently served as a Board Director for the National Indian Education Association (NIEA), is currently the President of the National Indian Youth Council (NIYC), and Board Director for the National Coalition for the Advancement of Natives in Higher Education (NCANHE). She is also a former NASPA IPKC (Indigenous Peoples Knowledge Community) Chair. Dr. Minthorn is also the coeditor of *Indigenous Leadership in Higher Education*, published by Routledge Educational Leadership Research Series, and *Reclaiming Indigenous Research in Higher Education*, published by Rutgers University Press.

ANN L. MULLEN

Ann L. Mullen is an Associate Professor of Sociology at the University of Toronto. Her research interests include culture, social inequality, gender, and higher education. Her recent work examines access to higher education, the gendered segregation of fields of study, and competing cultural narratives about the purpose and value of higher education. Her first book, *Degrees of Inequality: Culture, Class and Gender in American Higher Education*, was published by Johns Hopkins University press in 2010. The book was awarded the Outstanding Publication in Postsecondary Education, by the American Educational Research Association, and the Educators Award, by the Delta

Kappa Gamma Society International. She is currently conducting an audit study to assess the relative value of bachelors' degrees from three Ontario universities in terms of labor market payoffs.

DELMA RAMOS

Delma Ramos is pursuing a PhD in Higher Education with an emphasis on Research Methods and Statistics at the University of Denver. Her background as a first-generation immigrant and college student guides her work on asset based approaches to college access and completion, with an emphasis on underserved populations. Delma is also interested in the influence of public policy on issues related to college success, which has led her to collaborate with policy organizations and think tanks including the RAND corporation, the American Council on Education, and the College Board. Delma's dissertation research embodies her focus on asset based perspectives through an exploration of Funds of Knowledge and the college success of first-generation, low-income, and students of color. Delma currently serves as graduate assistant for the Interdisciplinary Research Incubator for the Study of (In)equality (IRISE) and the Office of Diversity and Inclusion (ODI) at the University of Denver.

BEDELIA NICOLA RICHARDS

Bedelia Nicola Richards is an Associate Professor of Sociology in the Department of Sociology and Anthropology at the University of Richmond. She holds a PhD in Sociology from Johns Hopkins University in Baltimore, MD. As a race/ethnicity, immigration, and education scholar, she interrogates the role of educational institutions in reproducing institutionalized racism and classism, and produces research that promotes critical thinking in regards to how institutions of higher education can better work for students and faculty from diverse backgrounds and communities. She is currently working on two research projects designed to produce knowledge that will make higher education institutions more inclusive for racially and socioeconomically marginalized students and faculty. The first project investigates how schools can provide first-generation college students with the cultural and social capital to transition from high school to college successfully. The second project examines the relationship between "race-talk" and racial (in)justice in higher education institutions.

Dr. Richards has held a number of positions in organizations that advocate for underserved, racially and ethnically diverse youth in furthering their educational and occupational goals. Her work has appeared in *Ethnic & Racial Studies; Sociology of Race and Ethnicity; Black Women, Gender and Families; International Journal of Teaching and Learning in Higher Education;* and as chapters in edited volumes. She is available to lecture or conduct workshops on a range of topics related to issues of race and class diversity and inclusion in higher education institutions such as: race-talk in the classroom, minimizing race and gender bias in the classroom, and supporting first-generation college students.

ASHLEY C. RONDINI

Ashley C. Rondini is an Assistant Professor in the Department of Sociology at Franklin and Marshall College. She holds an MA in Women's Studies from the University of Sussex in Brighton, England, as well as an MA in Social Policy and a joint PhD in Sociology and Social Policy from Brandeis University. She was the 2010 recipient of the American Sociological Association's (ASA) Sydney S. Spivack Post-Doctoral Congressional Fellowship, through which she worked with the US House of Representatives Committee on Education and Labor as well as the Congressional Research Service Division on Domestic Social Policy in Higher Education. Her research and teaching interests integrate qualitative analyses of social justice and social policy issues in educational and healthcare settings with critical, intersectional inquiry. Her ongoing work focuses on the intergenerational meanings of educational mobility within families of low-income, first-generation college students. She is currently undertaking intersectional research on institutional approaches to campus sexual violence prevention and response in relation to dynamics of race, gender/gender identity, socioeconomic class, sexuality, and immigration status.

Dr. Rondini has worked with the Posse Foundation and Brandeis University's Myra T. Kraft Transitional Year Program. She is committed to critical and community-engaged pedagogical praxis, and received a 2012 Carla B. Howard Teaching Grant from the ASA. She is the editor of the Race, Gender, and Class section of the ASA's online *Teaching Research And Innovations Library In Sociology* (TRAILS), and she is a member of the *Teaching Sociology* Editorial Board. Her work has been published in *Sociological Forum*, *Sociology Compass, The DuBois Review: Social Science Research on Race*, *Teaching Sociology*, and as chapters in edited volumes.

THOMAS PIÑEROS SHIELDS

Thomas Piñeros Shields is lecturer in the Department of Sociology and Director of the Master of Public Administration (MPA) program at the University
of Massachusetts at Lowell. He grew up in the New York and New Jersey
area. As a small child, Tom watched his father complete his associate's degree and later his bachelor's degree by taking night classes at a local business
technical school. His father's example and encouragement instilled in him an
appreciation of college. Tom attended Cornell University as an undergraduate
student, where he became interested in community based research and social
justice. He worked for over a decade in the field of service-learning civic engagement, cultural exchange, and action research before becoming a full-time
research associate at the Heller School for Social Policy and Management at
Brandeis University, where he conducted multisite, mixed-methods evaluations, including studies about first-generation college student access to higher
education and community-based participatory research. At Brandeis, Tom
completed a joint doctoral degree in social policy and sociology. His dissertation is an ethnography of the student immigrant movement that explains how
the DREAMers emerged as new political actors. He teaches a social problems
course as a community-based learning project with the Public Higher Education Network of Massachusetts (PHENOM) to identify and address issues
related to access to public higher education.

NICOLAS P. SIMON

Nicolas P. Simon is an Assistant Professor at Eastern Connecticut State University in the Department of Sociology, Anthropology, Criminology, and Social Work. After graduating with a MA in Geography and a MA in Sociology
from Université de Caen—Basse-Normandie, France, he immigrated to the
United States to pursue a career in higher education. He earned his doctoral
degree from the Department of Sociology at the University of Connecticut.
Using the intersection of race, class, and gender, his dissertation examines
how first-generation college students use their social capital to navigate their
experience in higher education.

His research and teaching interests focus on helping underserved students
graduate from institutions of higher education by developing their social
and cultural capital. His pedagogy emphasizes a student-centered approach
to learning by incorporating the strategies of asset-based learning in the
classroom. Working closely with the Center for Community Engagement, he

emphasizes civic involvement in his teaching and encourages students to volunteer in the community by participating in asset-based community service.

JENNY STUBER

Jenny Stuber is an Associate Professor of Sociology at the University of North Florida. After growing up in Minnesota, she went on to receive a PhD in Sociology from Indiana University, after obtaining earlier degrees in sociology from Northwestern University and Brown University. Motivated by her own experiences with feelings of social class alienation and being a first-generation college student, her research focuses on the cultural aspects of social class inequality. By looking at the cultural underpinnings of class inequality, Stuber's research asks questions about how people understand, enact, and use social class in their everyday lives. Her 2011 book, *Inside the College Gates: How Class and Culture Matter in Higher Education*, investigates the how social class and first-generation status shape how students navigate the college environment, focusing specifically on their social interactions and extracurricular involvement. Her recent work translates sociological research for broader undergraduate audiences, and includes the textbook *Exploring Inequality: A Sociological Approach* (Oxford) and *Sociology of Education: A Systematic Approach* (Routledge, with Jeanne Ballantine and Floyd Hammack). Her research has also appeared in *Sociological Forum, The Journal of Contemporary Sociology, The International Journal of Qualitative Studies in Education*, and *Teaching in Higher Education*.

FANNY YEUNG

Fanny Yeung joined California State University, East Bay as the Educational Effectiveness Research Manager in September 2014 after completing a postdoctoral fellowship and doctorate from the Higher Education and Organizational Change program at the University of California, Los Angeles (UCLA). Trained in both quantitative and qualitative methodologies, Fanny brings over a decade of institutional research experience in the areas of learning and development outcomes, program assessment and evaluation, and equity initiatives. As a first-generation college student from an immigrant family, Fanny's research and life story is rooted in the interwoven complexities of contemporary immigration patterns, multigenerational experiences, and rich educational opportunities that uniquely shaped her trajectory. By finding strength in her immigrant history, she seeks to incorporate photography, participant voices, and data to contextualize and honor students' rich experiences within education.

NATALIE ROSE YOUNGBULL

Natalie Rose Youngbull is enrolled in the Cheyenne & Arapaho Tribes of Oklahoma and descended from the Ft. Peck Assiniboine & Sioux tribes of Montana. She grew up in El Reno, OK and returns as often as she can to visit family and friends. Natalie earned her PhD in the Educational Policy Studies and Practice department with an emphasis in Higher Education from the University of Arizona. Currently, she serves as the Faculty Development Program Officer where she administers fellowships to assist Tribal College and University (TCU) faculty in the completion of their Master's and terminal degrees, plans the annual TCU Faculty Research Convening, and oversees the annual publication of the TCU Research Journal. As an American Indian Gates Millennium Scholar (AIGMS) alum, Natalie believes this research on AIGMS' nonpersistence within institutions of higher education is an important piece in understanding the experiences of Native American first-generation college students.

Made in the USA
Las Vegas, NV
27 March 2022